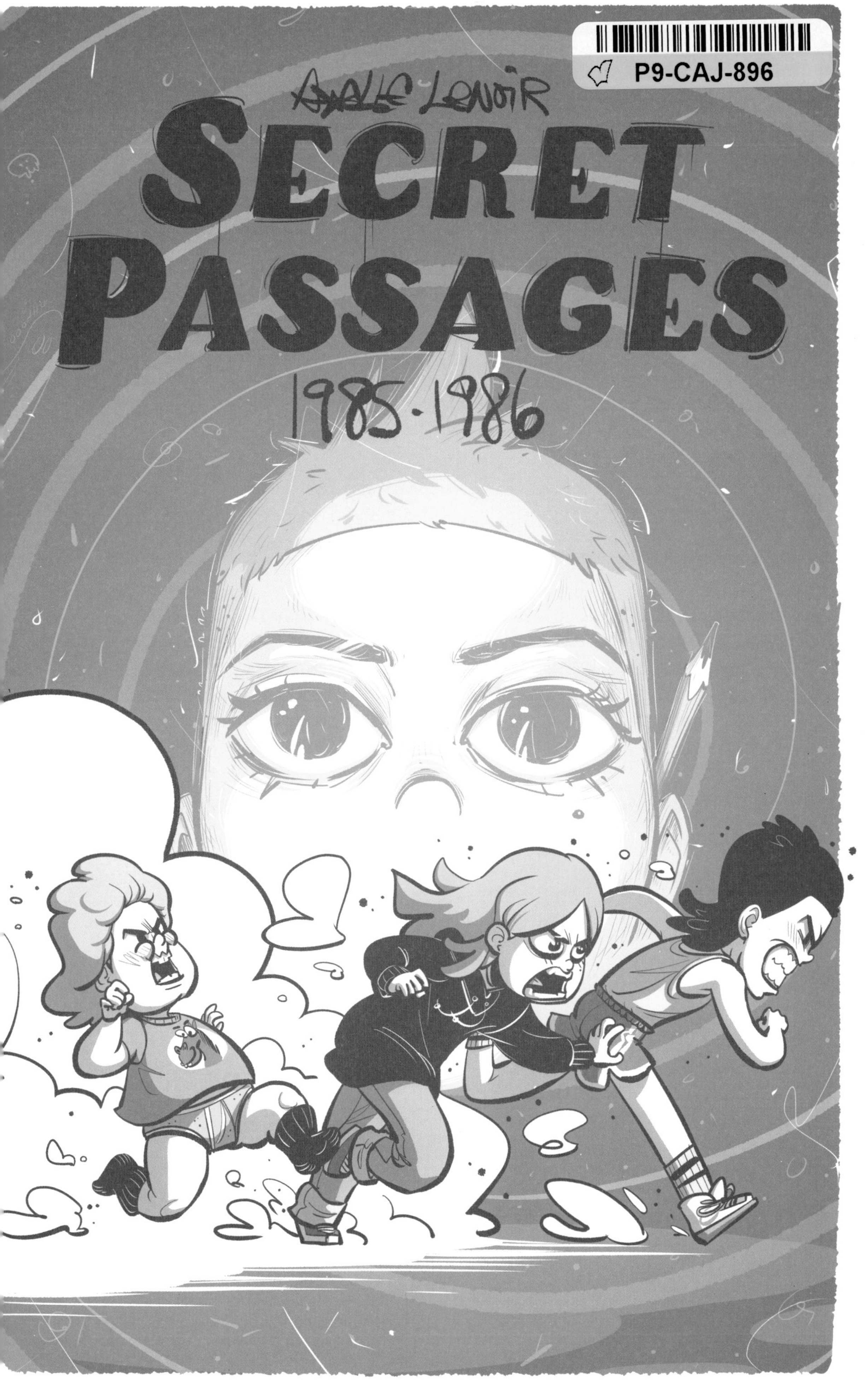
SECRET
PASSAGES
1985-1986

Published by Top Shelf Productions, an imprint of IDW Publishing, a division of Idea and Design Works, LLC. Offices: Top Shelf Productions, c/o Idea & Design Works, LLC, 2765 Truxtun Road, San Diego, CA 92106. Top Shelf Productions®, the Top Shelf logo, Idea and Design Works®, and the IDW logo are registered trademarks of Idea and Design Works, LLC. All Rights Reserved. With the exception of small excerpts of artwork used for review purposes, none of the contents of this publication may be reprinted without the permission of IDW Publishing.

IDW Publishing does not read or accept unsolicited submissions of ideas, stories, or artwork.

Editor-in-Chief: Chris Staros

ISBN: 978-1-60309-499-3 24 23 22 21 4 3 2 1

Visit our online catalog at topshelfcomix.com.

Printed in Korea.

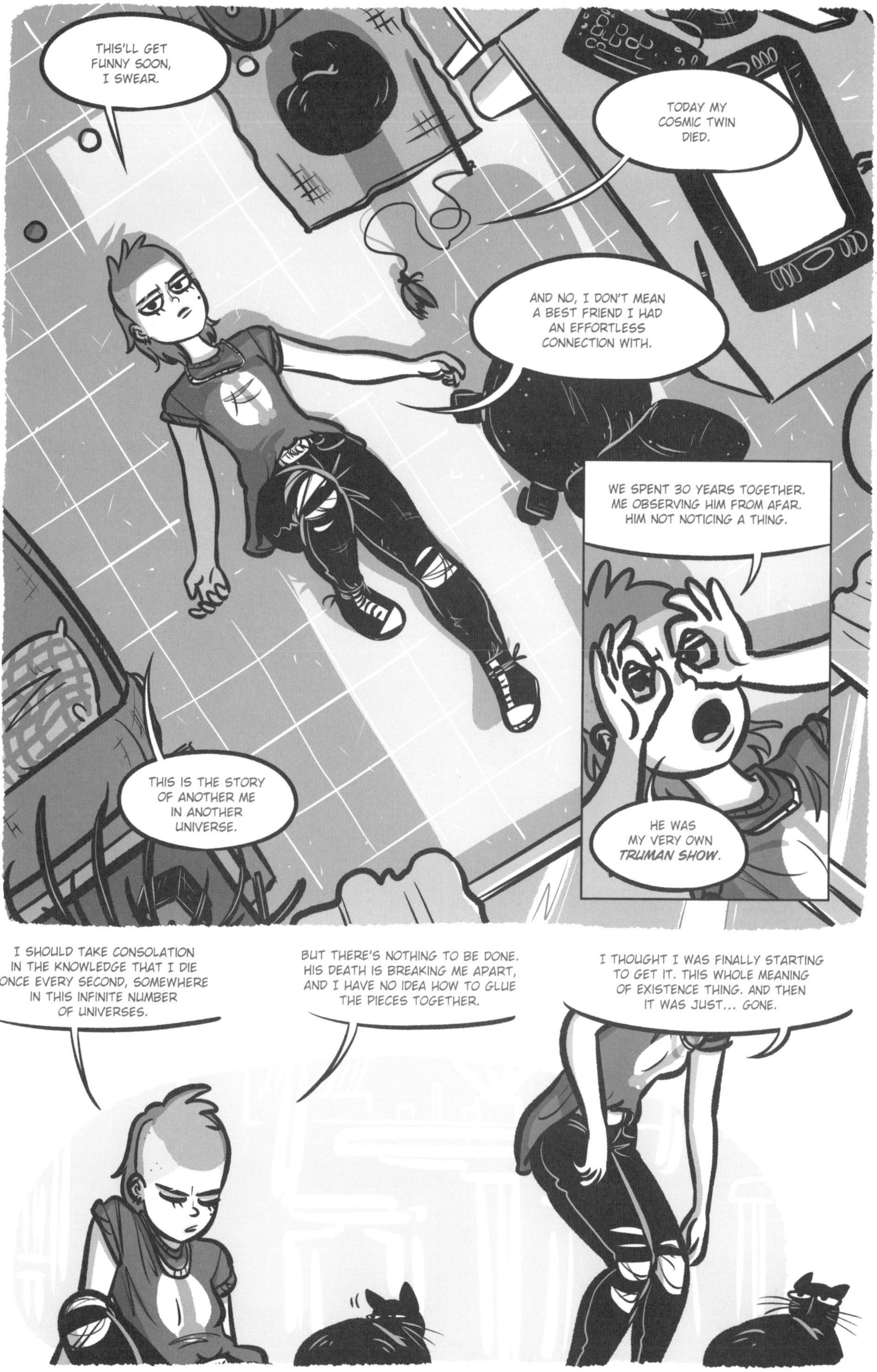

THIS'LL GET FUNNY SOON, I SWEAR.
TODAY MY COSMIC TWIN DIED.
AND NO, I DON'T MEAN A BEST FRIEND I HAD AN EFFORTLESS CONNECTION WITH.
THIS IS THE STORY OF ANOTHER ME IN ANOTHER UNIVERSE.
WE SPENT 30 YEARS TOGETHER. ME OBSERVING HIM FROM AFAR. HIM NOT NOTICING A THING.
HE WAS MY VERY OWN ***TRUMAN SHOW***.
I SHOULD TAKE CONSOLATION IN THE KNOWLEDGE THAT I DIE ONCE EVERY SECOND, SOMEWHERE IN THIS INFINITE NUMBER OF UNIVERSES.
BUT THERE'S NOTHING TO BE DONE. HIS DEATH IS BREAKING ME APART, AND I HAVE NO IDEA HOW TO GLUE THE PIECES TOGETHER.
I THOUGHT I WAS FINALLY STARTING TO GET IT. THIS WHOLE MEANING OF EXISTENCE THING. AND THEN IT WAS JUST... GONE.

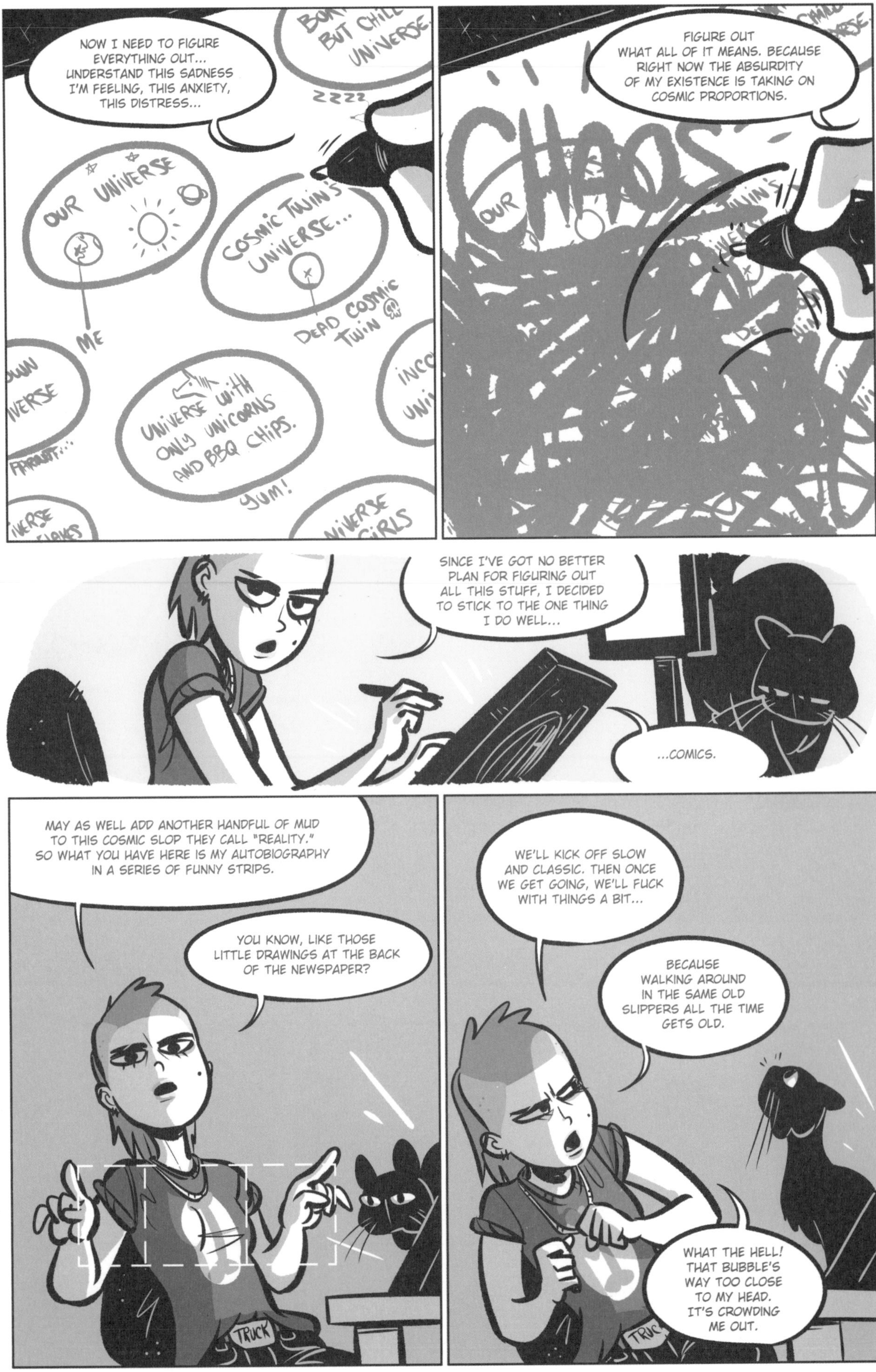
NOW I NEED TO FIGURE EVERYTHING OUT... UNDERSTAND THIS SADNESS I'M FEELING, THIS ANXIETY, THIS DISTRESS...
BUT CHILL UNIVERSE.
ZZZZ
OUR UNIVERSE
ME
COSMIC TWIN'S UNIVERSE...
DEAD COSMIC TWIN
UNIVERSE WITH ONLY UNICORNS AND BBQ CHIPS.
YUM!
FIGURE OUT WHAT ALL OF IT MEANS. BECAUSE RIGHT NOW THE ABSURDITY OF MY EXISTENCE IS TAKING ON COSMIC PROPORTIONS.
CHAOS
SINCE I'VE GOT NO BETTER PLAN FOR FIGURING OUT ALL THIS STUFF, I DECIDED TO STICK TO THE ONE THING I DO WELL...
...COMICS.
MAY AS WELL ADD ANOTHER HANDFUL OF MUD TO THIS COSMIC SLOP THEY CALL "REALITY." SO WHAT YOU HAVE HERE IS MY AUTOBIOGRAPHY IN A SERIES OF FUNNY STRIPS.
YOU KNOW, LIKE THOSE LITTLE DRAWINGS AT THE BACK OF THE NEWSPAPER?
TRUCK
WE'LL KICK OFF SLOW AND CLASSIC. THEN ONCE WE GET GOING, WE'LL FUCK WITH THINGS A BIT...
BECAUSE WALKING AROUND IN THE SAME OLD SLIPPERS ALL THE TIME GETS OLD.
WHAT THE HELL! THAT BUBBLE'S WAY TOO CLOSE TO MY HEAD. IT'S CROWDING ME OUT.

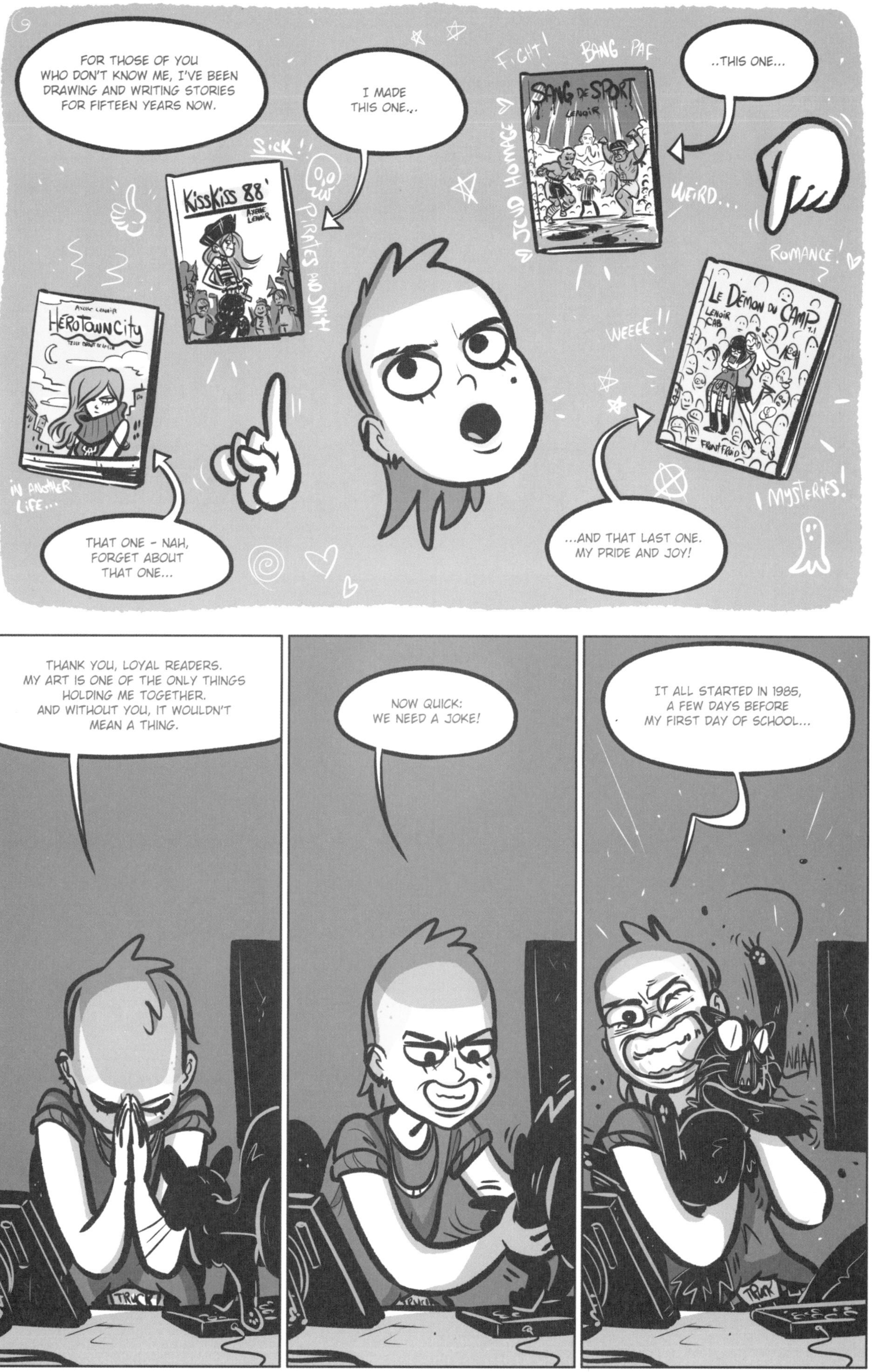
FOR THOSE OF YOU WHO DON'T KNOW ME, I'VE BEEN DRAWING AND WRITING STORIES FOR FIFTEEN YEARS NOW.
I MADE THIS ONE...
..THIS ONE...
THAT ONE - NAH, FORGET ABOUT THAT ONE...
...AND THAT LAST ONE. MY PRIDE AND JOY!
KissKiss 88'
SANG DE SPORT
LENOIR
HeroTownCity
LE DÉMON DU CAMP
SICK!
PIRATES AND SHIT
FIGHT!
BANG · PAF
JCVD HOMAGE
WEIRD...
ROMANCE!
WEEEE!!
MYSTERIES!
IN ANOTHER LIFE...
THANK YOU, LOYAL READERS. MY ART IS ONE OF THE ONLY THINGS HOLDING ME TOGETHER. AND WITHOUT YOU, IT WOULDN'T MEAN A THING.
NOW QUICK: WE NEED A JOKE!
IT ALL STARTED IN 1985, A FEW DAYS BEFORE MY FIRST DAY OF SCHOOL...
NAAA
TRUCK

CHAPTER 1

ALIEN PARENTS, ACTION FIGURES & A TALK WITH A FOREST

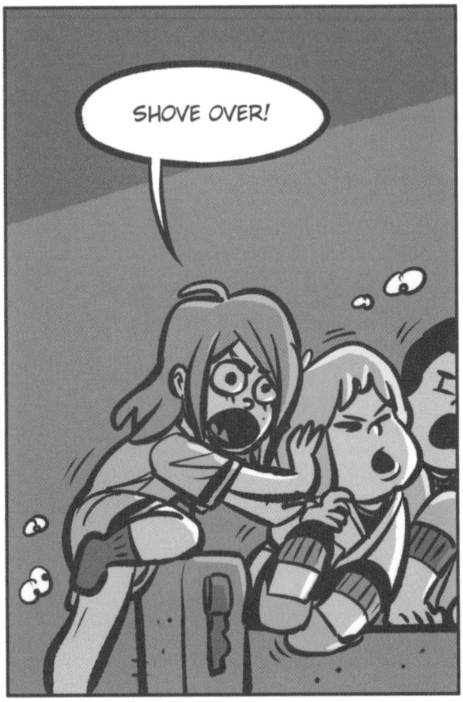
SHOVE OVER!

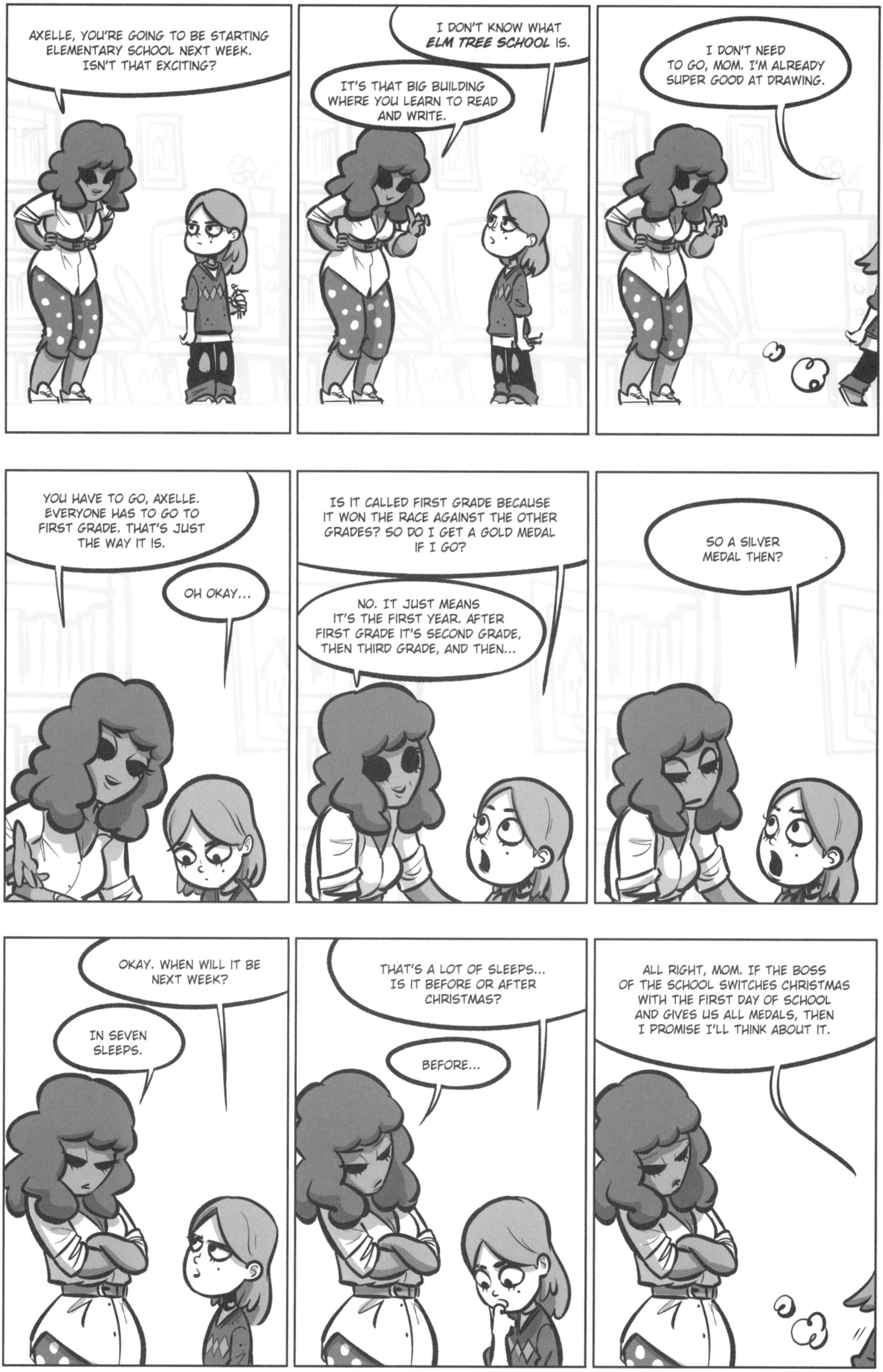
AXELLE, YOU'RE GOING TO BE STARTING ELEMENTARY SCHOOL NEXT WEEK. ISN'T THAT EXCITING?
I DON'T KNOW WHAT ***ELM TREE SCHOOL*** IS.
IT'S THAT BIG BUILDING WHERE YOU LEARN TO READ AND WRITE.
I DON'T NEED TO GO, MOM. I'M ALREADY SUPER GOOD AT DRAWING.
YOU HAVE TO GO, AXELLE. EVERYONE HAS TO GO TO FIRST GRADE. THAT'S JUST THE WAY IT IS.
OH OKAY...
IS IT CALLED FIRST GRADE BECAUSE IT WON THE RACE AGAINST THE OTHER GRADES? SO DO I GET A GOLD MEDAL IF I GO?
NO. IT JUST MEANS IT'S THE FIRST YEAR. AFTER FIRST GRADE IT'S SECOND GRADE, THEN THIRD GRADE, AND THEN...
SO A SILVER MEDAL THEN?
OKAY. WHEN WILL IT BE NEXT WEEK?
IN SEVEN SLEEPS.
THAT'S A LOT OF SLEEPS... IS IT BEFORE OR AFTER CHRISTMAS?
BEFORE...
ALL RIGHT, MOM. IF THE BOSS OF THE SCHOOL SWITCHES CHRISTMAS WITH THE FIRST DAY OF SCHOOL AND GIVES US ALL MEDALS, THEN I PROMISE I'LL THINK ABOUT IT.

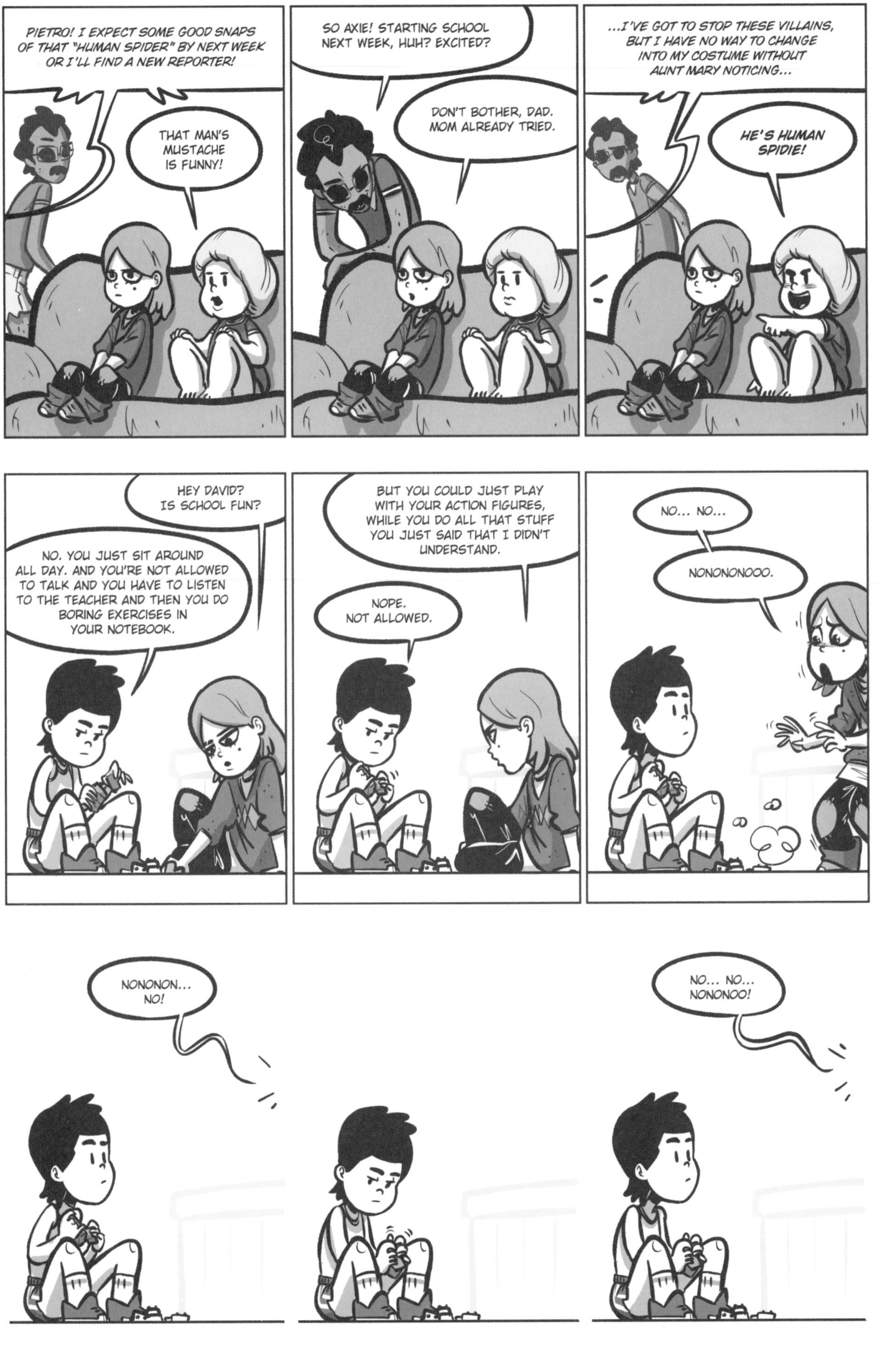
PIETRO! I EXPECT SOME GOOD SNAPS OF THAT "HUMAN SPIDER" BY NEXT WEEK OR I'LL FIND A NEW REPORTER!
THAT MAN'S MUSTACHE IS FUNNY!
SO AXIE! STARTING SCHOOL NEXT WEEK, HUH? EXCITED?
DON'T BOTHER, DAD. MOM ALREADY TRIED.
...I'VE GOT TO STOP THESE VILLAINS, BUT I HAVE NO WAY TO CHANGE INTO MY COSTUME WITHOUT AUNT MARY NOTICING...
HE'S HUMAN SPIDIE!
HEY DAVID? IS SCHOOL FUN?
NO. YOU JUST SIT AROUND ALL DAY. AND YOU'RE NOT ALLOWED TO TALK AND YOU HAVE TO LISTEN TO THE TEACHER AND THEN YOU DO BORING EXERCISES IN YOUR NOTEBOOK.
BUT YOU COULD JUST PLAY WITH YOUR ACTION FIGURES, WHILE YOU DO ALL THAT STUFF YOU JUST SAID THAT I DIDN'T UNDERSTAND.
NOPE. NOT ALLOWED.
NO... NO...
NONONONOOO.
NONONON... NO!
NO... NO... NONONOO!

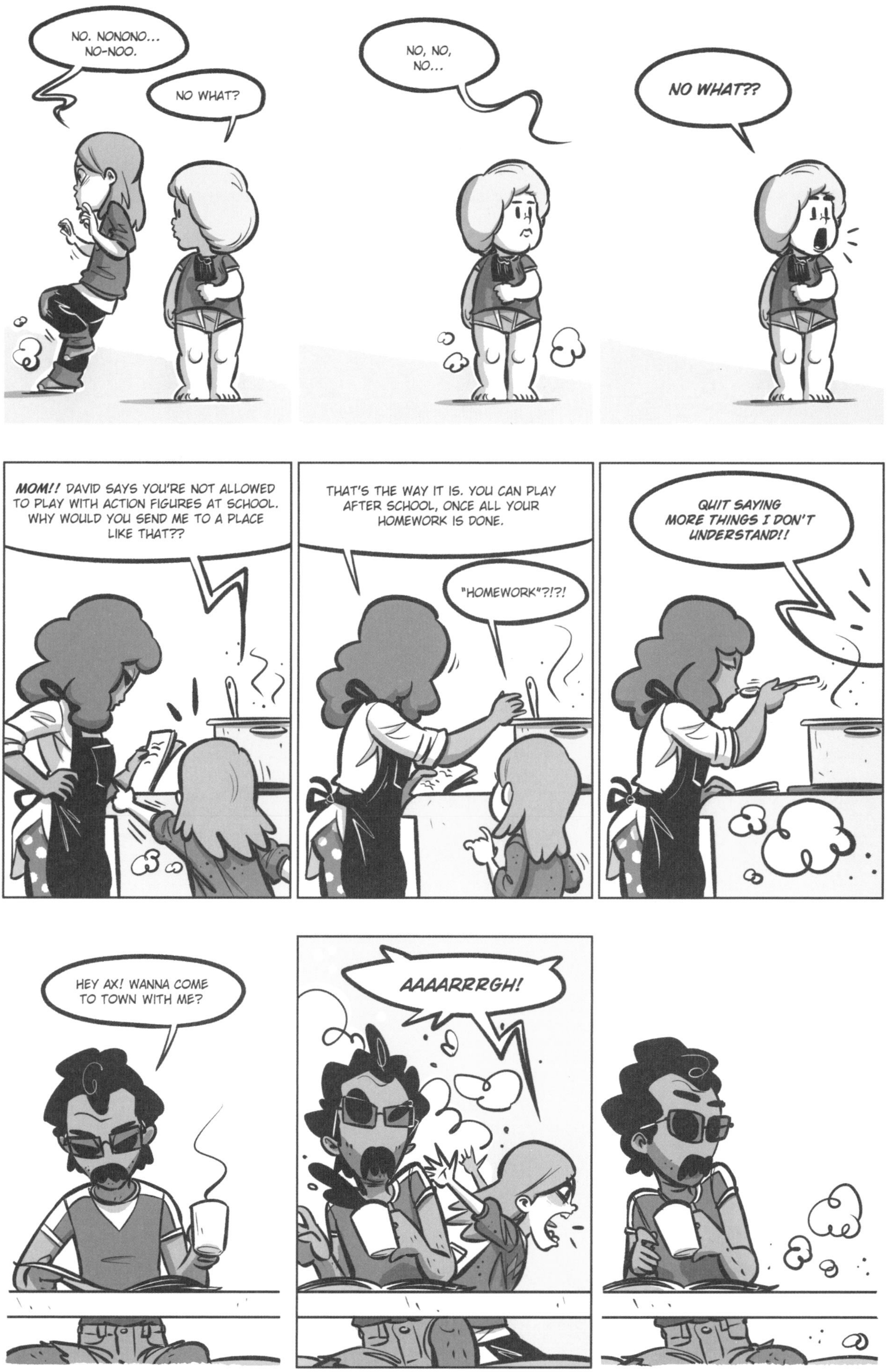
NO. NONONO...
NO-NOO.
NO WHAT?
NO, NO,
NO...
NO WHAT??
MOM!! DAVID SAYS YOU'RE NOT ALLOWED TO PLAY WITH ACTION FIGURES AT SCHOOL. WHY WOULD YOU SEND ME TO A PLACE LIKE THAT??
THAT'S THE WAY IT IS. YOU CAN PLAY AFTER SCHOOL, ONCE ALL YOUR HOMEWORK IS DONE.
"HOMEWORK"?!?!
QUIT SAYING MORE THINGS I DON'T UNDERSTAND!!
HEY AX! WANNA COME TO TOWN WITH ME?
AAAARRRGH!

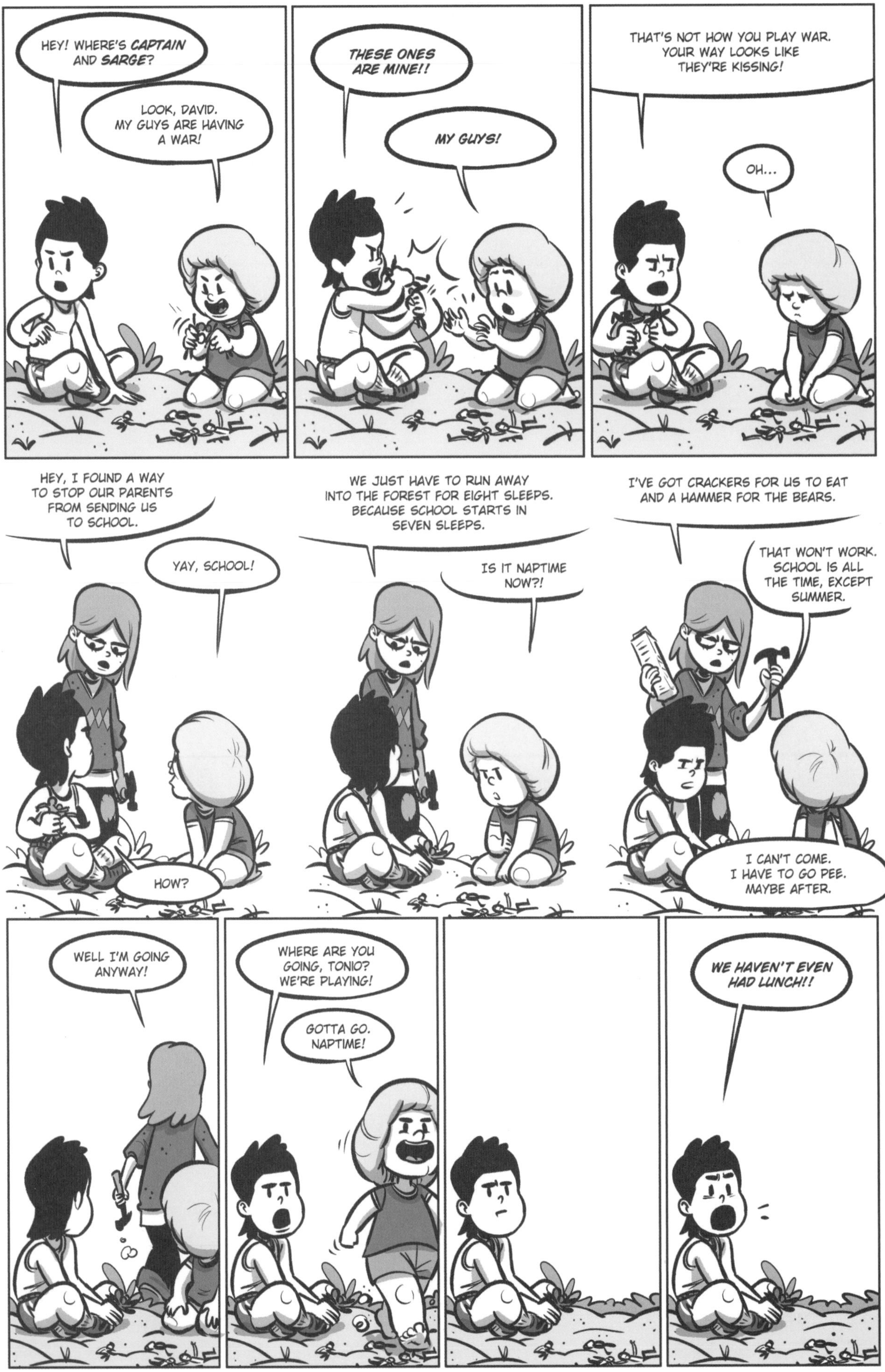
HEY! WHERE'S CAPTAIN AND SARGE?
LOOK, DAVID. MY GUYS ARE HAVING A WAR!
THESE ONES ARE MINE!!
MY GUYS!
THAT'S NOT HOW YOU PLAY WAR. YOUR WAY LOOKS LIKE THEY'RE KISSING!
OH...
HEY, I FOUND A WAY TO STOP OUR PARENTS FROM SENDING US TO SCHOOL.
YAY, SCHOOL!
HOW?
WE JUST HAVE TO RUN AWAY INTO THE FOREST FOR EIGHT SLEEPS. BECAUSE SCHOOL STARTS IN SEVEN SLEEPS.
IS IT NAPTIME NOW?!
I'VE GOT CRACKERS FOR US TO EAT AND A HAMMER FOR THE BEARS.
THAT WON'T WORK. SCHOOL IS ALL THE TIME, EXCEPT SUMMER.
I CAN'T COME. I HAVE TO GO PEE. MAYBE AFTER.
WELL I'M GOING ANYWAY!
WHERE ARE YOU GOING, TONIO? WE'RE PLAYING!
GOTTA GO. NAPTIME!
WE HAVEN'T EVEN HAD LUNCH!!

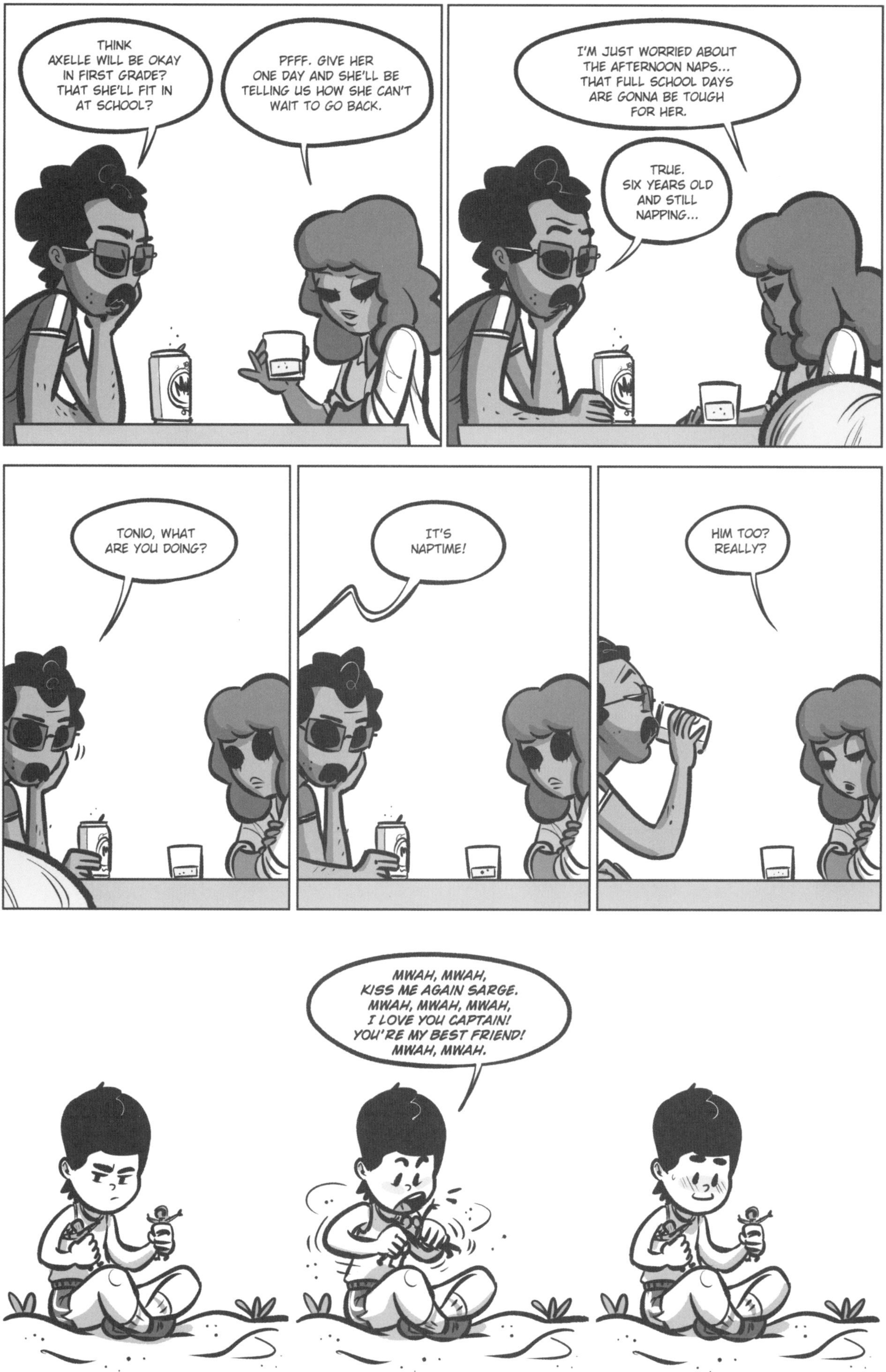
THINK AXELLE WILL BE OKAY IN FIRST GRADE? THAT SHE'LL FIT IN AT SCHOOL?
PFFF. GIVE HER ONE DAY AND SHE'LL BE TELLING US HOW SHE CAN'T WAIT TO GO BACK.
I'M JUST WORRIED ABOUT THE AFTERNOON NAPS... THAT FULL SCHOOL DAYS ARE GONNA BE TOUGH FOR HER.
TRUE. SIX YEARS OLD AND STILL NAPPING...
TONIO, WHAT ARE YOU DOING?
IT'S NAPTIME!
HIM TOO? REALLY?
MWAH, MWAH, KISS ME AGAIN SARGE. MWAH, MWAH, MWAH, I LOVE YOU CAPTAIN! YOU'RE MY BEST FRIEND! MWAH, MWAH.

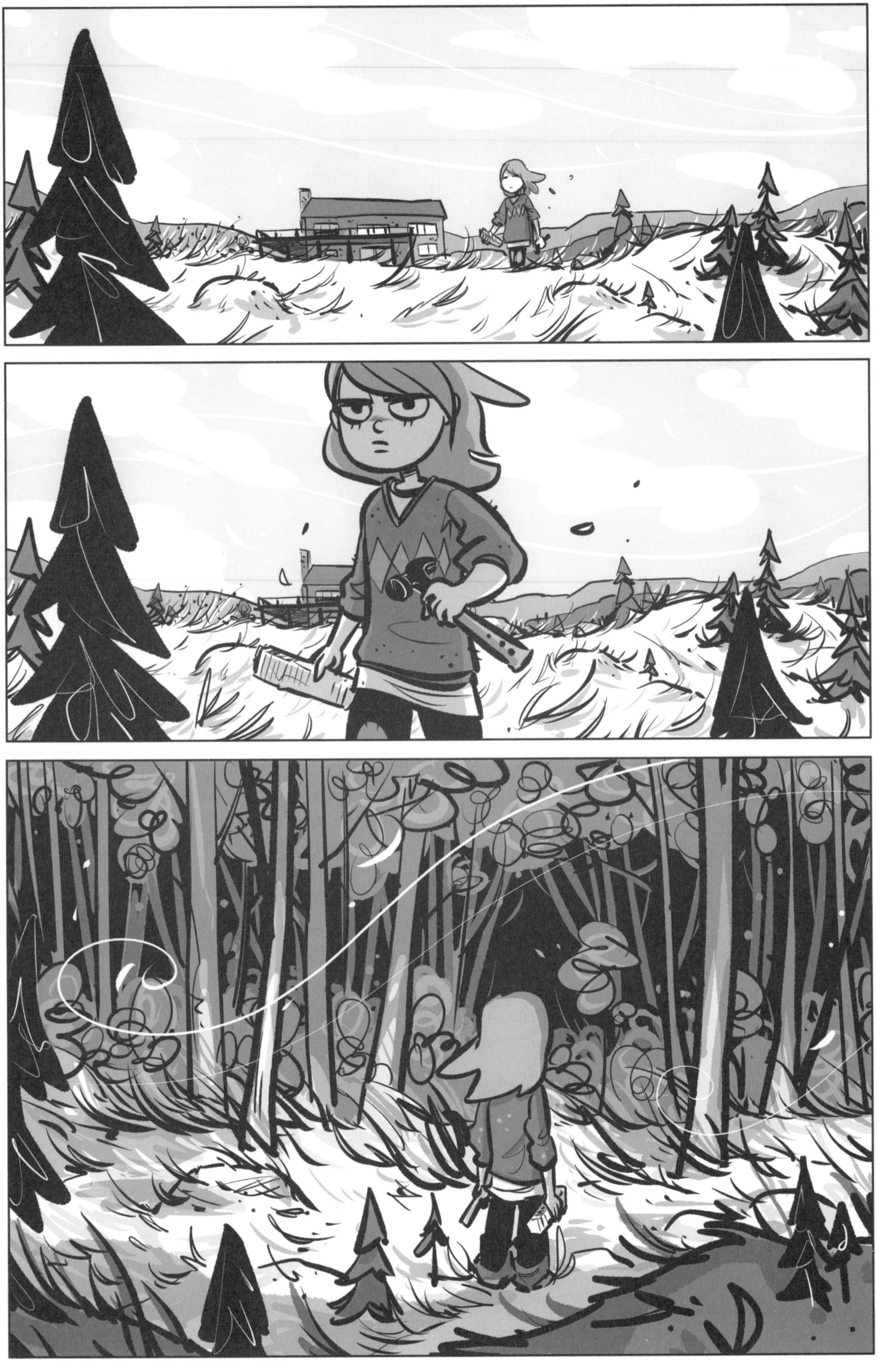

UHH... HI, FOREST. I HAVE TO GO INSIDE YOU. BECAUSE I'VE GOT TO RUN AWAY FROM SCHOOL.

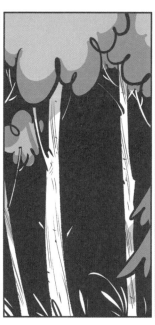

I'M KINDA SCARED OF YOU, SO MAYBE YOU COULD GIVE ME A SIGN THAT YOU WON'T HURT ME?

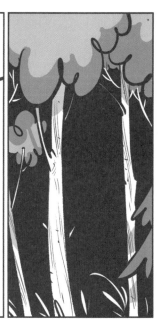

HEY! ANSWER ME! I'M NOT SCARED YOU KNOW! AND I'VE GOT A HAMMER FOR THE BEARS!!

I'M GOING TO WALK IN SLOW, JUST IN CASE YOU WERE ABOUT TO GIVE ME A SIGN, OK?

WOOOOOO-OOOO...

OKAY, THANKS.

NOW CAN YOU SEND ANOTHER SIGN? SO I KNOW IF THE LAST ONE WAS A GOOD OR BAD SIGN?

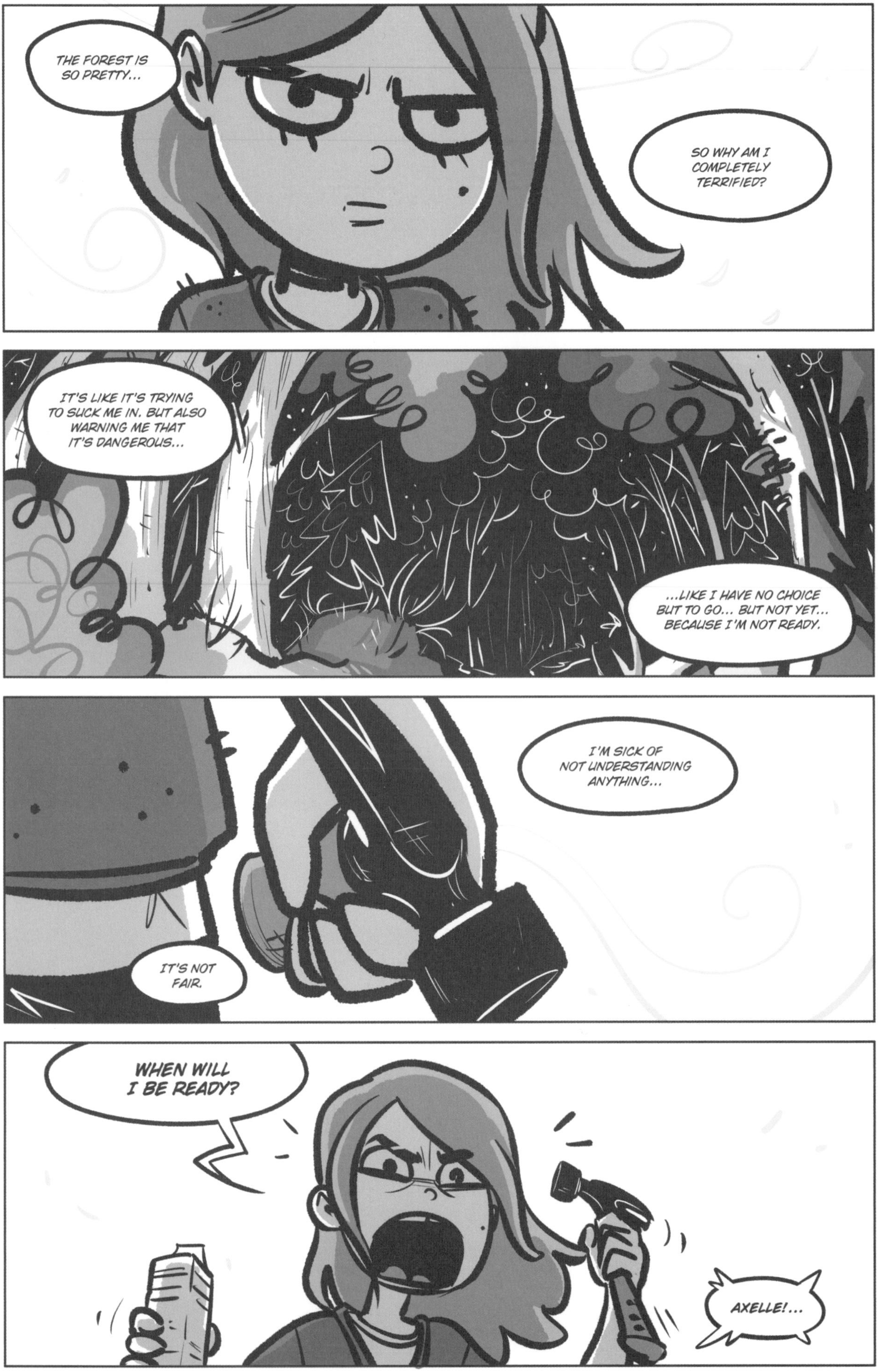

THE FOREST IS SO PRETTY...
SO WHY AM I COMPLETELY TERRIFIED?
IT'S LIKE IT'S TRYING TO SUCK ME IN. BUT ALSO WARNING ME THAT IT'S DANGEROUS...
...LIKE I HAVE NO CHOICE BUT TO GO... BUT NOT YET... BECAUSE I'M NOT READY.
I'M SICK OF NOT UNDERSTANDING ANYTHING...
IT'S NOT FAIR.
WHEN WILL I BE READY?
AXELLE!...

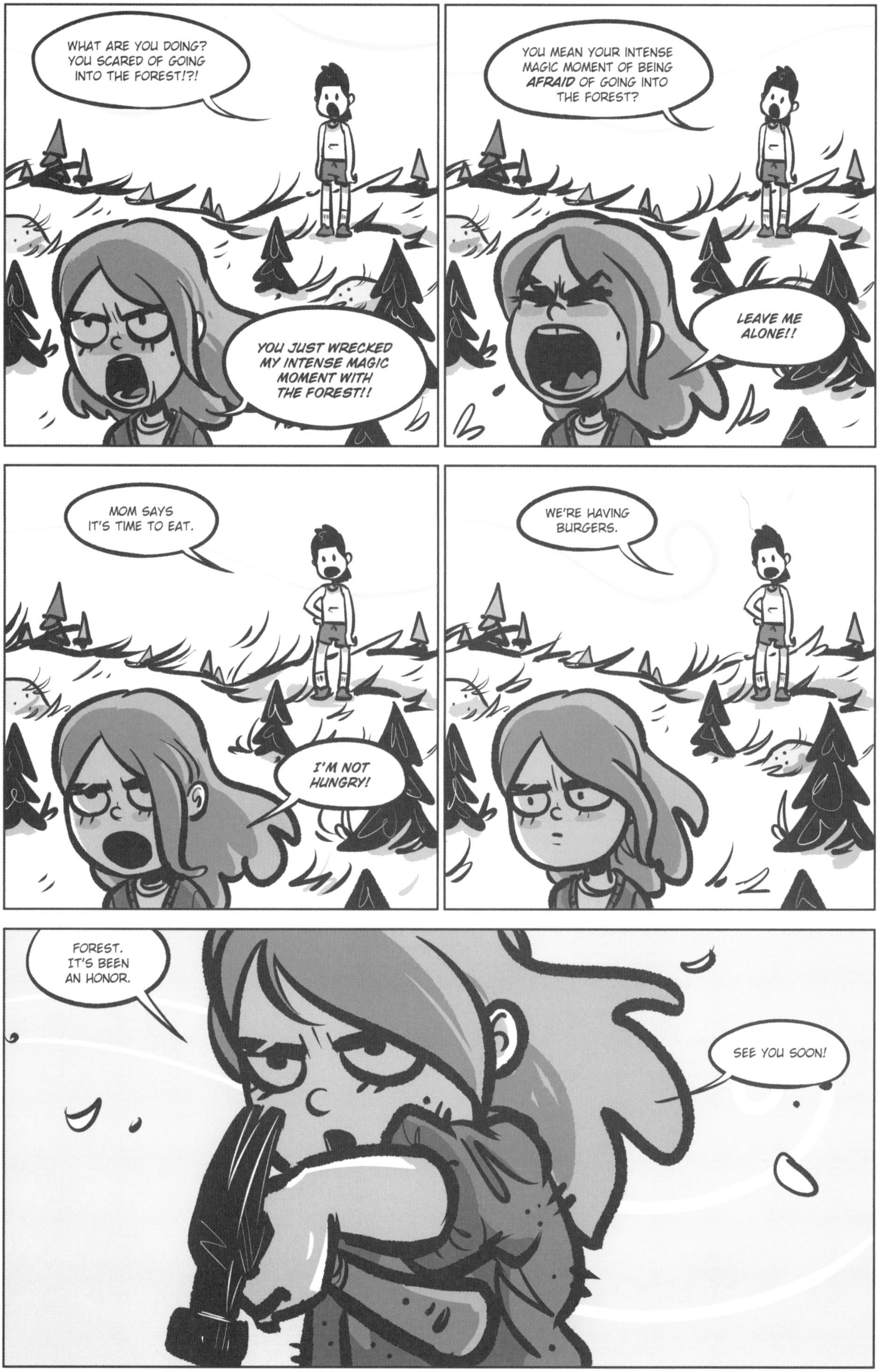
WHAT ARE YOU DOING? YOU SCARED OF GOING INTO THE FOREST!?!
YOU JUST WRECKED MY INTENSE MAGIC MOMENT WITH THE FOREST!!
YOU MEAN YOUR INTENSE MAGIC MOMENT OF BEING AFRAID OF GOING INTO THE FOREST?
LEAVE ME ALONE!!
MOM SAYS IT'S TIME TO EAT.
I'M NOT HUNGRY!
WE'RE HAVING BURGERS.
FOREST. IT'S BEEN AN HONOR.
SEE YOU SOON!

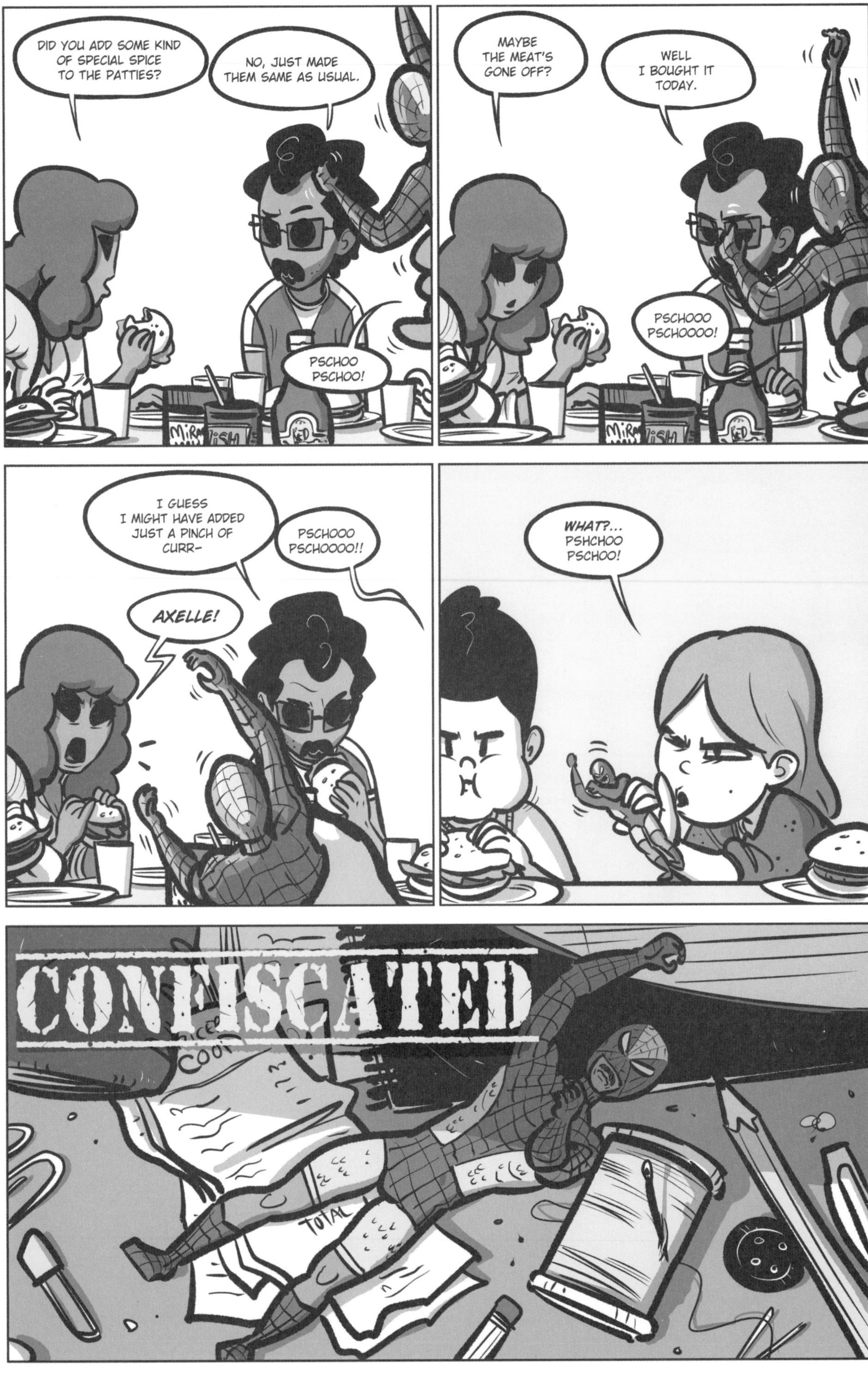
DID YOU ADD SOME KIND OF SPECIAL SPICE TO THE PATTIES?
NO, JUST MADE THEM SAME AS USUAL.
PSCHOO PSCHOO!
MAYBE THE MEAT'S GONE OFF?
WELL I BOUGHT IT TODAY.
PSCHOOO PSCHOOOO!
I GUESS I MIGHT HAVE ADDED JUST A PINCH OF CURR-
PSCHOOO PSCHOOOO!!
AXELLE!
WHAT?... PSHCHOO PSCHOO!
CONFISCATED
TOTAL

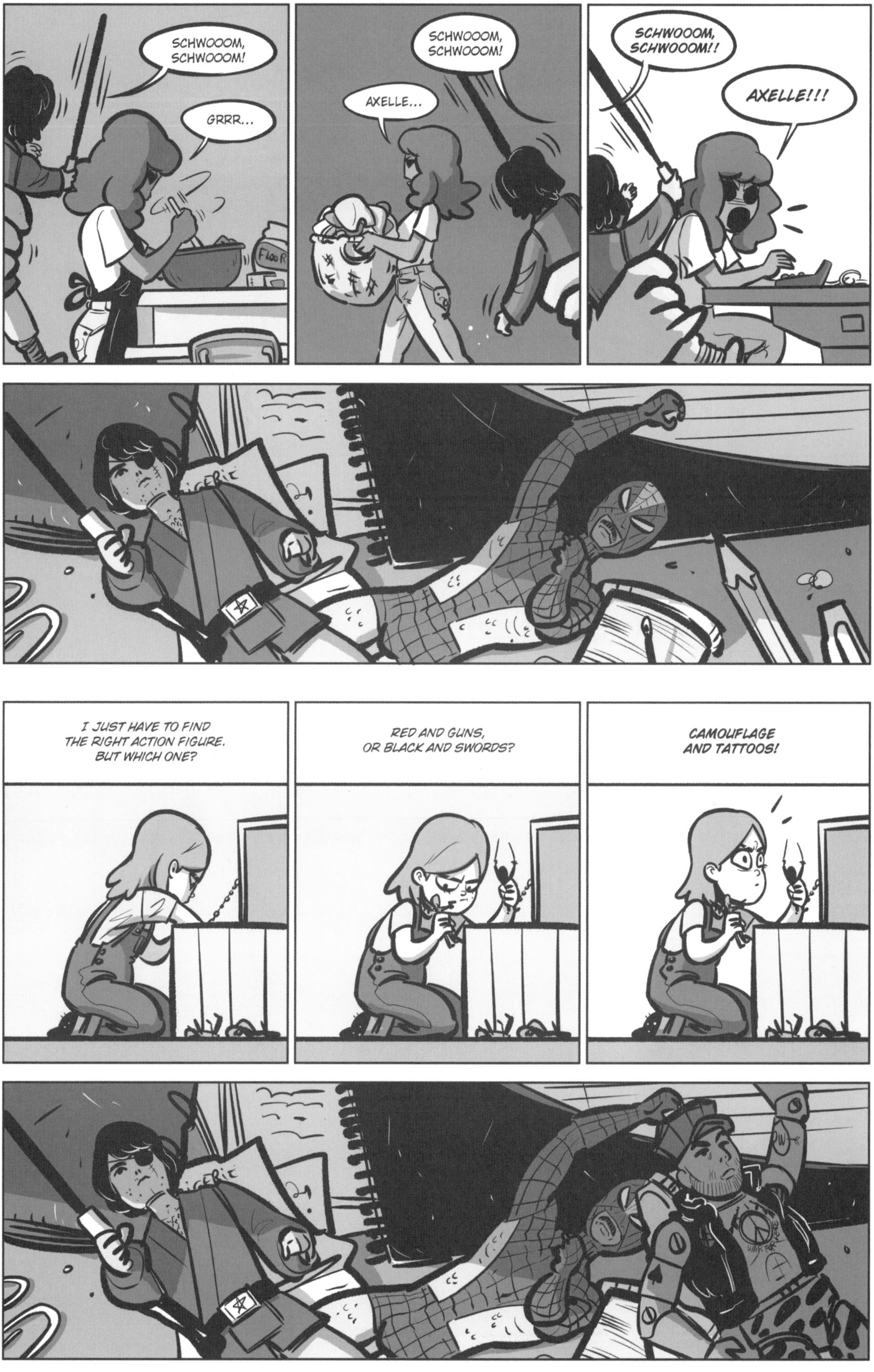

SCHWOOOM, SCHWOOOM!
GRRR...
SCHWOOOM, SCHWOOOM!
AXELLE...
SCHWOOOM, SCHWOOOM!!
AXELLE!!!
I JUST HAVE TO FIND THE RIGHT ACTION FIGURE. BUT WHICH ONE?
RED AND GUNS, OR BLACK AND SWORDS?
CAMOUFLAGE AND TATTOOS!

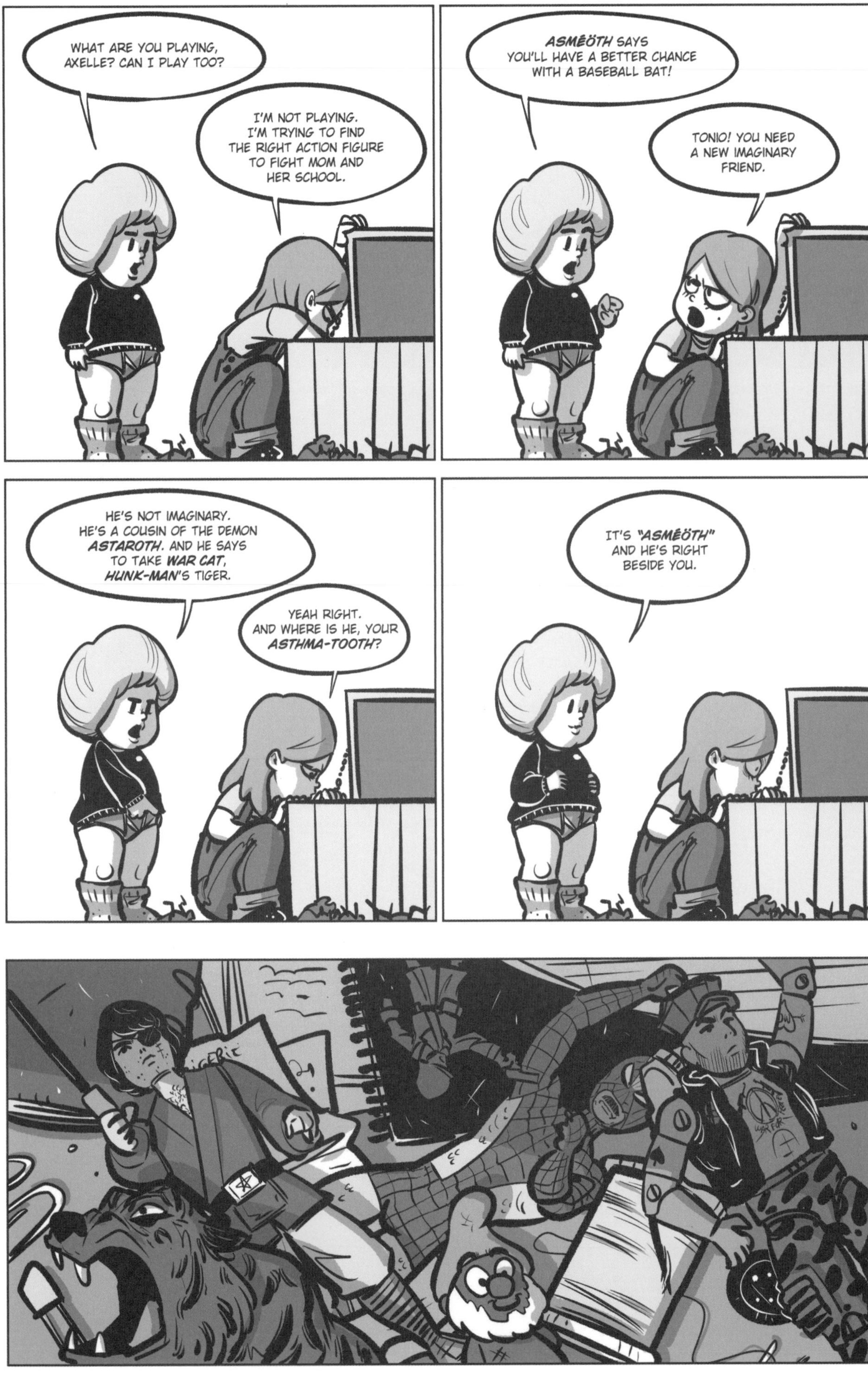
WHAT ARE YOU PLAYING, AXELLE? CAN I PLAY TOO?
I'M NOT PLAYING. I'M TRYING TO FIND THE RIGHT ACTION FIGURE TO FIGHT MOM AND HER SCHOOL.
ASMÊÖTH SAYS YOU'LL HAVE A BETTER CHANCE WITH A BASEBALL BAT!
TONIO! YOU NEED A NEW IMAGINARY FRIEND.
HE'S NOT IMAGINARY. HE'S A COUSIN OF THE DEMON ASTAROTH. AND HE SAYS TO TAKE WAR CAT, HUNK-MAN'S TIGER.
YEAH RIGHT. AND WHERE IS HE, YOUR ASTHMA-TOOTH?
IT'S "ASMÊÖTH" AND HE'S RIGHT BESIDE YOU.

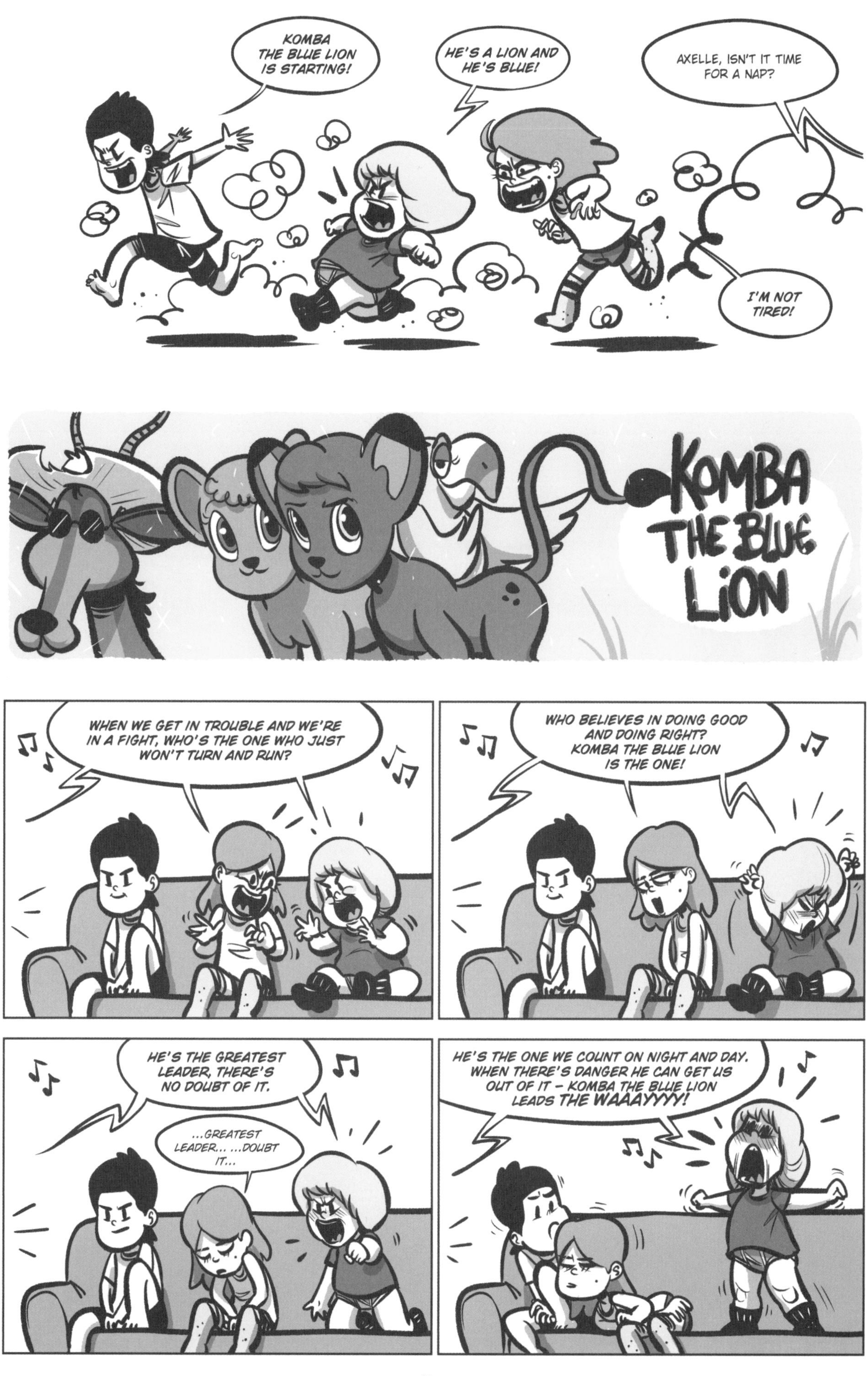
KOMBA THE BLUE LION IS STARTING!
HE'S A LION AND HE'S BLUE!
AXELLE, ISN'T IT TIME FOR A NAP?
I'M NOT TIRED!
KOMBA THE BLUE LION
WHEN WE GET IN TROUBLE AND WE'RE IN A FIGHT, WHO'S THE ONE WHO JUST WON'T TURN AND RUN?
WHO BELIEVES IN DOING GOOD AND DOING RIGHT? KOMBA THE BLUE LION IS THE ONE!
HE'S THE GREATEST LEADER, THERE'S NO DOUBT OF IT.
...GREATEST LEADER... ...DOUBT IT...
HE'S THE ONE WE COUNT ON NIGHT AND DAY. WHEN THERE'S DANGER HE CAN GET US OUT OF IT – KOMBA THE BLUE LION LEADS THE WAAAYYYY!

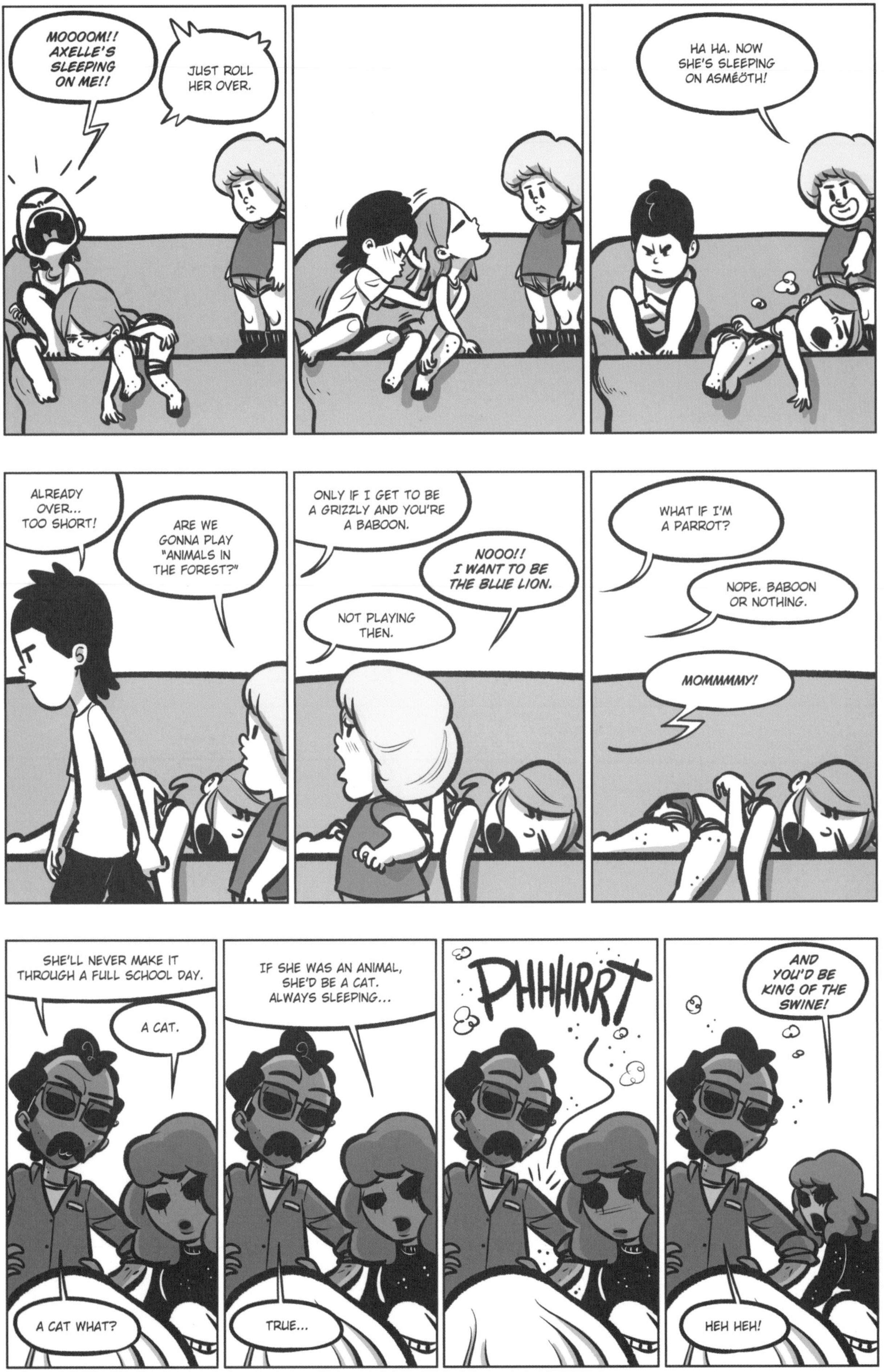
MOOOOM!! AXELLE'S SLEEPING ON ME!!
JUST ROLL HER OVER.
HA HA. NOW SHE'S SLEEPING ON ASMÉÖTH!
ALREADY OVER... TOO SHORT!
ARE WE GONNA PLAY "ANIMALS IN THE FOREST?"
ONLY IF I GET TO BE A GRIZZLY AND YOU'RE A BABOON.
NOOO!! I WANT TO BE THE BLUE LION.
NOT PLAYING THEN.
WHAT IF I'M A PARROT?
NOPE. BABOON OR NOTHING.
MOMMMMY!
SHE'LL NEVER MAKE IT THROUGH A FULL SCHOOL DAY.
A CAT.
A CAT WHAT?
IF SHE WAS AN ANIMAL, SHE'D BE A CAT. ALWAYS SLEEPING...
TRUE...
PHHHRRT
AND YOU'D BE KING OF THE SWINE!
HEH HEH!

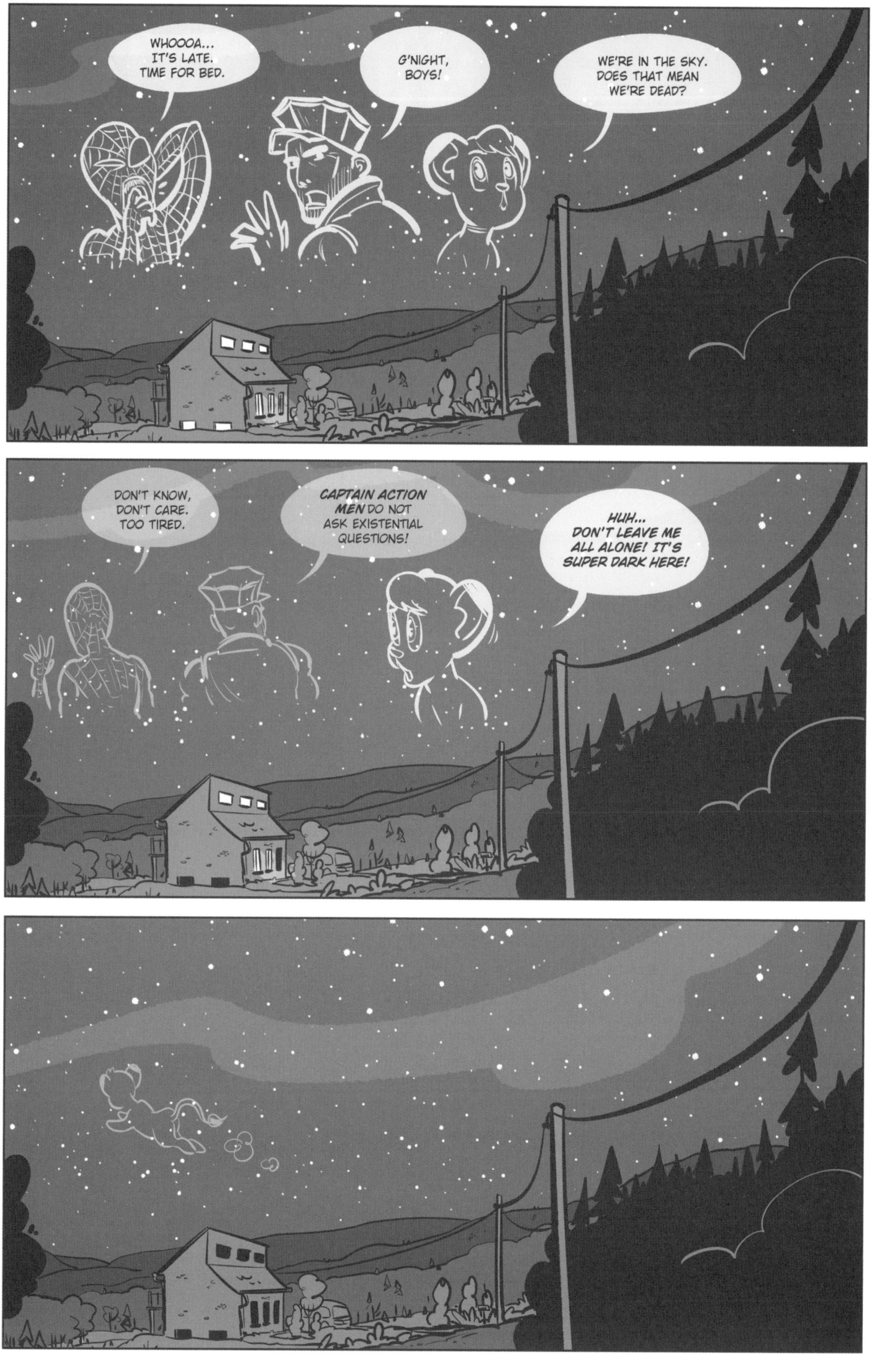
WHOOOA... IT'S LATE. TIME FOR BED.
G'NIGHT, BOYS!
WE'RE IN THE SKY. DOES THAT MEAN WE'RE DEAD?
DON'T KNOW, DON'T CARE. TOO TIRED.
CAPTAIN ACTION MEN DO NOT ASK EXISTENTIAL QUESTIONS!
HUH... DON'T LEAVE ME ALL ALONE! IT'S SUPER DARK HERE!

SATURDAY MORNING CARTOONS

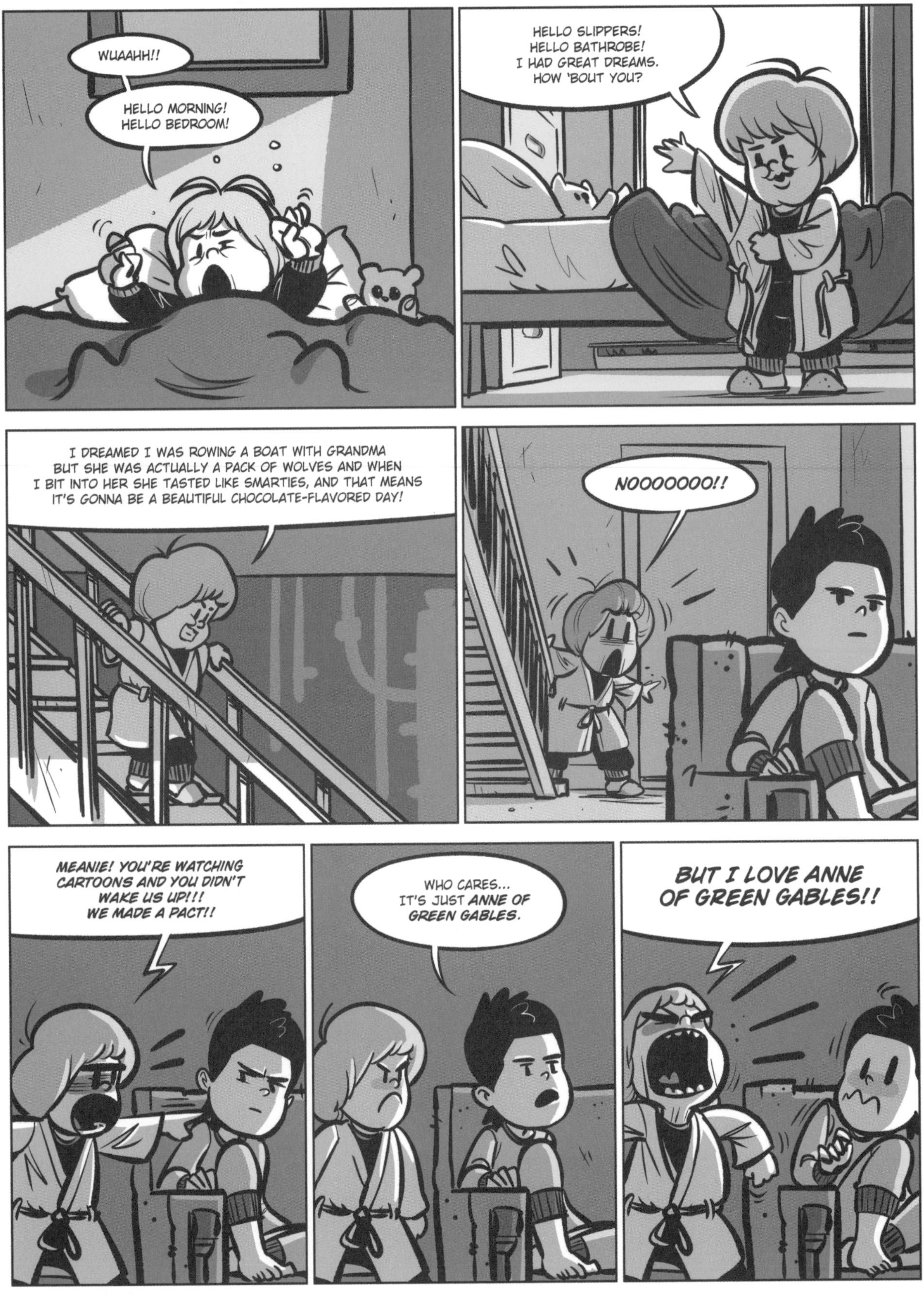

WUAAHH!!
HELLO MORNING! HELLO BEDROOM!
HELLO SLIPPERS! HELLO BATHROBE! I HAD GREAT DREAMS. HOW 'BOUT YOU?
I DREAMED I WAS ROWING A BOAT WITH GRANDMA BUT SHE WAS ACTUALLY A PACK OF WOLVES AND WHEN I BIT INTO HER SHE TASTED LIKE SMARTIES, AND THAT MEANS IT'S GONNA BE A BEAUTIFUL CHOCOLATE-FLAVORED DAY!
NOOOOOOO!!
MEANIE! YOU'RE WATCHING CARTOONS AND YOU DIDN'T WAKE US UP!!! WE MADE A PACT!!
WHO CARES... IT'S JUST ANNE OF GREEN GABLES.
BUT I LOVE ANNE OF GREEN GABLES!!

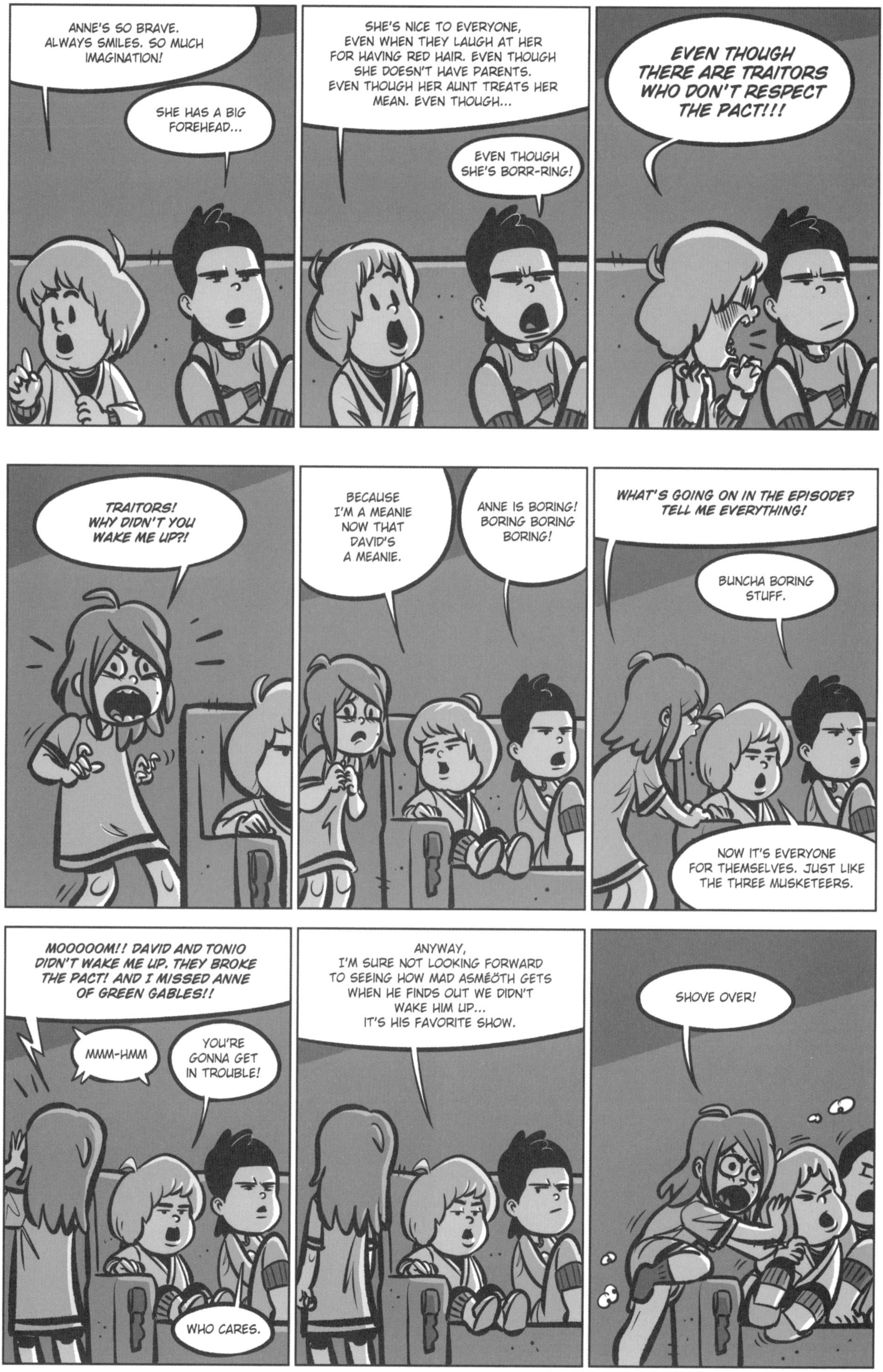
ANNE'S SO BRAVE. ALWAYS SMILES. SO MUCH IMAGINATION!
SHE HAS A BIG FOREHEAD...
SHE'S NICE TO EVERYONE, EVEN WHEN THEY LAUGH AT HER FOR HAVING RED HAIR. EVEN THOUGH SHE DOESN'T HAVE PARENTS. EVEN THOUGH HER AUNT TREATS HER MEAN. EVEN THOUGH...
EVEN THOUGH SHE'S BORR-RING!
EVEN THOUGH THERE ARE TRAITORS WHO DON'T RESPECT THE PACT!!!
TRAITORS! WHY DIDN'T YOU WAKE ME UP?!
BECAUSE I'M A MEANIE NOW THAT DAVID'S A MEANIE.
ANNE IS BORING! BORING BORING BORING!
WHAT'S GOING ON IN THE EPISODE? TELL ME EVERYTHING!
BUNCHA BORING STUFF.
NOW IT'S EVERYONE FOR THEMSELVES. JUST LIKE THE THREE MUSKETEERS.
MOOOOOM!! DAVID AND TONIO DIDN'T WAKE ME UP. THEY BROKE THE PACT! AND I MISSED ANNE OF GREEN GABLES!!
MMM-HMM
YOU'RE GONNA GET IN TROUBLE!
WHO CARES.
ANYWAY, I'M SURE NOT LOOKING FORWARD TO SEEING HOW MAD ASMÉÖTH GETS WHEN HE FINDS OUT WE DIDN'T WAKE HIM UP... IT'S HIS FAVORITE SHOW.
SHOVE OVER!

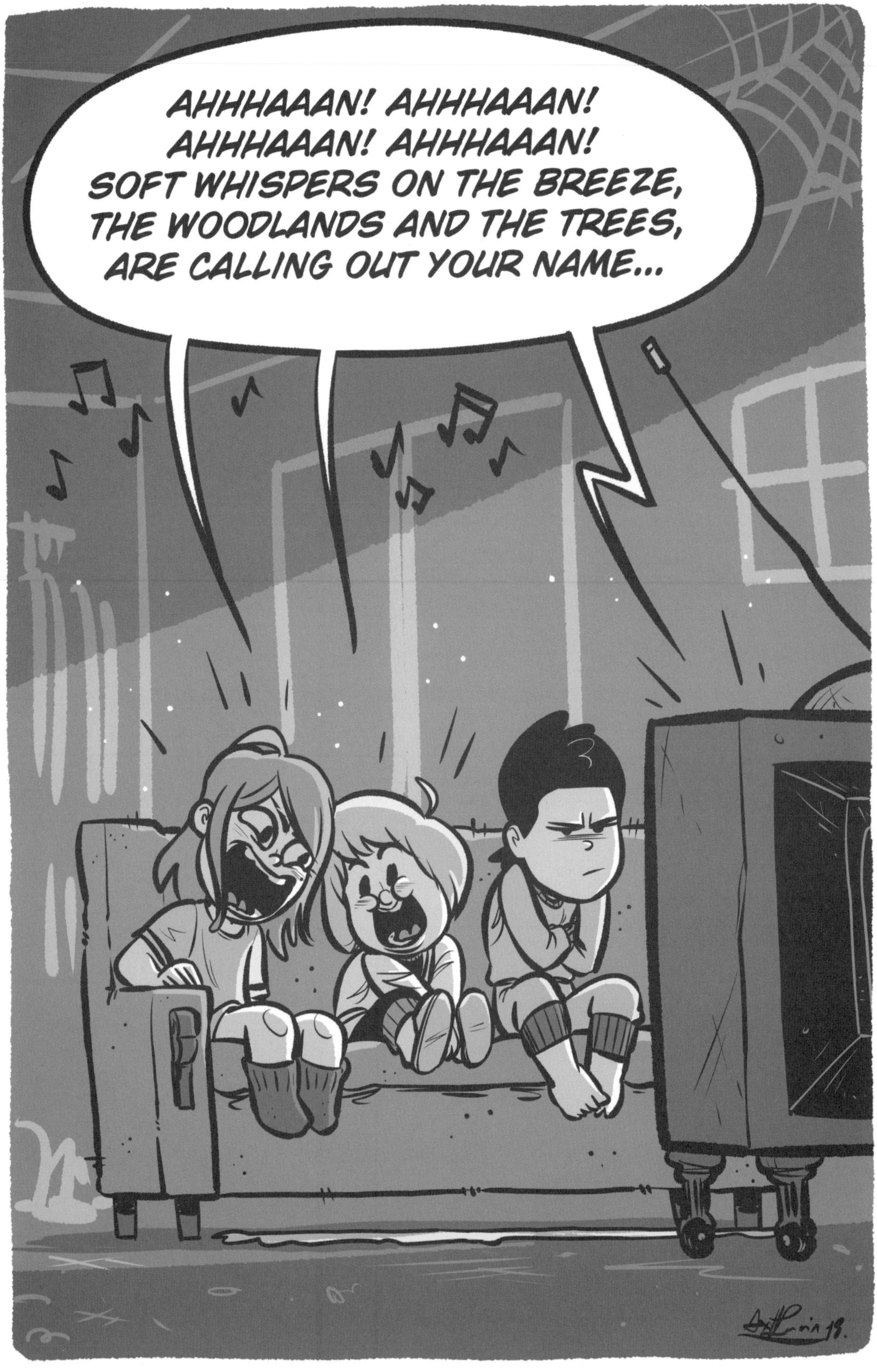
AHHHAAAN! AHHHAAAN! AHHHAAAN! AHHHAAAN! SOFT WHISPERS ON THE BREEZE, THE WOODLANDS AND THE TREES, ARE CALLING OUT YOUR NAME...

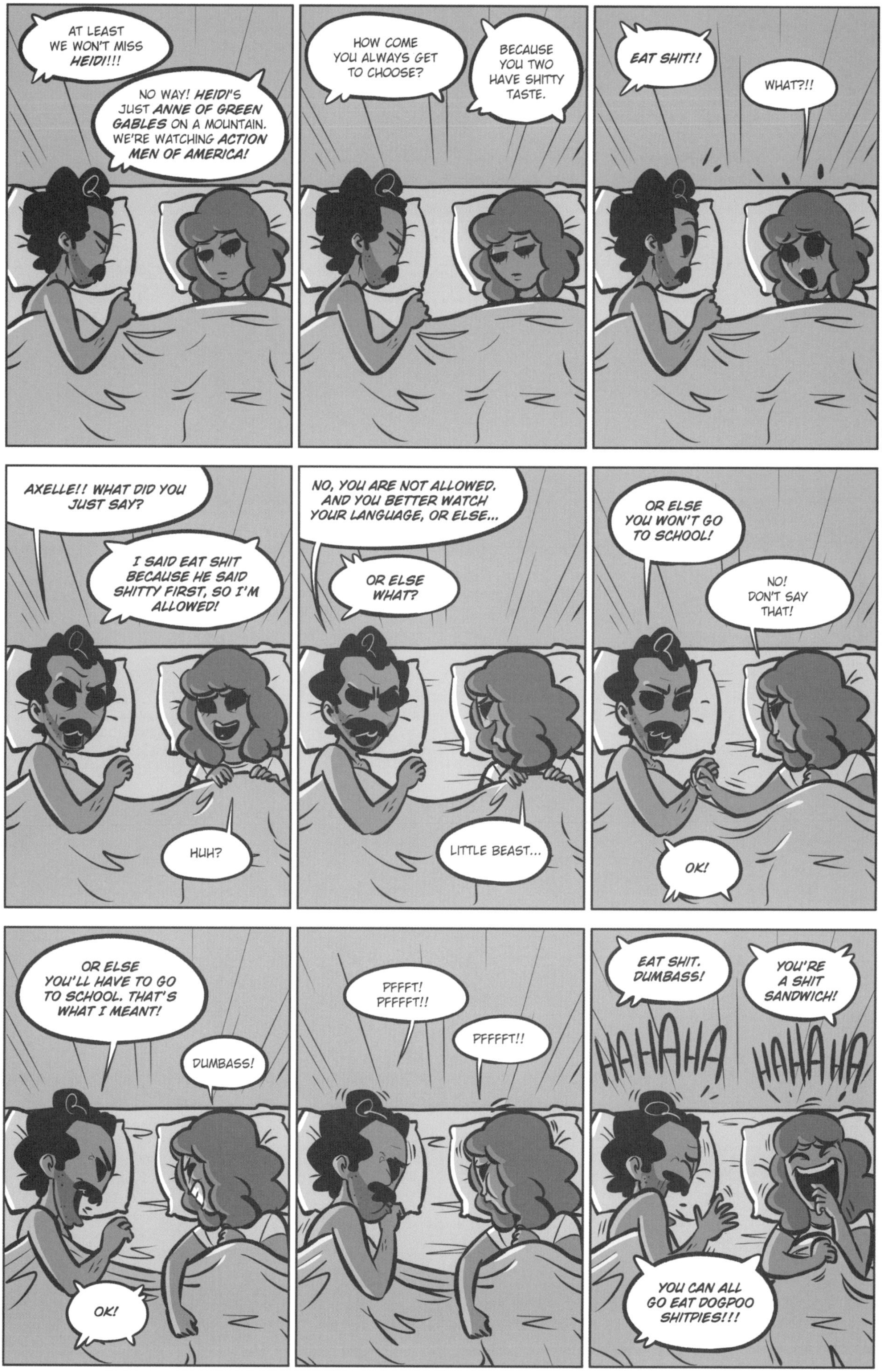
AT LEAST WE WON'T MISS HEIDI!!!
NO WAY! HEIDI'S JUST ANNE OF GREEN GABLES ON A MOUNTAIN. WE'RE WATCHING ACTION MEN OF AMERICA!
HOW COME YOU ALWAYS GET TO CHOOSE?
BECAUSE YOU TWO HAVE SHITTY TASTE.
EAT SHIT!!
WHAT?!!
AXELLE!! WHAT DID YOU JUST SAY?
I SAID EAT SHIT BECAUSE HE SAID SHITTY FIRST, SO I'M ALLOWED!
HUH?
NO, YOU ARE NOT ALLOWED. AND YOU BETTER WATCH YOUR LANGUAGE, OR ELSE...
OR ELSE WHAT?
LITTLE BEAST...
OR ELSE YOU WON'T GO TO SCHOOL!
NO! DON'T SAY THAT!
OK!
OR ELSE YOU'LL HAVE TO GO TO SCHOOL. THAT'S WHAT I MEANT!
DUMBASS!
OK!
PFFFT! PFFFFT!!
PFFFFT!!
EAT SHIT. DUMBASS!
YOU'RE A SHIT SANDWICH!
HAHAHA
HAHAHA
YOU CAN ALL GO EAT DOGPOO SHITPIES!!!

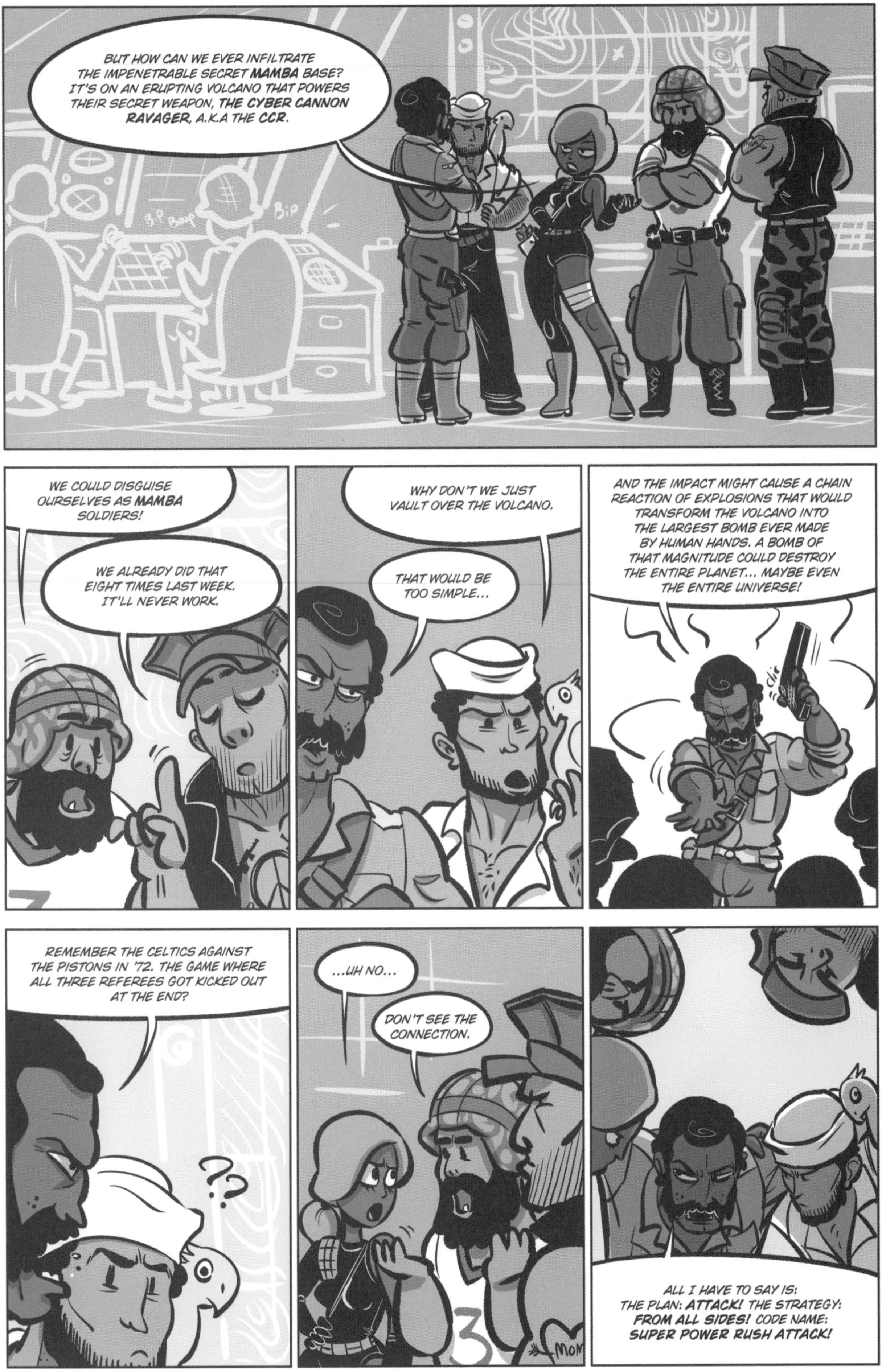
BUT HOW CAN WE EVER INFILTRATE THE IMPENETRABLE SECRET MAMBA BASE? IT'S ON AN ERUPTING VOLCANO THAT POWERS THEIR SECRET WEAPON, THE CYBER CANNON RAVAGER, A.K.A THE CCR.
BIP BOOP BIP
WE COULD DISGUISE OURSELVES AS MAMBA SOLDIERS!
WE ALREADY DID THAT EIGHT TIMES LAST WEEK. IT'LL NEVER WORK.
WHY DON'T WE JUST VAULT OVER THE VOLCANO.
THAT WOULD BE TOO SIMPLE...
AND THE IMPACT MIGHT CAUSE A CHAIN REACTION OF EXPLOSIONS THAT WOULD TRANSFORM THE VOLCANO INTO THE LARGEST BOMB EVER MADE BY HUMAN HANDS. A BOMB OF THAT MAGNITUDE COULD DESTROY THE ENTIRE PLANET... MAYBE EVEN THE ENTIRE UNIVERSE!
CLIC
REMEMBER THE CELTICS AGAINST THE PISTONS IN '72. THE GAME WHERE ALL THREE REFEREES GOT KICKED OUT AT THE END?
??
...UH NO...
DON'T SEE THE CONNECTION.
MOM
ALL I HAVE TO SAY IS: THE PLAN: ATTACK! THE STRATEGY: FROM ALL SIDES! CODE NAME: SUPER POWER RUSH ATTACK!

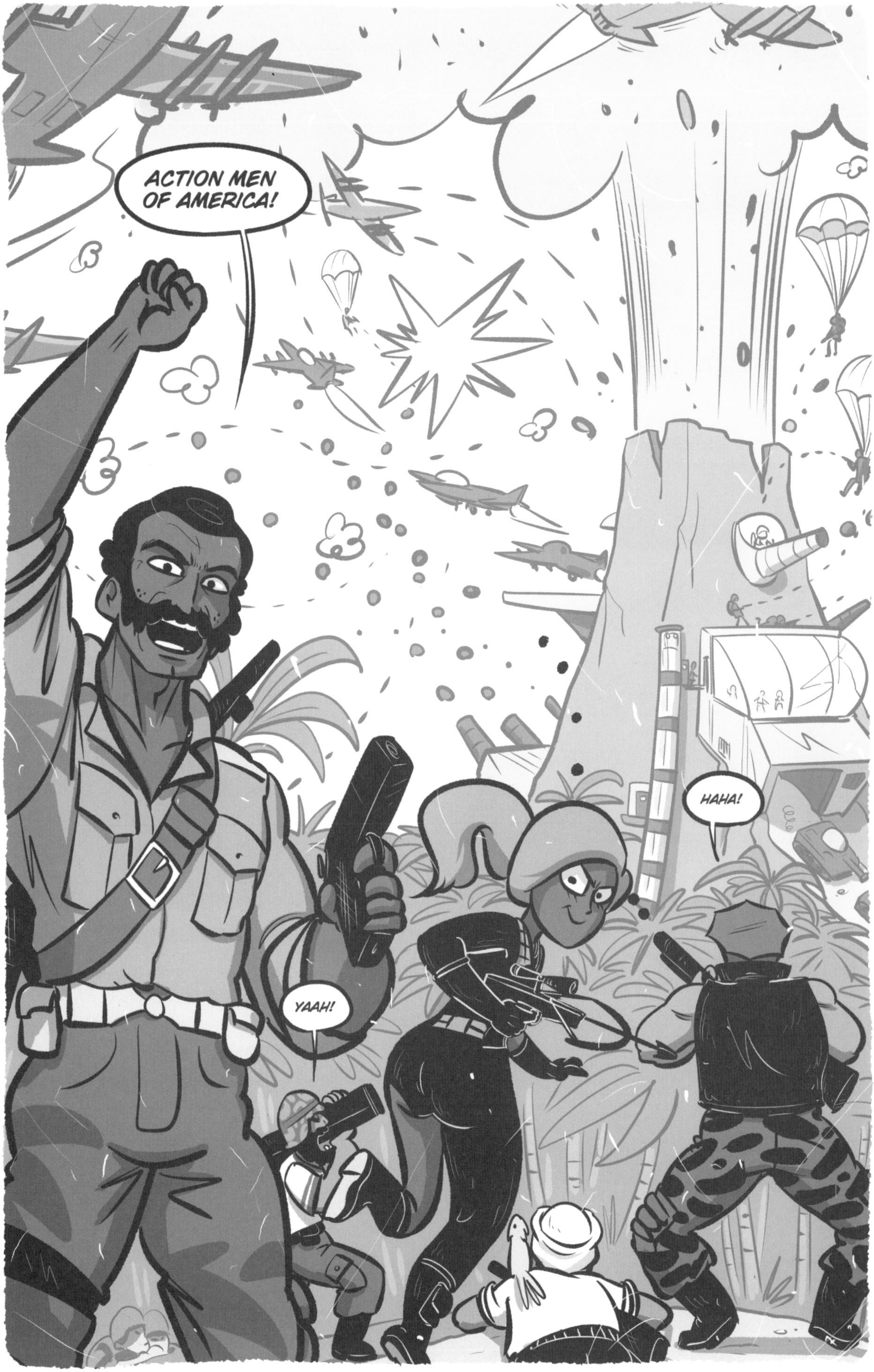
ACTION MEN OF AMERICA!
HAHA!
YAAH!

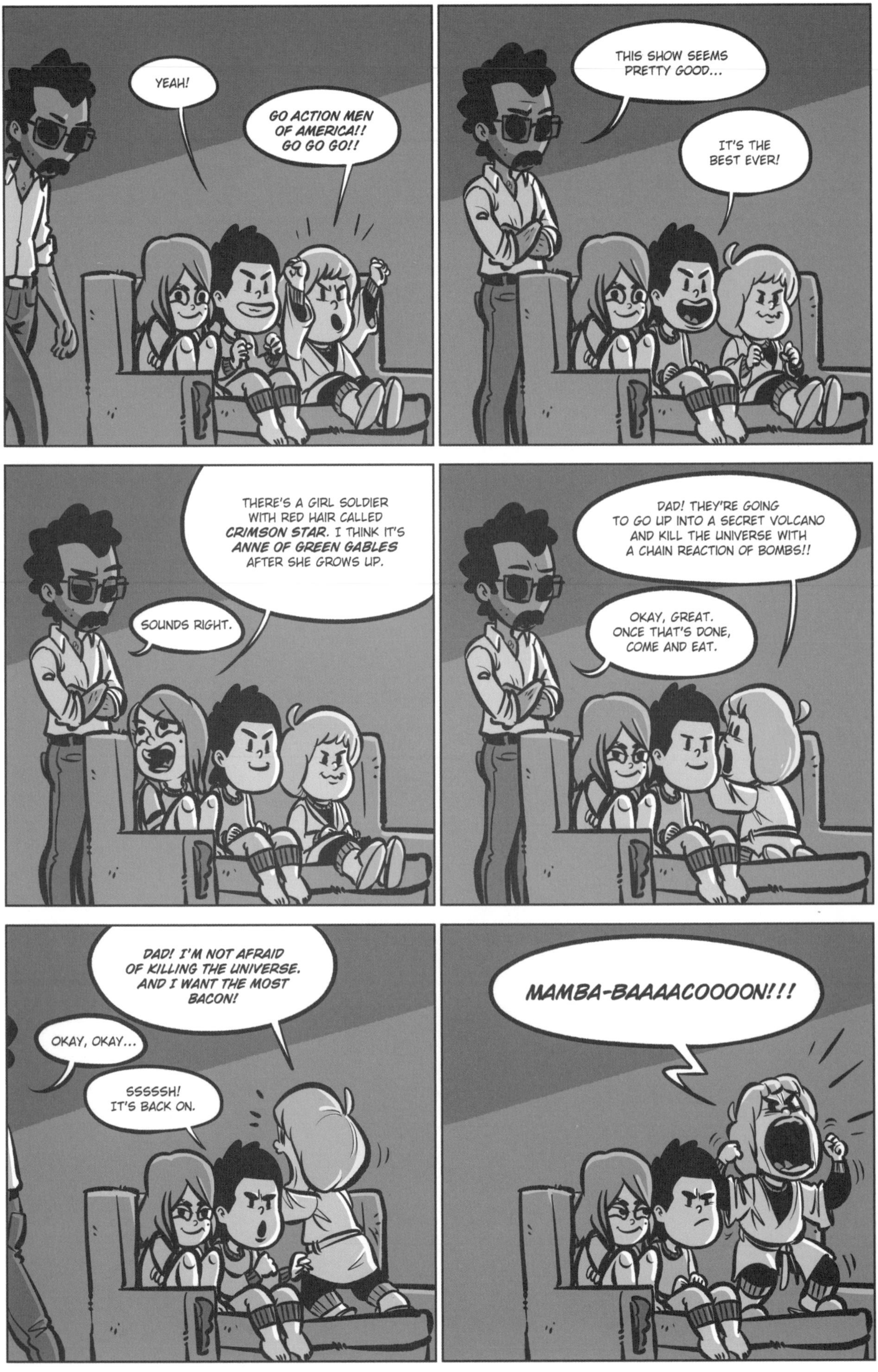

YEAH!
GO ACTION MEN OF AMERICA!! GO GO GO!!
THIS SHOW SEEMS PRETTY GOOD...
IT'S THE BEST EVER!
THERE'S A GIRL SOLDIER WITH RED HAIR CALLED *CRIMSON STAR*. I THINK IT'S *ANNE OF GREEN GABLES* AFTER SHE GROWS UP.
SOUNDS RIGHT.
DAD! THEY'RE GOING TO GO UP INTO A SECRET VOLCANO AND KILL THE UNIVERSE WITH A CHAIN REACTION OF BOMBS!!
OKAY, GREAT. ONCE THAT'S DONE, COME AND EAT.
DAD! I'M NOT AFRAID OF KILLING THE UNIVERSE. AND I WANT THE MOST BACON!
OKAY, OKAY...
SSSSSH! IT'S BACK ON.
MAMBA-BAAAACOOOON!!!

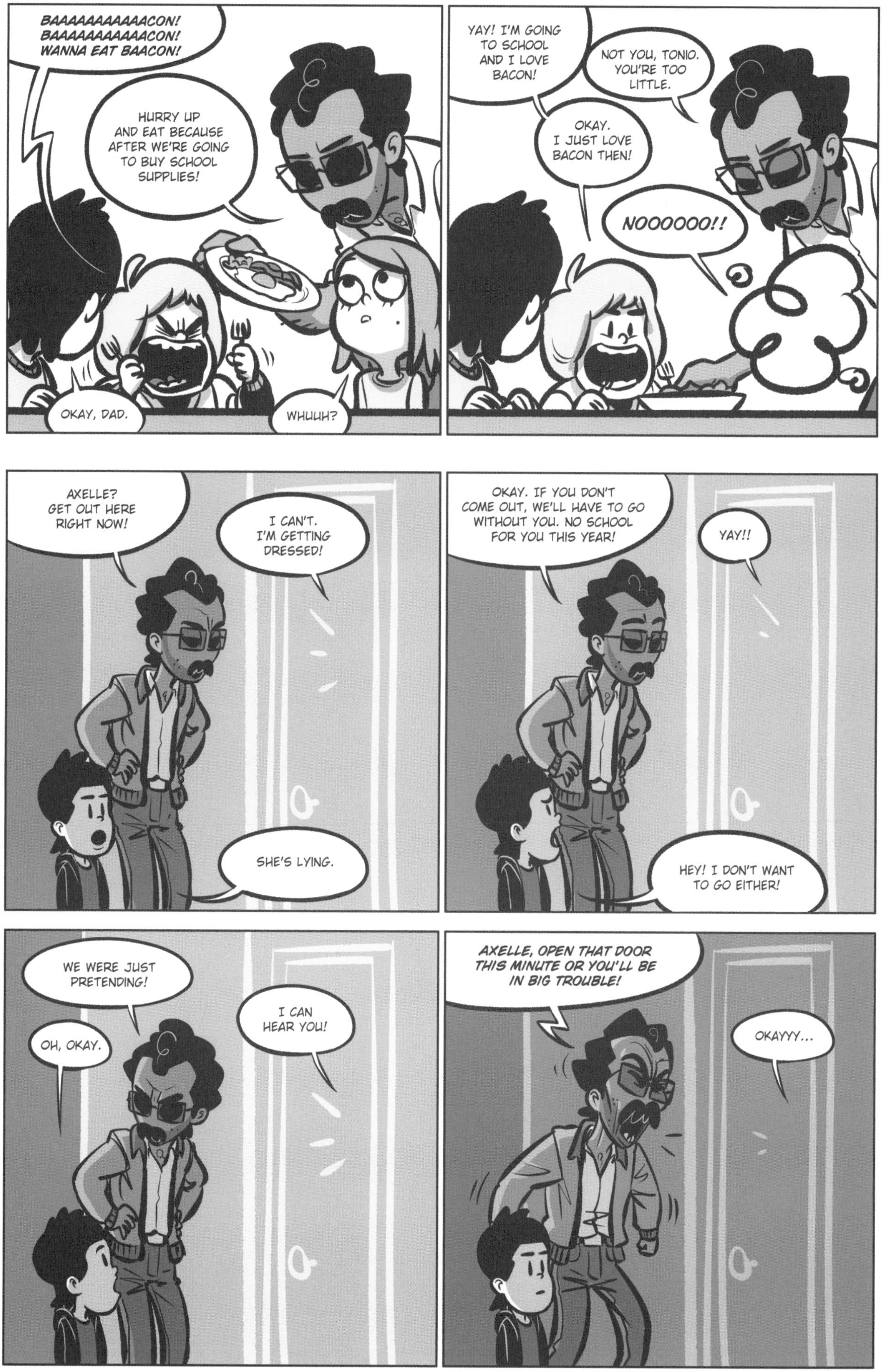

BAAAAAAAAAAAACON!
BAAAAAAAAAAAACON!
WANNA EAT BAACON!
HURRY UP AND EAT BECAUSE AFTER WE'RE GOING TO BUY SCHOOL SUPPLIES!
OKAY, DAD.
WHUUH?
YAY! I'M GOING TO SCHOOL AND I LOVE BACON!
NOT YOU, TONIO. YOU'RE TOO LITTLE.
OKAY. I JUST LOVE BACON THEN!
NOOOOOO!!
AXELLE? GET OUT HERE RIGHT NOW!
I CAN'T. I'M GETTING DRESSED!
SHE'S LYING.
OKAY. IF YOU DON'T COME OUT, WE'LL HAVE TO GO WITHOUT YOU. NO SCHOOL FOR YOU THIS YEAR!
YAY!!
HEY! I DON'T WANT TO GO EITHER!
WE WERE JUST PRETENDING!
OH, OKAY.
I CAN HEAR YOU!
AXELLE, OPEN THAT DOOR THIS MINUTE OR YOU'LL BE IN BIG TROUBLE!
OKAYYY...

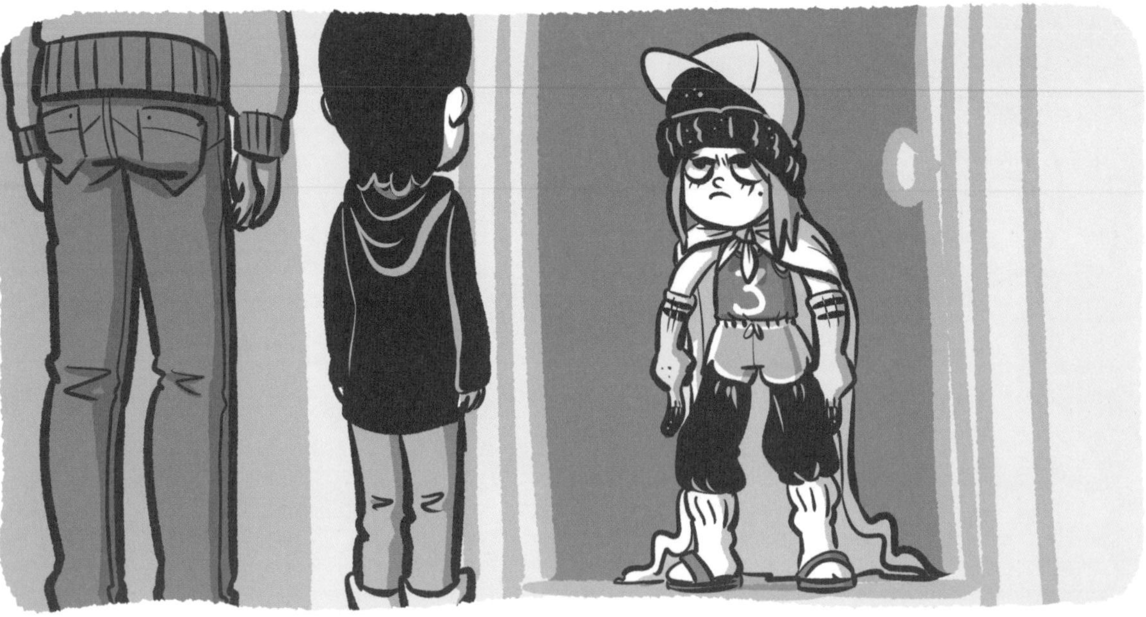

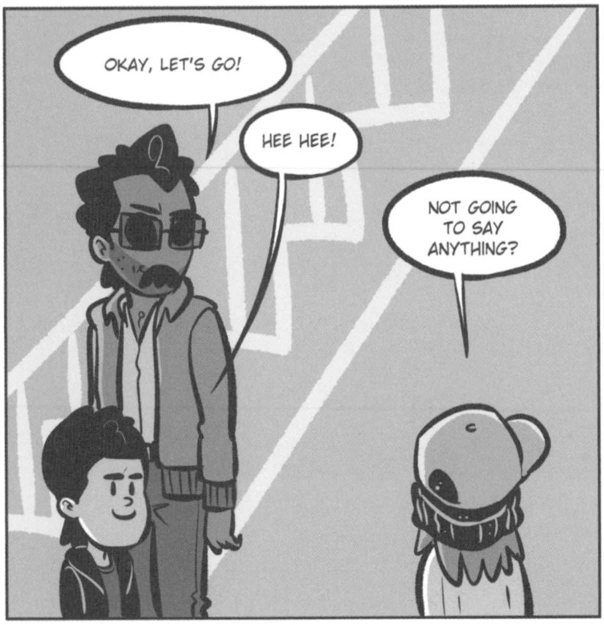
OKAY, LET'S GO!
HEE HEE!
NOT GOING TO SAY ANYTHING?

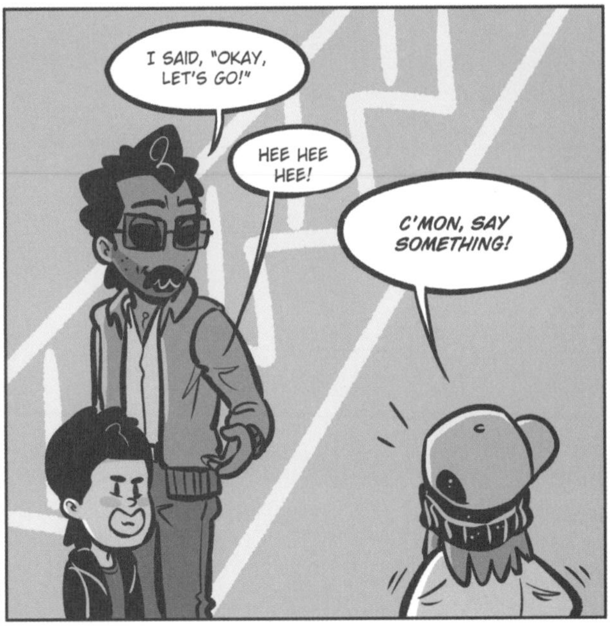
I SAID, "OKAY, LET'S GO!"
HEE HEE HEE!
C'MON, SAY SOMETHING!

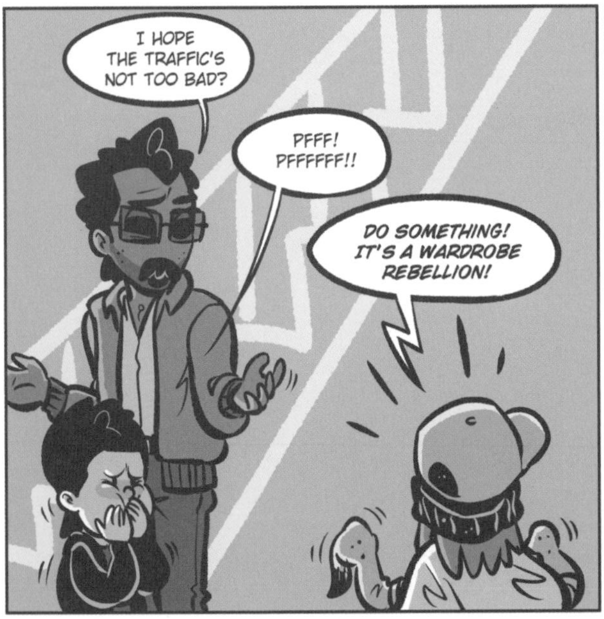
I HOPE THE TRAFFIC'S NOT TOO BAD?
PFFF! PFFFFFF!!
DO SOMETHING! IT'S A WARDROBE REBELLION!

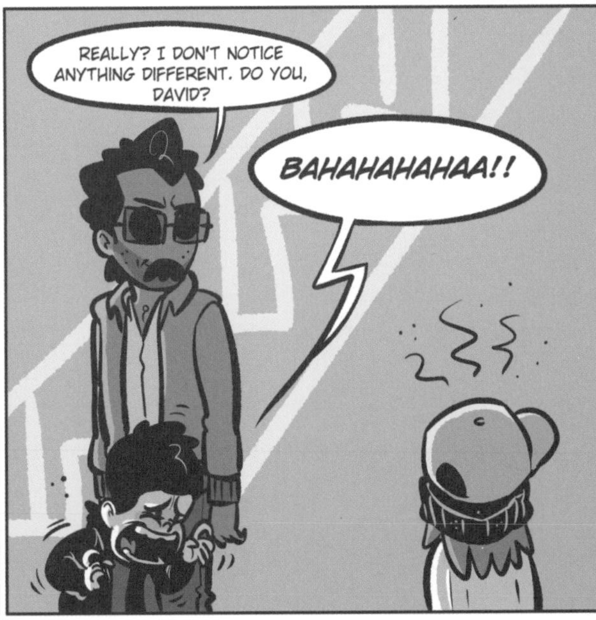
REALLY? I DON'T NOTICE ANYTHING DIFFERENT. DO YOU, DAVID?
BAHAHAHAHAA!!

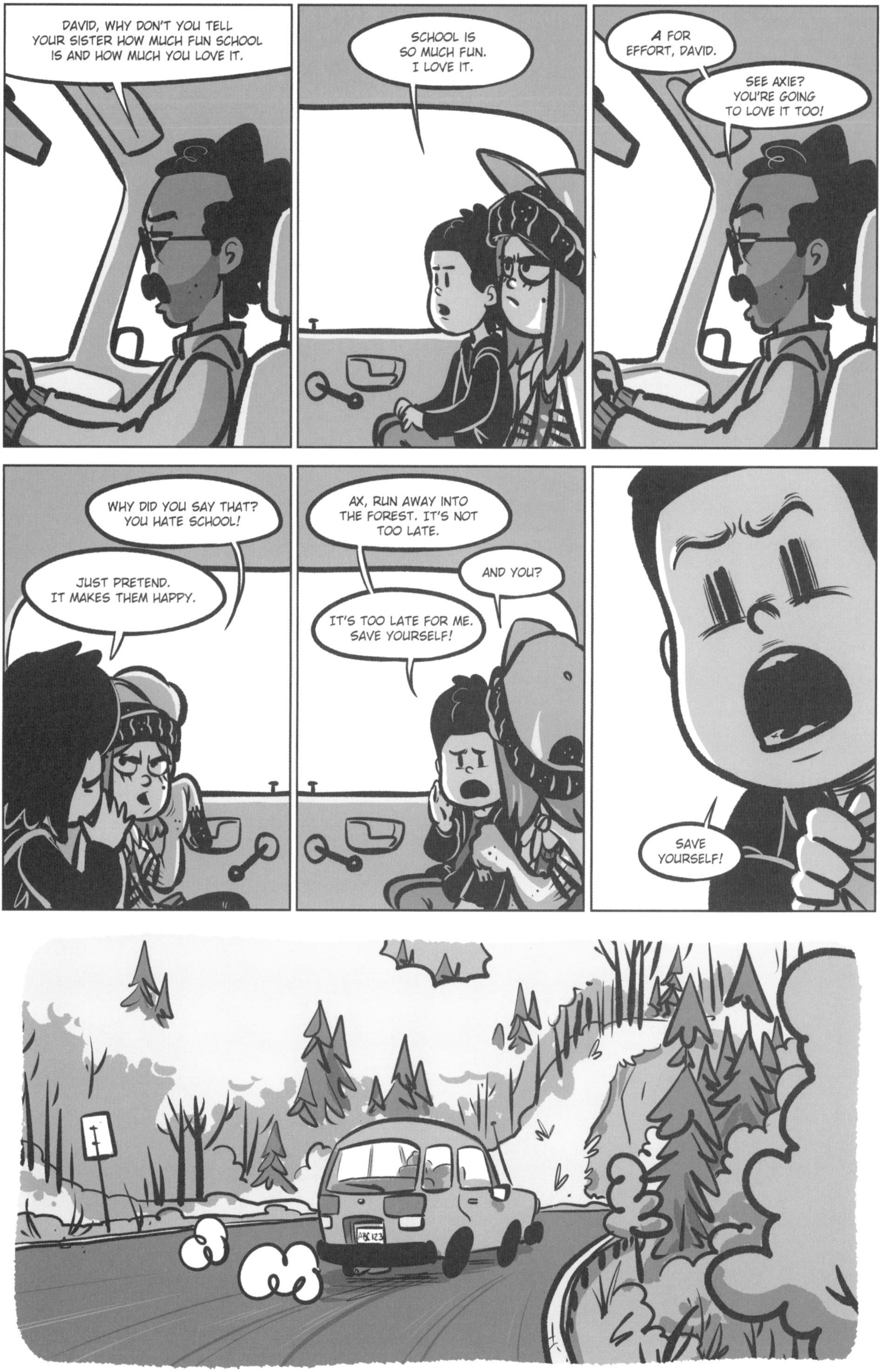
DAVID, WHY DON'T YOU TELL YOUR SISTER HOW MUCH FUN SCHOOL IS AND HOW MUCH YOU LOVE IT.
SCHOOL IS SO MUCH FUN. I LOVE IT.
A FOR EFFORT, DAVID.
SEE AXIE? YOU'RE GOING TO LOVE IT TOO!
WHY DID YOU SAY THAT? YOU HATE SCHOOL!
JUST PRETEND. IT MAKES THEM HAPPY.
AX, RUN AWAY INTO THE FOREST. IT'S NOT TOO LATE.
AND YOU?
IT'S TOO LATE FOR ME. SAVE YOURSELF!
SAVE YOURSELF!
ABC123

YOU GUYS AREN'T GONNA SAY A WORD, HUH?

I KNOW! LET'S HAVE A POUTING CONTEST!
...
OH, LOOKS LIKE WE'VE GOT TWO WINNERS ALREADY!

SECRET WEAPON...

A SMASH HIT FROM THE 80s.

THE MUSIC RIGHTS ARE TOO EXPENSIVE FOR ME TO INCLUDE IT HERE...

YOU WANT ICE CREAM BUT TARA TAKES THE SPOON BEFORE YOU MAKE IT!

BUT HERE'S A CLUE: I USED TO BE TERRIFIED OF THE ZOMBIES IN THE MUSIC VIDEO"

YOU START TO SNEEZE AS THE PEPPER GOES RIGHT INTO YOUR EYES, YOU'RE PARALYZED!

CAUSE THIS IS TO THRILL HER! THRILL HER TONIGHT!!

MOTEL

AUBER

BIENVENU
NOTRE-DAME DU DÉ

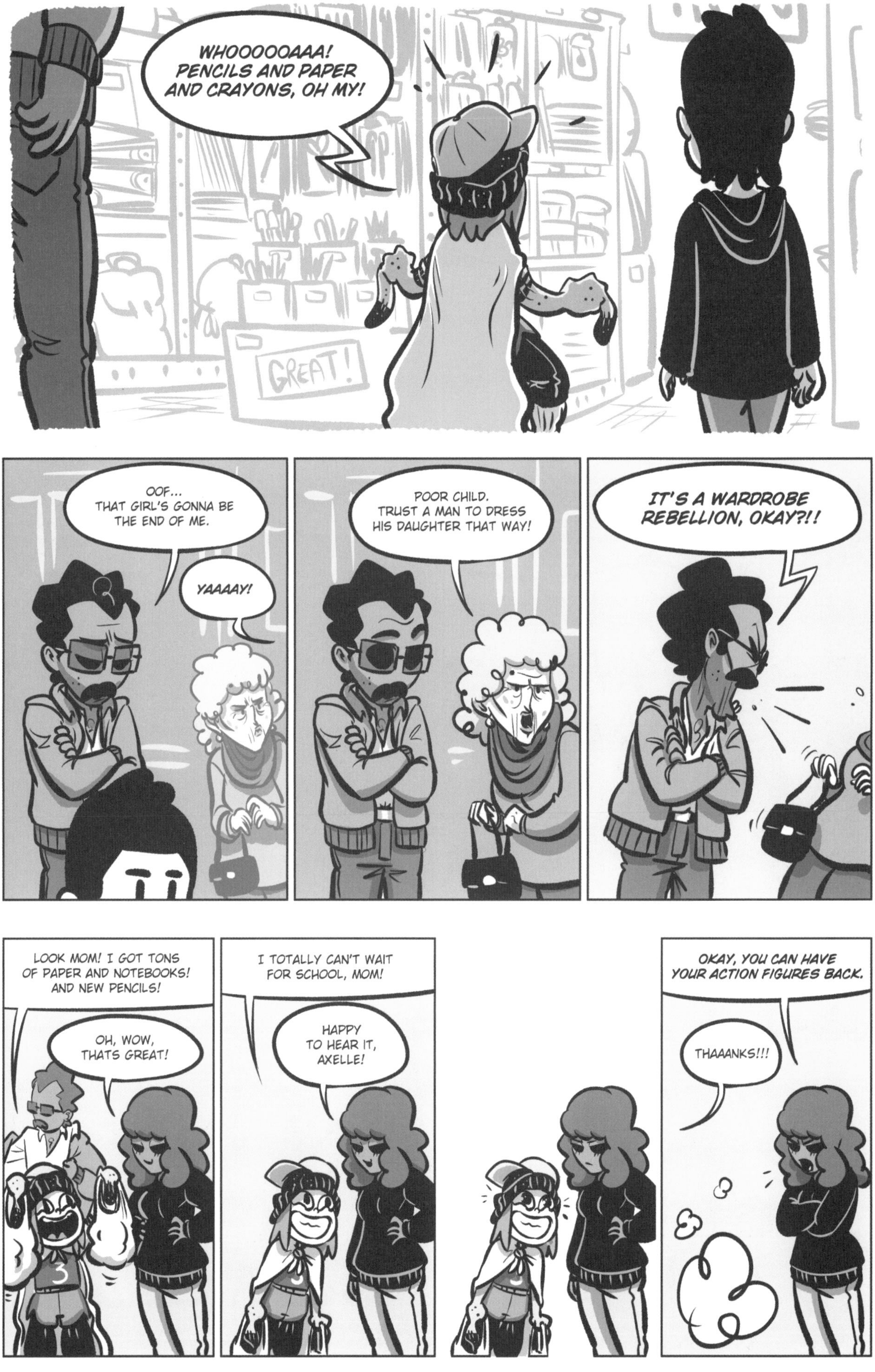
WHOOOOOAAA! PENCILS AND PAPER AND CRAYONS, OH MY!
GREAT!
OOF... THAT GIRL'S GONNA BE THE END OF ME.
YAAAAY!
POOR CHILD. TRUST A MAN TO DRESS HIS DAUGHTER THAT WAY!
IT'S A WARDROBE REBELLION, OKAY?!!
LOOK MOM! I GOT TONS OF PAPER AND NOTEBOOKS! AND NEW PENCILS!
OH, WOW, THATS GREAT!
I TOTALLY CAN'T WAIT FOR SCHOOL, MOM!
HAPPY TO HEAR IT, AXELLE!
OKAY, YOU CAN HAVE YOUR ACTION FIGURES BACK.
THAAANKS!!!

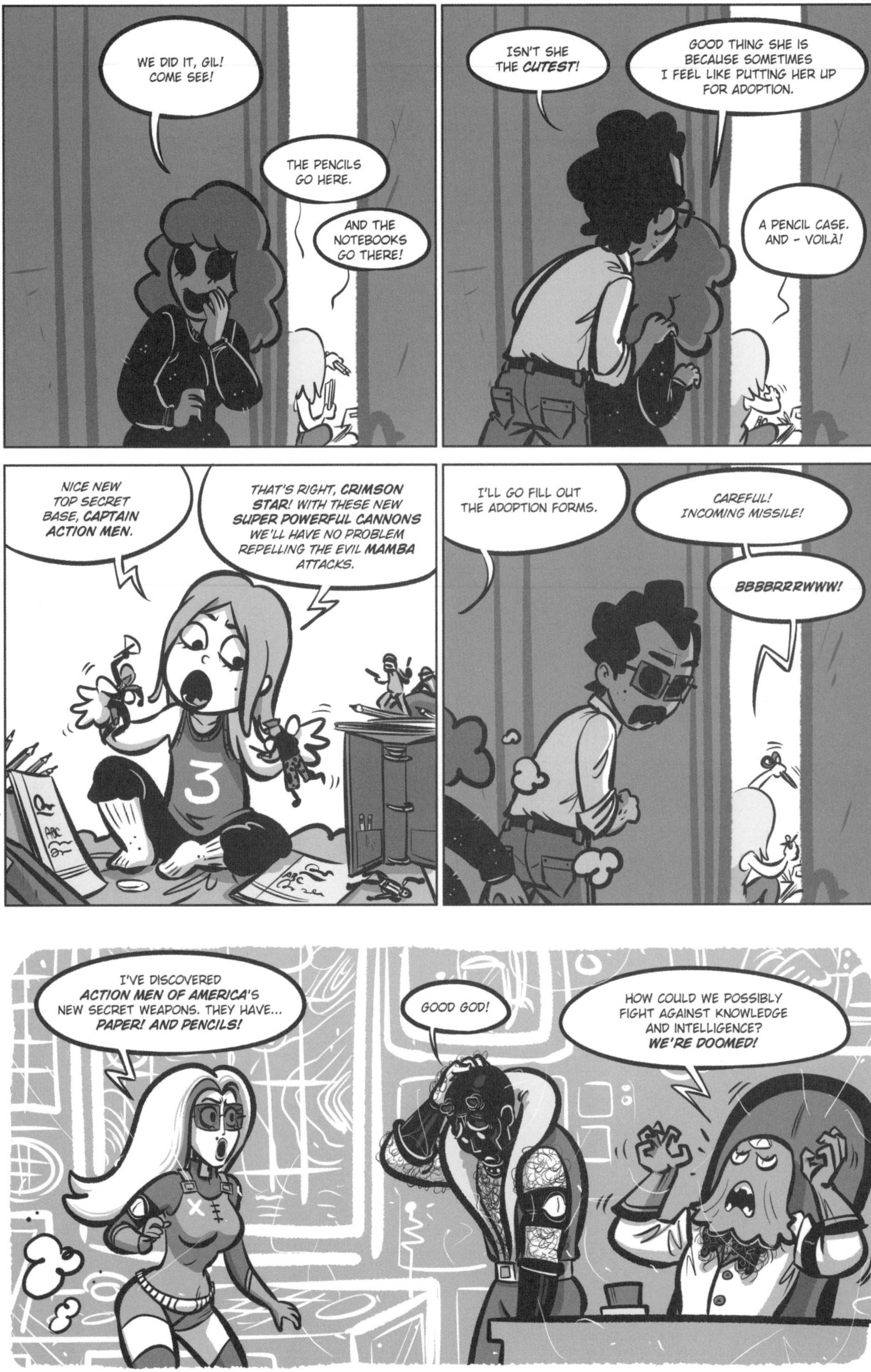
WE DID IT, GIL! COME SEE!
THE PENCILS GO HERE.
AND THE NOTEBOOKS GO THERE!
ISN'T SHE THE *CUTEST!*
GOOD THING SHE IS BECAUSE SOMETIMES I FEEL LIKE PUTTING HER UP FOR ADOPTION.
A PENCIL CASE. AND - VOILÀ!
NICE NEW TOP SECRET BASE, **CAPTAIN ACTION MEN.**
THAT'S RIGHT, **CRIMSON STAR!** WITH THESE NEW **SUPER POWERFUL CANNONS** WE'LL HAVE NO PROBLEM REPELLING THE EVIL **MAMBA** ATTACKS.
I'LL GO FILL OUT THE ADOPTION FORMS.
CAREFUL! INCOMING MISSILE!
BBBBRRRWWW!
I'VE DISCOVERED **ACTION MEN OF AMERICA**'S NEW SECRET WEAPONS. THEY HAVE... **PAPER! AND PENCILS!**
GOOD GOD!
HOW COULD WE POSSIBLY FIGHT AGAINST KNOWLEDGE AND INTELLIGENCE? **WE'RE DOOMED!**

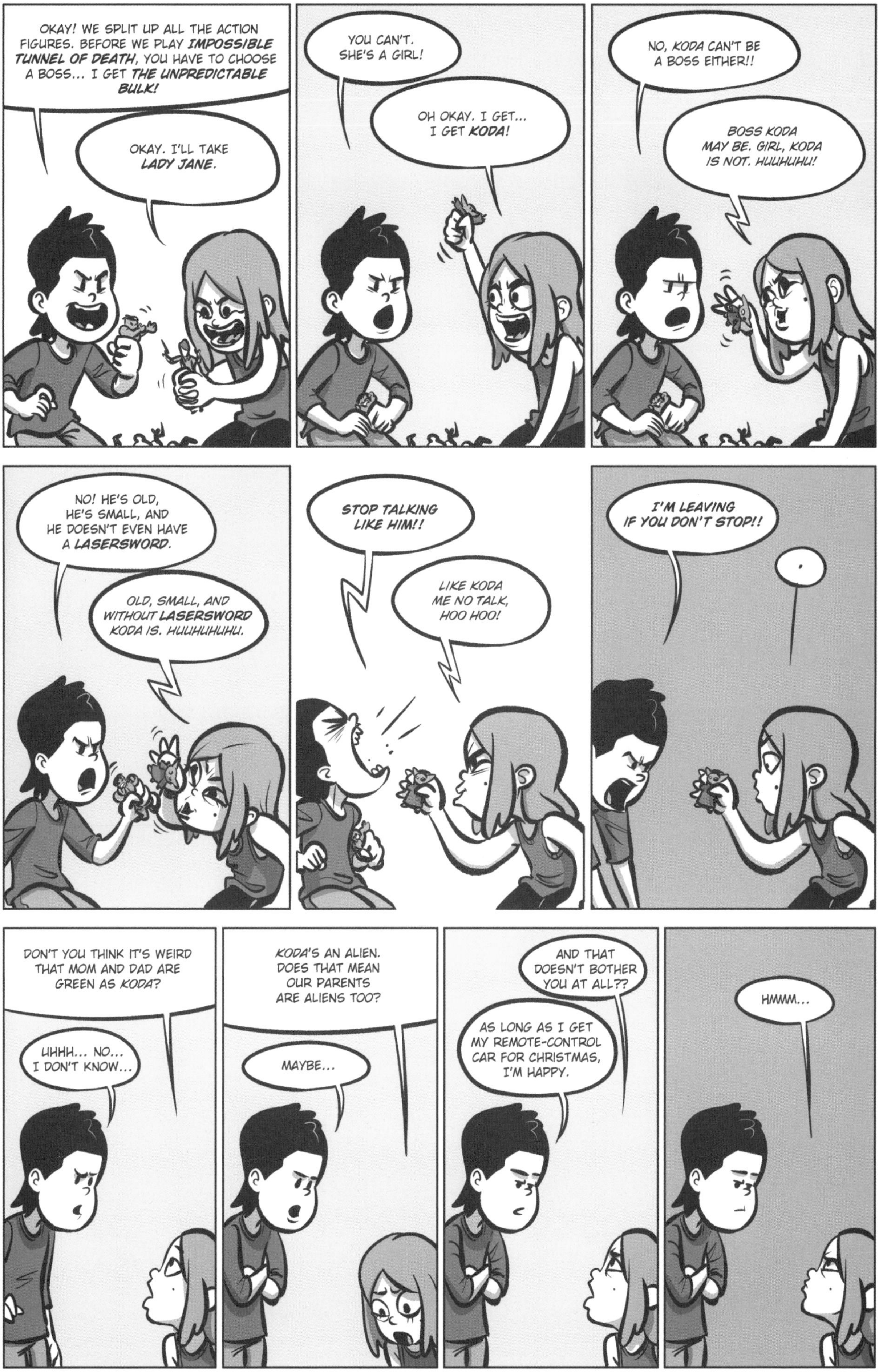
OKAY! WE SPLIT UP ALL THE ACTION FIGURES. BEFORE WE PLAY IMPOSSIBLE TUNNEL OF DEATH, YOU HAVE TO CHOOSE A BOSS... I GET THE UNPREDICTABLE BULK!
OKAY. I'LL TAKE LADY JANE.
YOU CAN'T. SHE'S A GIRL!
OH OKAY. I GET... I GET KODA!
NO, KODA CAN'T BE A BOSS EITHER!!
BOSS KODA MAY BE. GIRL, KODA IS NOT. HUUHUHU!
NO! HE'S OLD, HE'S SMALL, AND HE DOESN'T EVEN HAVE A LASERSWORD.
OLD, SMALL, AND WITHOUT LASERSWORD KODA IS. HUUHUHUHU.
STOP TALKING LIKE HIM!!
LIKE KODA ME NO TALK, HOO HOO!
I'M LEAVING IF YOU DON'T STOP!!
DON'T YOU THINK IT'S WEIRD THAT MOM AND DAD ARE GREEN AS KODA?
UHHH... NO... I DON'T KNOW...
KODA'S AN ALIEN. DOES THAT MEAN OUR PARENTS ARE ALIENS TOO?
MAYBE...
AND THAT DOESN'T BOTHER YOU AT ALL??
AS LONG AS I GET MY REMOTE-CONTROL CAR FOR CHRISTMAS, I'M HAPPY.
HMMM...

GOODNIGHT AXELLE... SLEEP TIGHT.
SMACK
I DON'T GET A GOODNIGHT?
EVERYTHING OKAY, AXELLE?
OK, NIGHTIE-NIGHT THEN.
IF MOM AND DAD ARE ALIENS, DOES THAT MAKE ME AN ALIEN CHILD?
I DON'T HAVE GREEN SKIN OR GIANT BLACK EYES LIKE THEM...
UNLESS THEY FOUND US! LIKE IN THE CARTOONS, WHEN POOR PARENTS LEAVE THEIR KIDS IN BASKETS ON RICH PEOPLE'S DOORSTEPS.
DAMN YOU, POOR, REAL PARENTS! YOU COULD HAVE AT LEAST FOUND SOME RICHER ALIENS.

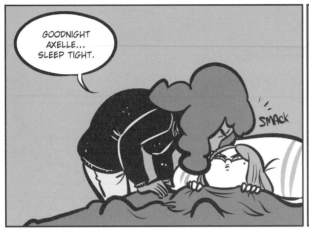

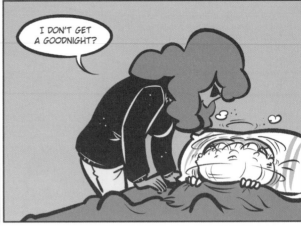

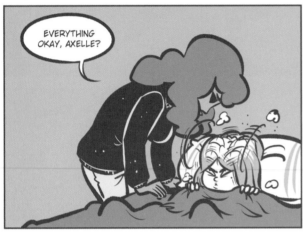

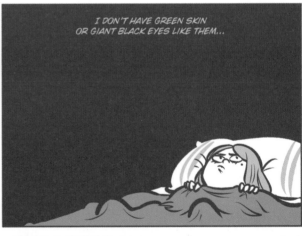

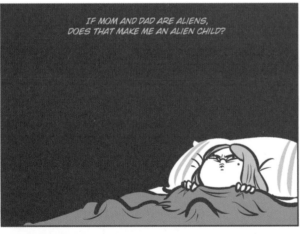

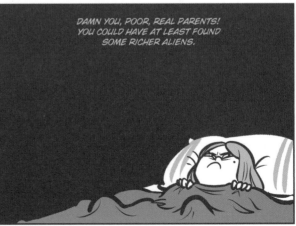

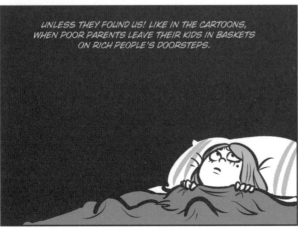

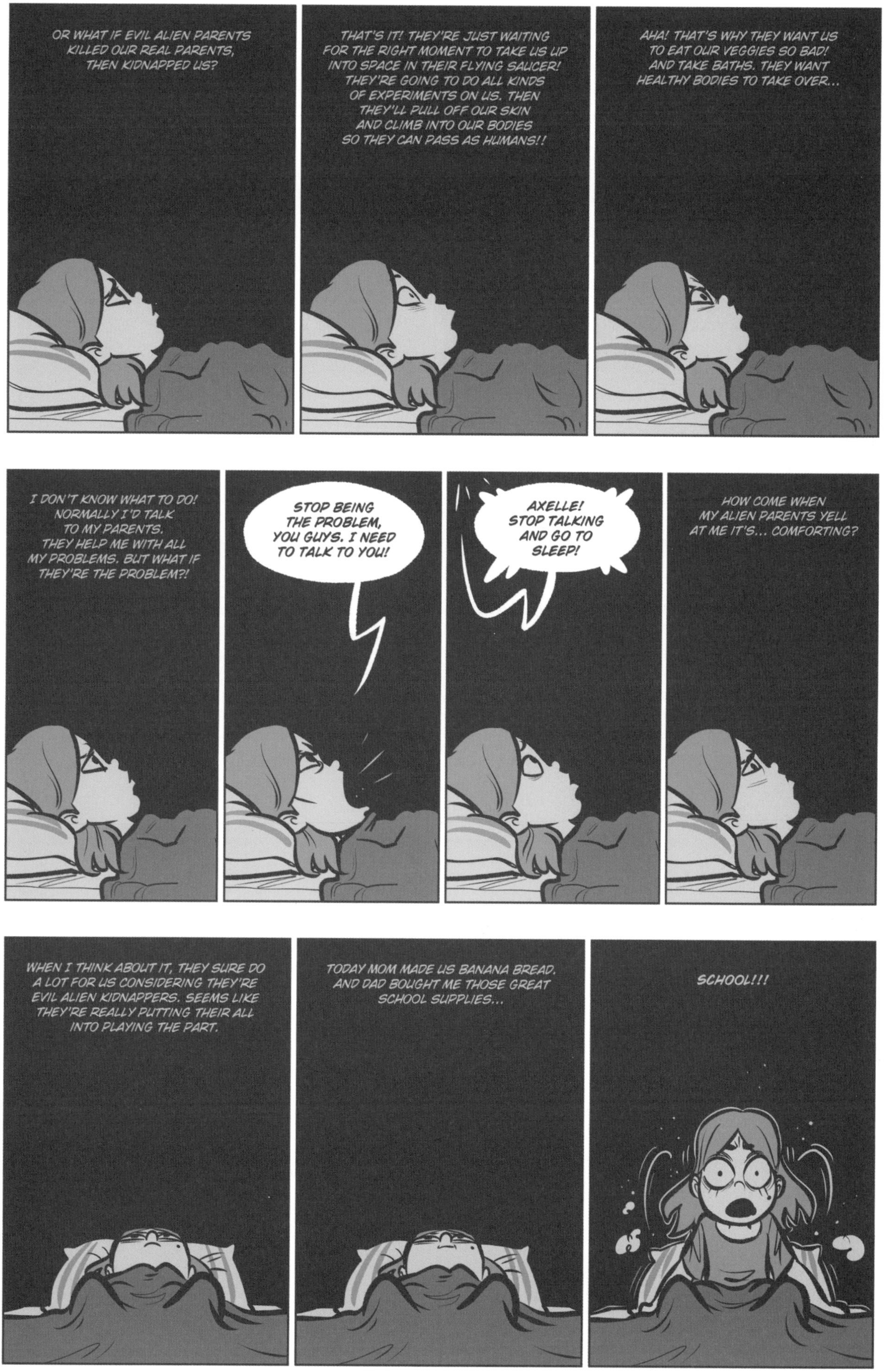

OR WHAT IF EVIL ALIEN PARENTS KILLED OUR REAL PARENTS, THEN KIDNAPPED US?
THAT'S IT! THEY'RE JUST WAITING FOR THE RIGHT MOMENT TO TAKE US UP INTO SPACE IN THEIR FLYING SAUCER! THEY'RE GOING TO DO ALL KINDS OF EXPERIMENTS ON US. THEN THEY'LL PULL OFF OUR SKIN AND CLIMB INTO OUR BODIES SO THEY CAN PASS AS HUMANS!!
AHA! THAT'S WHY THEY WANT US TO EAT OUR VEGGIES SO BAD! AND TAKE BATHS. THEY WANT HEALTHY BODIES TO TAKE OVER...
I DON'T KNOW WHAT TO DO! NORMALLY I'D TALK TO MY PARENTS. THEY HELP ME WITH ALL MY PROBLEMS. BUT WHAT IF THEY'RE THE PROBLEM?!
STOP BEING THE PROBLEM, YOU GUYS. I NEED TO TALK TO YOU!
AXELLE! STOP TALKING AND GO TO SLEEP!
HOW COME WHEN MY ALIEN PARENTS YELL AT ME IT'S... COMFORTING?
WHEN I THINK ABOUT IT, THEY SURE DO A LOT FOR US CONSIDERING THEY'RE EVIL ALIEN KIDNAPPERS. SEEMS LIKE THEY'RE REALLY PUTTING THEIR ALL INTO PLAYING THE PART.
TODAY MOM MADE US BANANA BREAD. AND DAD BOUGHT ME THOSE GREAT SCHOOL SUPPLIES...
SCHOOL!!!

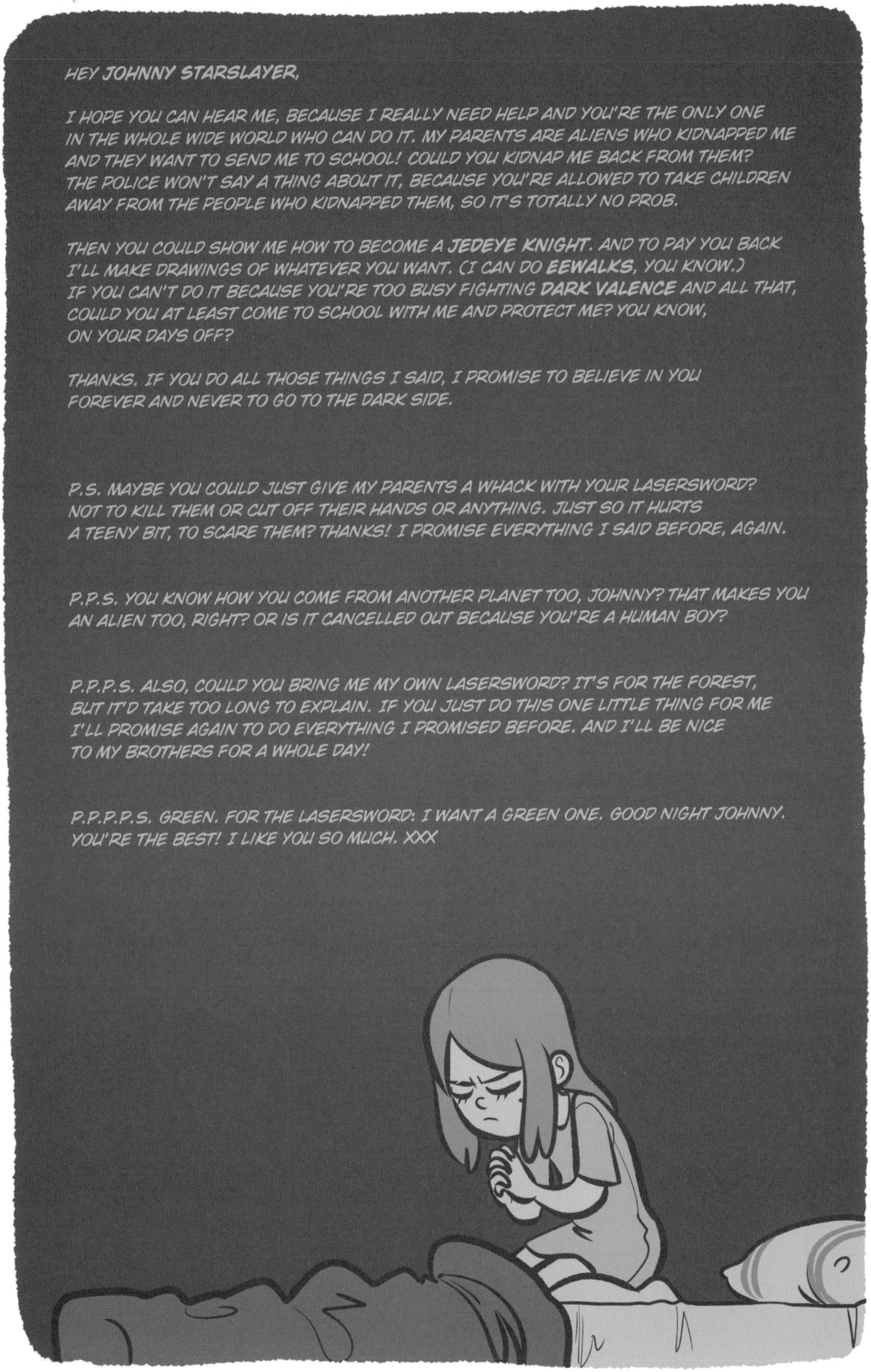
HEY JOHNNY STARSLAYER,
I HOPE YOU CAN HEAR ME, BECAUSE I REALLY NEED HELP AND YOU'RE THE ONLY ONE IN THE WHOLE WIDE WORLD WHO CAN DO IT. MY PARENTS ARE ALIENS WHO KIDNAPPED ME AND THEY WANT TO SEND ME TO SCHOOL! COULD YOU KIDNAP ME BACK FROM THEM? THE POLICE WON'T SAY A THING ABOUT IT, BECAUSE YOU'RE ALLOWED TO TAKE CHILDREN AWAY FROM THE PEOPLE WHO KIDNAPPED THEM, SO IT'S TOTALLY NO PROB.
THEN YOU COULD SHOW ME HOW TO BECOME A JEDEYE KNIGHT. AND TO PAY YOU BACK I'LL MAKE DRAWINGS OF WHATEVER YOU WANT. (I CAN DO EEWALKS, YOU KNOW.) IF YOU CAN'T DO IT BECAUSE YOU'RE TOO BUSY FIGHTING DARK VALENCE AND ALL THAT, COULD YOU AT LEAST COME TO SCHOOL WITH ME AND PROTECT ME? YOU KNOW, ON YOUR DAYS OFF?
THANKS. IF YOU DO ALL THOSE THINGS I SAID, I PROMISE TO BELIEVE IN YOU FOREVER AND NEVER TO GO TO THE DARK SIDE.
P.S. MAYBE YOU COULD JUST GIVE MY PARENTS A WHACK WITH YOUR LASERSWORD? NOT TO KILL THEM OR CUT OFF THEIR HANDS OR ANYTHING. JUST SO IT HURTS A TEENY BIT, TO SCARE THEM? THANKS! I PROMISE EVERYTHING I SAID BEFORE, AGAIN.
P.P.S. YOU KNOW HOW YOU COME FROM ANOTHER PLANET TOO, JOHNNY? THAT MAKES YOU AN ALIEN TOO, RIGHT? OR IS IT CANCELLED OUT BECAUSE YOU'RE A HUMAN BOY?
P.P.P.S. ALSO, COULD YOU BRING ME MY OWN LASERSWORD? IT'S FOR THE FOREST, BUT IT'D TAKE TOO LONG TO EXPLAIN. IF YOU JUST DO THIS ONE LITTLE THING FOR ME I'LL PROMISE AGAIN TO DO EVERYTHING I PROMISED BEFORE. AND I'LL BE NICE TO MY BROTHERS FOR A WHOLE DAY!
P.P.P.P.S. GREEN. FOR THE LASERSWORD: I WANT A GREEN ONE. GOOD NIGHT JOHNNY. YOU'RE THE BEST! I LIKE YOU SO MUCH. XXX

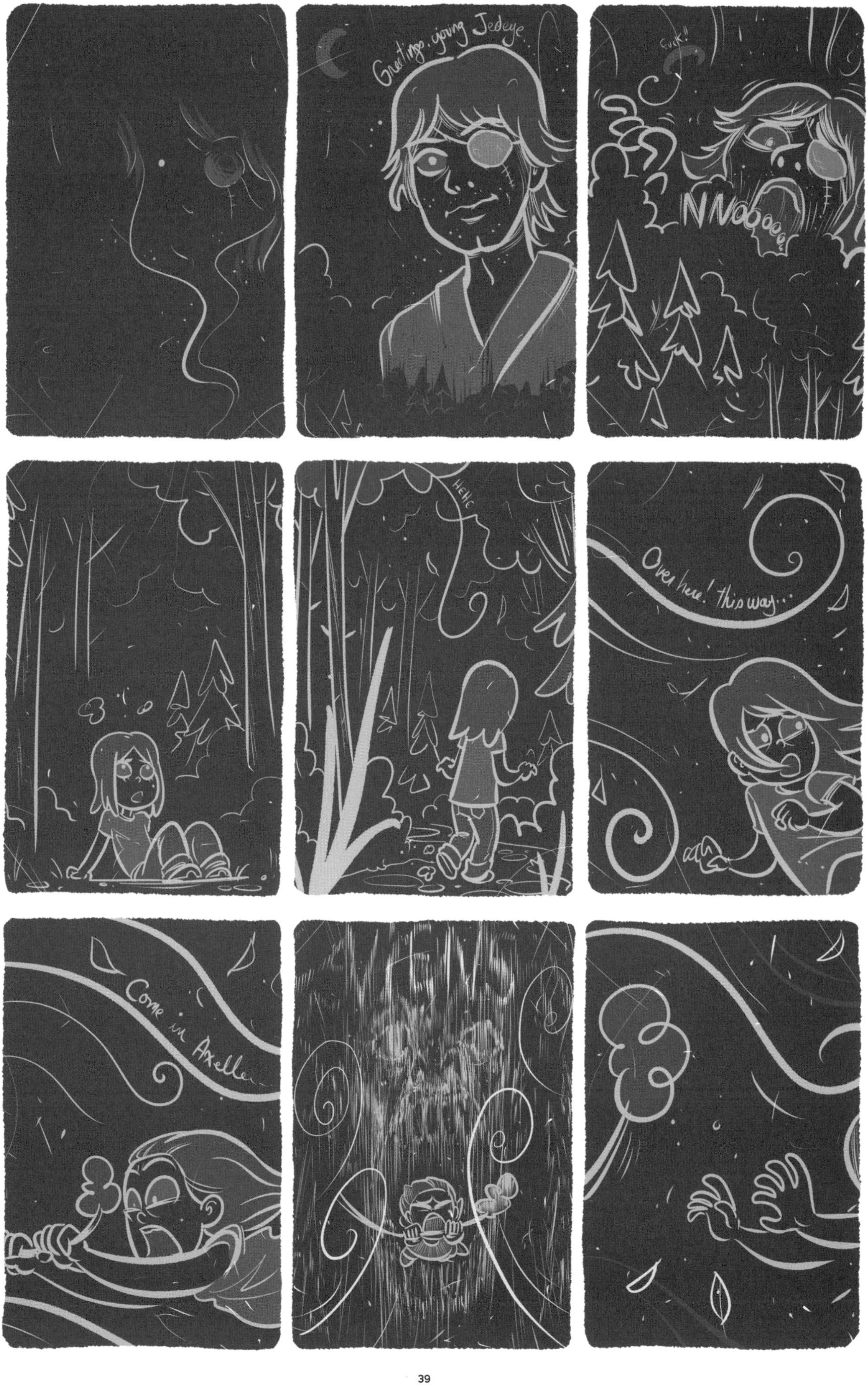
Greetings, young Jedeye.
Fuck!!
NNOoooo
HEHE
Over here! this way...
Come in Axelle...

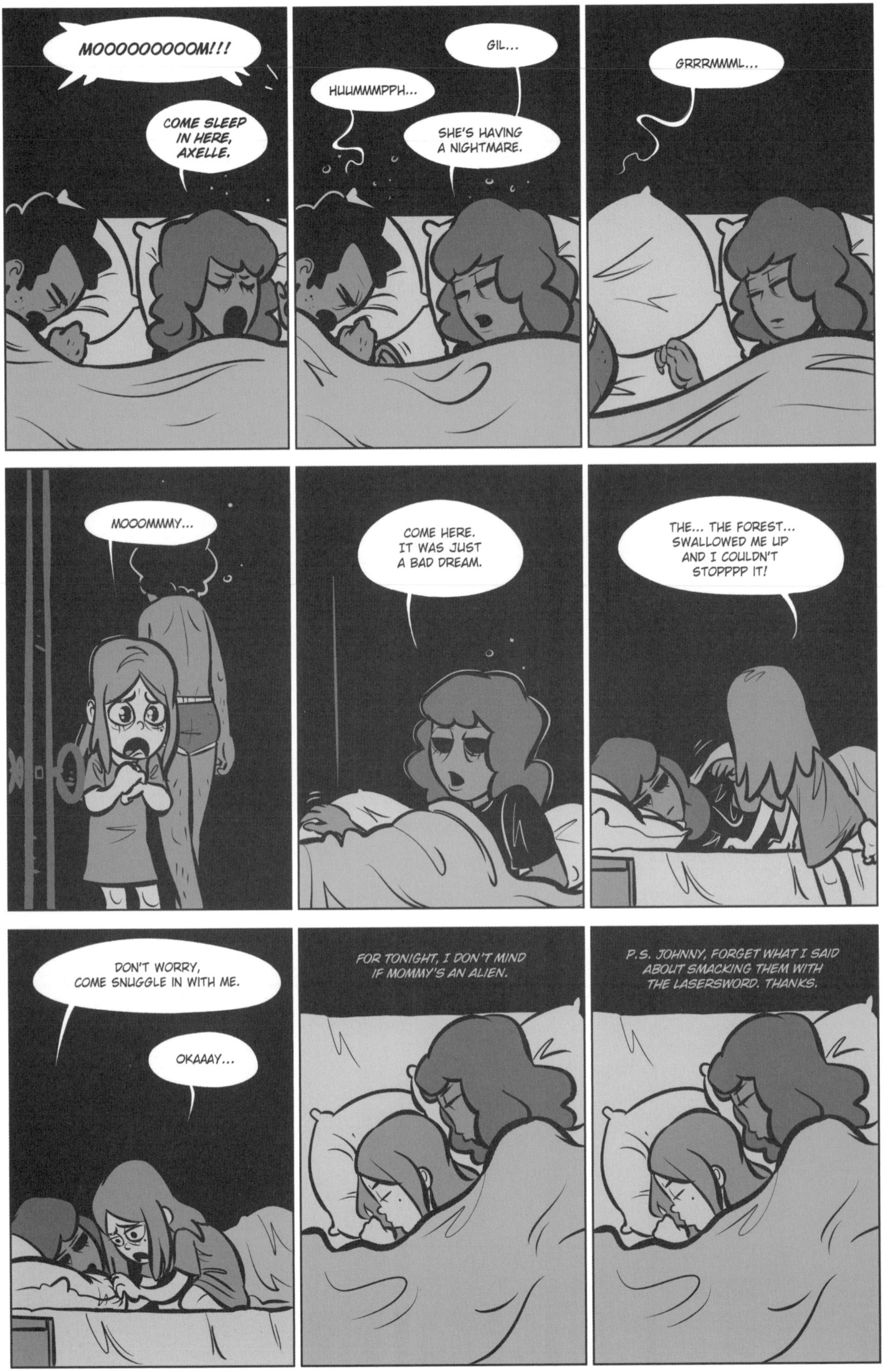
MOOOOOOOOOM!!!
COME SLEEP IN HERE, AXELLE.
HUUMMMPPH...
GIL...
SHE'S HAVING A NIGHTMARE.
GRRRMMML...
MOOOMMMY...
COME HERE. IT WAS JUST A BAD DREAM.
THE... THE FOREST... SWALLOWED ME UP AND I COULDN'T STOPPPP IT!
DON'T WORRY, COME SNUGGLE IN WITH ME.
OKAAAY...
FOR TONIGHT, I DON'T MIND IF MOMMY'S AN ALIEN.
P.S. JOHNNY, FORGET WHAT I SAID ABOUT SMACKING THEM WITH THE LASERSWORD. THANKS.

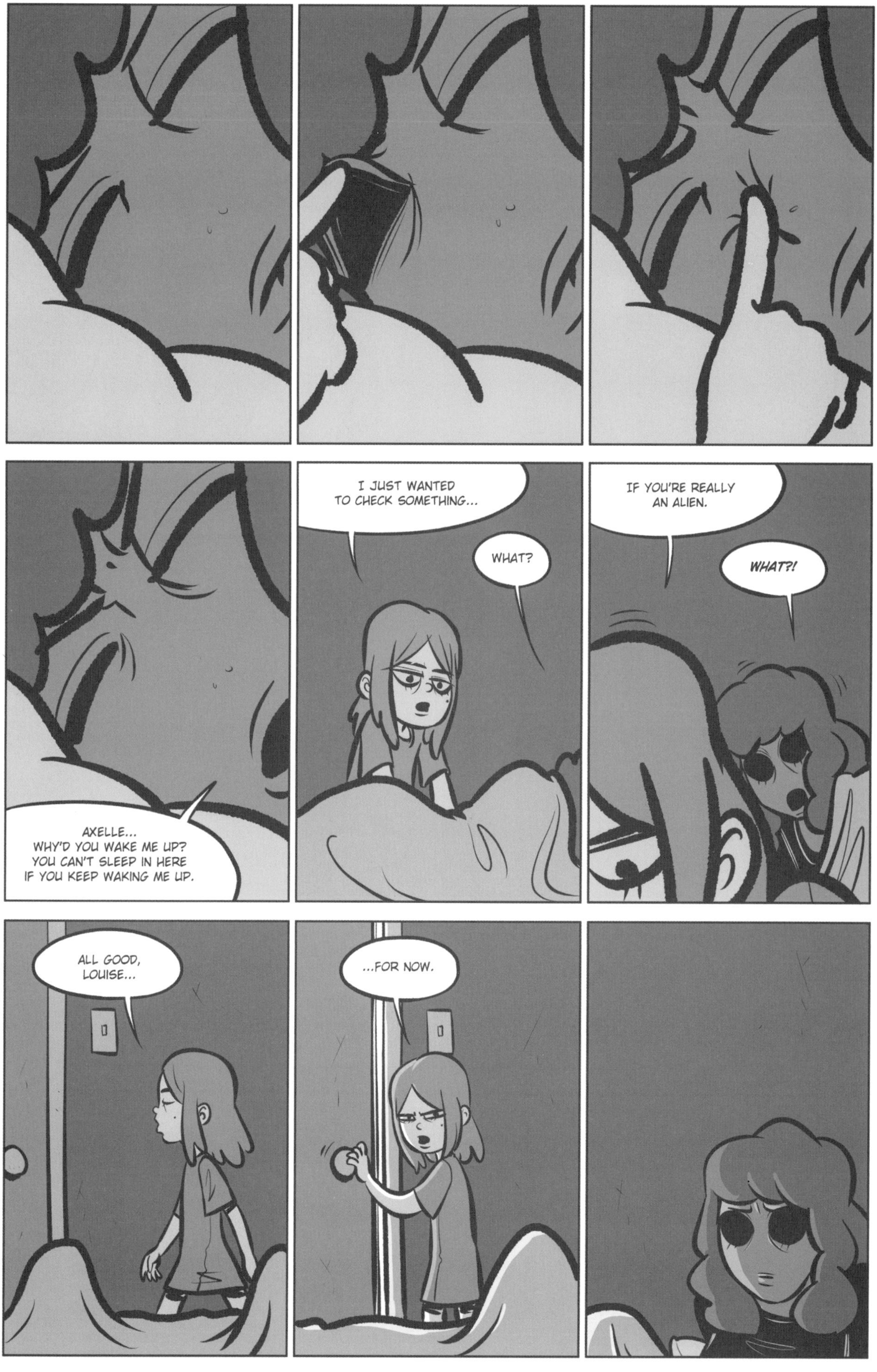
AXELLE...
WHY'D YOU WAKE ME UP?
YOU CAN'T SLEEP IN HERE
IF YOU KEEP WAKING ME UP.
I JUST WANTED
TO CHECK SOMETHING...
WHAT?
IF YOU'RE REALLY
AN ALIEN.
WHAT?!
ALL GOOD,
LOUISE...
...FOR NOW.

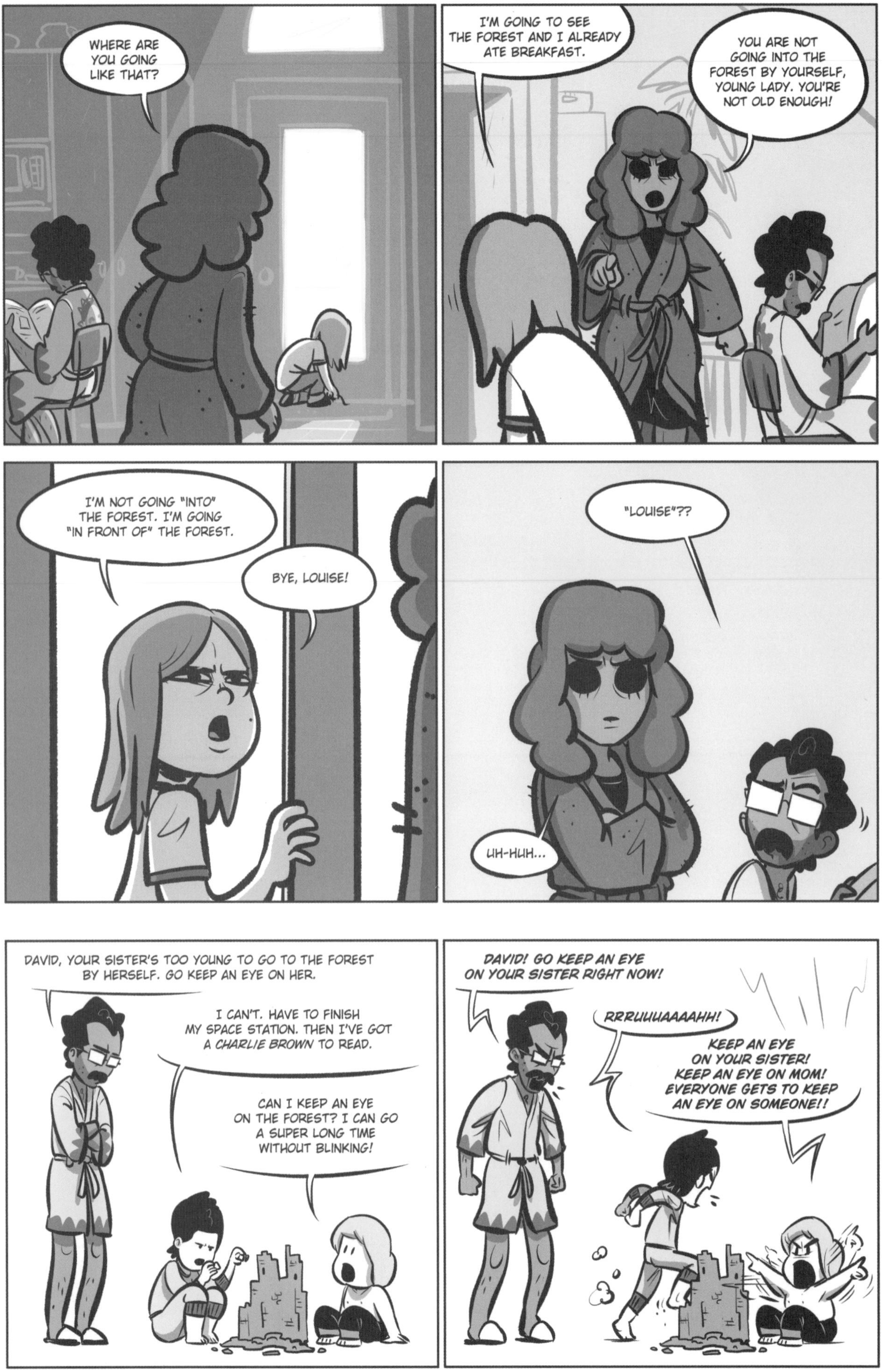

WHERE ARE YOU GOING LIKE THAT?
I'M GOING TO SEE THE FOREST AND I ALREADY ATE BREAKFAST.
YOU ARE NOT GOING INTO THE FOREST BY YOURSELF, YOUNG LADY. YOU'RE NOT OLD ENOUGH!
I'M NOT GOING "INTO" THE FOREST. I'M GOING "IN FRONT OF" THE FOREST.
BYE, LOUISE!
"LOUISE"??
UH-HUH...
DAVID, YOUR SISTER'S TOO YOUNG TO GO TO THE FOREST BY HERSELF. GO KEEP AN EYE ON HER.
I CAN'T. HAVE TO FINISH MY SPACE STATION. THEN I'VE GOT A *CHARLIE BROWN* TO READ.
CAN I KEEP AN EYE ON THE FOREST? I CAN GO A SUPER LONG TIME WITHOUT BLINKING!
DAVID! GO KEEP AN EYE ON YOUR SISTER RIGHT NOW!
RRRUUUAAAAHH!
KEEP AN EYE ON YOUR SISTER! KEEP AN EYE ON MOM! EVERYONE GETS TO KEEP AN EYE ON SOMEONE!!

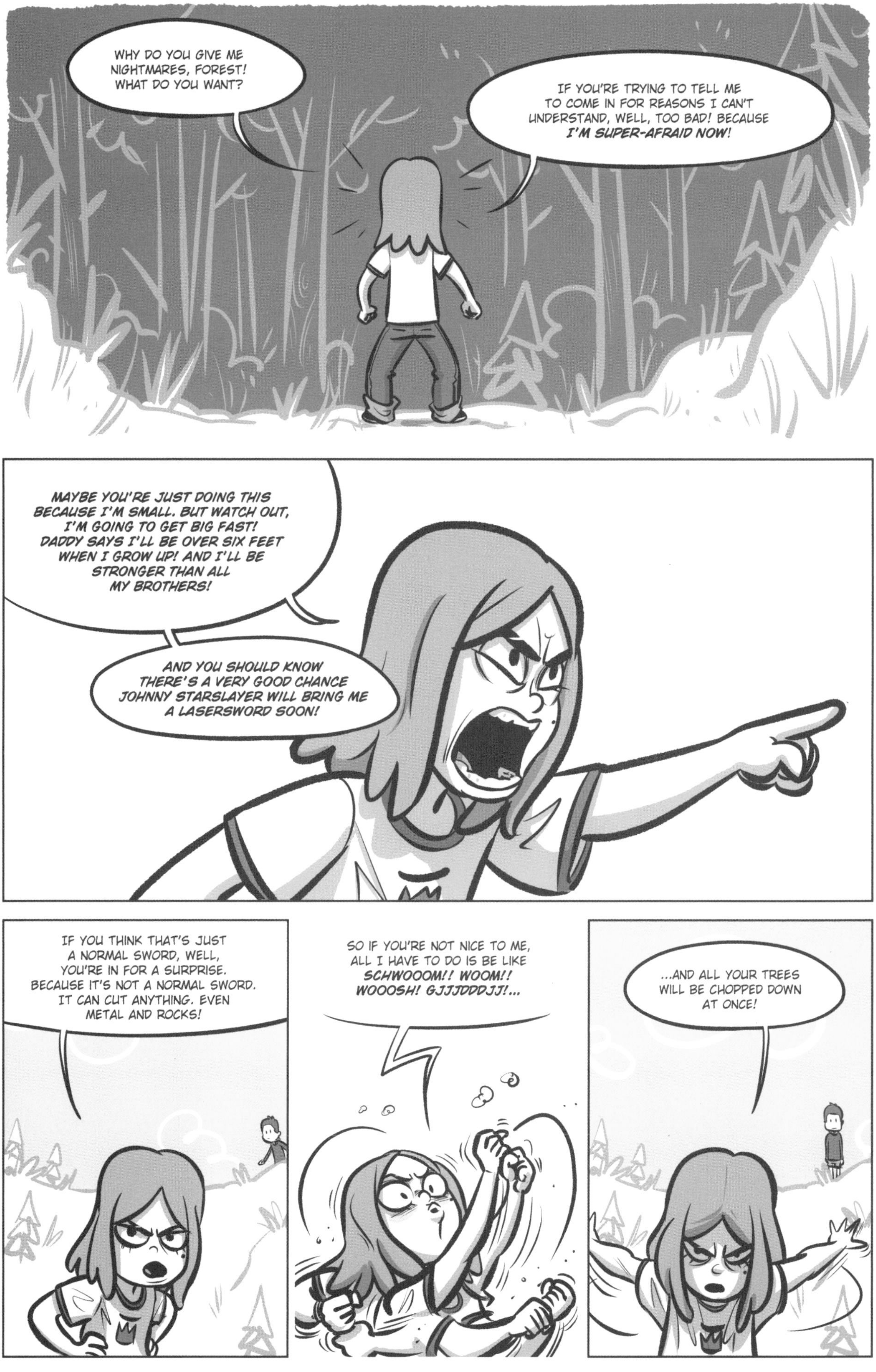
WHY DO YOU GIVE ME NIGHTMARES, FOREST! WHAT DO YOU WANT?
IF YOU'RE TRYING TO TELL ME TO COME IN FOR REASONS I CAN'T UNDERSTAND, WELL, TOO BAD! BECAUSE *I'M SUPER-AFRAID NOW*!
MAYBE YOU'RE JUST DOING THIS BECAUSE I'M SMALL. BUT WATCH OUT, I'M GOING TO GET BIG FAST! DADDY SAYS I'LL BE OVER SIX FEET WHEN I GROW UP! AND I'LL BE STRONGER THAN ALL MY BROTHERS!
AND YOU SHOULD KNOW THERE'S A VERY GOOD CHANCE JOHNNY STARSLAYER WILL BRING ME A LASERSWORD SOON!
IF YOU THINK THAT'S JUST A NORMAL SWORD, WELL, YOU'RE IN FOR A SURPRISE. BECAUSE IT'S NOT A NORMAL SWORD. IT CAN CUT ANYTHING. EVEN METAL AND ROCKS!
SO IF YOU'RE NOT NICE TO ME, ALL I HAVE TO DO IS BE LIKE ***SCHWOOOM!! WOOM!! WOOOSH! GJJJDDDJJ!...***
...AND ALL YOUR TREES WILL BE CHOPPED DOWN AT ONCE!

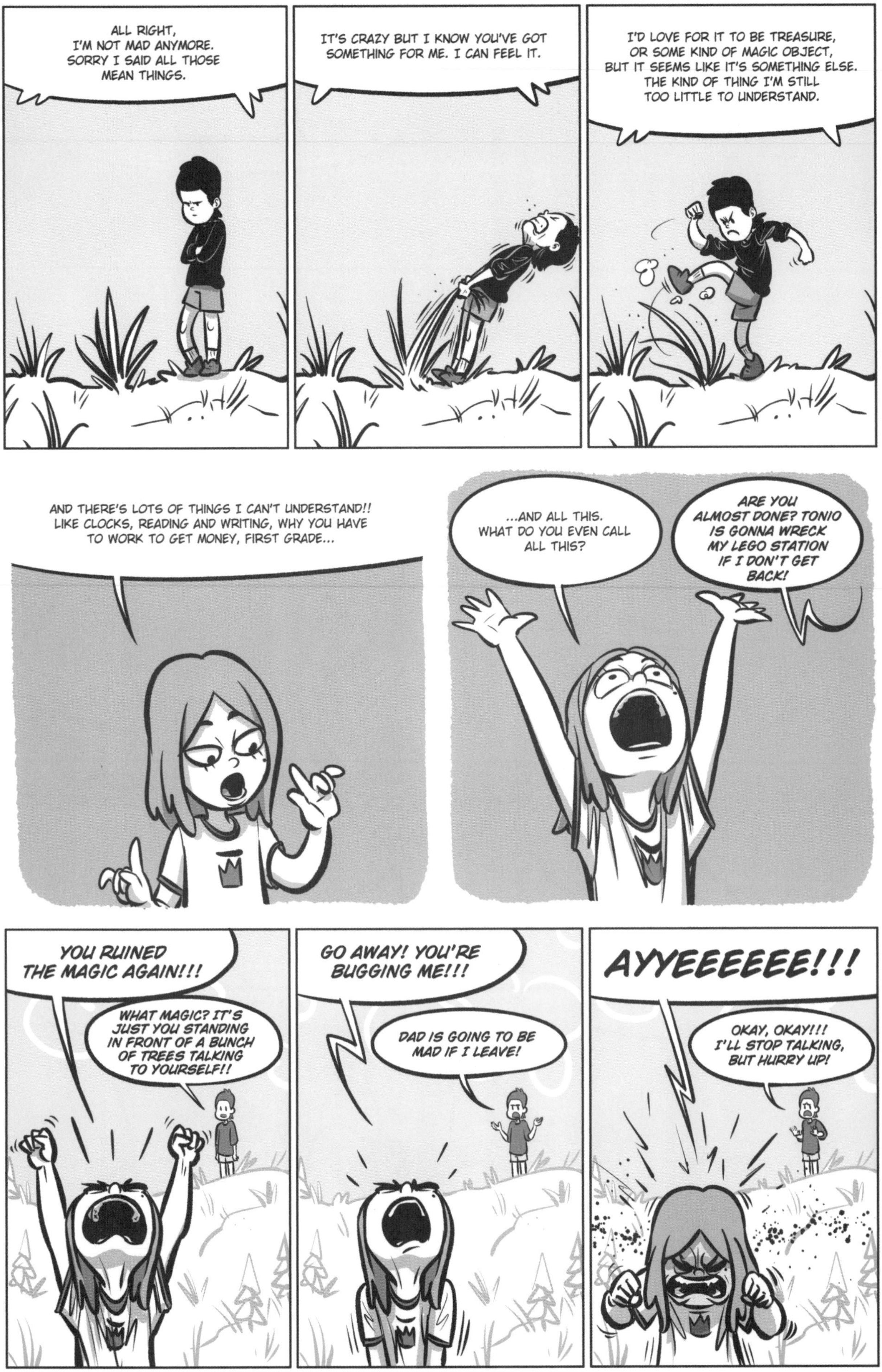
ALL RIGHT, I'M NOT MAD ANYMORE. SORRY I SAID ALL THOSE MEAN THINGS.
IT'S CRAZY BUT I KNOW YOU'VE GOT SOMETHING FOR ME. I CAN FEEL IT.
I'D LOVE FOR IT TO BE TREASURE, OR SOME KIND OF MAGIC OBJECT, BUT IT SEEMS LIKE IT'S SOMETHING ELSE. THE KIND OF THING I'M STILL TOO LITTLE TO UNDERSTAND.
AND THERE'S LOTS OF THINGS I CAN'T UNDERSTAND!! LIKE CLOCKS, READING AND WRITING, WHY YOU HAVE TO WORK TO GET MONEY, FIRST GRADE...
...AND ALL THIS. WHAT DO YOU EVEN CALL ALL THIS?
ARE YOU ALMOST DONE? TONIO IS GONNA WRECK MY LEGO STATION IF I DON'T GET BACK!
YOU RUINED THE MAGIC AGAIN!!!
WHAT MAGIC? IT'S JUST YOU STANDING IN FRONT OF A BUNCH OF TREES TALKING TO YOURSELF!!
GO AWAY! YOU'RE BUGGING ME!!!
DAD IS GOING TO BE MAD IF I LEAVE!
AYYEEEEEEE!!!
OKAY, OKAY!!! I'LL STOP TALKING, BUT HURRY UP!

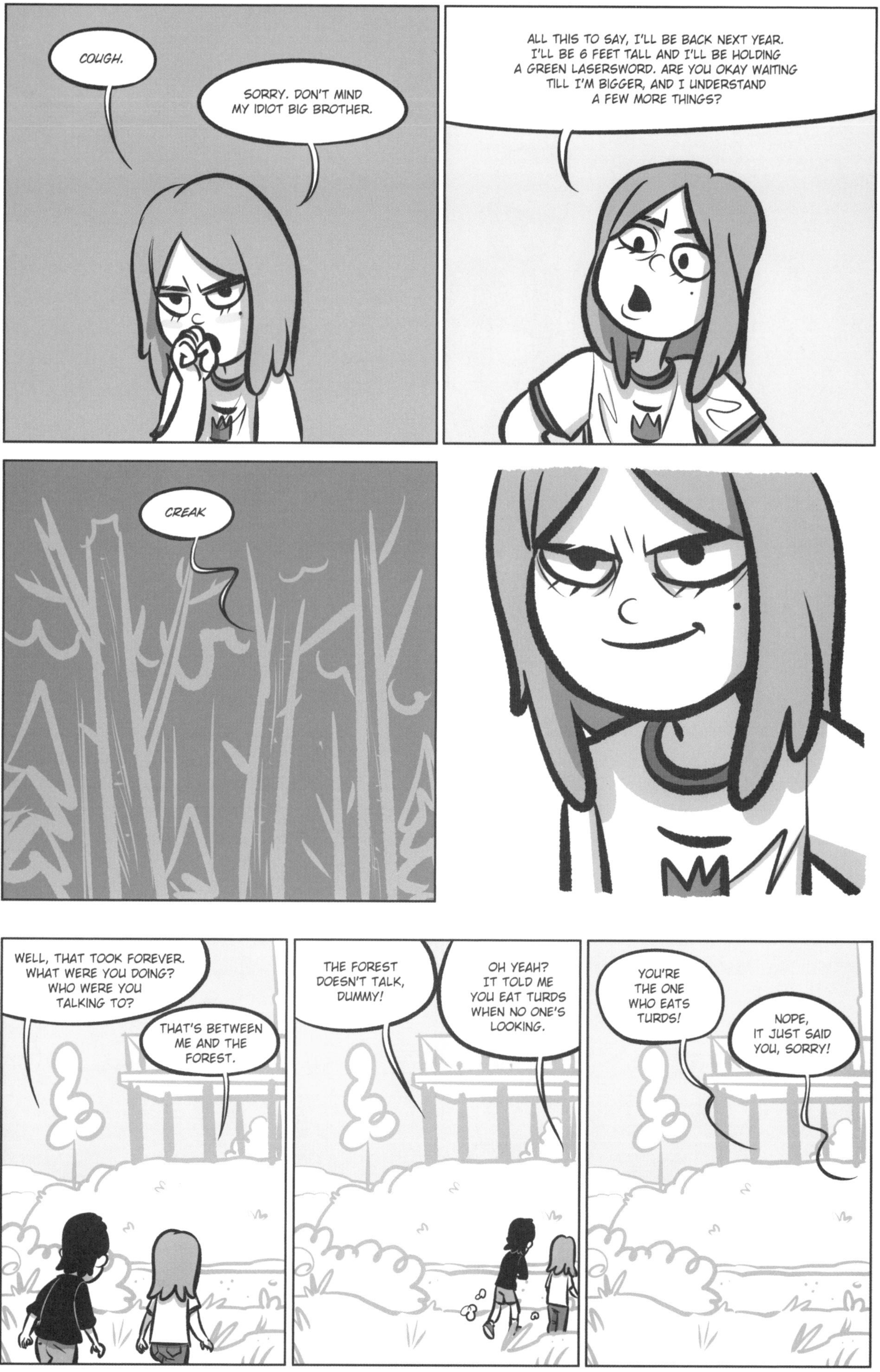
COUGH.
SORRY. DON'T MIND MY IDIOT BIG BROTHER.
ALL THIS TO SAY, I'LL BE BACK NEXT YEAR. I'LL BE 6 FEET TALL AND I'LL BE HOLDING A GREEN LASERSWORD. ARE YOU OKAY WAITING TILL I'M BIGGER, AND I UNDERSTAND A FEW MORE THINGS?
CREAK
WELL, THAT TOOK FOREVER. WHAT WERE YOU DOING? WHO WERE YOU TALKING TO?
THAT'S BETWEEN ME AND THE FOREST.
THE FOREST DOESN'T TALK, DUMMY!
OH YEAH? IT TOLD ME YOU EAT TURDS WHEN NO ONE'S LOOKING.
YOU'RE THE ONE WHO EATS TURDS!
NOPE, IT JUST SAID YOU, SORRY!

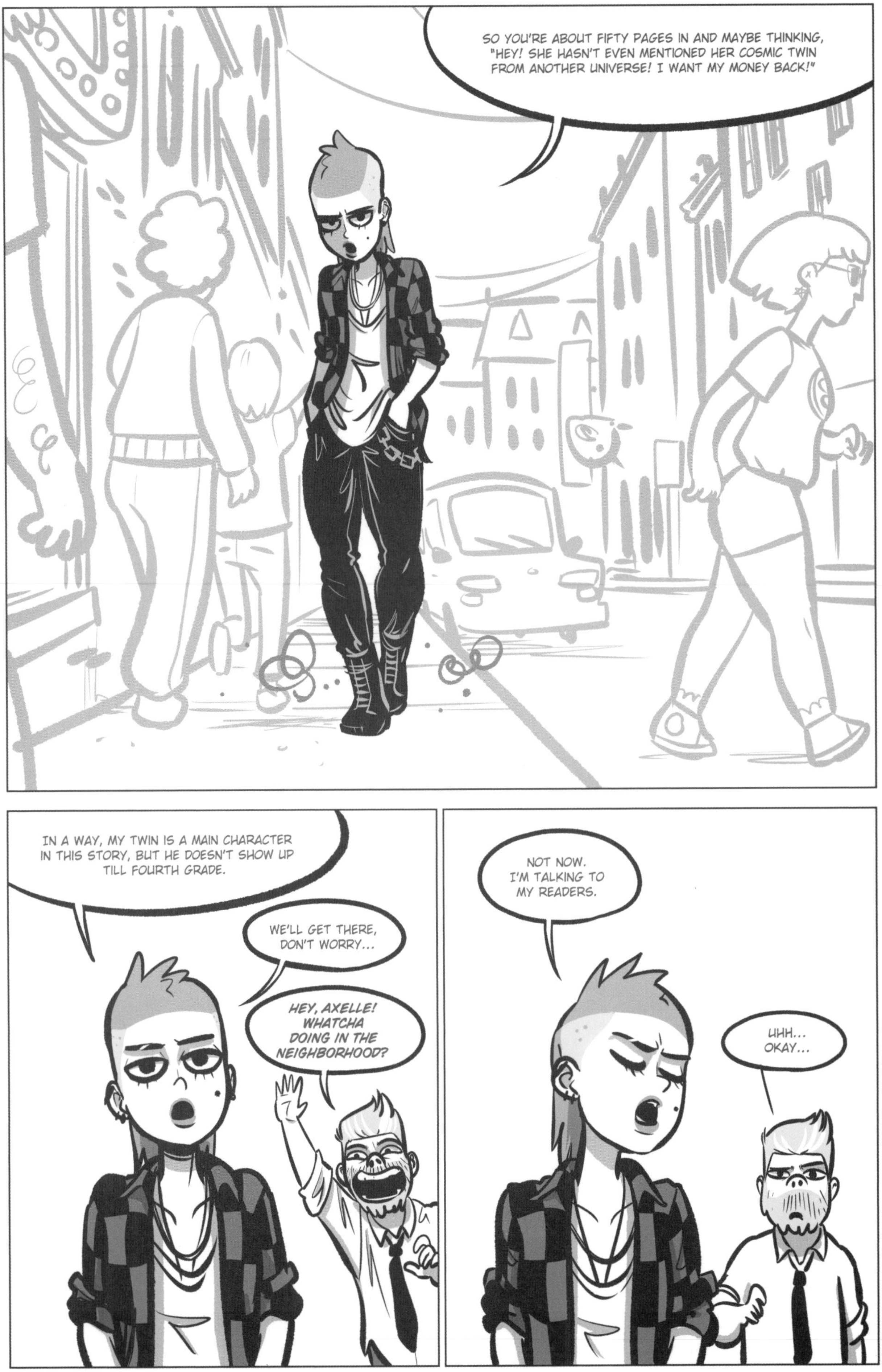
SO YOU'RE ABOUT FIFTY PAGES IN AND MAYBE THINKING, "HEY! SHE HASN'T EVEN MENTIONED HER COSMIC TWIN FROM ANOTHER UNIVERSE! I WANT MY MONEY BACK!"
IN A WAY, MY TWIN IS A MAIN CHARACTER IN THIS STORY, BUT HE DOESN'T SHOW UP TILL FOURTH GRADE.
WE'LL GET THERE, DON'T WORRY...
HEY, AXELLE! WHATCHA DOING IN THE NEIGHBORHOOD?
NOT NOW. I'M TALKING TO MY READERS.
UHH... OKAY...

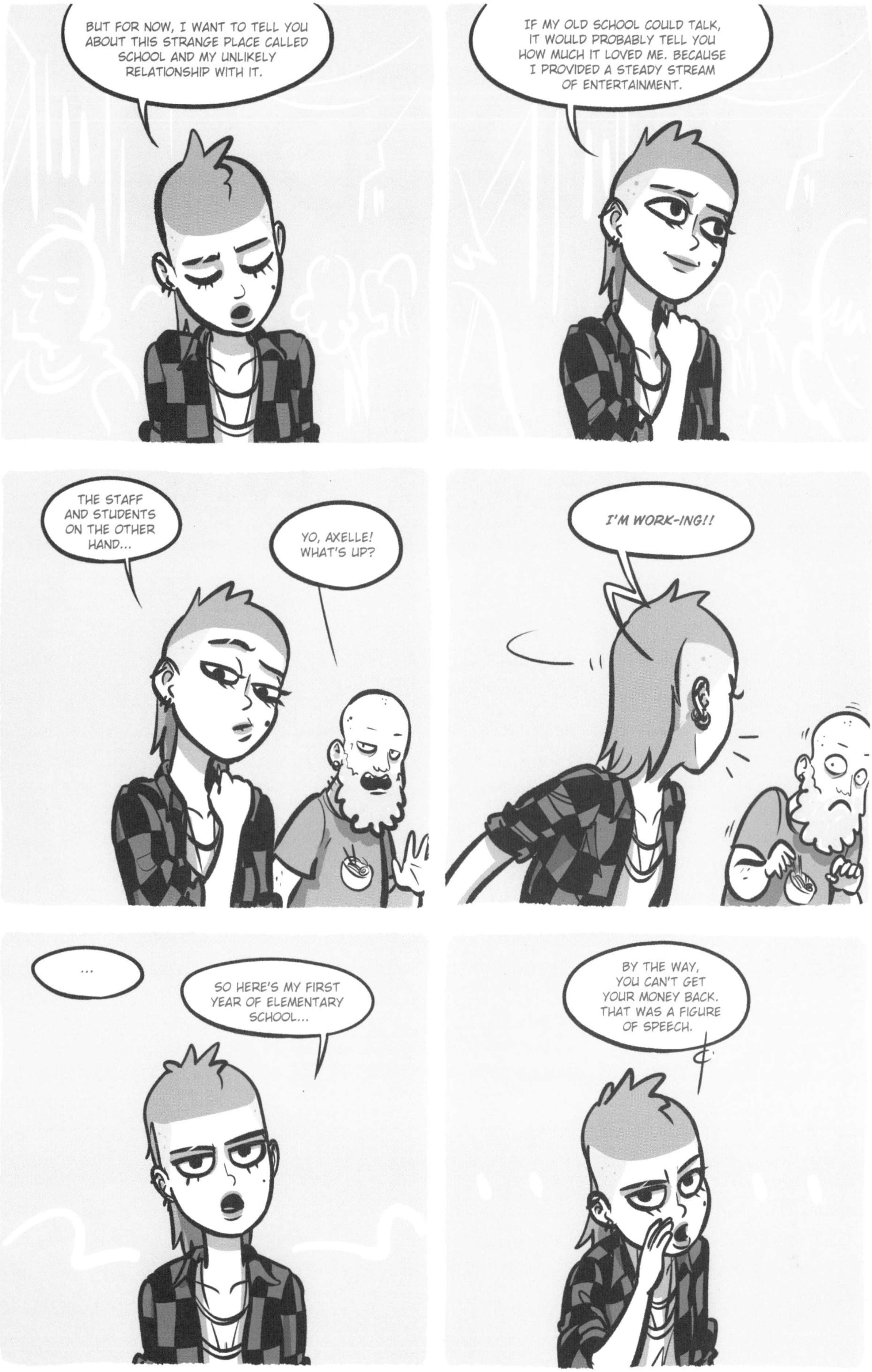
BUT FOR NOW, I WANT TO TELL YOU ABOUT THIS STRANGE PLACE CALLED SCHOOL AND MY UNLIKELY RELATIONSHIP WITH IT.
IF MY OLD SCHOOL COULD TALK, IT WOULD PROBABLY TELL YOU HOW MUCH IT LOVED ME. BECAUSE I PROVIDED A STEADY STREAM OF ENTERTAINMENT.
THE STAFF AND STUDENTS ON THE OTHER HAND...
YO, AXELLE! WHAT'S UP?
I'M WORK-ING!!
...
SO HERE'S MY FIRST YEAR OF ELEMENTARY SCHOOL...
BY THE WAY, YOU CAN'T GET YOUR MONEY BACK. THAT WAS A FIGURE OF SPEECH.

CHAPTER II

THE LONGEST DAY OF SCHOOL IN THE HISTORY OF THE UNIVERSE

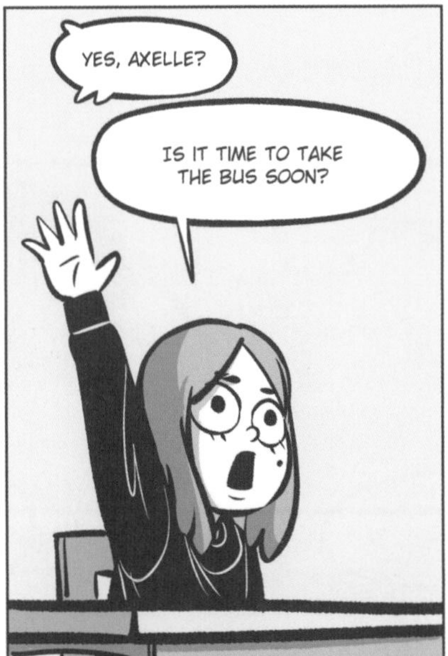
YES, AXELLE?
IS IT TIME TO TAKE THE BUS SOON?

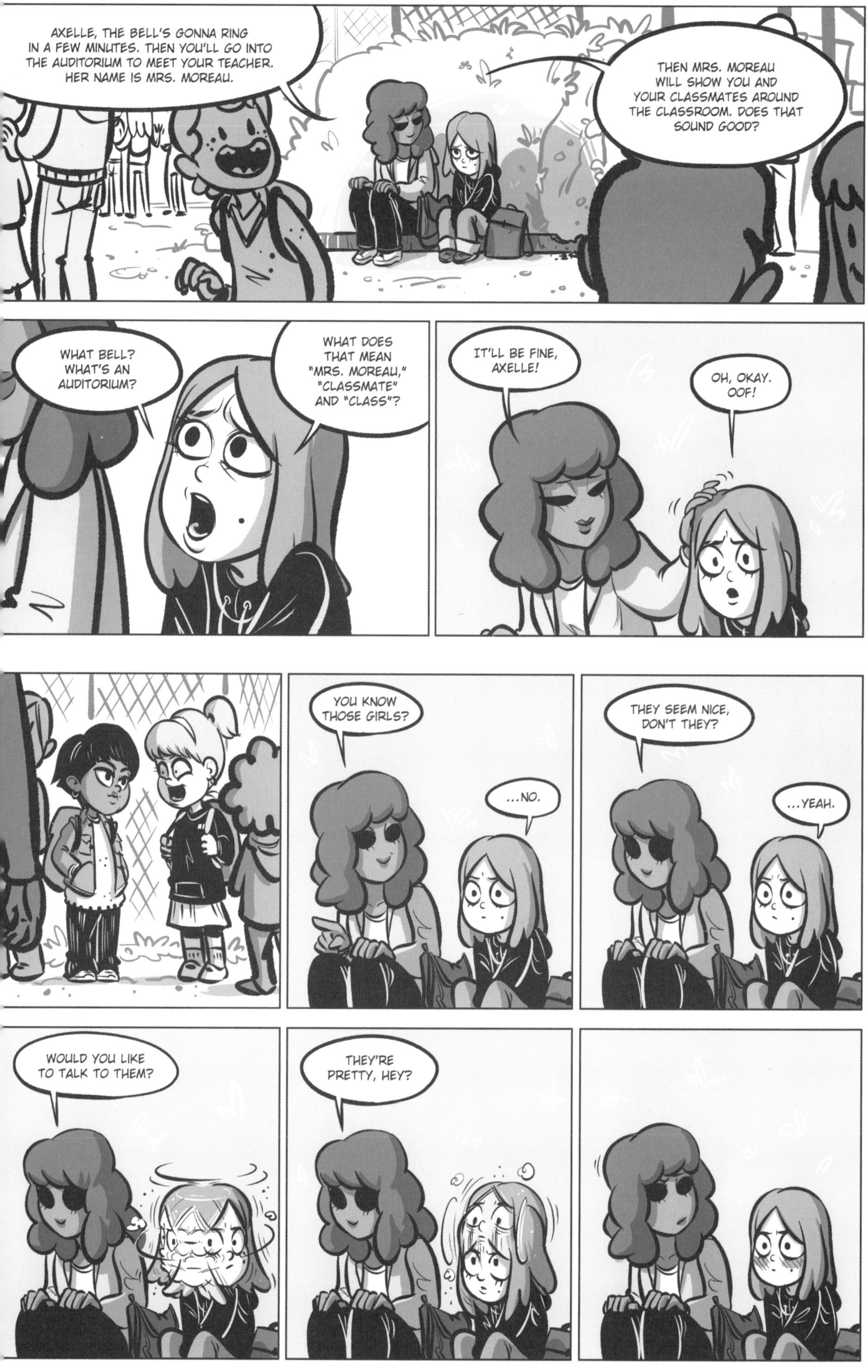
AXELLE, THE BELL'S GONNA RING IN A FEW MINUTES. THEN YOU'LL GO INTO THE AUDITORIUM TO MEET YOUR TEACHER. HER NAME IS MRS. MOREAU.
THEN MRS. MOREAU WILL SHOW YOU AND YOUR CLASSMATES AROUND THE CLASSROOM. DOES THAT SOUND GOOD?
WHAT BELL? WHAT'S AN AUDITORIUM?
WHAT DOES THAT MEAN "MRS. MOREAU," "CLASSMATE" AND "CLASS"?
IT'LL BE FINE, AXELLE!
OH, OKAY. OOF!
YOU KNOW THOSE GIRLS?
...NO.
THEY SEEM NICE, DON'T THEY?
...YEAH.
WOULD YOU LIKE TO TALK TO THEM?
THEY'RE PRETTY, HEY?

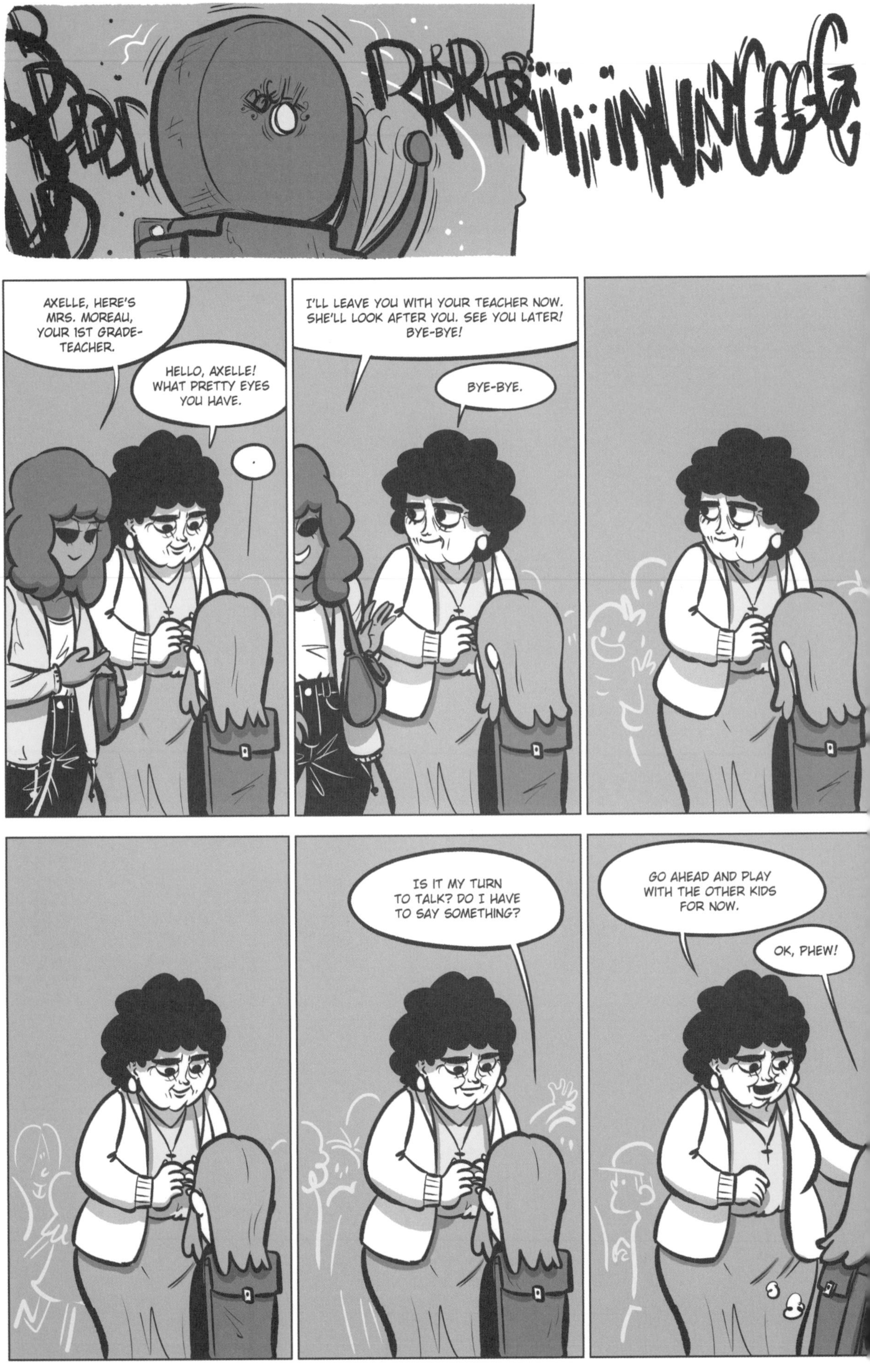
AXELLE, HERE'S MRS. MOREAU, YOUR 1ST GRADE-TEACHER.
HELLO, AXELLE! WHAT PRETTY EYES YOU HAVE.
I'LL LEAVE YOU WITH YOUR TEACHER NOW. SHE'LL LOOK AFTER YOU. SEE YOU LATER! BYE-BYE!
BYE-BYE.
IS IT MY TURN TO TALK? DO I HAVE TO SAY SOMETHING?
GO AHEAD AND PLAY WITH THE OTHER KIDS FOR NOW.
OK, PHEW!

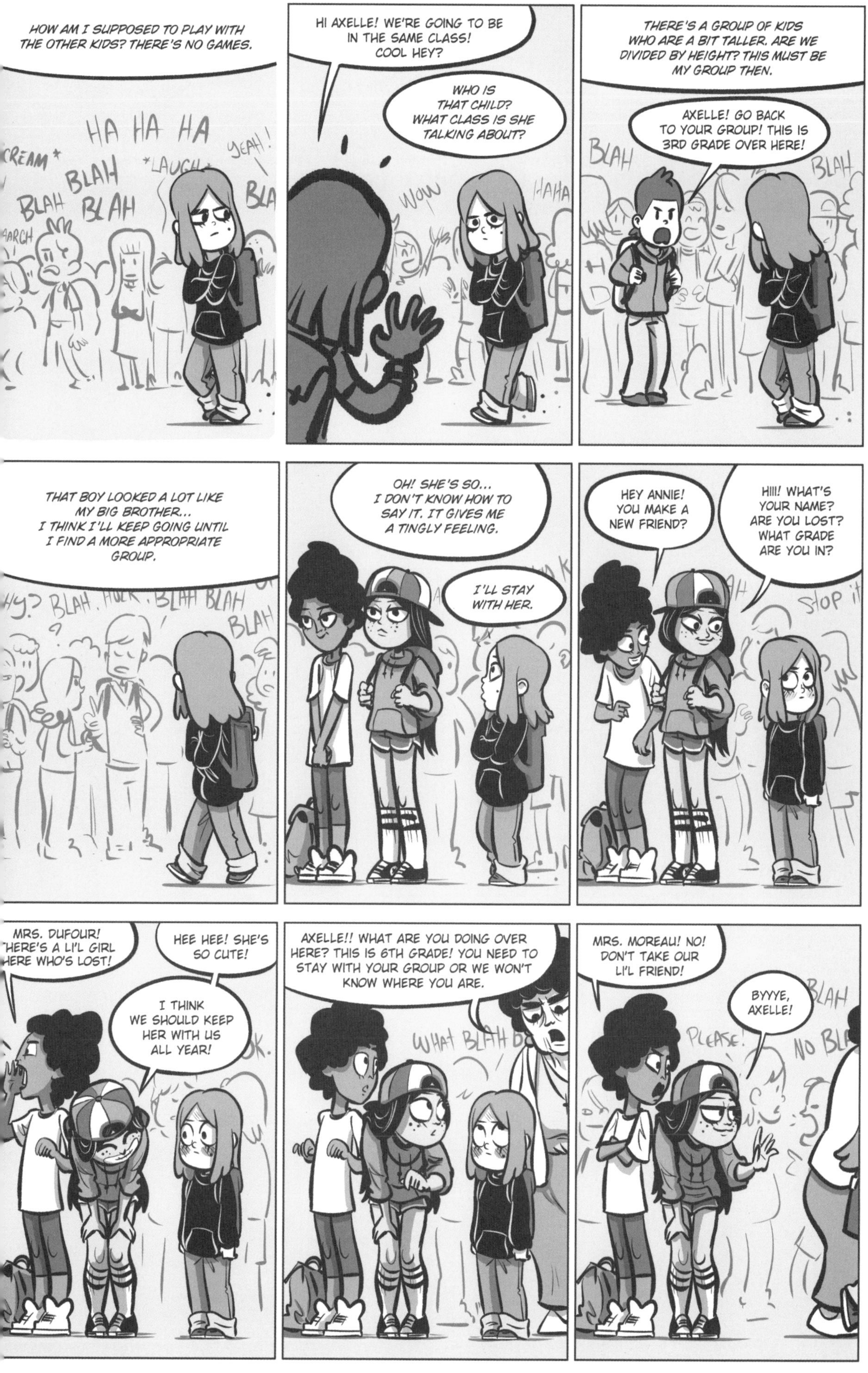
HOW AM I SUPPOSED TO PLAY WITH THE OTHER KIDS? THERE'S NO GAMES.
HA HA HA
BLAH BLAH
BLAH BLAH
YEAH!
HI AXELLE! WE'RE GOING TO BE IN THE SAME CLASS! COOL HEY?
WHO IS THAT CHILD? WHAT CLASS IS SHE TALKING ABOUT?
WOW
HAHA
THERE'S A GROUP OF KIDS WHO ARE A BIT TALLER. ARE WE DIVIDED BY HEIGHT? THIS MUST BE MY GROUP THEN.
AXELLE! GO BACK TO YOUR GROUP! THIS IS 3RD GRADE OVER HERE!
BLAH
BLAH
THAT BOY LOOKED A LOT LIKE MY BIG BROTHER... I THINK I'LL KEEP GOING UNTIL I FIND A MORE APPROPRIATE GROUP.
BLAH BLAH BLAH BLAH
OH! SHE'S SO... I DON'T KNOW HOW TO SAY IT. IT GIVES ME A TINGLY FEELING.
I'LL STAY WITH HER.
HEY ANNIE! YOU MAKE A NEW FRIEND?
HIII! WHAT'S YOUR NAME? ARE YOU LOST? WHAT GRADE ARE YOU IN?
MRS. DUFOUR! THERE'S A LI'L GIRL HERE WHO'S LOST!
HEE HEE! SHE'S SO CUTE!
I THINK WE SHOULD KEEP HER WITH US ALL YEAR!
AXELLE!! WHAT ARE YOU DOING OVER HERE? THIS IS 6TH GRADE! YOU NEED TO STAY WITH YOUR GROUP OR WE WON'T KNOW WHERE YOU ARE.
WHAT BLAH
MRS. MOREAU! NO! DON'T TAKE OUR LI'L FRIEND!
BYYYE, AXELLE!
PLEASE!
BLAH

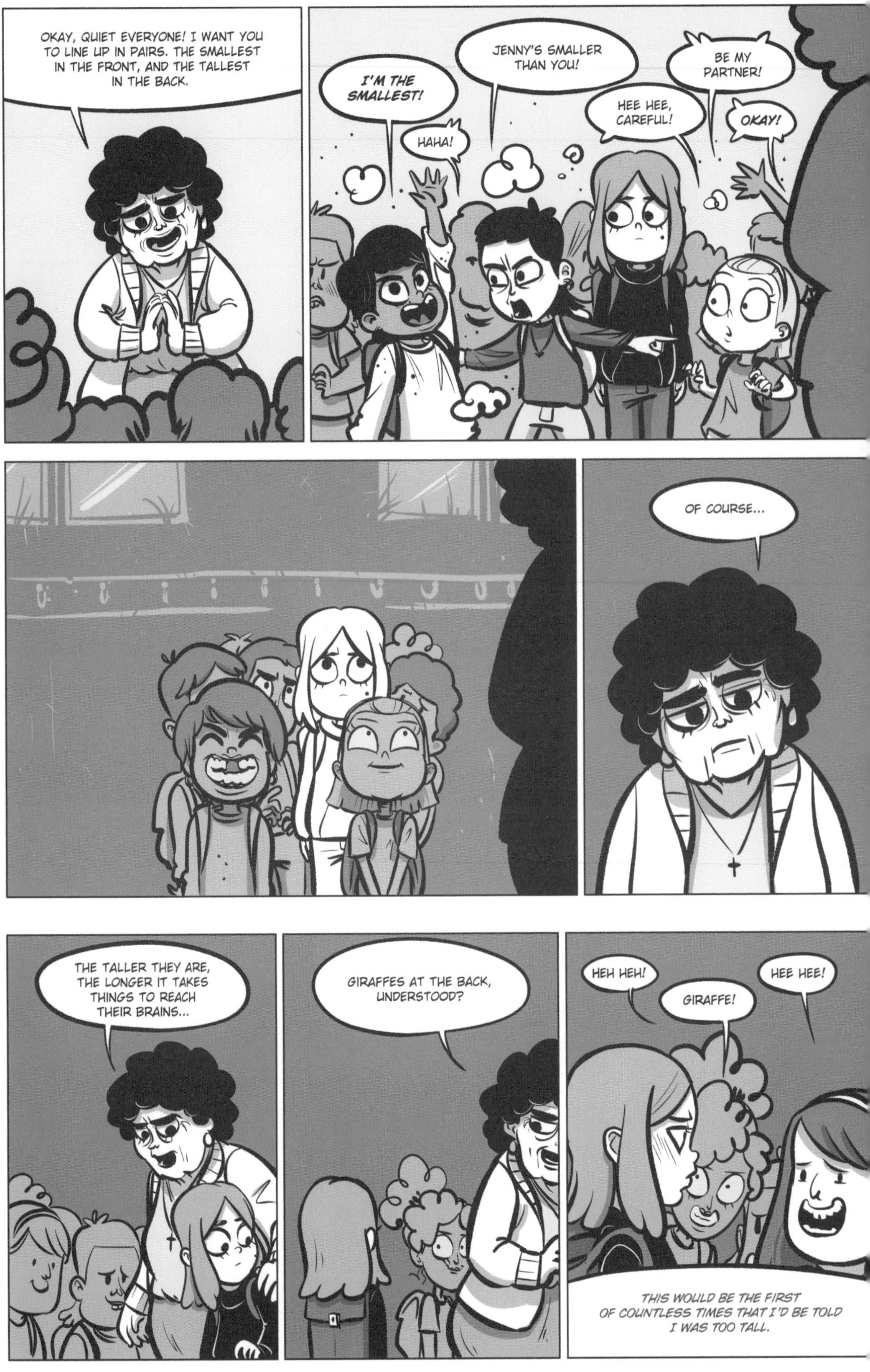
OKAY, QUIET EVERYONE! I WANT YOU TO LINE UP IN PAIRS. THE SMALLEST IN THE FRONT, AND THE TALLEST IN THE BACK.
I'M THE SMALLEST!
HAHA!
JENNY'S SMALLER THAN YOU!
HEE HEE, CAREFUL!
BE MY PARTNER!
OKAY!
OF COURSE...
THE TALLER THEY ARE, THE LONGER IT TAKES THINGS TO REACH THEIR BRAINS...
GIRAFFES AT THE BACK, UNDERSTOOD?
HEH HEH!
GIRAFFE!
HEE HEE!
THIS WOULD BE THE FIRST OF COUNTLESS TIMES THAT I'D BE TOLD I WAS TOO TALL.

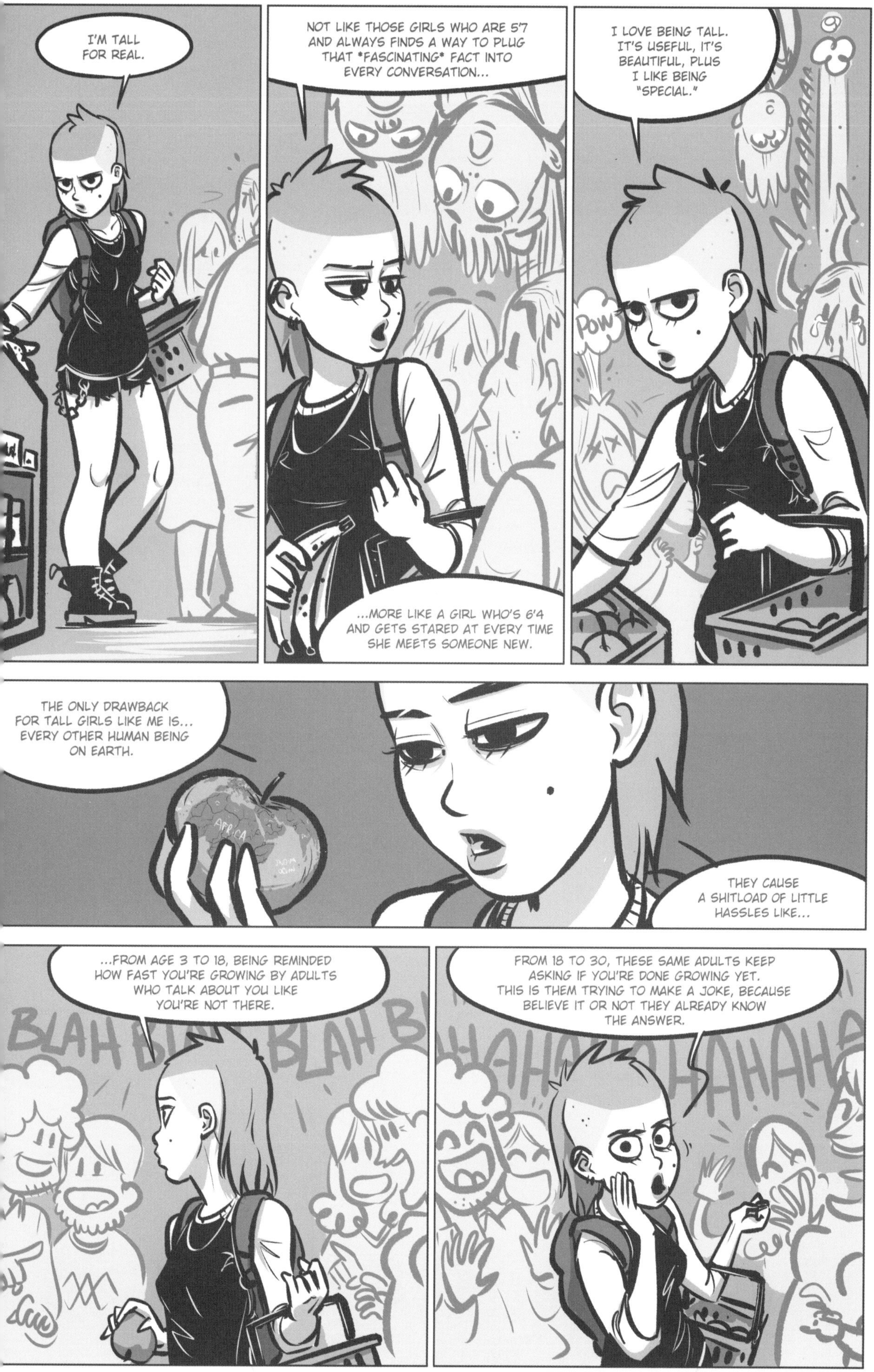
I'M TALL FOR REAL.
NOT LIKE THOSE GIRLS WHO ARE 5'7 AND ALWAYS FINDS A WAY TO PLUG THAT *FASCINATING* FACT INTO EVERY CONVERSATION...
...MORE LIKE A GIRL WHO'S 6'4 AND GETS STARED AT EVERY TIME SHE MEETS SOMEONE NEW.
I LOVE BEING TALL. IT'S USEFUL, IT'S BEAUTIFUL, PLUS I LIKE BEING "SPECIAL."
POW
THE ONLY DRAWBACK FOR TALL GIRLS LIKE ME IS... EVERY OTHER HUMAN BEING ON EARTH.
AFRICA
THEY CAUSE A SHITLOAD OF LITTLE HASSLES LIKE...
...FROM AGE 3 TO 18, BEING REMINDED HOW FAST YOU'RE GROWING BY ADULTS WHO TALK ABOUT YOU LIKE YOU'RE NOT THERE.
FROM 18 TO 30, THESE SAME ADULTS KEEP ASKING IF YOU'RE DONE GROWING YET. THIS IS THEM TRYING TO MAKE A JOKE, BECAUSE BELIEVE IT OR NOT THEY ALREADY KNOW THE ANSWER.

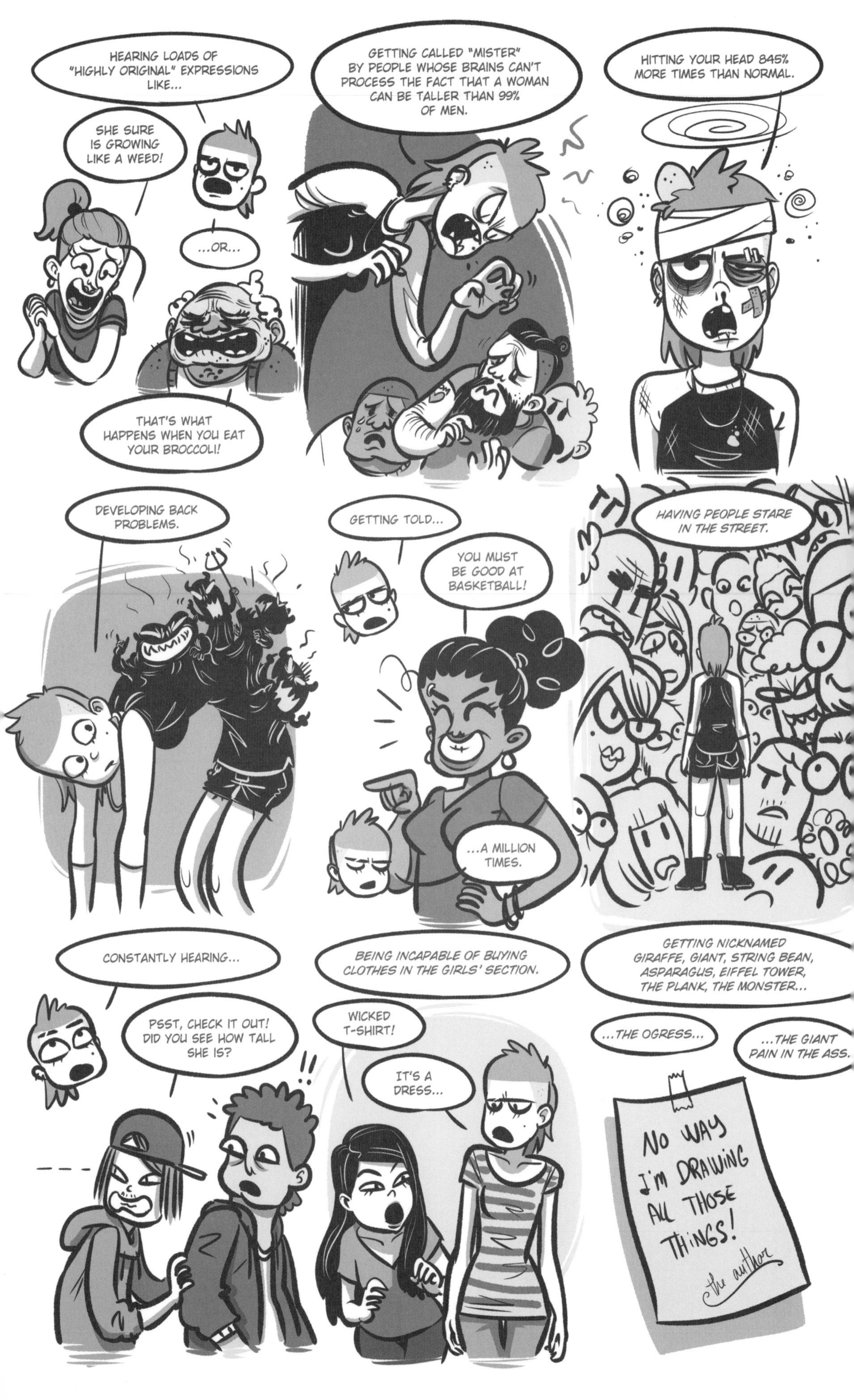
HEARING LOADS OF "HIGHLY ORIGINAL" EXPRESSIONS LIKE...
SHE SURE IS GROWING LIKE A WEED!
...OR...
THAT'S WHAT HAPPENS WHEN YOU EAT YOUR BROCCOLI!
GETTING CALLED "MISTER" BY PEOPLE WHOSE BRAINS CAN'T PROCESS THE FACT THAT A WOMAN CAN BE TALLER THAN 99% OF MEN.
HITTING YOUR HEAD 845% MORE TIMES THAN NORMAL.
DEVELOPING BACK PROBLEMS.
GETTING TOLD...
YOU MUST BE GOOD AT BASKETBALL!
...A MILLION TIMES.
HAVING PEOPLE STARE IN THE STREET.
CONSTANTLY HEARING...
PSST, CHECK IT OUT! DID YOU SEE HOW TALL SHE IS?
BEING INCAPABLE OF BUYING CLOTHES IN THE GIRLS' SECTION.
WICKED T-SHIRT!
IT'S A DRESS...
GETTING NICKNAMED GIRAFFE, GIANT, STRING BEAN, ASPARAGUS, EIFFEL TOWER, THE PLANK, THE MONSTER...
...THE OGRESS...
...THE GIANT PAIN IN THE ASS.
NO WAY I'M DRAWING ALL THOSE THINGS!
the author

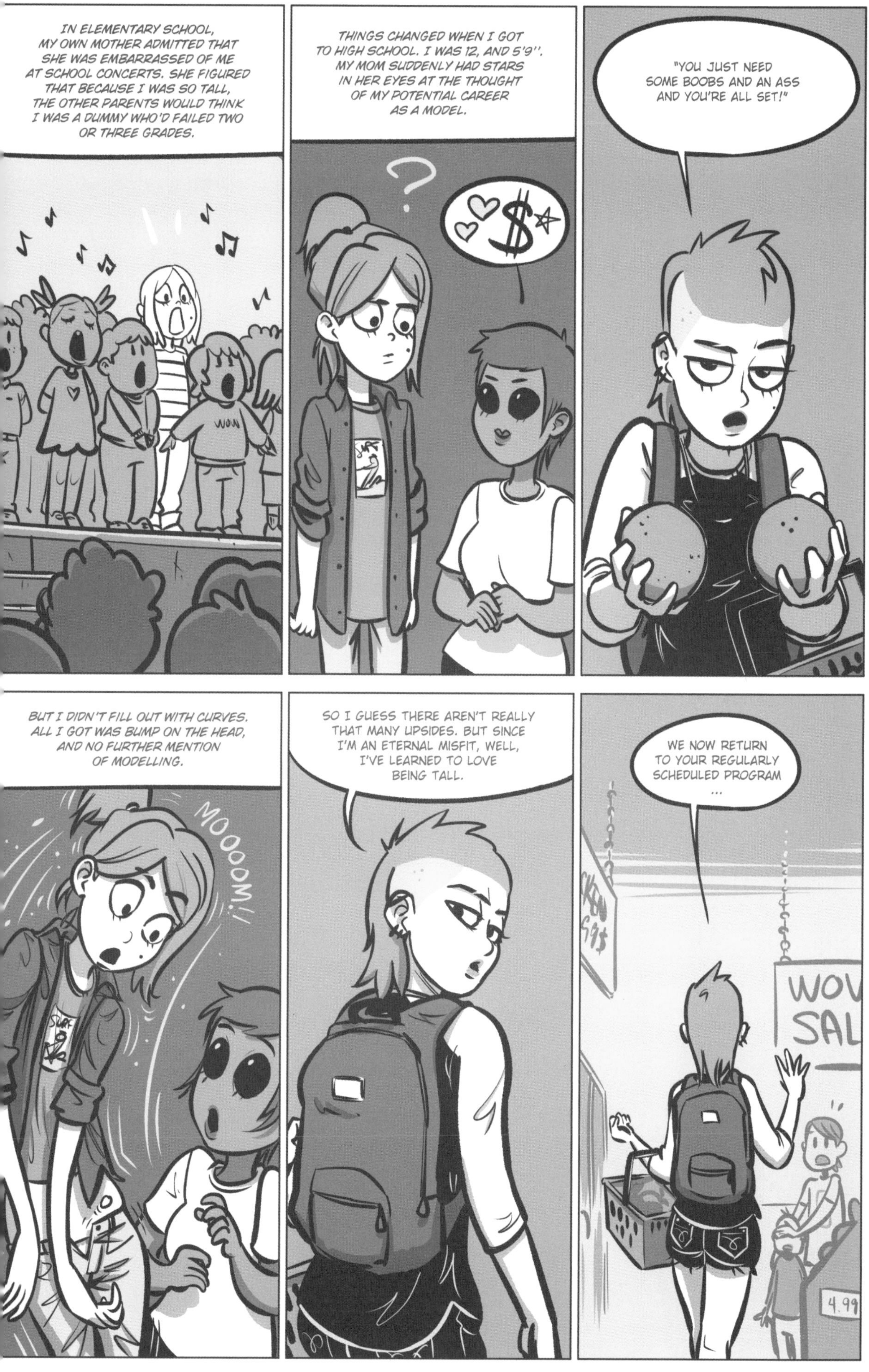
IN ELEMENTARY SCHOOL, MY OWN MOTHER ADMITTED THAT SHE WAS EMBARRASSED OF ME AT SCHOOL CONCERTS. SHE FIGURED THAT BECAUSE I WAS SO TALL, THE OTHER PARENTS WOULD THINK I WAS A DUMMY WHO'D FAILED TWO OR THREE GRADES.
WOW
THINGS CHANGED WHEN I GOT TO HIGH SCHOOL. I WAS 12, AND 5'9''. MY MOM SUDDENLY HAD STARS IN HER EYES AT THE THOUGHT OF MY POTENTIAL CAREER AS A MODEL.
?
$
"YOU JUST NEED SOME BOOBS AND AN ASS AND YOU'RE ALL SET!"
BUT I DIDN'T FILL OUT WITH CURVES. ALL I GOT WAS BUMP ON THE HEAD, AND NO FURTHER MENTION OF MODELLING.
MOOOOM!!
SO I GUESS THERE AREN'T REALLY THAT MANY UPSIDES. BUT SINCE I'M AN ETERNAL MISFIT, WELL, I'VE LEARNED TO LOVE BEING TALL.
WE NOW RETURN TO YOUR REGULARLY SCHEDULED PROGRAM
...
4.99

SO THIS IS A CLASSROOM... IT'S HUUUUUGE!

I DIDN'T KNOW THIS MANY KIDS MY AGE EVEN EXISTED.

WHY ARE THEY ALL SUPER EXCITED LIKE IT'S THEIR BIRTHDAY?

THEY MUST BE BROKEN...

BLAH BLAH BLAH BLAH BLAH BLAH BLAH

BLAH BLAH BLAH BLAH BLAH BLAH! ...BLAH

BLAH BLAH... BLAH BLAH BLAH BLAH-BLAH! BLAH.

BLAH BLAH BLAH BLAH BLAH BLAH BLAH BLAH

AXELLE!

WHAA?

IT'S YOUR TURN TO INTRODUCE YOURSELF.

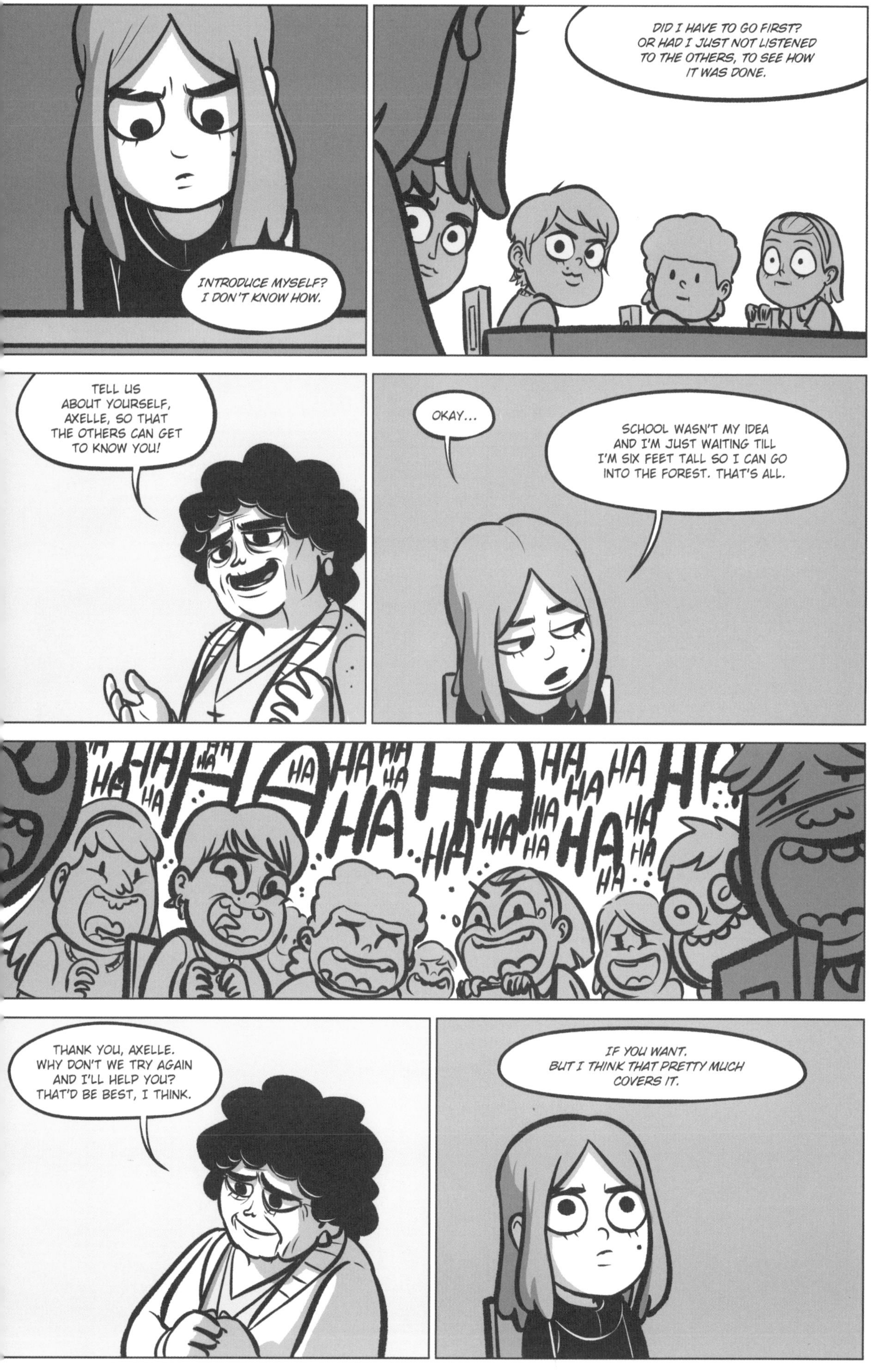
INTRODUCE MYSELF?
I DON'T KNOW HOW.
DID I HAVE TO GO FIRST?
OR HAD I JUST NOT LISTENED
TO THE OTHERS, TO SEE HOW
IT WAS DONE.
TELL US ABOUT YOURSELF, AXELLE, SO THAT THE OTHERS CAN GET TO KNOW YOU!
OKAY...
SCHOOL WASN'T MY IDEA AND I'M JUST WAITING TILL I'M SIX FEET TALL SO I CAN GO INTO THE FOREST. THAT'S ALL.
HA HA HA HA HA HA HA HA HA HA HA HA HA HA HA HA HA HA HA HA HA HA HA
THANK YOU, AXELLE. WHY DON'T WE TRY AGAIN AND I'LL HELP YOU? THAT'D BE BEST, I THINK.
IF YOU WANT.
BUT I THINK THAT PRETTY MUCH
COVERS IT.

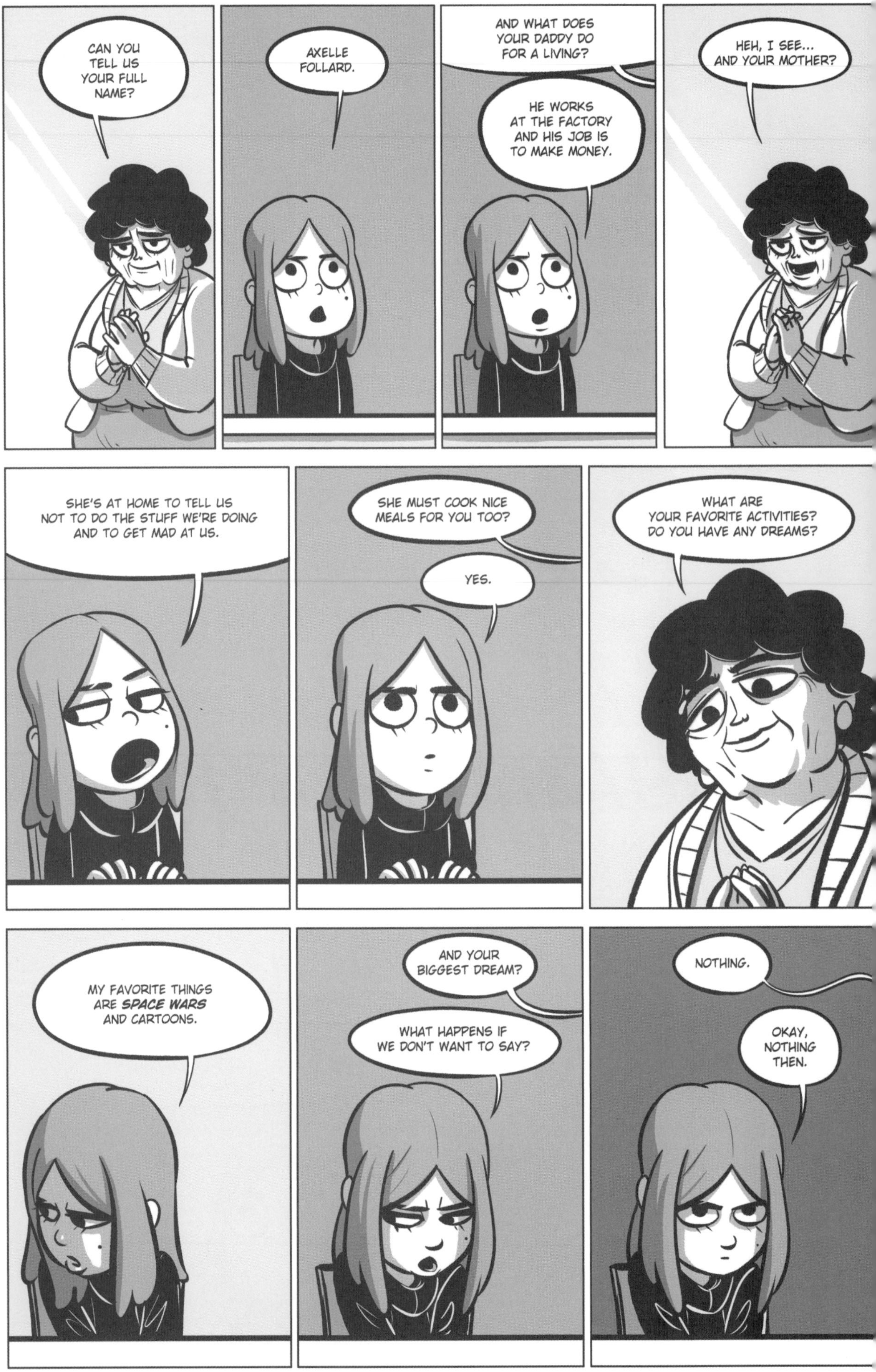
CAN YOU TELL US YOUR FULL NAME?
AXELLE FOLLARD.
AND WHAT DOES YOUR DADDY DO FOR A LIVING?
HE WORKS AT THE FACTORY AND HIS JOB IS TO MAKE MONEY.
HEH, I SEE... AND YOUR MOTHER?
SHE'S AT HOME TO TELL US NOT TO DO THE STUFF WE'RE DOING AND TO GET MAD AT US.
SHE MUST COOK NICE MEALS FOR YOU TOO?
YES.
WHAT ARE YOUR FAVORITE ACTIVITIES? DO YOU HAVE ANY DREAMS?
MY FAVORITE THINGS ARE *SPACE WARS* AND CARTOONS.
AND YOUR BIGGEST DREAM?
WHAT HAPPENS IF WE DON'T WANT TO SAY?
NOTHING.
OKAY, NOTHING THEN.

WELL MY DADDY MAKES MEDICINE FOR SICK PEOPLE. AND MY MOMMY MAKES GIANT CAKES! I LIKE THEM A LOT...

I FEEL WEIRD THAT I SAID ALL THOSE THINGS.

...AND WHAT I LIKE MOST ARE HORSIES AND DOLPHINS BECAUSE THEY'RE NICE AND I LIKE THEM!

I SHOULDN'T HAVE GIVEN IN TO THE PRESSURE. I FEEL LIKE I'VE BETRAYED MYSELF... I WONDER IF WE CAN START OVER?

...MY BIGGEST DREAM IS TO CATCH A RAINBOW AND DECORATE MY ROOM WITH IT!

HOLD ON?!? WE'RE ALLOWED TO GIVE DUMB ANSWERS LIKE THAT?

MRS. MOREAU TEACHER? CAN I DO MINE OVER AND SAY DUMB THINGS TOO?

AXELLE! BLAH BLAH BLAH BLAH BLAH BLAH BLAH

UH-OH. HERE SHE GOES AGAIN...

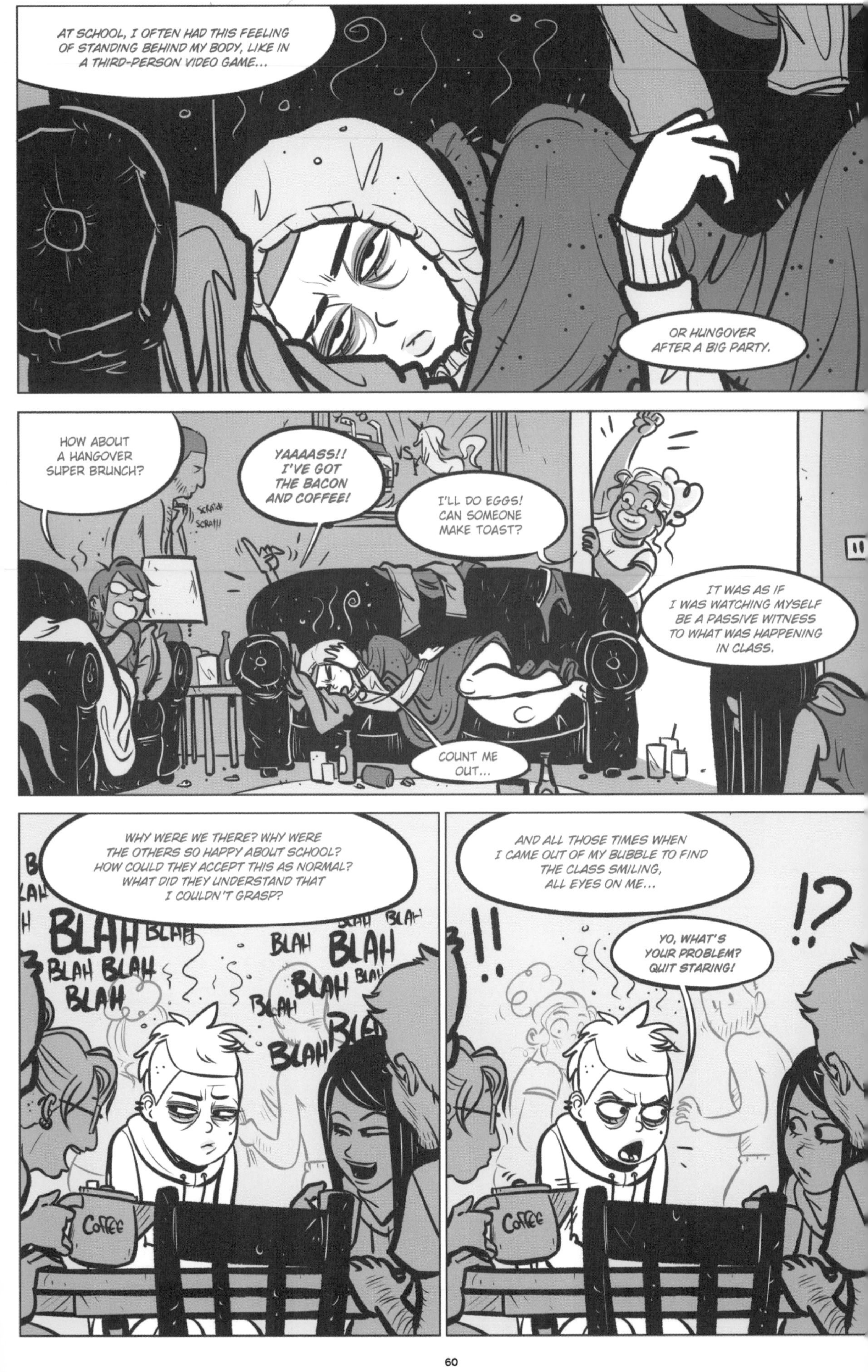
AT SCHOOL, I OFTEN HAD THIS FEELING OF STANDING BEHIND MY BODY, LIKE IN A THIRD-PERSON VIDEO GAME...
OR HUNGOVER AFTER A BIG PARTY.
HOW ABOUT A HANGOVER SUPER BRUNCH?
YAAAAASS!! I'VE GOT THE BACON AND COFFEE!
I'LL DO EGGS! CAN SOMEONE MAKE TOAST?
IT WAS AS IF I WAS WATCHING MYSELF BE A PASSIVE WITNESS TO WHAT WAS HAPPENING IN CLASS.
COUNT ME OUT...
WHY WERE WE THERE? WHY WERE THE OTHERS SO HAPPY ABOUT SCHOOL? HOW COULD THEY ACCEPT THIS AS NORMAL? WHAT DID THEY UNDERSTAND THAT I COULDN'T GRASP?
BLAH BLAH BLAH BLAH BLAH BLAH BLAH BLAH BLAH BLAH
COFFEE
AND ALL THOSE TIMES WHEN I CAME OUT OF MY BUBBLE TO FIND THE CLASS SMILING, ALL EYES ON ME...
!!
YO, WHAT'S YOUR PROBLEM? QUIT STARING!
!?
COFFEE

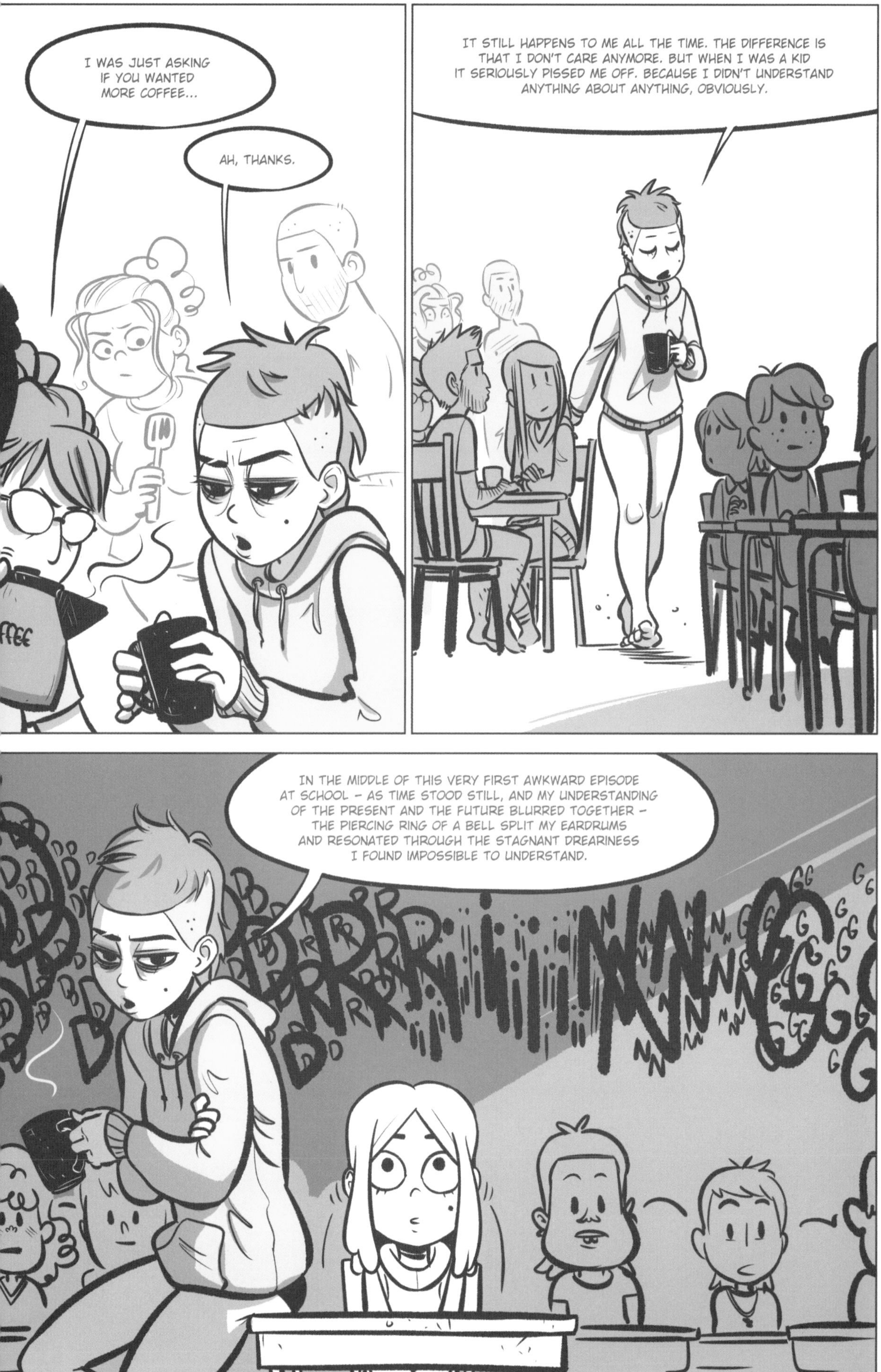
I WAS JUST ASKING IF YOU WANTED MORE COFFEE...
AH, THANKS.
IT STILL HAPPENS TO ME ALL THE TIME. THE DIFFERENCE IS THAT I DON'T CARE ANYMORE. BUT WHEN I WAS A KID IT SERIOUSLY PISSED ME OFF. BECAUSE I DIDN'T UNDERSTAND ANYTHING ABOUT ANYTHING, OBVIOUSLY.
IN THE MIDDLE OF THIS VERY FIRST AWKWARD EPISODE AT SCHOOL – AS TIME STOOD STILL, AND MY UNDERSTANDING OF THE PRESENT AND THE FUTURE BLURRED TOGETHER – THE PIERCING RING OF A BELL SPLIT MY EARDRUMS AND RESONATED THROUGH THE STAGNANT DREARINESS I FOUND IMPOSSIBLE TO UNDERSTAND.
BRRRiiiNNG

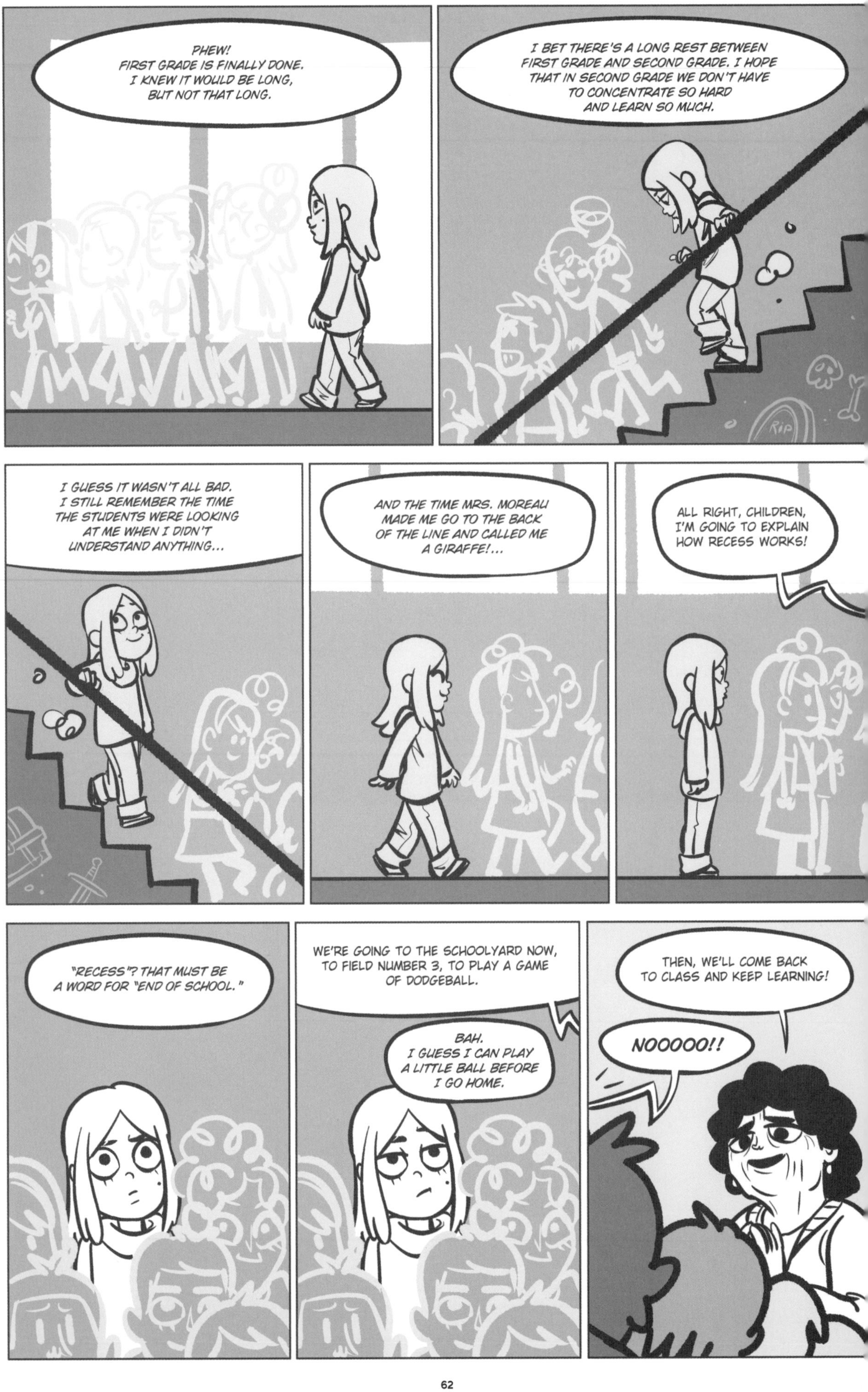
PHEW!
FIRST GRADE IS FINALLY DONE.
I KNEW IT WOULD BE LONG,
BUT NOT THAT LONG.
I BET THERE'S A LONG REST BETWEEN FIRST GRADE AND SECOND GRADE. I HOPE THAT IN SECOND GRADE WE DON'T HAVE TO CONCENTRATE SO HARD AND LEARN SO MUCH.
RIP
I GUESS IT WASN'T ALL BAD. I STILL REMEMBER THE TIME THE STUDENTS WERE LOOKING AT ME WHEN I DIDN'T UNDERSTAND ANYTHING...
AND THE TIME MRS. MOREAU MADE ME GO TO THE BACK OF THE LINE AND CALLED ME A GIRAFFE!...
ALL RIGHT, CHILDREN, I'M GOING TO EXPLAIN HOW RECESS WORKS!
"RECESS"? THAT MUST BE A WORD FOR "END OF SCHOOL."
WE'RE GOING TO THE SCHOOLYARD NOW, TO FIELD NUMBER 3, TO PLAY A GAME OF DODGEBALL.
BAH. I GUESS I CAN PLAY A LITTLE BALL BEFORE I GO HOME.
THEN, WE'LL COME BACK TO CLASS AND KEEP LEARNING!
NOOOOO!!

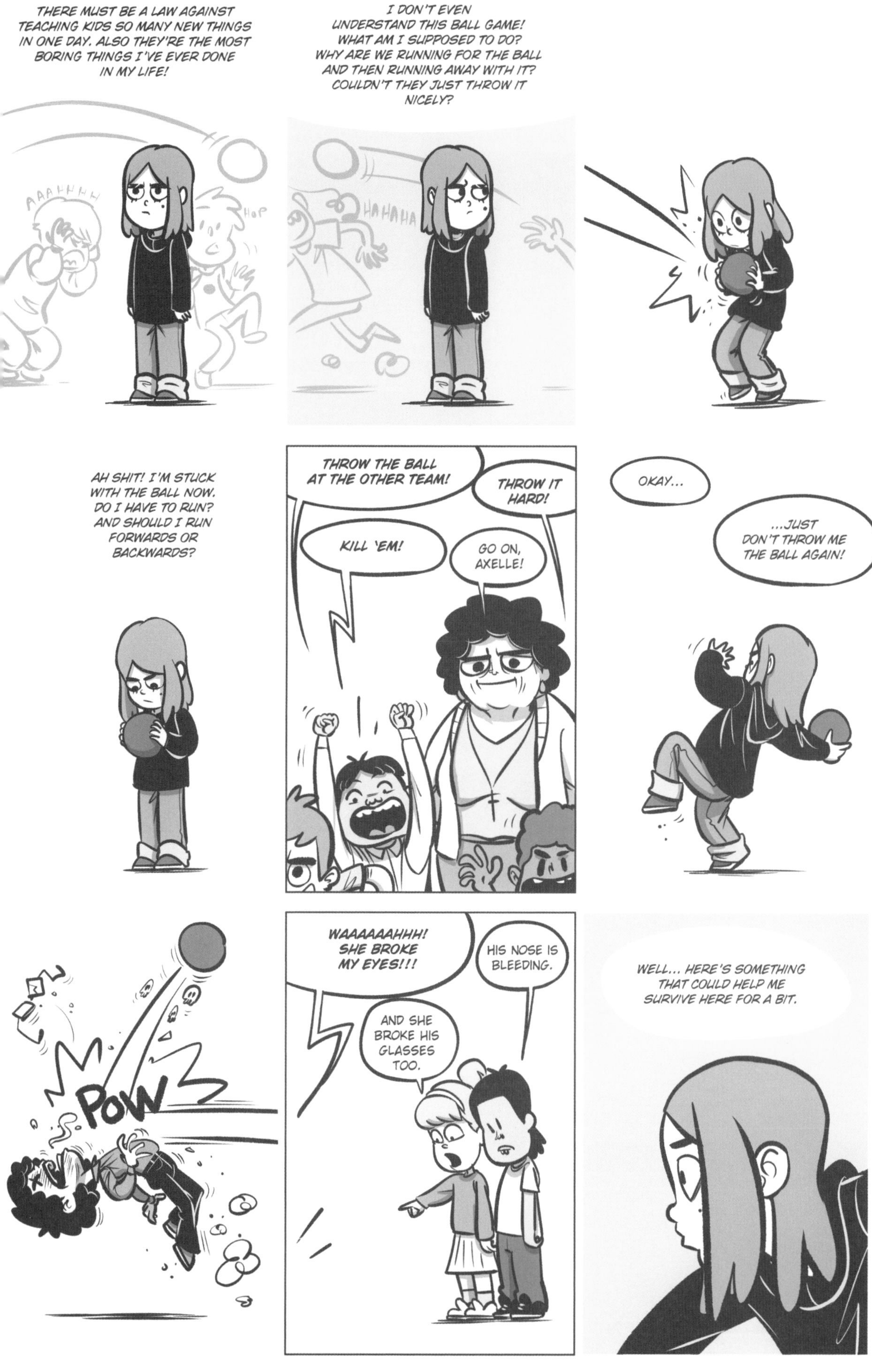
THERE MUST BE A LAW AGAINST TEACHING KIDS SO MANY NEW THINGS IN ONE DAY. ALSO THEY'RE THE MOST BORING THINGS I'VE EVER DONE IN MY LIFE!
HOP
I DON'T EVEN UNDERSTAND THIS BALL GAME! WHAT AM I SUPPOSED TO DO? WHY ARE WE RUNNING FOR THE BALL AND THEN RUNNING AWAY WITH IT? COULDN'T THEY JUST THROW IT NICELY?
HAHAHA
AH SHIT! I'M STUCK WITH THE BALL NOW. DO I HAVE TO RUN? AND SHOULD I RUN FORWARDS OR BACKWARDS?
THROW THE BALL AT THE OTHER TEAM!
THROW IT HARD!
KILL 'EM!
GO ON, AXELLE!
OKAY...
...JUST DON'T THROW ME THE BALL AGAIN!
POW
WAAAAAAHHH! SHE BROKE MY EYES!!!
HIS NOSE IS BLEEDING.
AND SHE BROKE HIS GLASSES TOO.
WELL... HERE'S SOMETHING THAT COULD HELP ME SURVIVE HERE FOR A BIT.

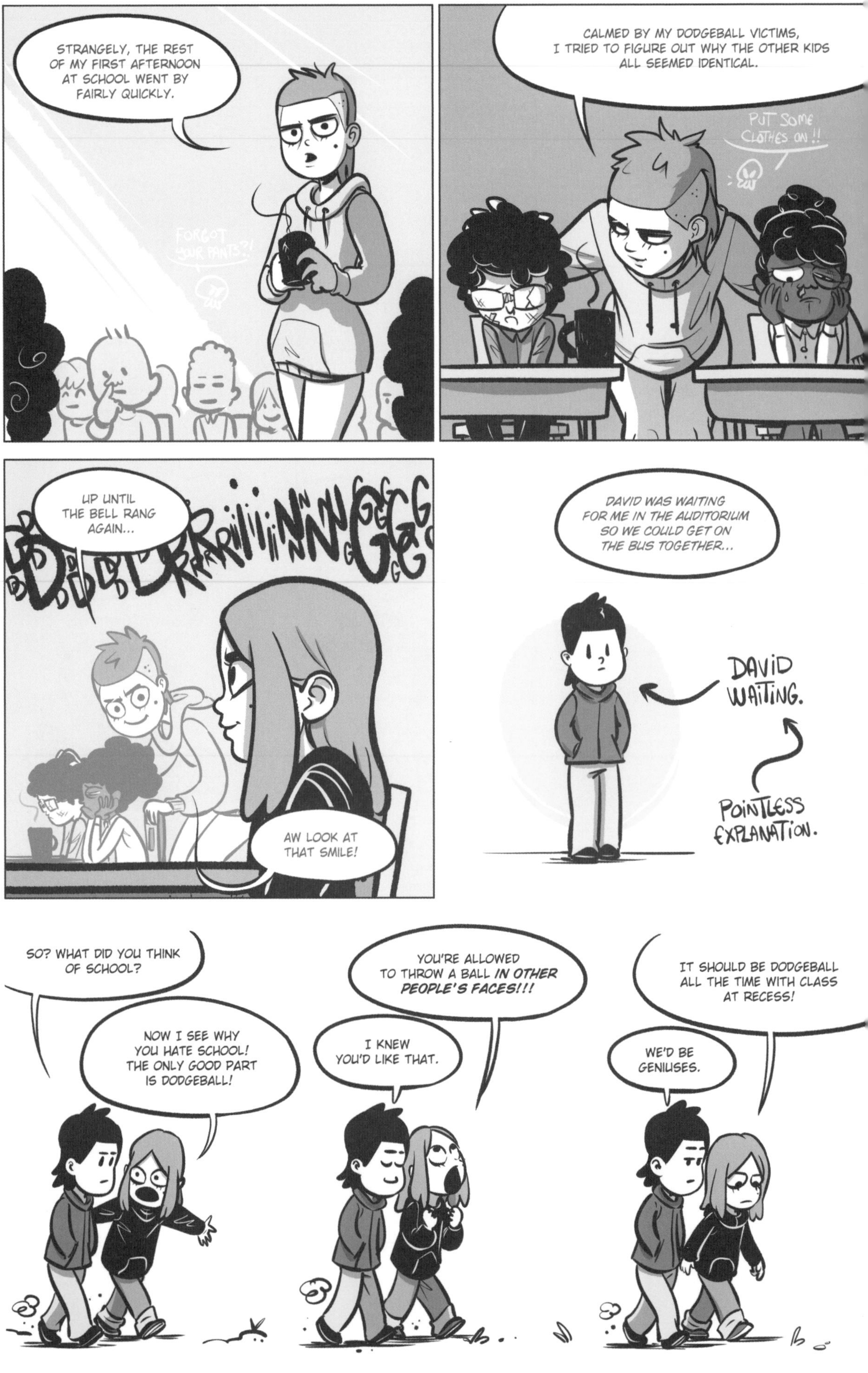

STRANGELY, THE REST OF MY FIRST AFTERNOON AT SCHOOL WENT BY FAIRLY QUICKLY.
FORGOT YOUR PANTS?!
CALMED BY MY DODGEBALL VICTIMS, I TRIED TO FIGURE OUT WHY THE OTHER KIDS ALL SEEMED IDENTICAL.
PUT SOME CLOTHES ON !!
UP UNTIL THE BELL RANG AGAIN...
AW LOOK AT THAT SMILE!
DAVID WAS WAITING FOR ME IN THE AUDITORIUM SO WE COULD GET ON THE BUS TOGETHER...
DAVID WAITING.
POINTLESS EXPLANATION.
SO? WHAT DID YOU THINK OF SCHOOL?
NOW I SEE WHY YOU HATE SCHOOL! THE ONLY GOOD PART IS DODGEBALL!
YOU'RE ALLOWED TO THROW A BALL *IN OTHER PEOPLE'S FACES!!!*
I KNEW YOU'D LIKE THAT.
IT SHOULD BE DODGEBALL ALL THE TIME WITH CLASS AT RECESS!
WE'D BE GENIUSES.

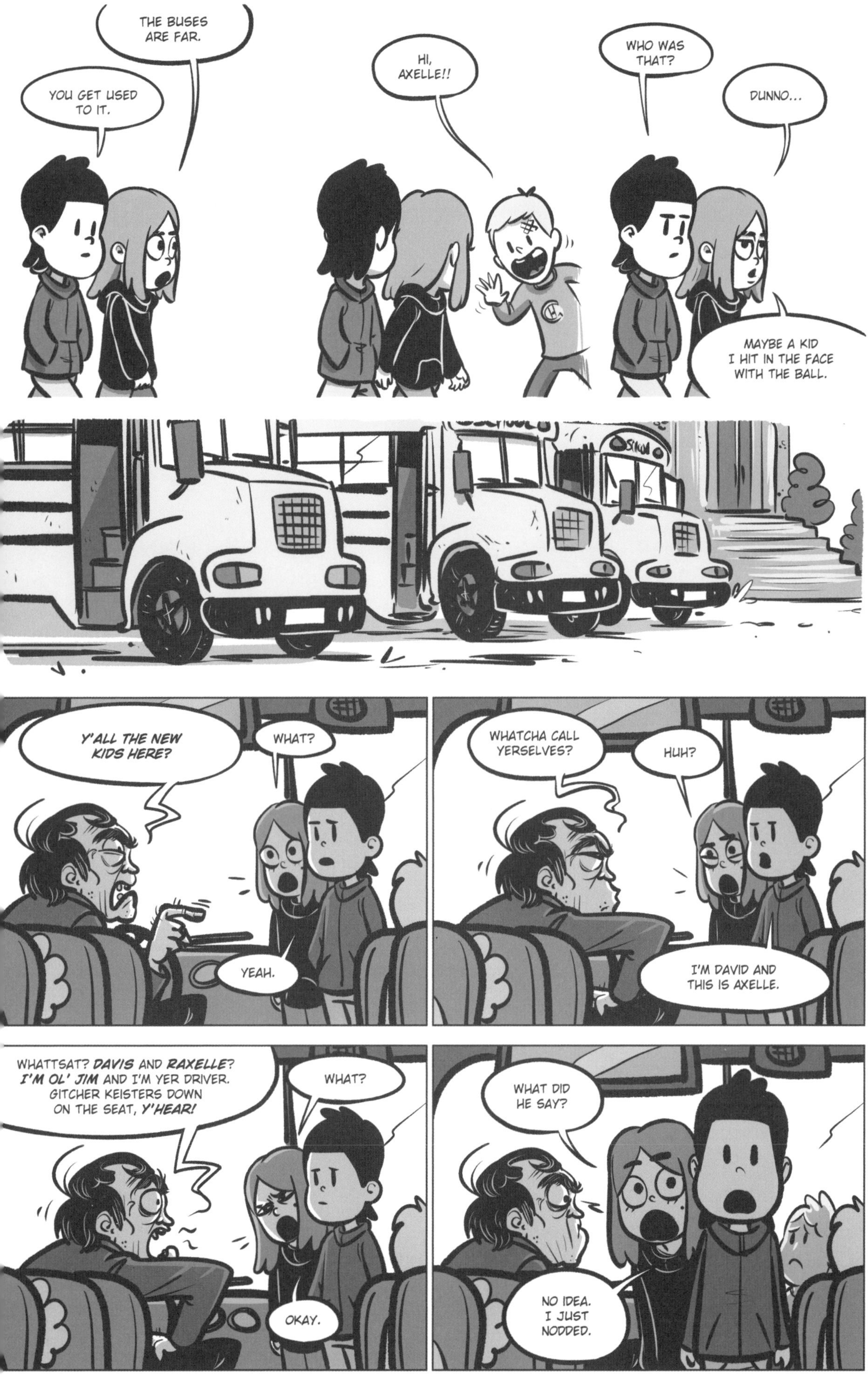
YOU GET USED TO IT.
THE BUSES ARE FAR.
HI, AXELLE!!
WHO WAS THAT?
DUNNO...
MAYBE A KID I HIT IN THE FACE WITH THE BALL.
Y'ALL THE NEW KIDS HERE?
WHAT?
YEAH.
WHATCHA CALL YERSELVES?
HUH?
I'M DAVID AND THIS IS AXELLE.
WHATTSAT? ***DAVIS*** AND ***RAXELLE***? ***I'M OL' JIM*** AND I'M YER DRIVER. GITCHER KEISTERS DOWN ON THE SEAT, ***Y'HEAR!***
WHAT?
OKAY.
WHAT DID HE SAY?
NO IDEA. I JUST NODDED.

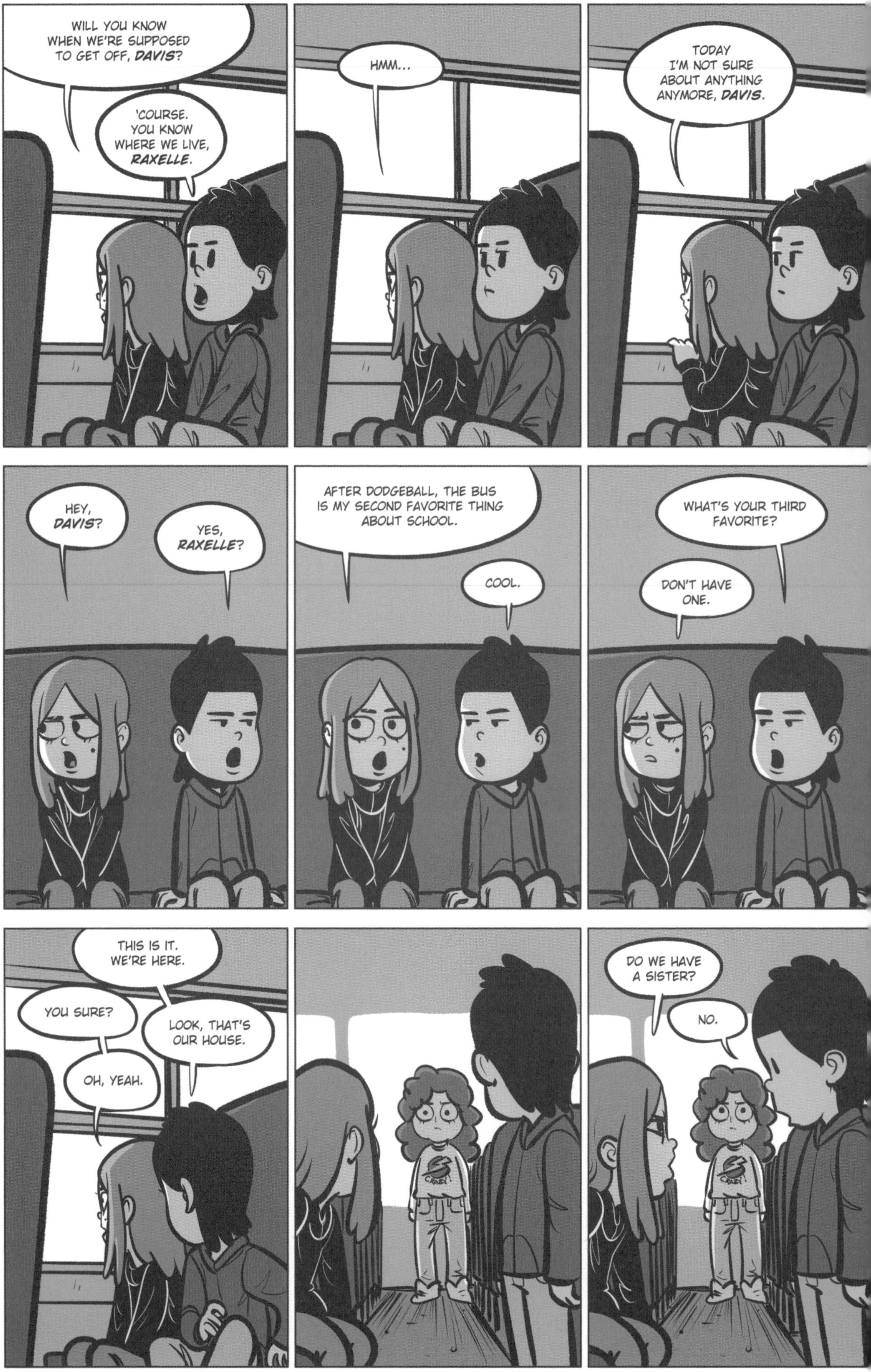
WILL YOU KNOW WHEN WE'RE SUPPOSED TO GET OFF, **DAVIS**?
'COURSE. YOU KNOW WHERE WE LIVE, **RAXELLE**.
HMM...
TODAY I'M NOT SURE ABOUT ANYTHING ANYMORE, **DAVIS**.
HEY, **DAVIS**?
YES, **RAXELLE**?
AFTER DODGEBALL, THE BUS IS MY SECOND FAVORITE THING ABOUT SCHOOL.
COOL.
WHAT'S YOUR THIRD FAVORITE?
DON'T HAVE ONE.
THIS IS IT. WE'RE HERE.
YOU SURE?
LOOK, THAT'S OUR HOUSE.
OH, YEAH.
CRAZY!
DO WE HAVE A SISTER?
NO.

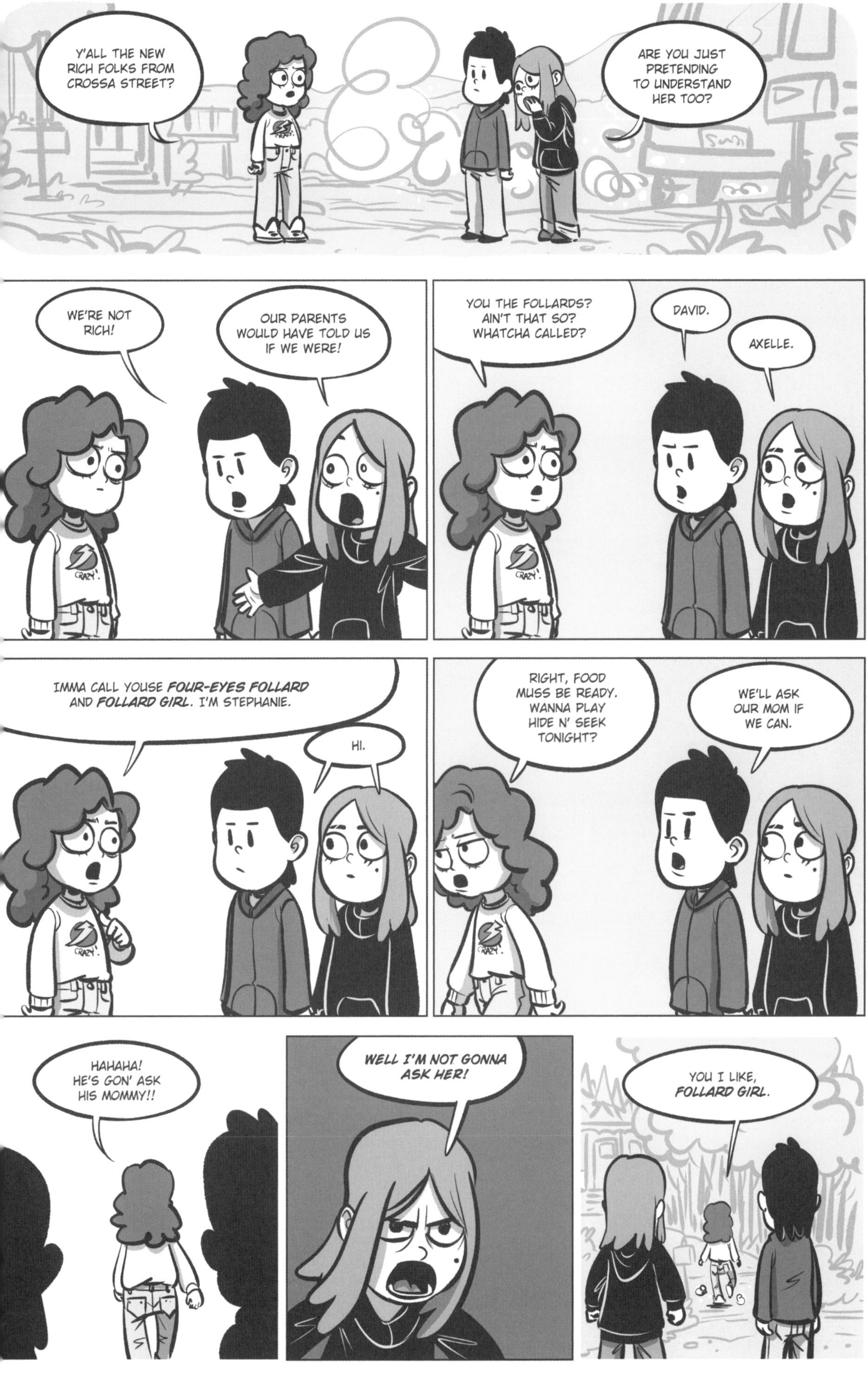
Y'ALL THE NEW RICH FOLKS FROM CROSSA STREET?
ARE YOU JUST PRETENDING TO UNDERSTAND HER TOO?
WE'RE NOT RICH!
OUR PARENTS WOULD HAVE TOLD US IF WE WERE!
YOU THE FOLLARDS? AIN'T THAT SO? WHATCHA CALLED?
DAVID.
AXELLE.
IMMA CALL YOUSE FOUR-EYES FOLLARD AND FOLLARD GIRL. I'M STEPHANIE.
HI.
RIGHT, FOOD MUSS BE READY. WANNA PLAY HIDE N' SEEK TONIGHT?
WE'LL ASK OUR MOM IF WE CAN.
HAHAHA! HE'S GON' ASK HIS MOMMY!!
WELL I'M NOT GONNA ASK HER!
YOU I LIKE, FOLLARD GIRL.

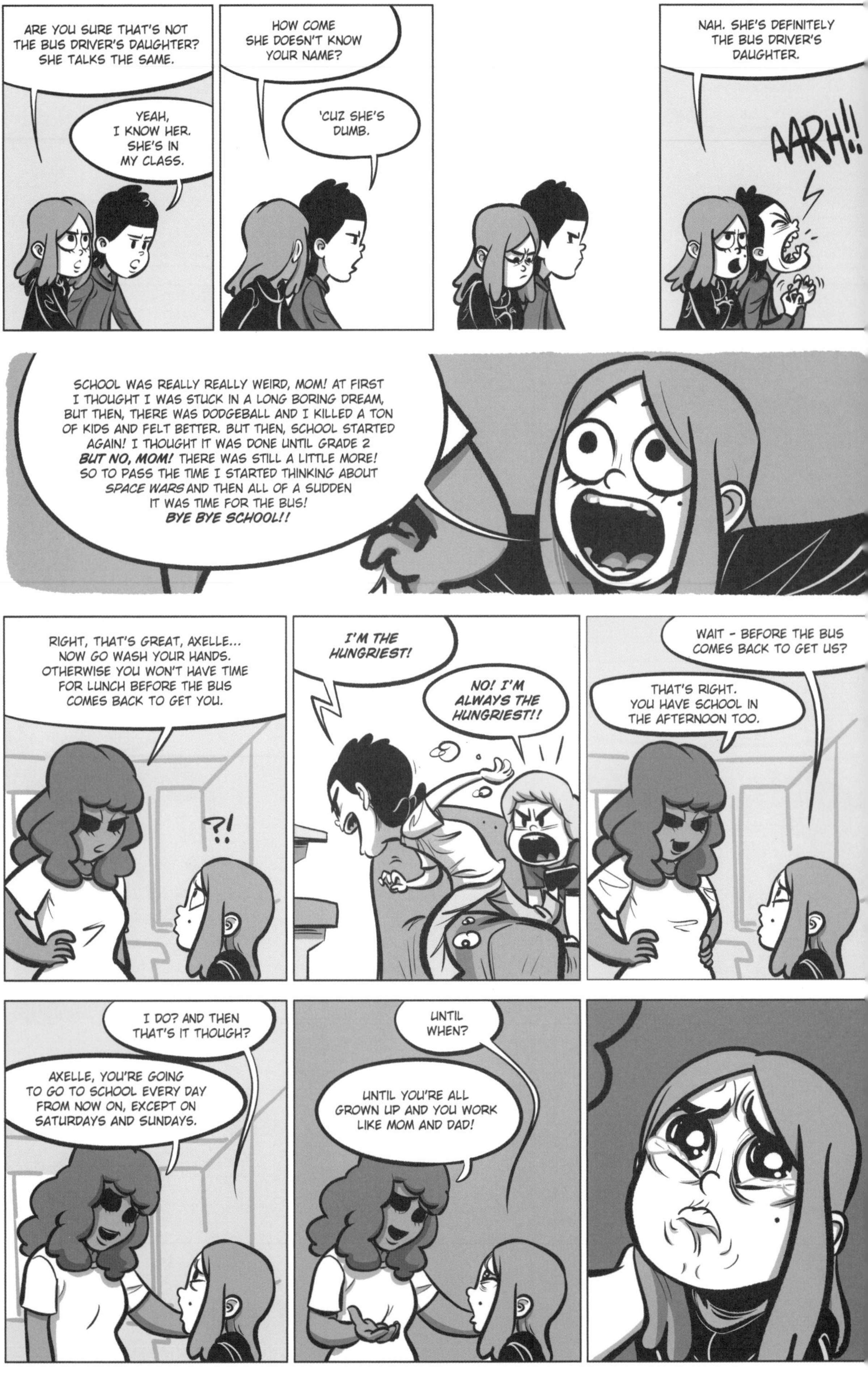
ARE YOU SURE THAT'S NOT THE BUS DRIVER'S DAUGHTER? SHE TALKS THE SAME.
YEAH, I KNOW HER. SHE'S IN MY CLASS.
HOW COME SHE DOESN'T KNOW YOUR NAME?
'CUZ SHE'S DUMB.
NAH. SHE'S DEFINITELY THE BUS DRIVER'S DAUGHTER.
AARH!!
SCHOOL WAS REALLY REALLY WEIRD, MOM! AT FIRST I THOUGHT I WAS STUCK IN A LONG BORING DREAM, BUT THEN, THERE WAS DODGEBALL AND I KILLED A TON OF KIDS AND FELT BETTER. BUT THEN, SCHOOL STARTED AGAIN! I THOUGHT IT WAS DONE UNTIL GRADE 2 BUT NO, MOM! THERE WAS STILL A LITTLE MORE! SO TO PASS THE TIME I STARTED THINKING ABOUT SPACE WARS AND THEN ALL OF A SUDDEN IT WAS TIME FOR THE BUS! BYE BYE SCHOOL!!
RIGHT, THAT'S GREAT, AXELLE... NOW GO WASH YOUR HANDS. OTHERWISE YOU WON'T HAVE TIME FOR LUNCH BEFORE THE BUS COMES BACK TO GET YOU.
?!
I'M THE HUNGRIEST!
NO! I'M ALWAYS THE HUNGRIEST!!
WAIT - BEFORE THE BUS COMES BACK TO GET US?
THAT'S RIGHT. YOU HAVE SCHOOL IN THE AFTERNOON TOO.
I DO? AND THEN THAT'S IT THOUGH?
AXELLE, YOU'RE GOING TO GO TO SCHOOL EVERY DAY FROM NOW ON, EXCEPT ON SATURDAYS AND SUNDAYS.
UNTIL WHEN?
UNTIL YOU'RE ALL GROWN UP AND YOU WORK LIKE MOM AND DAD!

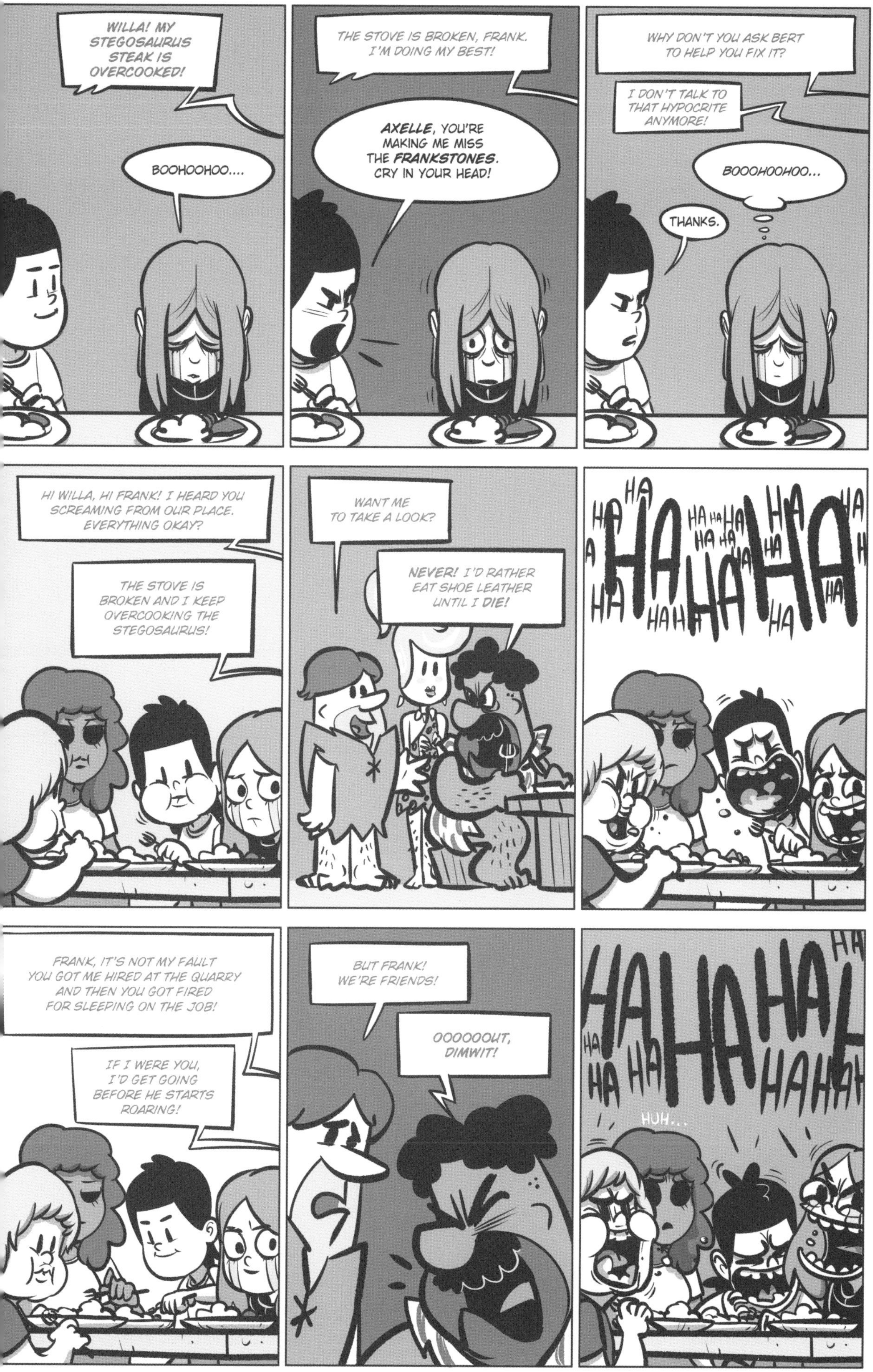
WILLA! MY STEGOSAURUS STEAK IS OVERCOOKED!
BOOHOOHOO....
THE STOVE IS BROKEN, FRANK. I'M DOING MY BEST!
AXELLE, YOU'RE MAKING ME MISS THE FRANKSTONES. CRY IN YOUR HEAD!
WHY DON'T YOU ASK BERT TO HELP YOU FIX IT?
I DON'T TALK TO THAT HYPOCRITE ANYMORE!
BOOOHOOHOO...
THANKS.
HI WILLA, HI FRANK! I HEARD YOU SCREAMING FROM OUR PLACE. EVERYTHING OKAY?
THE STOVE IS BROKEN AND I KEEP OVERCOOKING THE STEGOSAURUS!
WANT ME TO TAKE A LOOK?
NEVER! I'D RATHER EAT SHOE LEATHER UNTIL I DIE!
HA HA HA HA HA HA HA HA HA HA HA HA HA HA HA HA HA HA HA
FRANK, IT'S NOT MY FAULT YOU GOT ME HIRED AT THE QUARRY AND THEN YOU GOT FIRED FOR SLEEPING ON THE JOB!
IF I WERE YOU, I'D GET GOING BEFORE HE STARTS ROARING!
BUT FRANK! WE'RE FRIENDS!
OOOOOOUT, DIMWIT!
HAHAHAHAHA HA HA HA HA HAHAH
HUH...

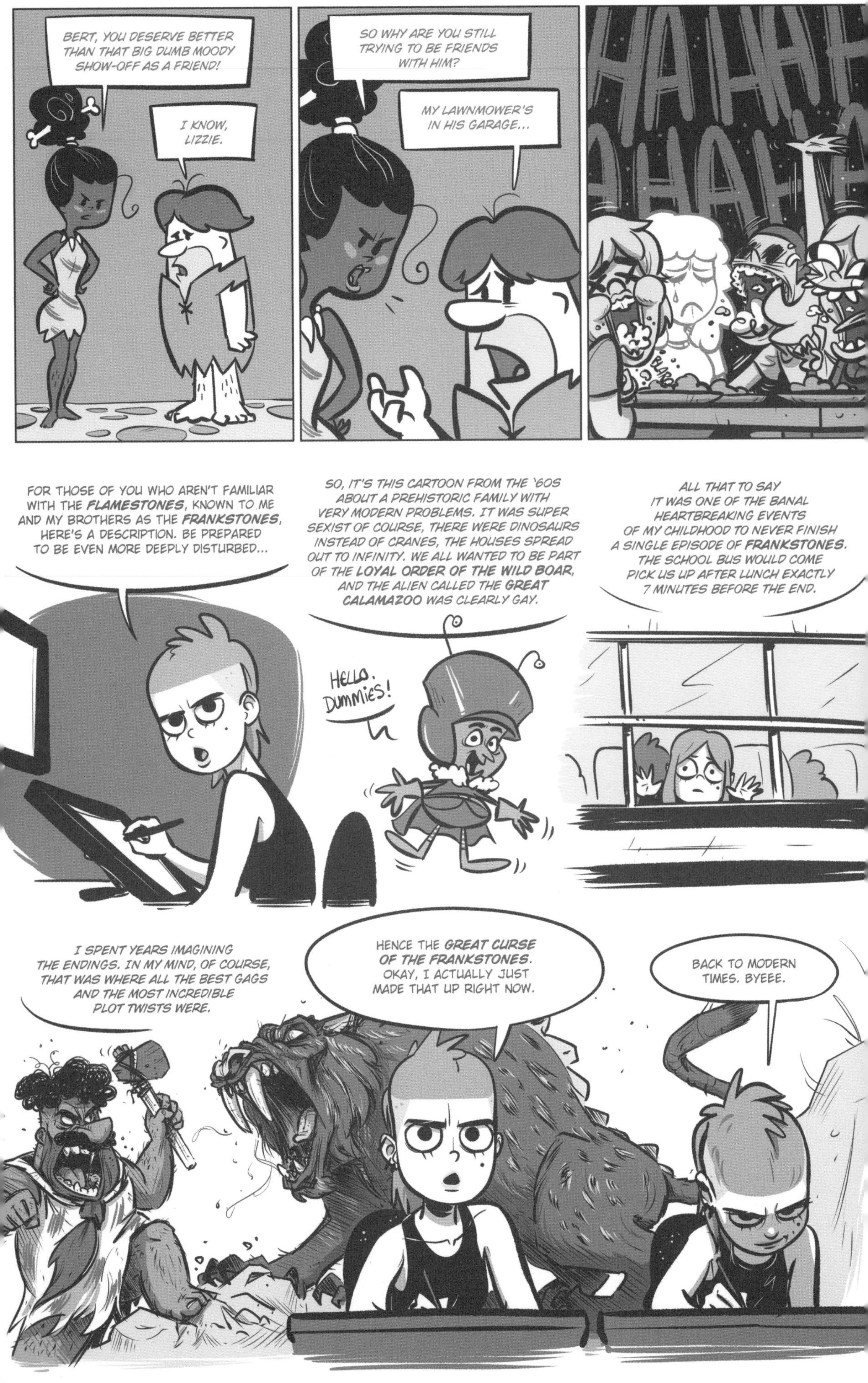
BERT, YOU DESERVE BETTER THAN THAT BIG DUMB MOODY SHOW-OFF AS A FRIEND!
I KNOW, LIZZIE.
SO WHY ARE YOU STILL TRYING TO BE FRIENDS WITH HIM?
MY LAWNMOWER'S IN HIS GARAGE...
FOR THOSE OF YOU WHO AREN'T FAMILIAR WITH THE FLAMESTONES, KNOWN TO ME AND MY BROTHERS AS THE FRANKSTONES, HERE'S A DESCRIPTION. BE PREPARED TO BE EVEN MORE DEEPLY DISTURBED...
SO, IT'S THIS CARTOON FROM THE '60S ABOUT A PREHISTORIC FAMILY WITH VERY MODERN PROBLEMS. IT WAS SUPER SEXIST OF COURSE, THERE WERE DINOSAURS INSTEAD OF CRANES, THE HOUSES SPREAD OUT TO INFINITY. WE ALL WANTED TO BE PART OF THE LOYAL ORDER OF THE WILD BOAR, AND THE ALIEN CALLED THE GREAT CALAMAZOO WAS CLEARLY GAY.
HELLO, DUMMIES!
ALL THAT TO SAY IT WAS ONE OF THE BANAL HEARTBREAKING EVENTS OF MY CHILDHOOD TO NEVER FINISH A SINGLE EPISODE OF FRANKSTONES. THE SCHOOL BUS WOULD COME PICK US UP AFTER LUNCH EXACTLY 7 MINUTES BEFORE THE END.
I SPENT YEARS IMAGINING THE ENDINGS. IN MY MIND, OF COURSE, THAT WAS WHERE ALL THE BEST GAGS AND THE MOST INCREDIBLE PLOT TWISTS WERE.
HENCE THE GREAT CURSE OF THE FRANKSTONES. OKAY, I ACTUALLY JUST MADE THAT UP RIGHT NOW.
BACK TO MODERN TIMES. BYEEE.

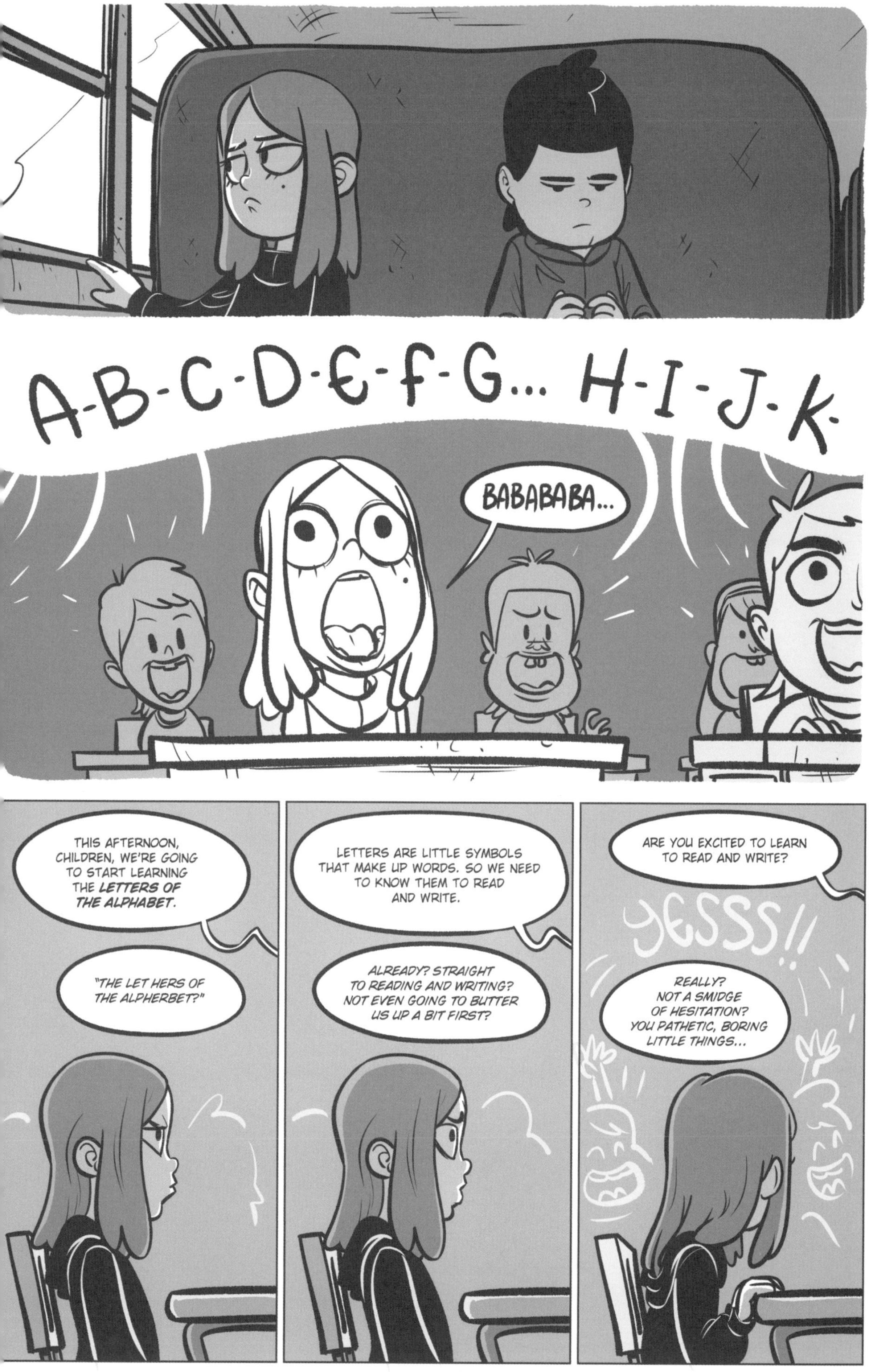
A-B-C-D-E-F-G... H-I-J-K-
BABABABA...
THIS AFTERNOON, CHILDREN, WE'RE GOING TO START LEARNING THE ***LETTERS OF THE ALPHABET***.
"THE LET HERS OF THE ALPHERBET?"
LETTERS ARE LITTLE SYMBOLS THAT MAKE UP WORDS. SO WE NEED TO KNOW THEM TO READ AND WRITE.
ALREADY? STRAIGHT TO READING AND WRITING? NOT EVEN GOING TO BUTTER US UP A BIT FIRST?
ARE YOU EXCITED TO LEARN TO READ AND WRITE?
YESSS!!
REALLY? NOT A SMIDGE OF HESITATION? YOU PATHETIC, BORING LITTLE THINGS...

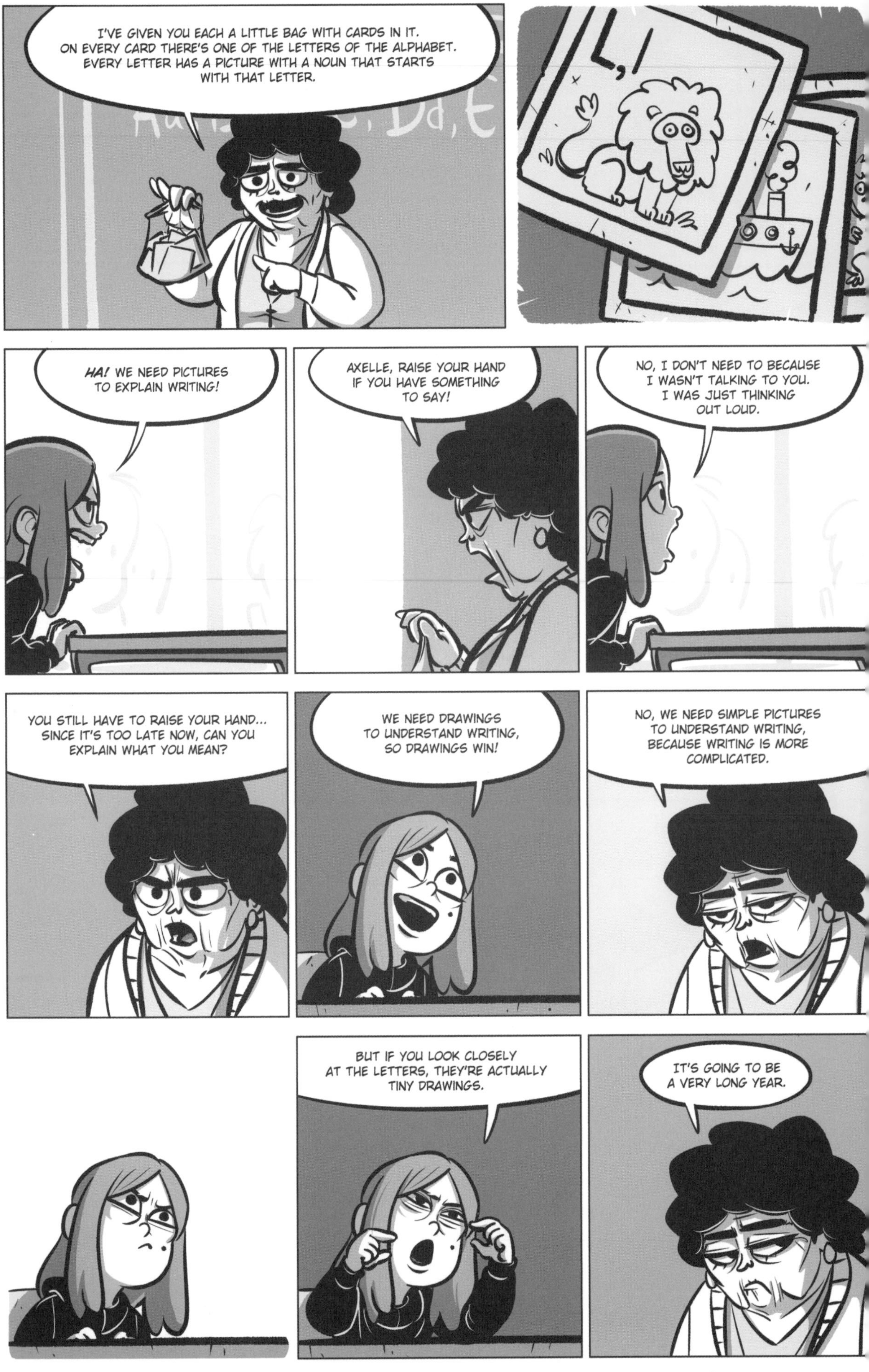
I'VE GIVEN YOU EACH A LITTLE BAG WITH CARDS IN IT. ON EVERY CARD THERE'S ONE OF THE LETTERS OF THE ALPHABET. EVERY LETTER HAS A PICTURE WITH A NOUN THAT STARTS WITH THAT LETTER.
L, l
HA! WE NEED PICTURES TO EXPLAIN WRITING!
AXELLE, RAISE YOUR HAND IF YOU HAVE SOMETHING TO SAY!
NO, I DON'T NEED TO BECAUSE I WASN'T TALKING TO YOU. I WAS JUST THINKING OUT LOUD.
YOU STILL HAVE TO RAISE YOUR HAND... SINCE IT'S TOO LATE NOW, CAN YOU EXPLAIN WHAT YOU MEAN?
WE NEED DRAWINGS TO UNDERSTAND WRITING, SO DRAWINGS WIN!
NO, WE NEED SIMPLE PICTURES TO UNDERSTAND WRITING, BECAUSE WRITING IS MORE COMPLICATED.
BUT IF YOU LOOK CLOSELY AT THE LETTERS, THEY'RE ACTUALLY TINY DRAWINGS.
IT'S GOING TO BE A VERY LONG YEAR.

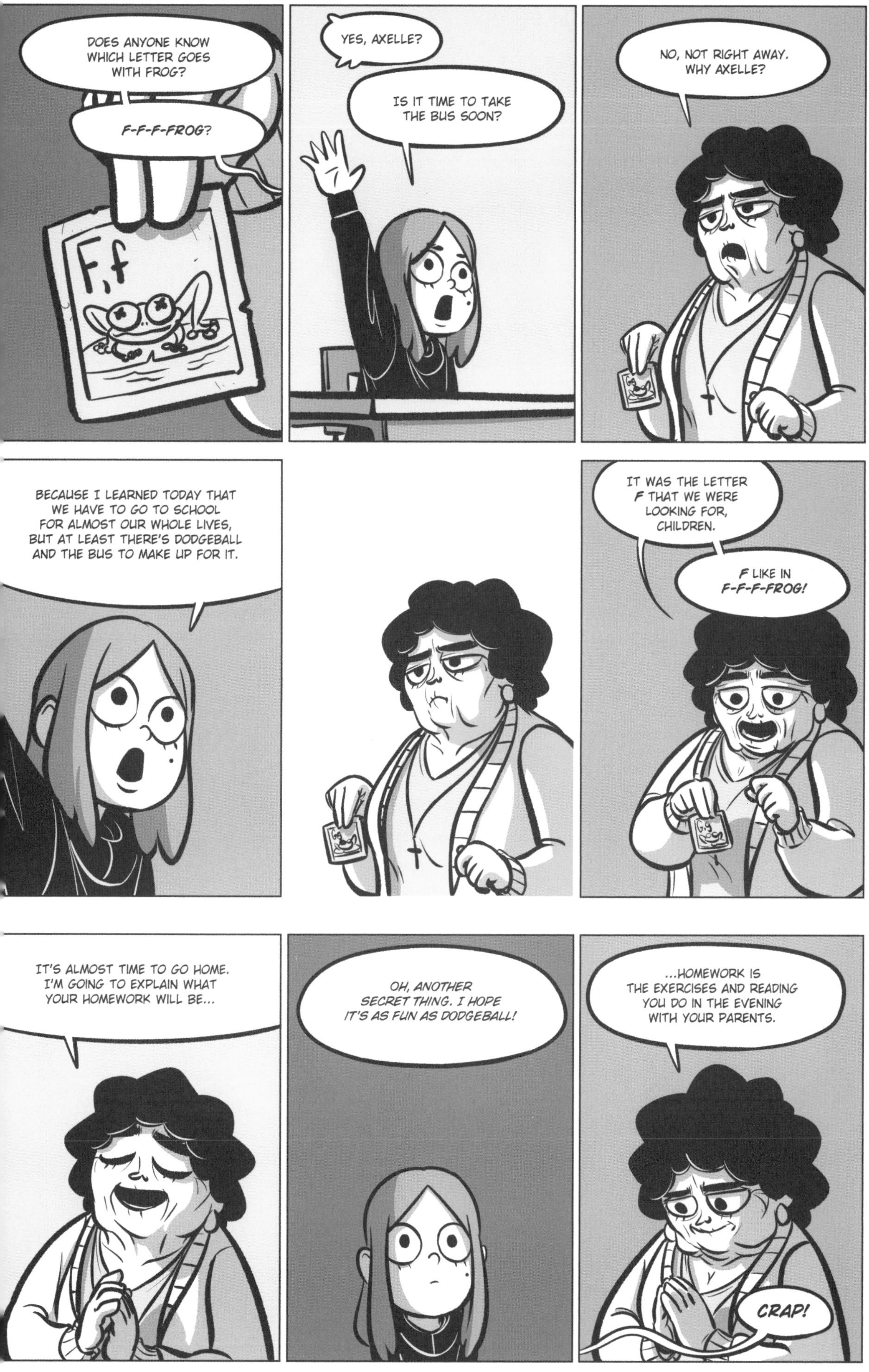
DOES ANYONE KNOW WHICH LETTER GOES WITH FROG?
F-F-F-FROG?
F, f
YES, AXELLE?
IS IT TIME TO TAKE THE BUS SOON?
NO, NOT RIGHT AWAY. WHY AXELLE?
BECAUSE I LEARNED TODAY THAT WE HAVE TO GO TO SCHOOL FOR ALMOST OUR WHOLE LIVES, BUT AT LEAST THERE'S DODGEBALL AND THE BUS TO MAKE UP FOR IT.
IT WAS THE LETTER F THAT WE WERE LOOKING FOR, CHILDREN.
F LIKE IN F-F-F-FROG!
IT'S ALMOST TIME TO GO HOME. I'M GOING TO EXPLAIN WHAT YOUR HOMEWORK WILL BE...
OH, ANOTHER SECRET THING. I HOPE IT'S AS FUN AS DODGEBALL!
...HOMEWORK IS THE EXERCISES AND READING YOU DO IN THE EVENING WITH YOUR PARENTS.
CRAP!

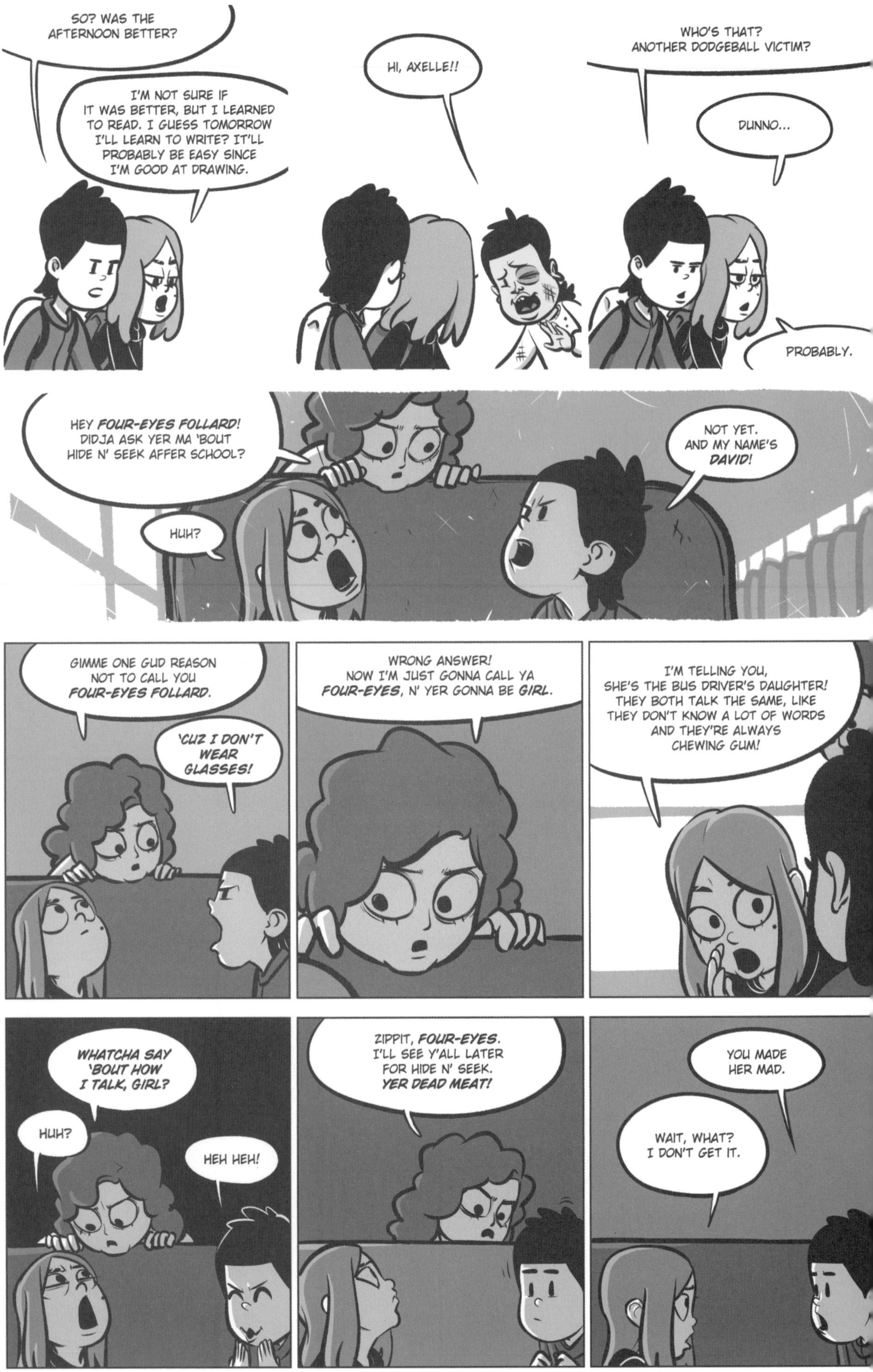
SO? WAS THE AFTERNOON BETTER?
I'M NOT SURE IF IT WAS BETTER, BUT I LEARNED TO READ. I GUESS TOMORROW I'LL LEARN TO WRITE? IT'LL PROBABLY BE EASY SINCE I'M GOOD AT DRAWING.
HI, AXELLE!!
WHO'S THAT? ANOTHER DODGEBALL VICTIM?
DUNNO...
PROBABLY.
HEY FOUR-EYES FOLLARD! DIDJA ASK YER MA 'BOUT HIDE N' SEEK AFFER SCHOOL?
HUH?
NOT YET. AND MY NAME'S DAVID!
GIMME ONE GUD REASON NOT TO CALL YOU FOUR-EYES FOLLARD.
'CUZ I DON'T WEAR GLASSES!
WRONG ANSWER! NOW I'M JUST GONNA CALL YA FOUR-EYES, N' YER GONNA BE GIRL.
I'M TELLING YOU, SHE'S THE BUS DRIVER'S DAUGHTER! THEY BOTH TALK THE SAME, LIKE THEY DON'T KNOW A LOT OF WORDS AND THEY'RE ALWAYS CHEWING GUM!
WHATCHA SAY 'BOUT HOW I TALK, GIRL?
HUH?
HEH HEH!
ZIPPIT, FOUR-EYES. I'LL SEE Y'ALL LATER FOR HIDE N' SEEK. YER DEAD MEAT!
YOU MADE HER MAD.
WAIT, WHAT? I DON'T GET IT.

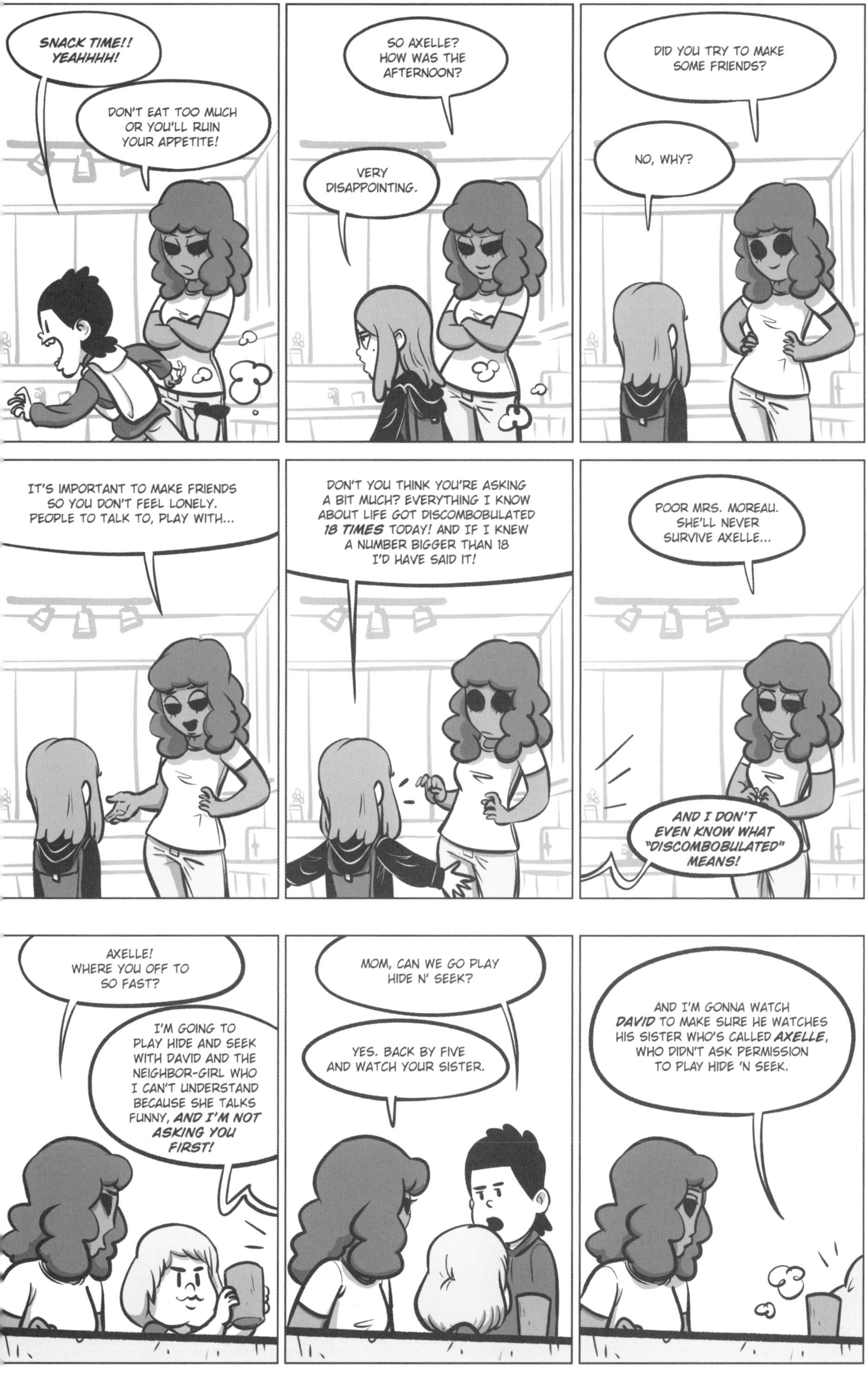
SNACK TIME!! YEAHHHH!
DON'T EAT TOO MUCH OR YOU'LL RUIN YOUR APPETITE!
SO AXELLE? HOW WAS THE AFTERNOON?
VERY DISAPPOINTING.
DID YOU TRY TO MAKE SOME FRIENDS?
NO, WHY?
IT'S IMPORTANT TO MAKE FRIENDS SO YOU DON'T FEEL LONELY. PEOPLE TO TALK TO, PLAY WITH...
DON'T YOU THINK YOU'RE ASKING A BIT MUCH? EVERYTHING I KNOW ABOUT LIFE GOT DISCOMBOBULATED 18 TIMES TODAY! AND IF I KNEW A NUMBER BIGGER THAN 18 I'D HAVE SAID IT!
POOR MRS. MOREAU. SHE'LL NEVER SURVIVE AXELLE...
AND I DON'T EVEN KNOW WHAT "DISCOMBOBULATED" MEANS!
AXELLE! WHERE YOU OFF TO SO FAST?
I'M GOING TO PLAY HIDE AND SEEK WITH DAVID AND THE NEIGHBOR-GIRL WHO I CAN'T UNDERSTAND BECAUSE SHE TALKS FUNNY, AND I'M NOT ASKING YOU FIRST!
MOM, CAN WE GO PLAY HIDE N' SEEK?
YES. BACK BY FIVE AND WATCH YOUR SISTER.
AND I'M GONNA WATCH DAVID TO MAKE SURE HE WATCHES HIS SISTER WHO'S CALLED AXELLE, WHO DIDN'T ASK PERMISSION TO PLAY HIDE 'N SEEK.

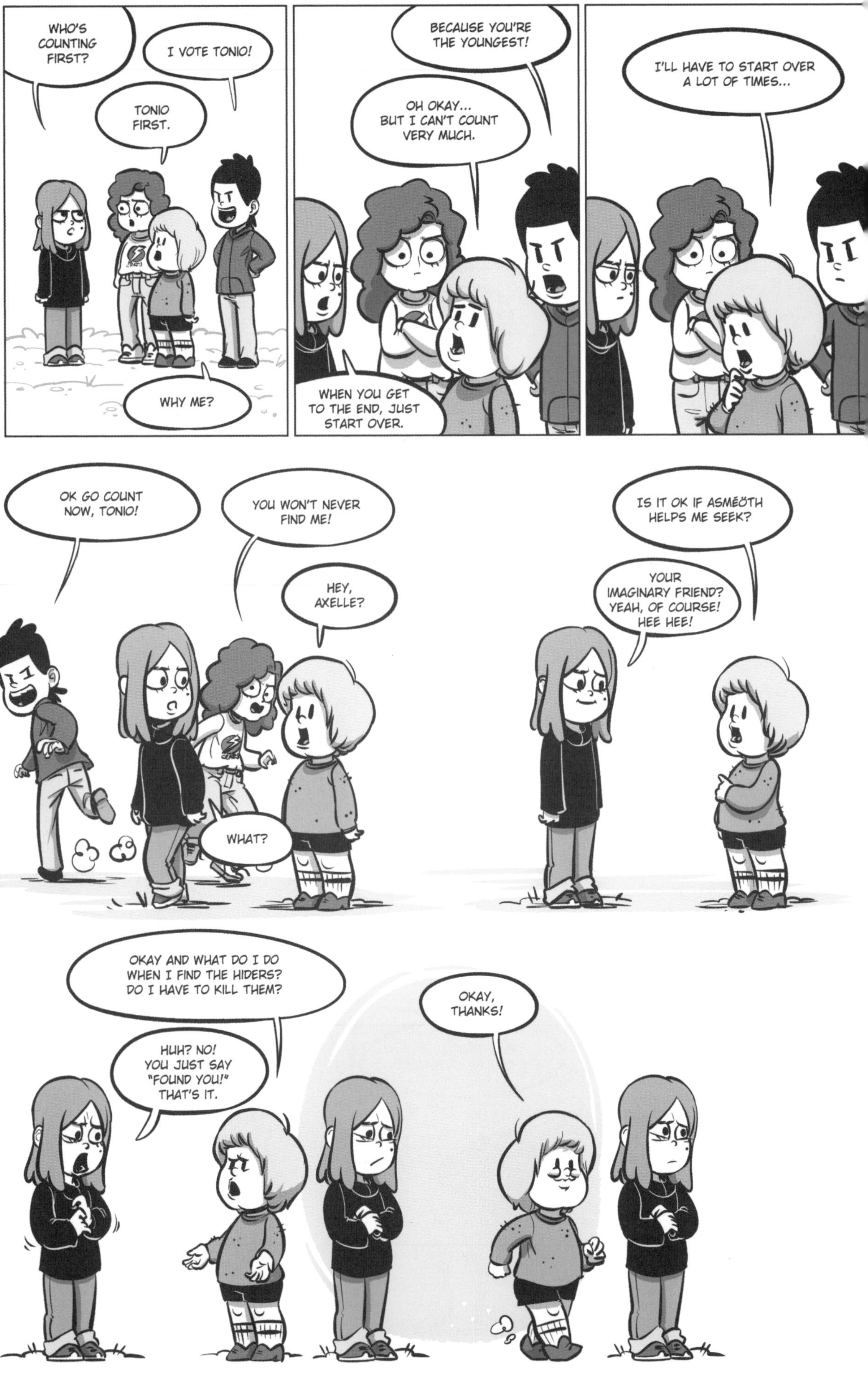
WHO'S COUNTING FIRST?
I VOTE TONIO!
TONIO FIRST.
WHY ME?
BECAUSE YOU'RE THE YOUNGEST!
OH OKAY... BUT I CAN'T COUNT VERY MUCH.
WHEN YOU GET TO THE END, JUST START OVER.
I'LL HAVE TO START OVER A LOT OF TIMES...
OK GO COUNT NOW, TONIO!
YOU WON'T NEVER FIND ME!
HEY, AXELLE?
WHAT?
IS IT OK IF ASMÉÖTH HELPS ME SEEK?
YOUR IMAGINARY FRIEND? YEAH, OF COURSE! HEE HEE!
OKAY AND WHAT DO I DO WHEN I FIND THE HIDERS? DO I HAVE TO KILL THEM?
HUH? NO! YOU JUST SAY "FOUND YOU!" THAT'S IT.
OKAY, THANKS!

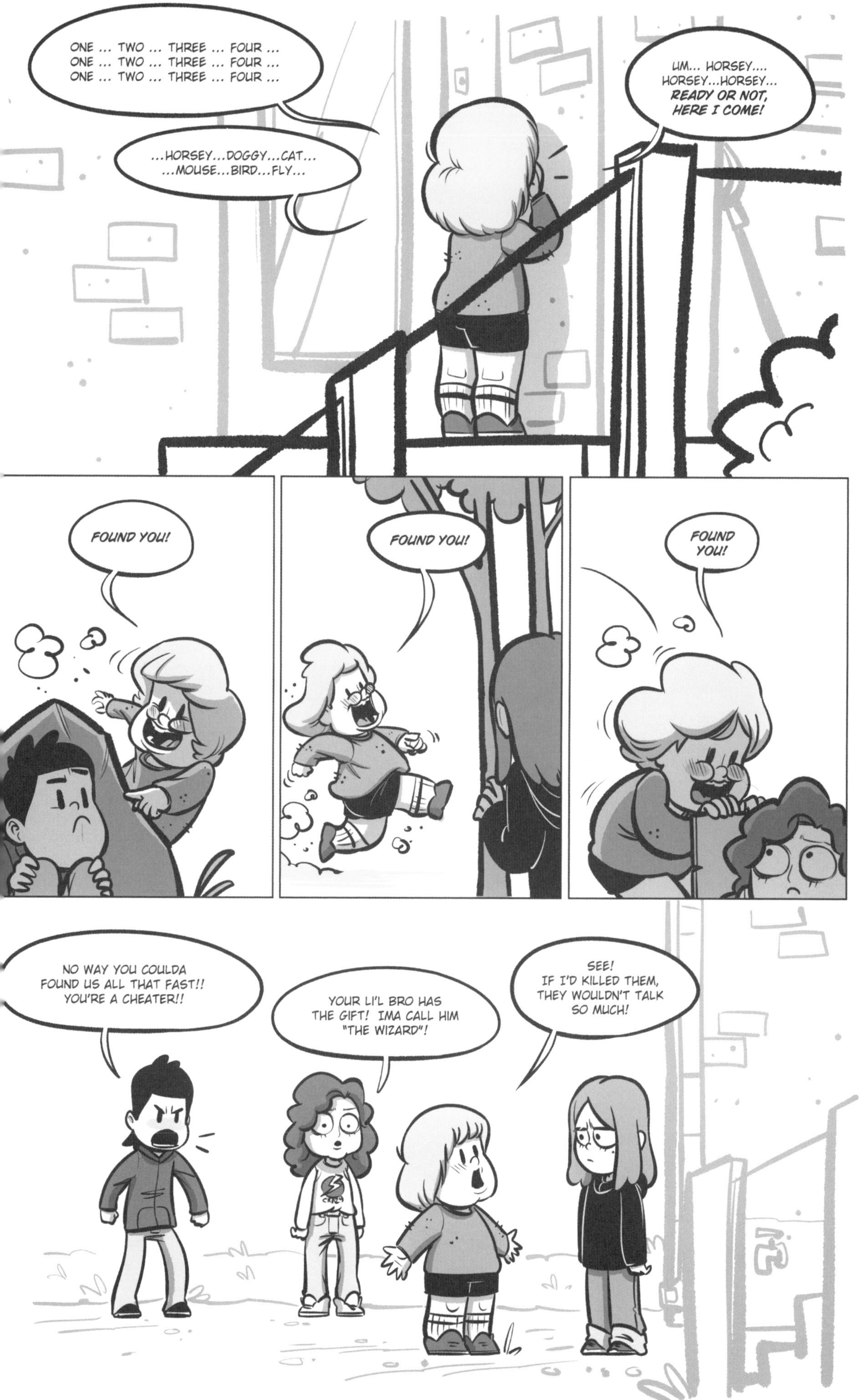

ONE ... TWO ... THREE ... FOUR ... ONE ... TWO ... THREE ... FOUR ... ONE ... TWO ... THREE ... FOUR ...
...HORSEY...DOGGY...CAT... ...MOUSE...BIRD...FLY...
UM... HORSEY.... HORSEY...HORSEY... READY OR NOT, HERE I COME!
FOUND YOU!
FOUND YOU!
FOUND YOU!
NO WAY YOU COULDA FOUND US ALL THAT FAST!! YOU'RE A CHEATER!!
YOUR LI'L BRO HAS THE GIFT! IMA CALL HIM "THE WIZARD"!
SEE! IF I'D KILLED THEM, THEY WOULDN'T TALK SO MUCH!

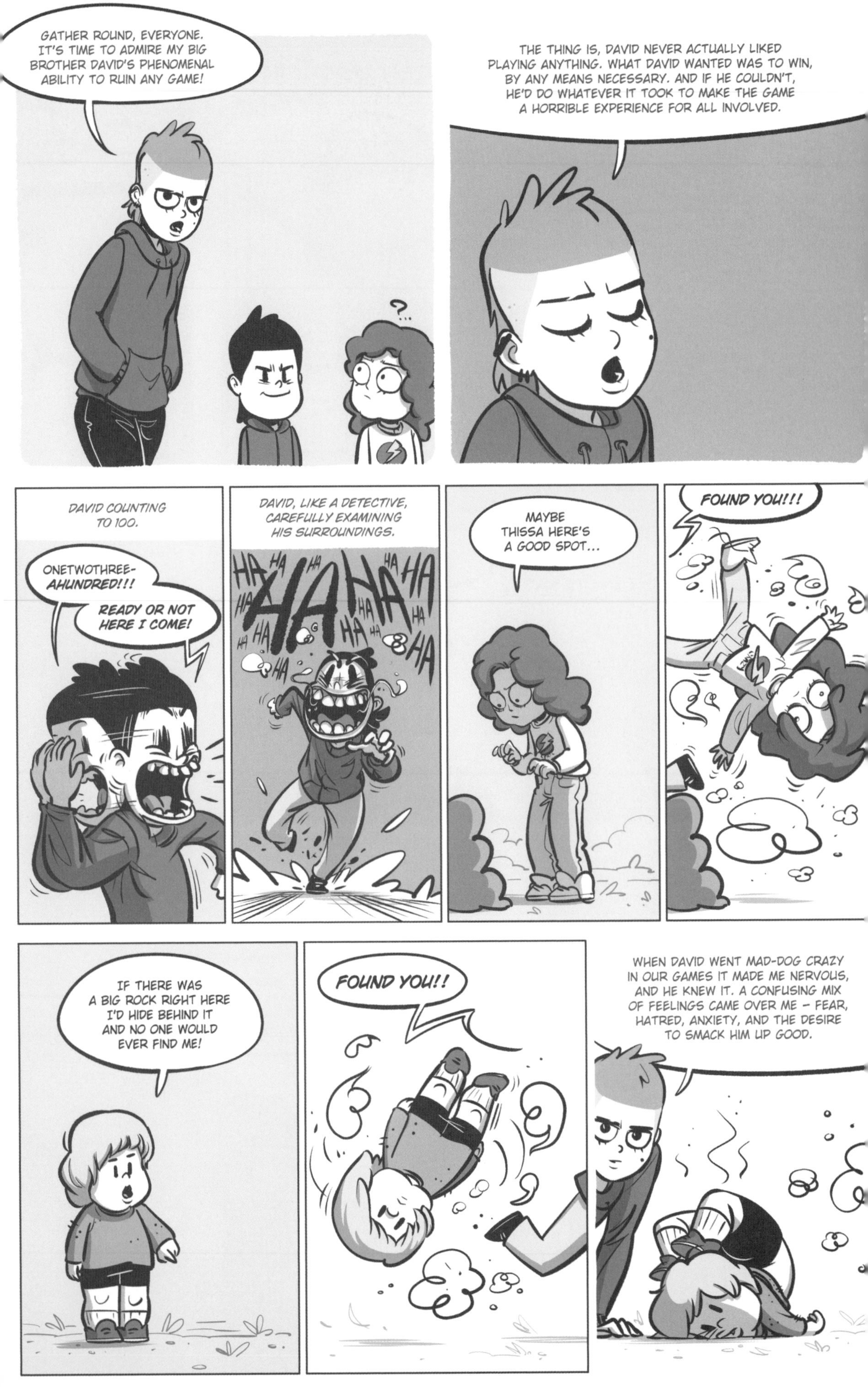
GATHER ROUND, EVERYONE. IT'S TIME TO ADMIRE MY BIG BROTHER DAVID'S PHENOMENAL ABILITY TO RUIN ANY GAME!
?...
THE THING IS, DAVID NEVER ACTUALLY LIKED PLAYING ANYTHING. WHAT DAVID WANTED WAS TO WIN, BY ANY MEANS NECESSARY. AND IF HE COULDN'T, HE'D DO WHATEVER IT TOOK TO MAKE THE GAME A HORRIBLE EXPERIENCE FOR ALL INVOLVED.
DAVID COUNTING TO 100.
ONETWOTHREE-AHUNDRED!!!
READY OR NOT HERE I COME!
DAVID, LIKE A DETECTIVE, CAREFULLY EXAMINING HIS SURROUNDINGS.
HA HA HA HAHA HA HA HA HA HA HA HA HA HA HA
MAYBE THISSA HERE'S A GOOD SPOT...
FOUND YOU!!!
IF THERE WAS A BIG ROCK RIGHT HERE I'D HIDE BEHIND IT AND NO ONE WOULD EVER FIND ME!
FOUND YOU!!
WHEN DAVID WENT MAD-DOG CRAZY IN OUR GAMES IT MADE ME NERVOUS, AND HE KNEW IT. A CONFUSING MIX OF FEELINGS CAME OVER ME – FEAR, HATRED, ANXIETY, AND THE DESIRE TO SMACK HIM UP GOOD.

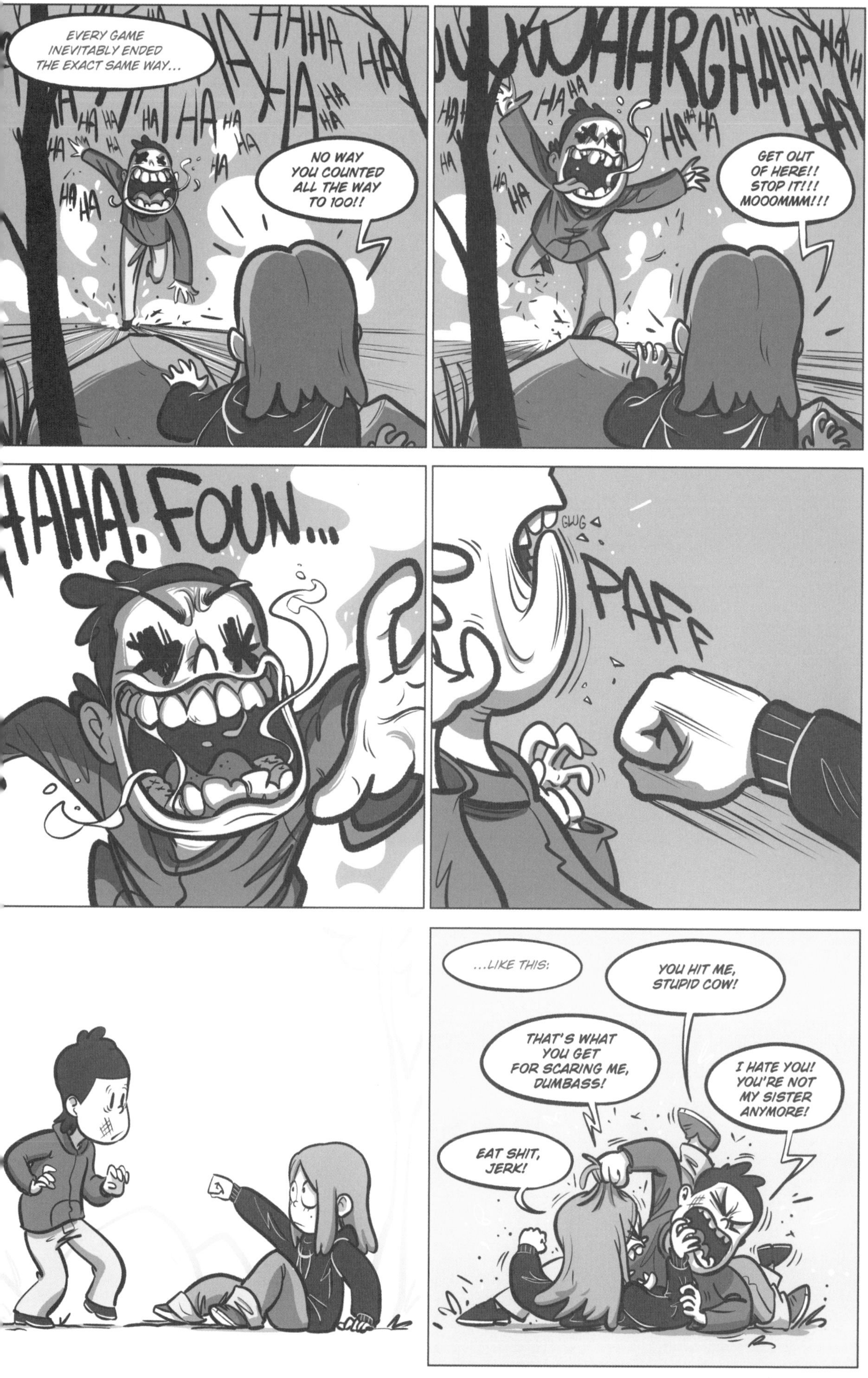
EVERY GAME INEVITABLY ENDED THE EXACT SAME WAY...
HAHA HA HA
NO WAY YOU COUNTED ALL THE WAY TO 100!!
WUAHRGHAHA HA HA
GET OUT OF HERE!! STOP IT!!! MOOOMMM!!!
HAHA! FOUN...
GLUG
PAFF
...LIKE THIS:
YOU HIT ME, STUPID COW!
THAT'S WHAT YOU GET FOR SCARING ME, DUMBASS!
I HATE YOU! YOU'RE NOT MY SISTER ANYMORE!
EAT SHIT, JERK!

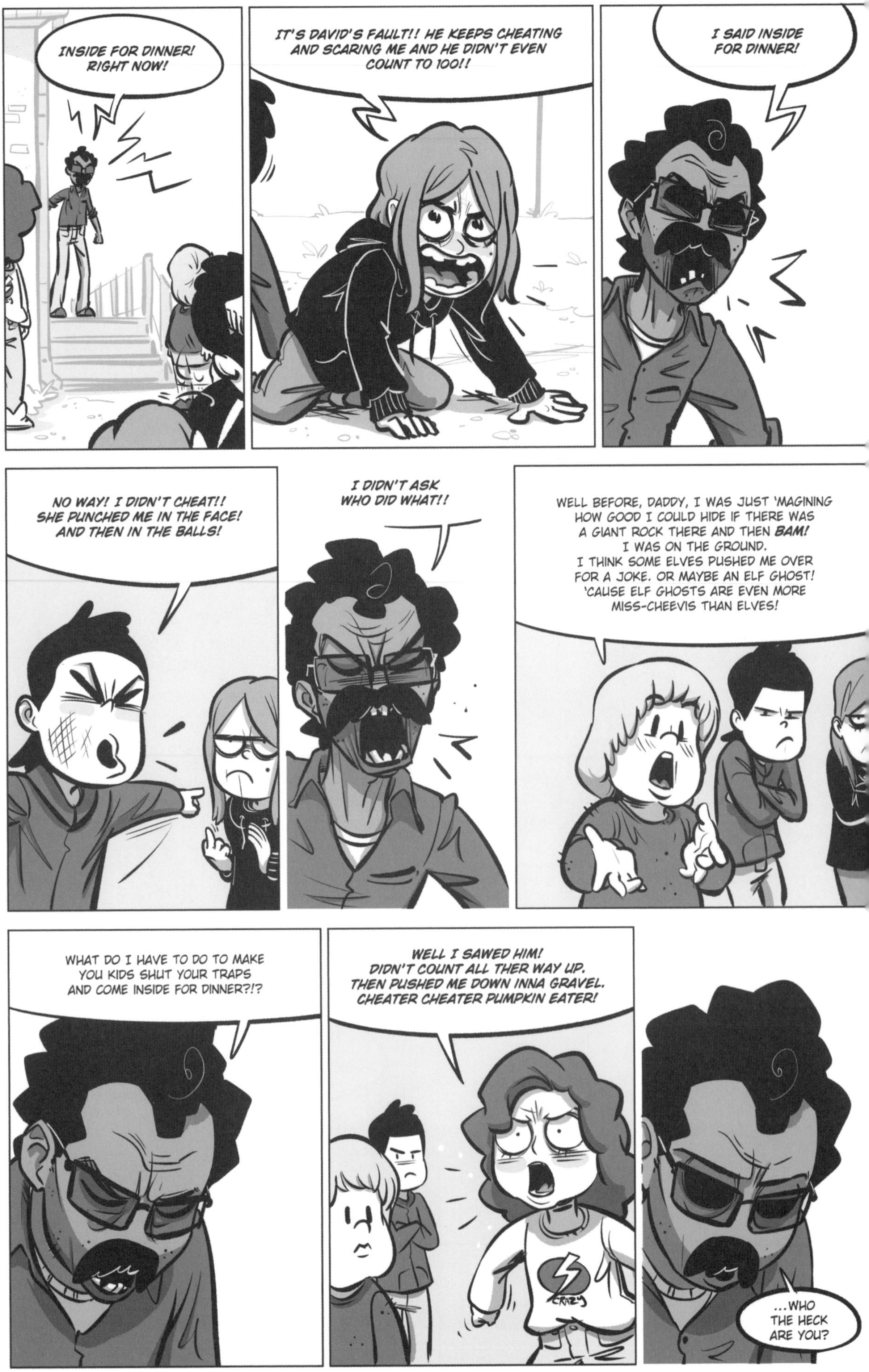
INSIDE FOR DINNER! RIGHT NOW!
IT'S DAVID'S FAULT!! HE KEEPS CHEATING AND SCARING ME AND HE DIDN'T EVEN COUNT TO 100!!
I SAID INSIDE FOR DINNER!
NO WAY! I DIDN'T CHEAT!! SHE PUNCHED ME IN THE FACE! AND THEN IN THE BALLS!
I DIDN'T ASK WHO DID WHAT!!
WELL BEFORE, DADDY, I WAS JUST 'MAGINING HOW GOOD I COULD HIDE IF THERE WAS A GIANT ROCK THERE AND THEN BAM! I WAS ON THE GROUND. I THINK SOME ELVES PUSHED ME OVER FOR A JOKE. OR MAYBE AN ELF GHOST! 'CAUSE ELF GHOSTS ARE EVEN MORE MISS-CHEEVIS THAN ELVES!
WHAT DO I HAVE TO DO TO MAKE YOU KIDS SHUT YOUR TRAPS AND COME INSIDE FOR DINNER?!?
WELL I SAWED HIM! DIDN'T COUNT ALL THER WAY UP. THEN PUSHED ME DOWN INNA GRAVEL. CHEATER CHEATER PUMPKIN EATER!
CRAZY
...WHO THE HECK ARE YOU?

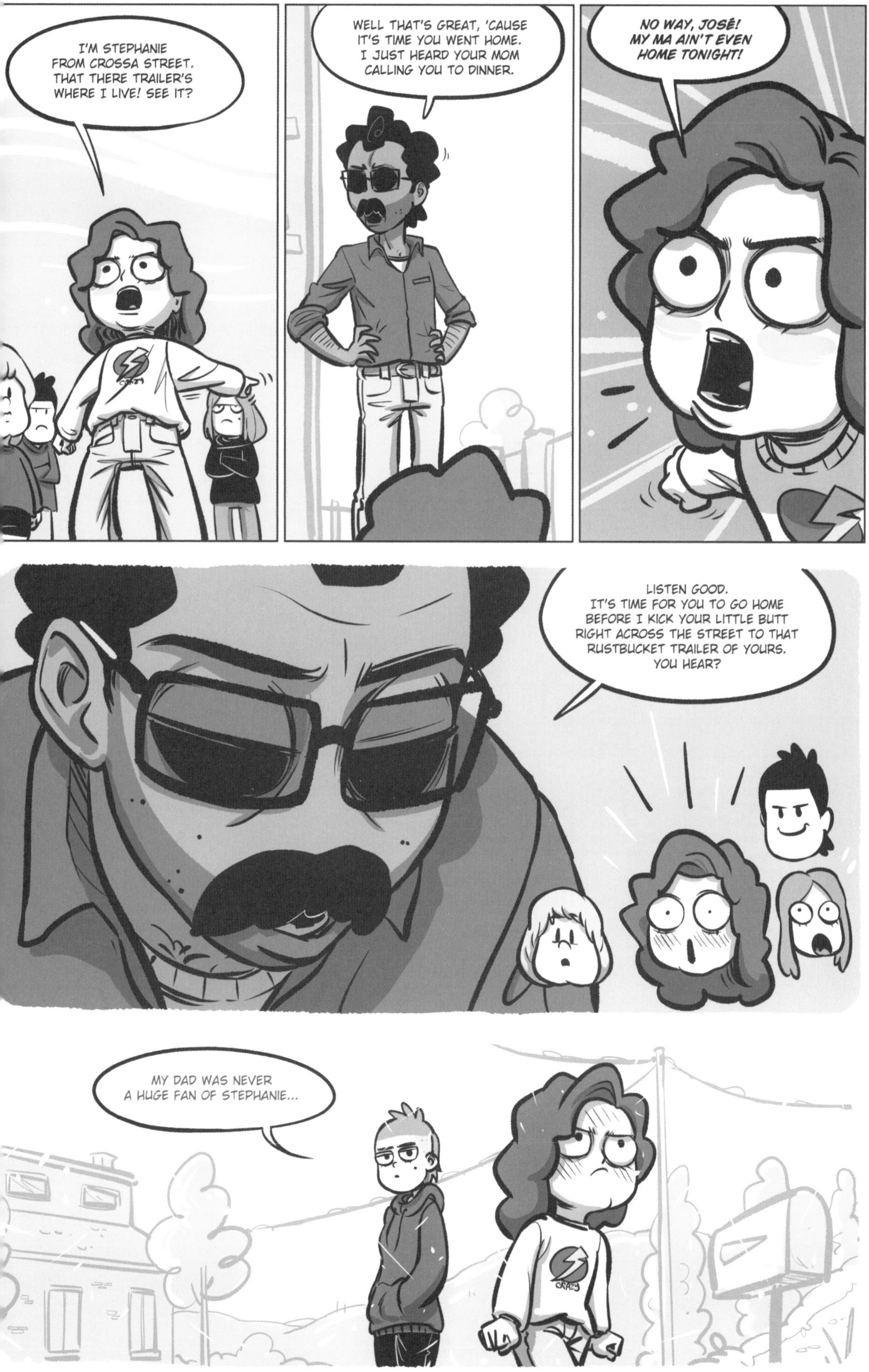
I'M STEPHANIE FROM CROSSA STREET. THAT THERE TRAILER'S WHERE I LIVE! SEE IT?
WELL THAT'S GREAT, 'CAUSE IT'S TIME YOU WENT HOME. I JUST HEARD YOUR MOM CALLING YOU TO DINNER.
NO WAY, JOSÉ! MY MA AIN'T EVEN HOME TONIGHT!
LISTEN GOOD. IT'S TIME FOR YOU TO GO HOME BEFORE I KICK YOUR LITTLE BUTT RIGHT ACROSS THE STREET TO THAT RUSTBUCKET TRAILER OF YOURS. YOU HEAR?
MY DAD WAS NEVER A HUGE FAN OF STEPHANIE...

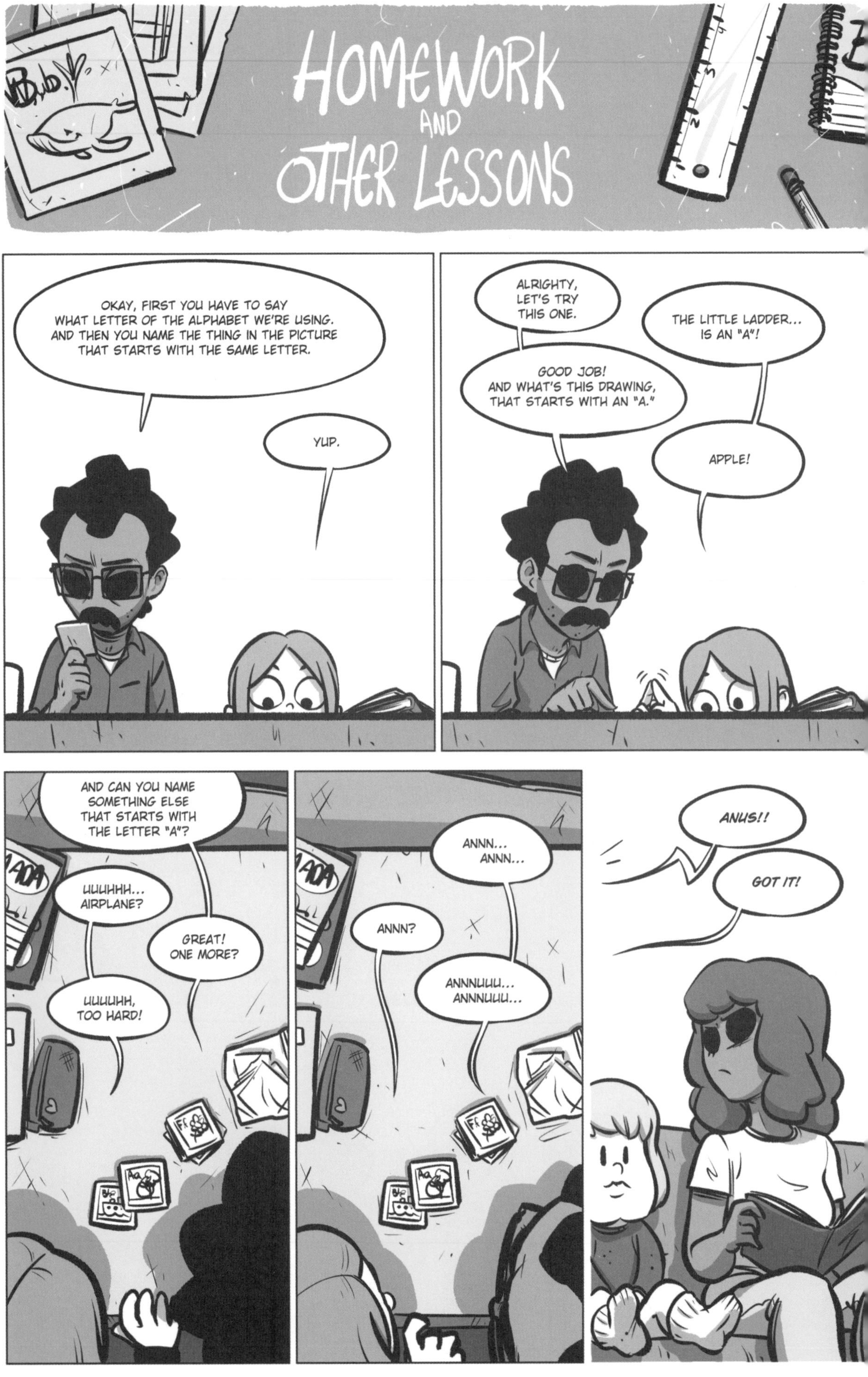
HOMEWORK AND OTHER LESSONS
OKAY, FIRST YOU HAVE TO SAY WHAT LETTER OF THE ALPHABET WE'RE USING. AND THEN YOU NAME THE THING IN THE PICTURE THAT STARTS WITH THE SAME LETTER.
YUP.
ALRIGHTY, LET'S TRY THIS ONE.
THE LITTLE LADDER... IS AN "A"!
GOOD JOB! AND WHAT'S THIS DRAWING, THAT STARTS WITH AN "A."
APPLE!
AND CAN YOU NAME SOMETHING ELSE THAT STARTS WITH THE LETTER "A"?
UUUHHH... AIRPLANE?
GREAT! ONE MORE?
UUUUHH, TOO HARD!
ANNN... ANNN...
ANNN?
ANNNUUU... ANNNUUU...
ANUS!!
GOT IT!

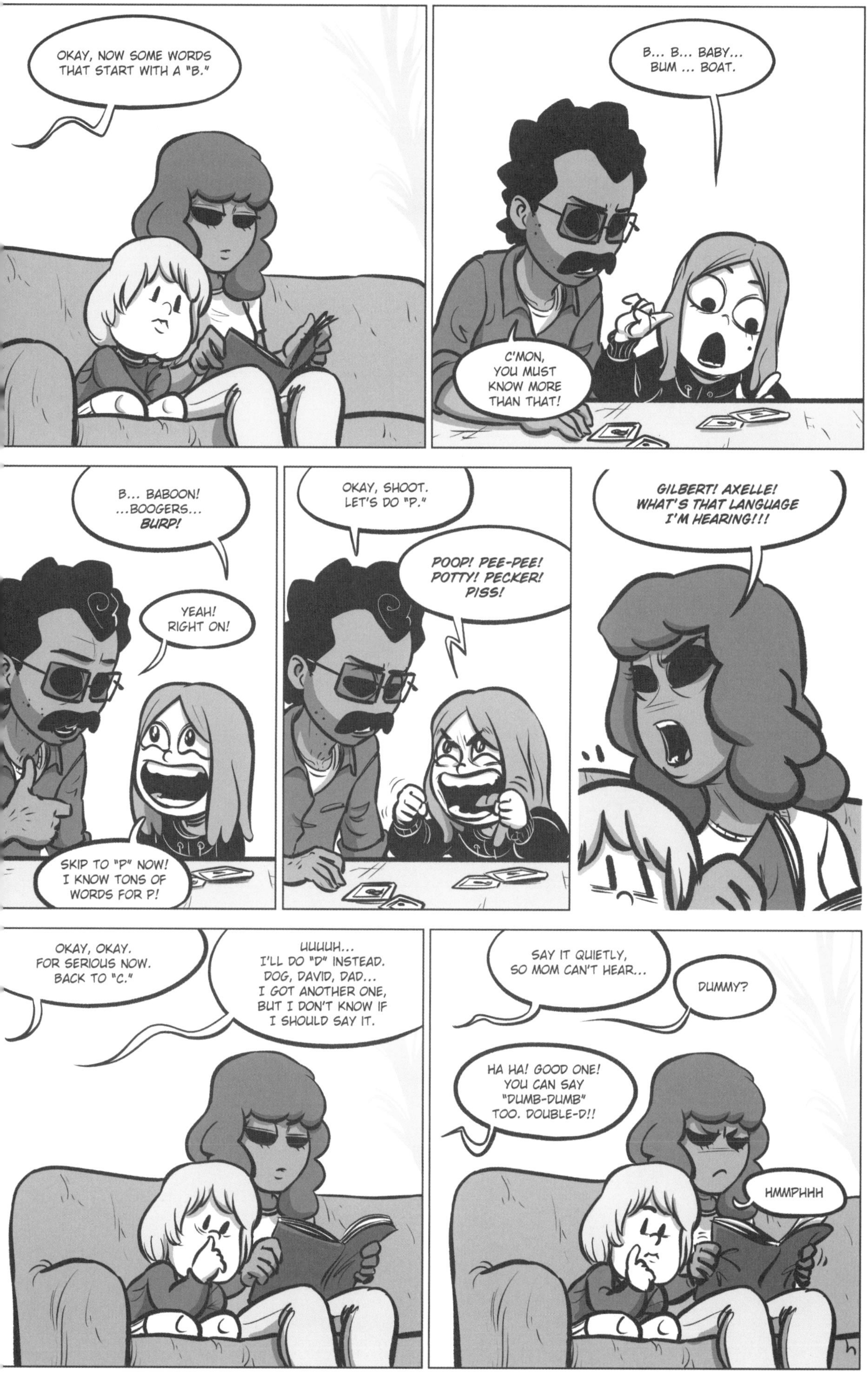
OKAY, NOW SOME WORDS THAT START WITH A "B."
B... B... BABY... BUM ... BOAT.
C'MON, YOU MUST KNOW MORE THAN THAT!
B... BABOON! ...BOOGERS... BURP!
YEAH! RIGHT ON!
SKIP TO "P" NOW! I KNOW TONS OF WORDS FOR P!
OKAY, SHOOT. LET'S DO "P."
POOP! PEE-PEE! POTTY! PECKER! PISS!
GILBERT! AXELLE! WHAT'S THAT LANGUAGE I'M HEARING!!!
OKAY, OKAY. FOR SERIOUS NOW. BACK TO "C."
UUUUH... I'LL DO "D" INSTEAD. DOG, DAVID, DAD... I GOT ANOTHER ONE, BUT I DON'T KNOW IF I SHOULD SAY IT.
SAY IT QUIETLY, SO MOM CAN'T HEAR...
DUMMY?
HA HA! GOOD ONE! YOU CAN SAY "DUMB-DUMB" TOO. DOUBLE-D!!
HMMPHHH

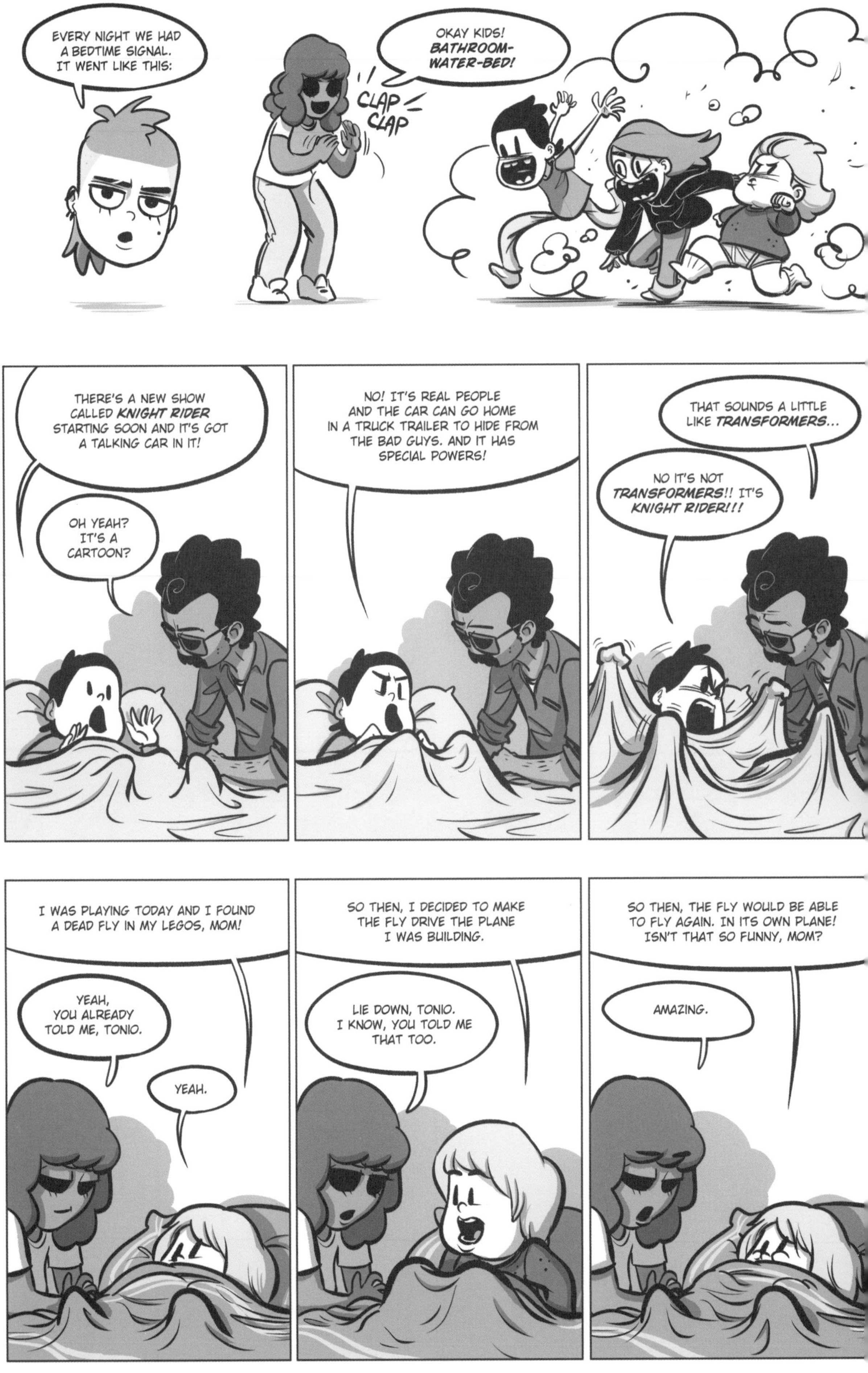
EVERY NIGHT WE HAD A BEDTIME SIGNAL. IT WENT LIKE THIS:
OKAY KIDS! BATHROOM-WATER-BED!
CLAP CLAP
THERE'S A NEW SHOW CALLED KNIGHT RIDER STARTING SOON AND IT'S GOT A TALKING CAR IN IT!
OH YEAH? IT'S A CARTOON?
NO! IT'S REAL PEOPLE AND THE CAR CAN GO HOME IN A TRUCK TRAILER TO HIDE FROM THE BAD GUYS. AND IT HAS SPECIAL POWERS!
THAT SOUNDS A LITTLE LIKE TRANSFORMERS...
NO IT'S NOT TRANSFORMERS!! IT'S KNIGHT RIDER!!!
I WAS PLAYING TODAY AND I FOUND A DEAD FLY IN MY LEGOS, MOM!
YEAH, YOU ALREADY TOLD ME, TONIO.
YEAH.
SO THEN, I DECIDED TO MAKE THE FLY DRIVE THE PLANE I WAS BUILDING.
LIE DOWN, TONIO. I KNOW, YOU TOLD ME THAT TOO.
SO THEN, THE FLY WOULD BE ABLE TO FLY AGAIN. IN ITS OWN PLANE! ISN'T THAT SO FUNNY, MOM?
AMAZING.

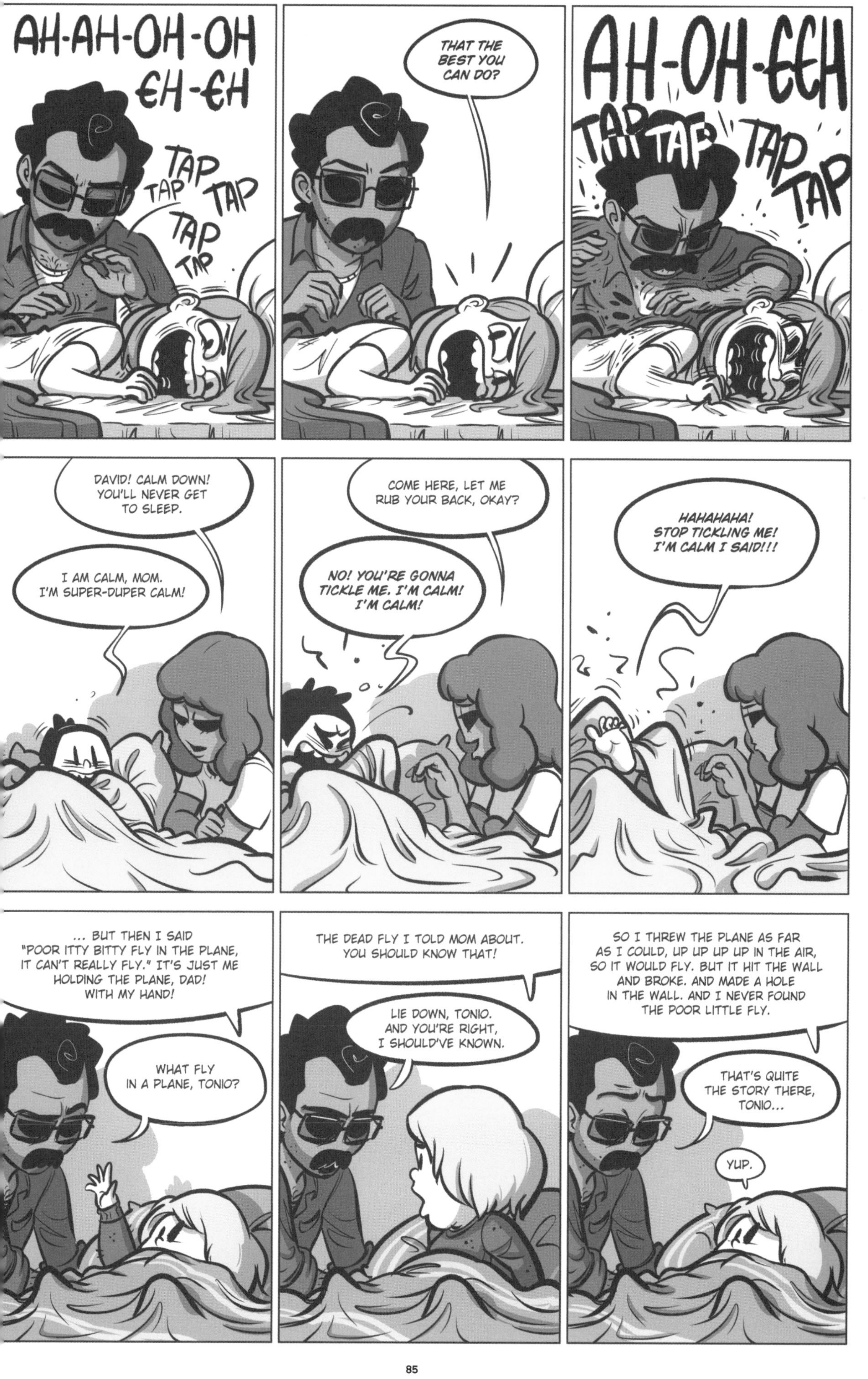
AH-AH-OH-OH EH-EH
TAP TAP TAP TAP TAP
THAT THE BEST YOU CAN DO?
AH-OH-EEH
TAP TAP TAP TAP
DAVID! CALM DOWN! YOU'LL NEVER GET TO SLEEP.
I AM CALM, MOM. I'M SUPER-DUPER CALM!
COME HERE, LET ME RUB YOUR BACK, OKAY?
NO! YOU'RE GONNA TICKLE ME. I'M CALM! I'M CALM!
HAHAHAHA! STOP TICKLING ME! I'M CALM I SAID!!!
... BUT THEN I SAID "POOR ITTY BITTY FLY IN THE PLANE, IT CAN'T REALLY FLY." IT'S JUST ME HOLDING THE PLANE, DAD! WITH MY HAND!
WHAT FLY IN A PLANE, TONIO?
THE DEAD FLY I TOLD MOM ABOUT. YOU SHOULD KNOW THAT!
LIE DOWN, TONIO. AND YOU'RE RIGHT, I SHOULD'VE KNOWN.
SO I THREW THE PLANE AS FAR AS I COULD, UP UP UP UP IN THE AIR, SO IT WOULD FLY. BUT IT HIT THE WALL AND BROKE. AND MADE A HOLE IN THE WALL. AND I NEVER FOUND THE POOR LITTLE FLY.
THAT'S QUITE THE STORY THERE, TONIO...
YUP.

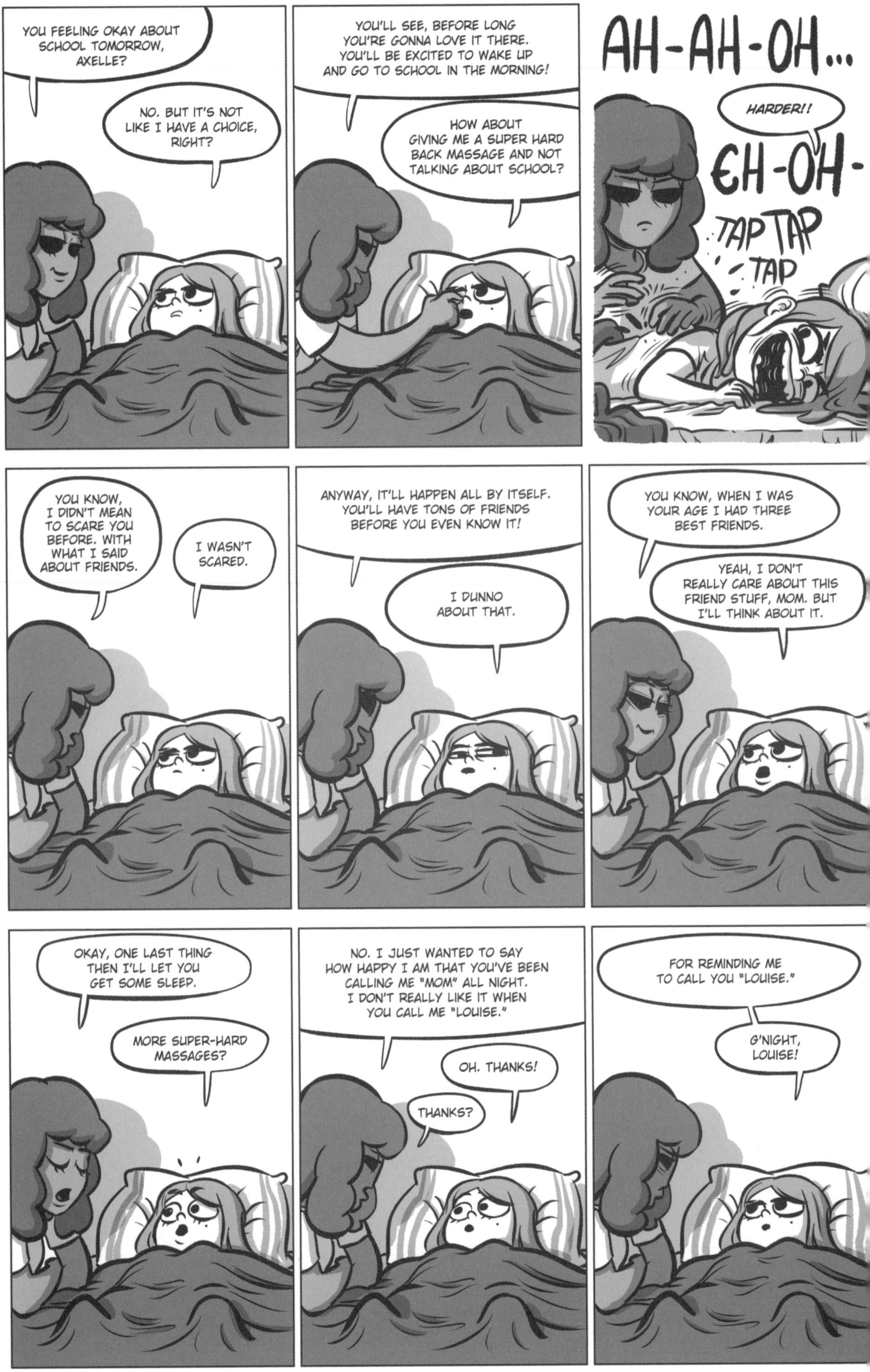

YOU FEELING OKAY ABOUT SCHOOL TOMORROW, AXELLE?
NO. BUT IT'S NOT LIKE I HAVE A CHOICE, RIGHT?
YOU'LL SEE, BEFORE LONG YOU'RE GONNA LOVE IT THERE. YOU'LL BE EXCITED TO WAKE UP AND GO TO SCHOOL IN THE MORNING!
HOW ABOUT GIVING ME A SUPER HARD BACK MASSAGE AND NOT TALKING ABOUT SCHOOL?
AH-AH-OH...
HARDER!!
EH-OH-
TAP TAP
TAP
YOU KNOW, I DIDN'T MEAN TO SCARE YOU BEFORE. WITH WHAT I SAID ABOUT FRIENDS.
I WASN'T SCARED.
ANYWAY, IT'LL HAPPEN ALL BY ITSELF. YOU'LL HAVE TONS OF FRIENDS BEFORE YOU EVEN KNOW IT!
I DUNNO ABOUT THAT.
YOU KNOW, WHEN I WAS YOUR AGE I HAD THREE BEST FRIENDS.
YEAH, I DON'T REALLY CARE ABOUT THIS FRIEND STUFF, MOM. BUT I'LL THINK ABOUT IT.
OKAY, ONE LAST THING THEN I'LL LET YOU GET SOME SLEEP.
MORE SUPER-HARD MASSAGES?
NO. I JUST WANTED TO SAY HOW HAPPY I AM THAT YOU'VE BEEN CALLING ME "MOM" ALL NIGHT. I DON'T REALLY LIKE IT WHEN YOU CALL ME "LOUISE."
OH. THANKS!
THANKS?
FOR REMINDING ME TO CALL YOU "LOUISE."
G'NIGHT, LOUISE!

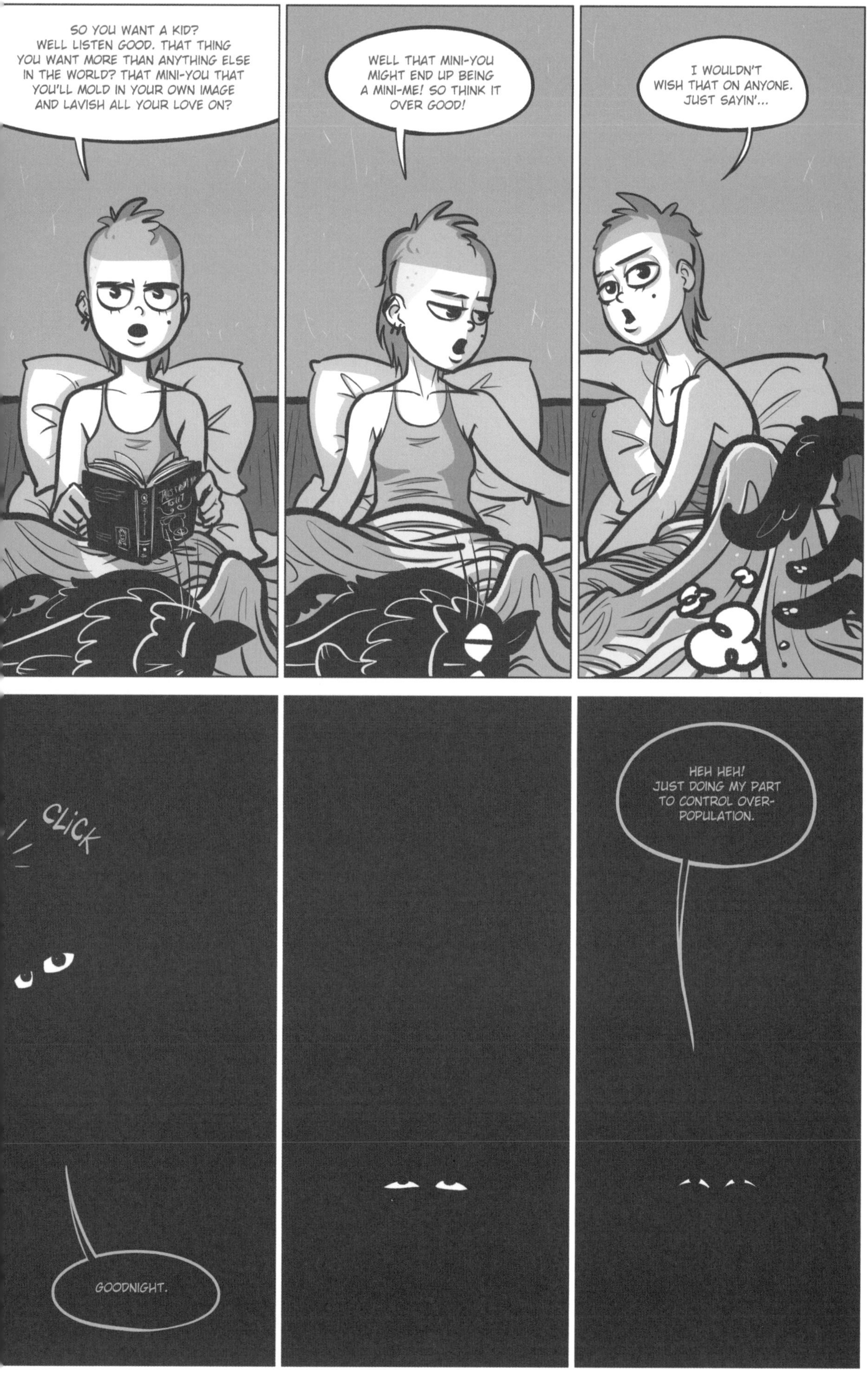
SO YOU WANT A KID? WELL LISTEN GOOD. THAT THING YOU WANT MORE THAN ANYTHING ELSE IN THE WORLD? THAT MINI-YOU THAT YOU'LL MOLD IN YOUR OWN IMAGE AND LAVISH ALL YOUR LOVE ON?
WELL THAT MINI-YOU MIGHT END UP BEING A MINI-ME! SO THINK IT OVER GOOD!
I WOULDN'T WISH THAT ON ANYONE. JUST SAYIN'...
CLICK
GOODNIGHT.
HEH HEH! JUST DOING MY PART TO CONTROL OVER-POPULATION.

THE ART OF MAKING FRIENDS

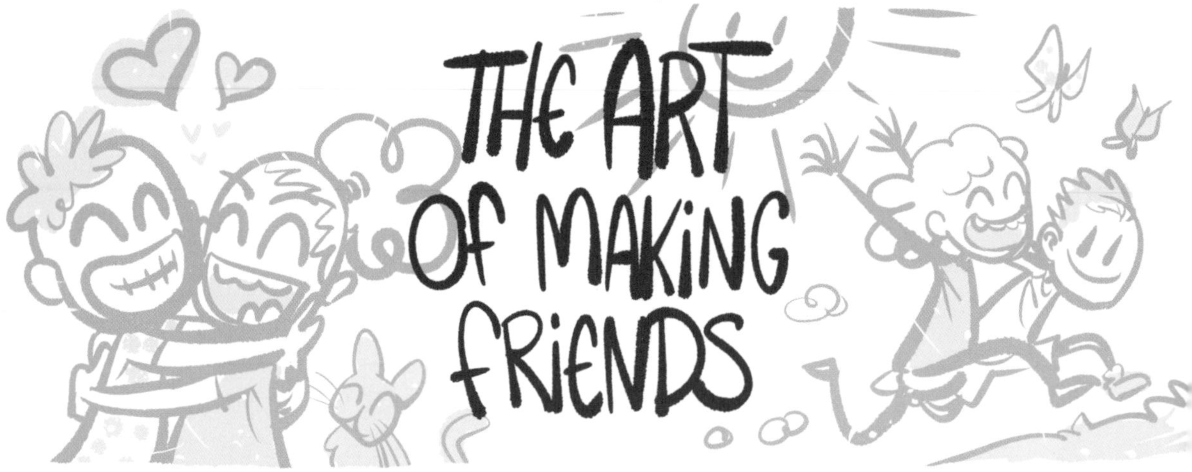

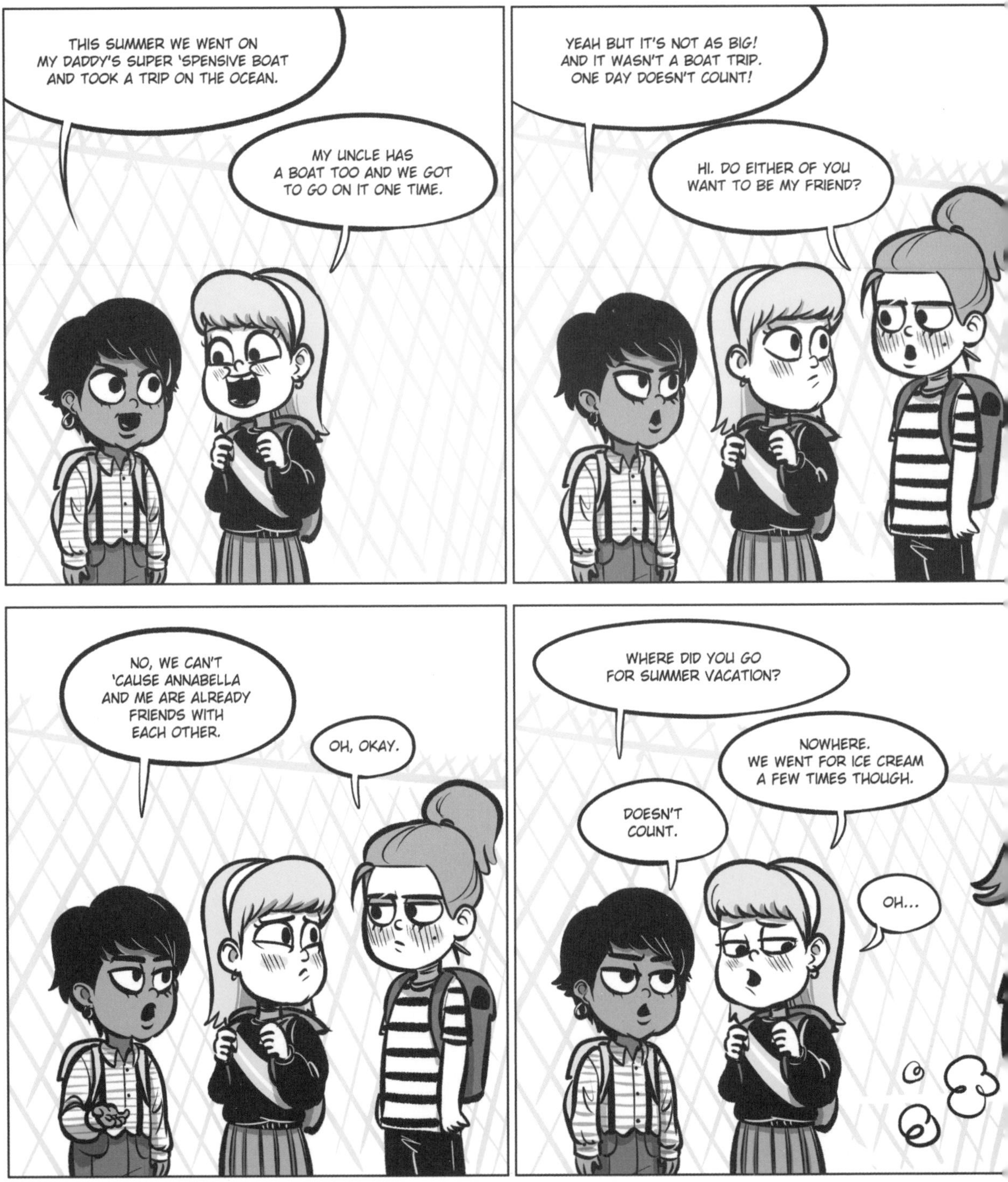
THIS SUMMER WE WENT ON MY DADDY'S SUPER 'SPENSIVE BOAT AND TOOK A TRIP ON THE OCEAN.
MY UNCLE HAS A BOAT TOO AND WE GOT TO GO ON IT ONE TIME.
YEAH BUT IT'S NOT AS BIG! AND IT WASN'T A BOAT TRIP. ONE DAY DOESN'T COUNT!
HI. DO EITHER OF YOU WANT TO BE MY FRIEND?
NO, WE CAN'T 'CAUSE ANNABELLA AND ME ARE ALREADY FRIENDS WITH EACH OTHER.
OH, OKAY.
WHERE DID YOU GO FOR SUMMER VACATION?
NOWHERE. WE WENT FOR ICE CREAM A FEW TIMES THOUGH.
DOESN'T COUNT.
OH...

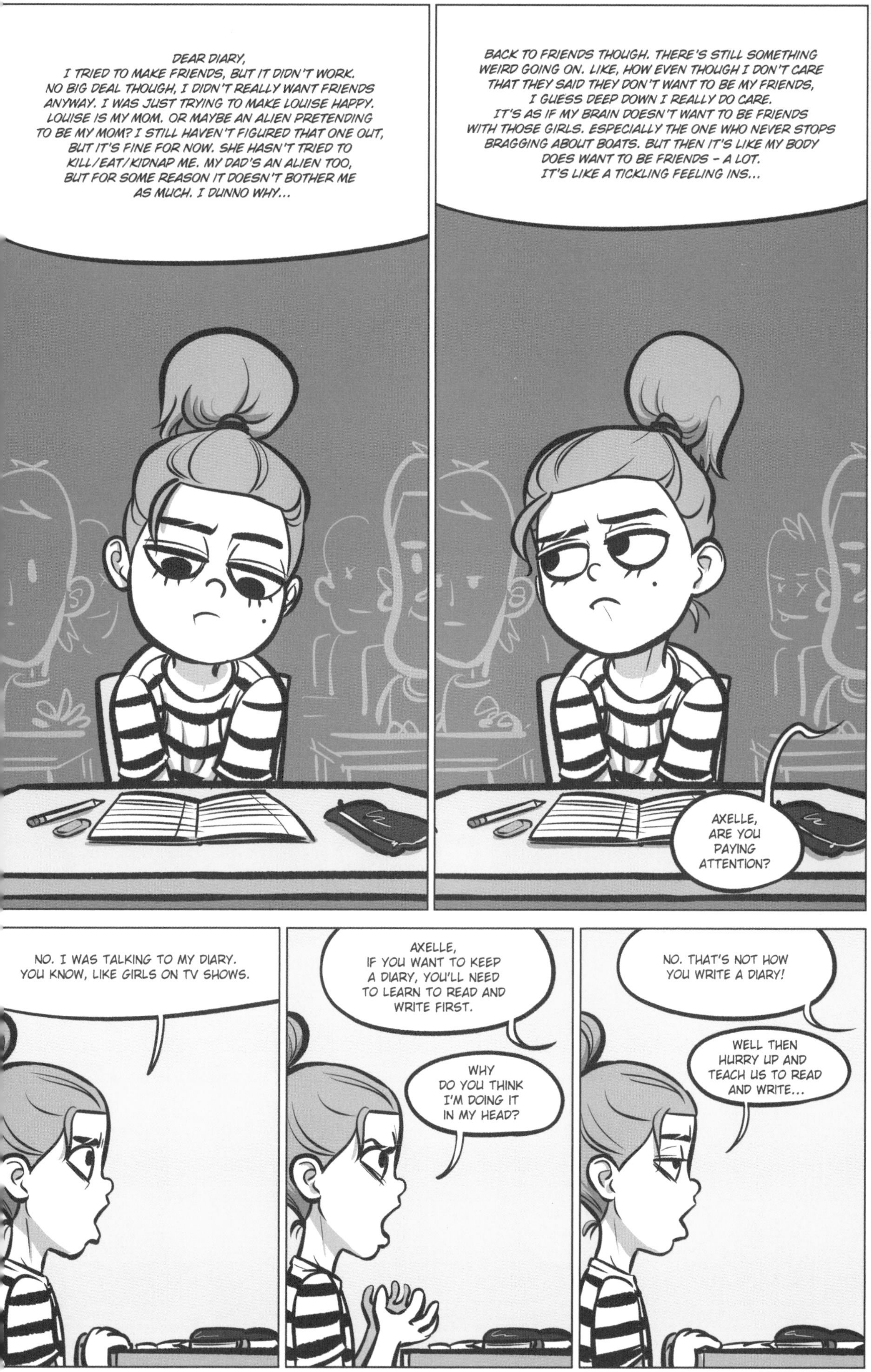
DEAR DIARY,
I TRIED TO MAKE FRIENDS, BUT IT DIDN'T WORK. NO BIG DEAL THOUGH, I DIDN'T REALLY WANT FRIENDS ANYWAY. I WAS JUST TRYING TO MAKE LOUISE HAPPY. LOUISE IS MY MOM. OR MAYBE AN ALIEN PRETENDING TO BE MY MOM? I STILL HAVEN'T FIGURED THAT ONE OUT, BUT IT'S FINE FOR NOW. SHE HASN'T TRIED TO KILL/EAT/KIDNAP ME. MY DAD'S AN ALIEN TOO, BUT FOR SOME REASON IT DOESN'T BOTHER ME AS MUCH. I DUNNO WHY...
BACK TO FRIENDS THOUGH. THERE'S STILL SOMETHING WEIRD GOING ON. LIKE, HOW EVEN THOUGH I DON'T CARE THAT THEY SAID THEY DON'T WANT TO BE MY FRIENDS, I GUESS DEEP DOWN I REALLY DO CARE. IT'S AS IF MY BRAIN DOESN'T WANT TO BE FRIENDS WITH THOSE GIRLS. ESPECIALLY THE ONE WHO NEVER STOPS BRAGGING ABOUT BOATS. BUT THEN IT'S LIKE MY BODY DOES WANT TO BE FRIENDS - A LOT. IT'S LIKE A TICKLING FEELING INS...
AXELLE, ARE YOU PAYING ATTENTION?
NO. I WAS TALKING TO MY DIARY. YOU KNOW, LIKE GIRLS ON TV SHOWS.
AXELLE, IF YOU WANT TO KEEP A DIARY, YOU'LL NEED TO LEARN TO READ AND WRITE FIRST.
WHY DO YOU THINK I'M DOING IT IN MY HEAD?
NO. THAT'S NOT HOW YOU WRITE A DIARY!
WELL THEN HURRY UP AND TEACH US TO READ AND WRITE...

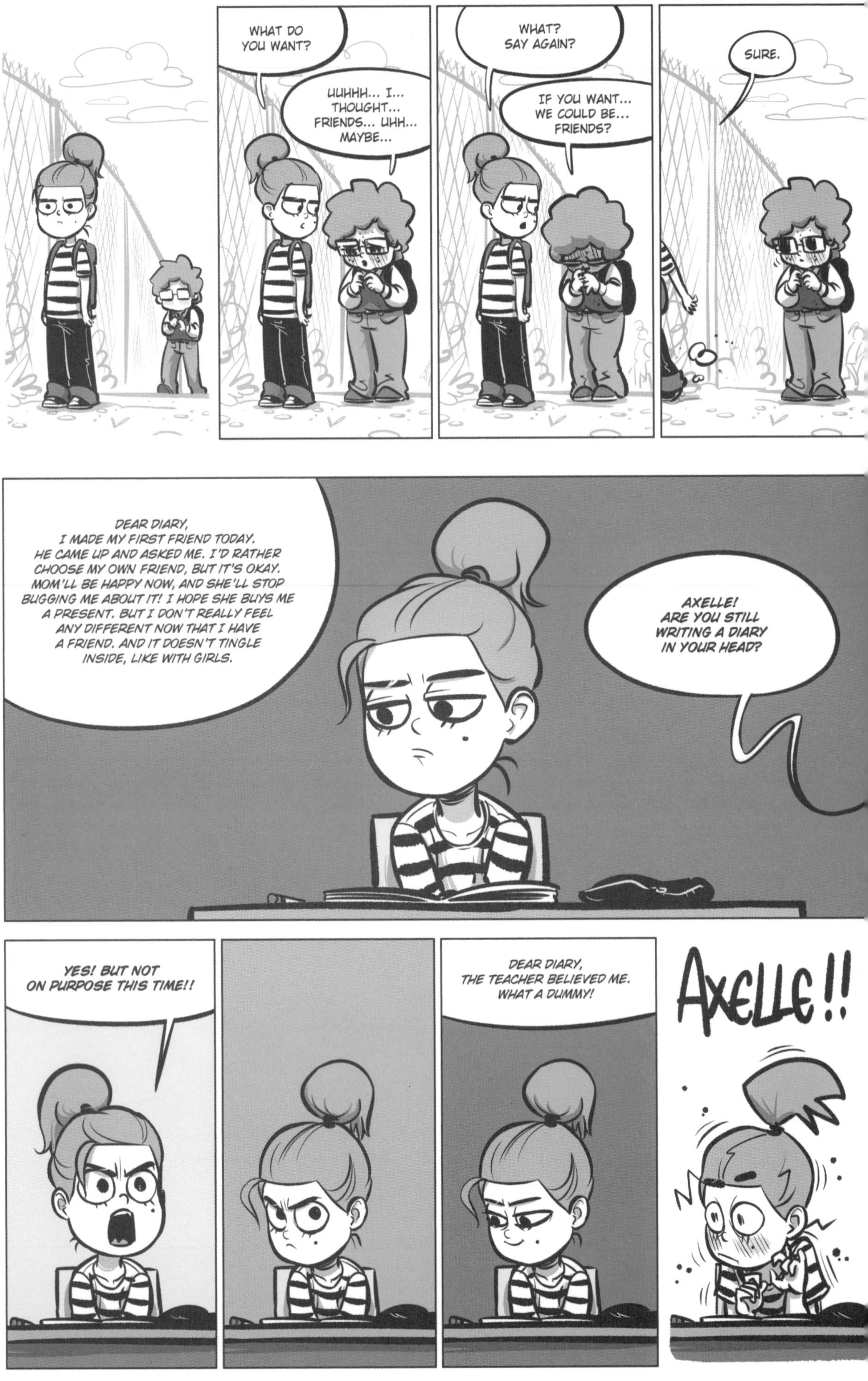
WHAT DO YOU WANT?
UUHHH... I... THOUGHT... FRIENDS... UHH... MAYBE...
WHAT? SAY AGAIN?
IF YOU WANT... WE COULD BE... FRIENDS?
SURE.
DEAR DIARY, I MADE MY FIRST FRIEND TODAY. HE CAME UP AND ASKED ME. I'D RATHER CHOOSE MY OWN FRIEND, BUT IT'S OKAY. MOM'LL BE HAPPY NOW, AND SHE'LL STOP BUGGING ME ABOUT IT! I HOPE SHE BUYS ME A PRESENT. BUT I DON'T REALLY FEEL ANY DIFFERENT NOW THAT I HAVE A FRIEND. AND IT DOESN'T TINGLE INSIDE, LIKE WITH GIRLS.
AXELLE! ARE YOU STILL WRITING A DIARY IN YOUR HEAD?
YES! BUT NOT ON PURPOSE THIS TIME!!
DEAR DIARY, THE TEACHER BELIEVED ME. WHAT A DUMMY!
AXELLE!!

DEAR DIARY,

TODAY WE HAD THE FIRST CLASS THAT'S ACTUALLY FUN.
IT'S CALLED "PHYSICAL EDUCATION," OR "PHYS. ED." FOR SHORT. IT'S JUST LIKE RECESS, EXCEPT IT'S A CLASS. I RAN AND KICKED THE BALL AND LAUGHED – I EVEN GOT TO HURT OTHER KIDS AND DIDN'T GET INTO THAT MUCH TROUBLE. HOW COULD THEY HAVE GIVEN SUCH A STUPID NAME TO SUCH AN AWESOME CLASS! IT SHOULD BE CALLED "AWESOME CLASS WHERE YOU RUN AROUND!"

P.S. MRS. MORIN, OUR GYM TEACHER, DOESN'T KNOW ABOUT DIARIES IN YOUR HEAD.

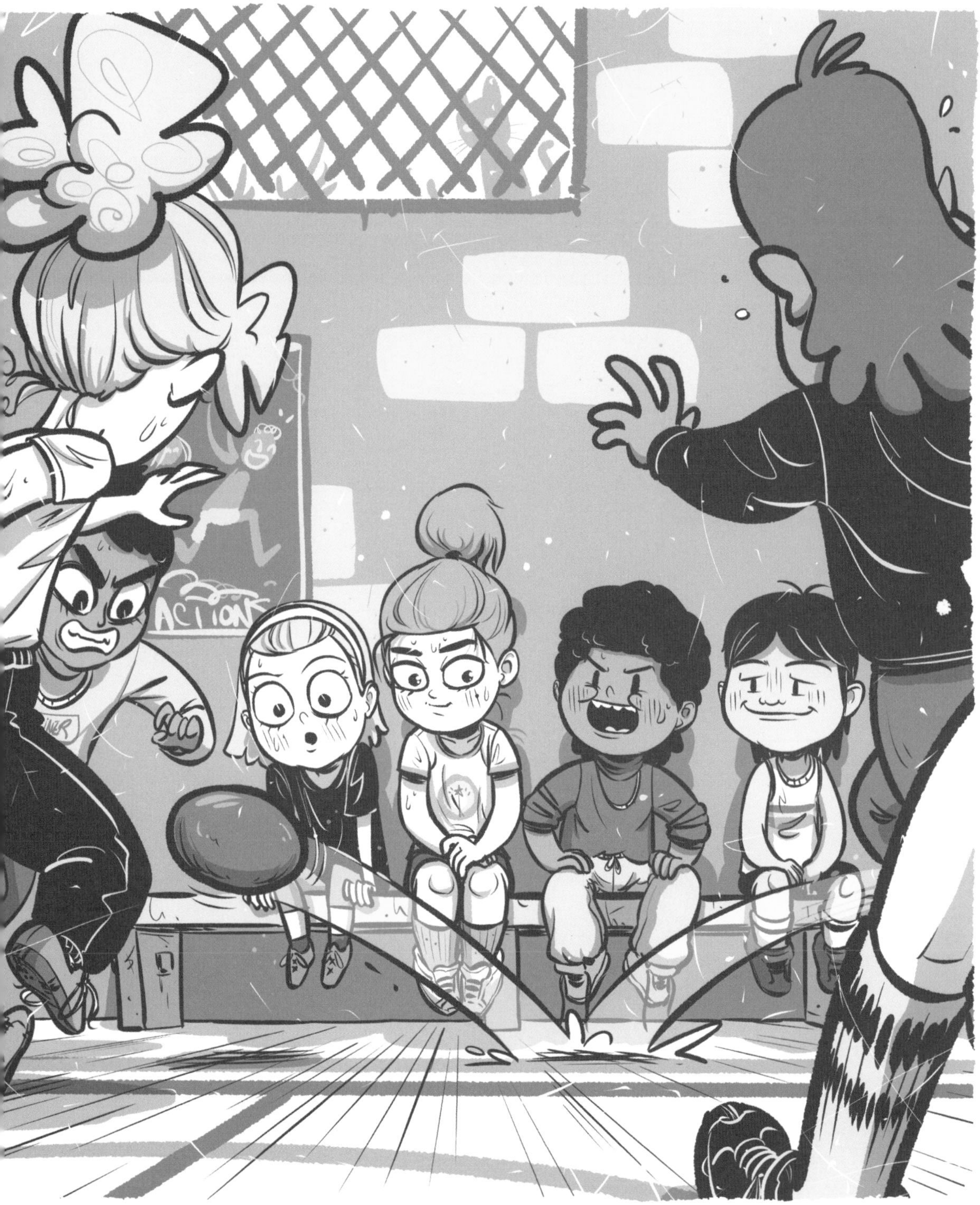

A FEW DAYS LATER: MY BIRTHDAY

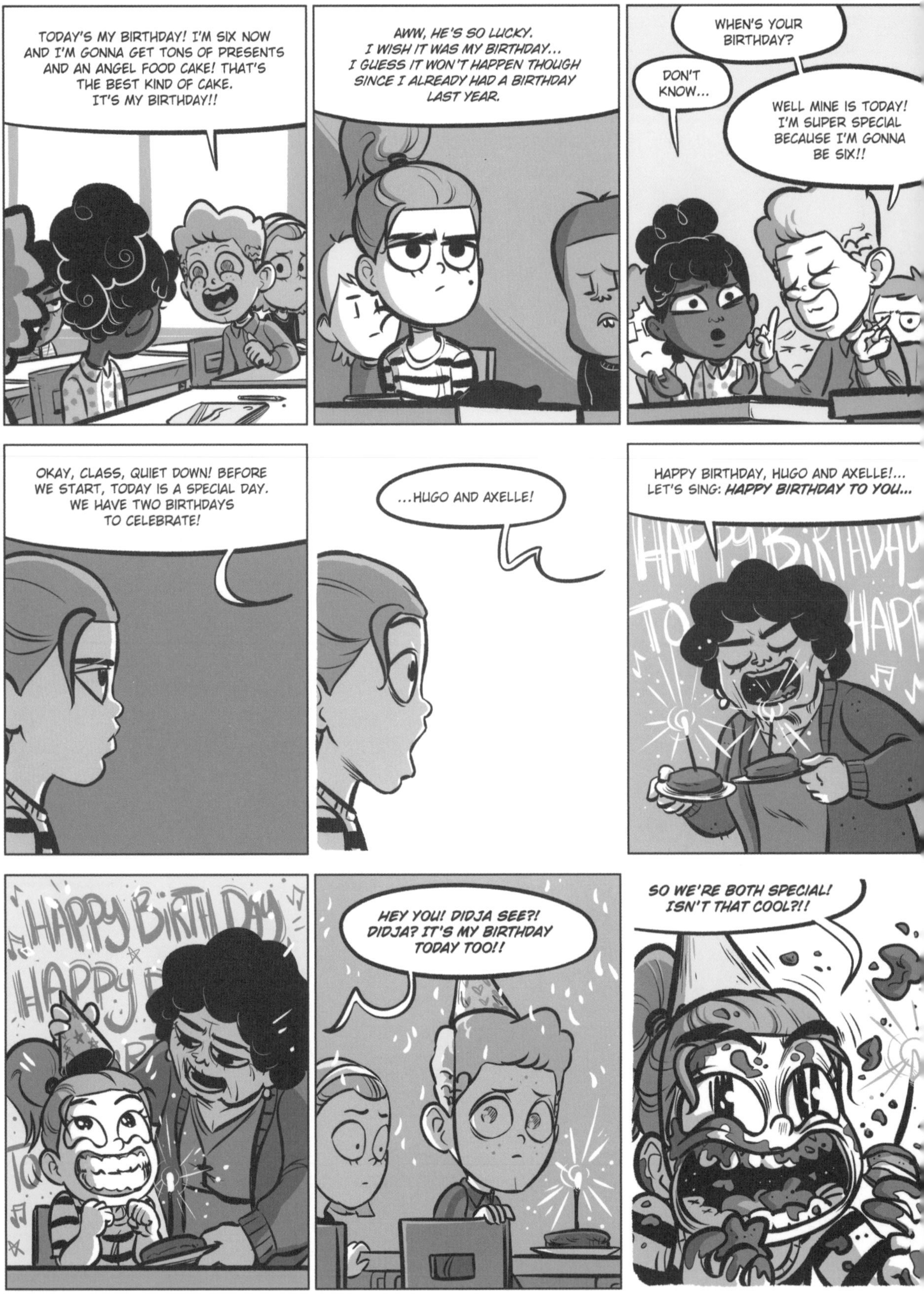

TODAY'S MY BIRTHDAY! I'M SIX NOW AND I'M GONNA GET TONS OF PRESENTS AND AN ANGEL FOOD CAKE! THAT'S THE BEST KIND OF CAKE. IT'S MY BIRTHDAY!!
AWW, HE'S SO LUCKY. I WISH IT WAS MY BIRTHDAY... I GUESS IT WON'T HAPPEN THOUGH SINCE I ALREADY HAD A BIRTHDAY LAST YEAR.
WHEN'S YOUR BIRTHDAY?
DON'T KNOW...
WELL MINE IS TODAY! I'M SUPER SPECIAL BECAUSE I'M GONNA BE SIX!!
OKAY, CLASS, QUIET DOWN! BEFORE WE START, TODAY IS A SPECIAL DAY. WE HAVE TWO BIRTHDAYS TO CELEBRATE!
...HUGO AND AXELLE!
HAPPY BIRTHDAY, HUGO AND AXELLE!... LET'S SING: *HAPPY BIRTHDAY TO YOU...*
HAPPY BIRTHDAY
HEY YOU! DIDJA SEE?! DIDJA? IT'S MY BIRTHDAY TODAY TOO!!
SO WE'RE BOTH SPECIAL! ISN'T THAT COOL?!!

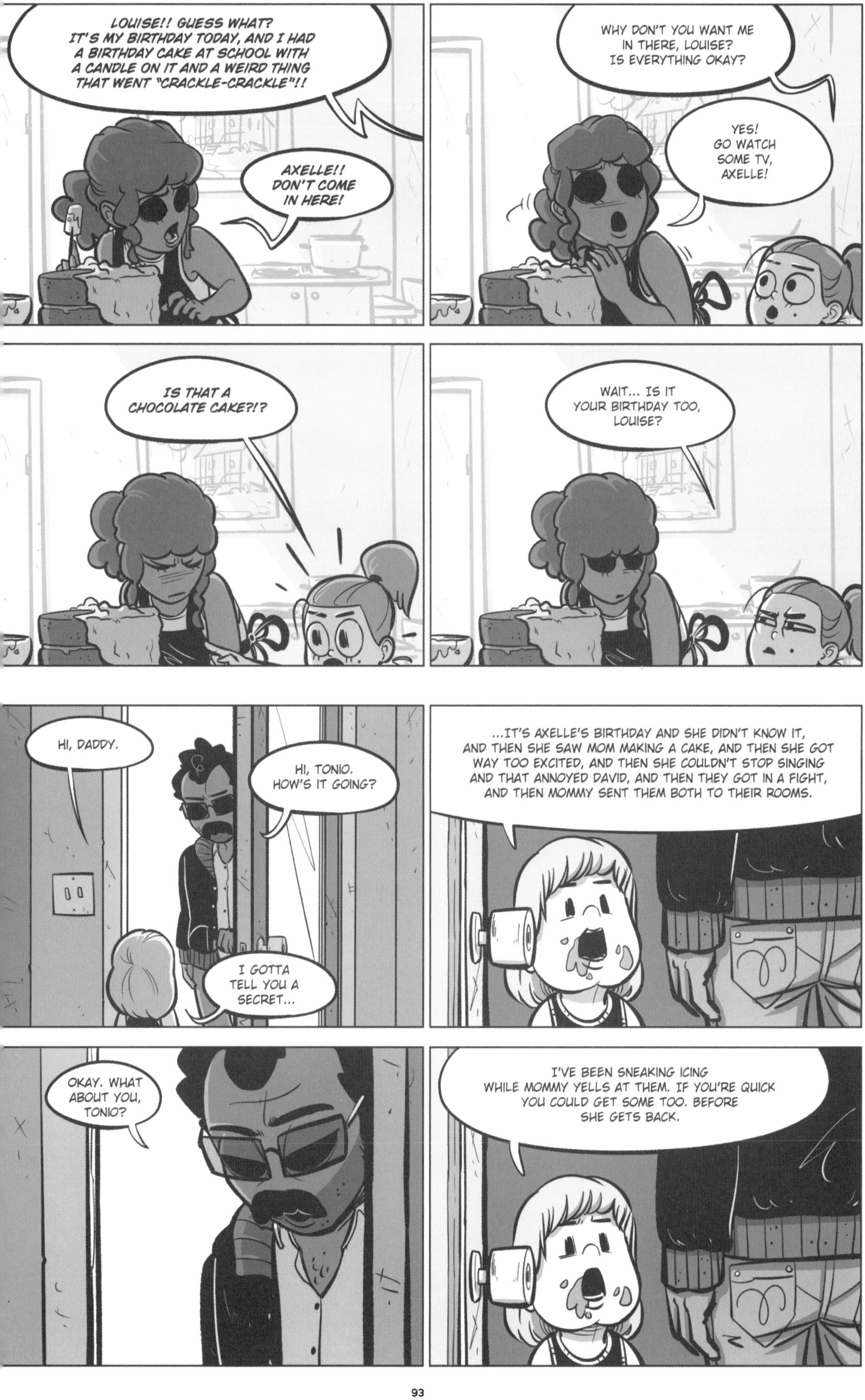
LOUISE!! GUESS WHAT? IT'S MY BIRTHDAY TODAY, AND I HAD A BIRTHDAY CAKE AT SCHOOL WITH A CANDLE ON IT AND A WEIRD THING THAT WENT "CRACKLE-CRACKLE"!!
AXELLE!! DON'T COME IN HERE!
WHY DON'T YOU WANT ME IN THERE, LOUISE? IS EVERYTHING OKAY?
YES! GO WATCH SOME TV, AXELLE!
IS THAT A CHOCOLATE CAKE?!?
WAIT... IS IT YOUR BIRTHDAY TOO, LOUISE?
HI, DADDY.
HI, TONIO. HOW'S IT GOING?
I GOTTA TELL YOU A SECRET...
...IT'S AXELLE'S BIRTHDAY AND SHE DIDN'T KNOW IT, AND THEN SHE SAW MOM MAKING A CAKE, AND THEN SHE GOT WAY TOO EXCITED, AND THEN SHE COULDN'T STOP SINGING AND THAT ANNOYED DAVID, AND THEN THEY GOT IN A FIGHT, AND THEN MOMMY SENT THEM BOTH TO THEIR ROOMS.
OKAY. WHAT ABOUT YOU, TONIO?
I'VE BEEN SNEAKING ICING WHILE MOMMY YELLS AT THEM. IF YOU'RE QUICK YOU COULD GET SOME TOO. BEFORE SHE GETS BACK.

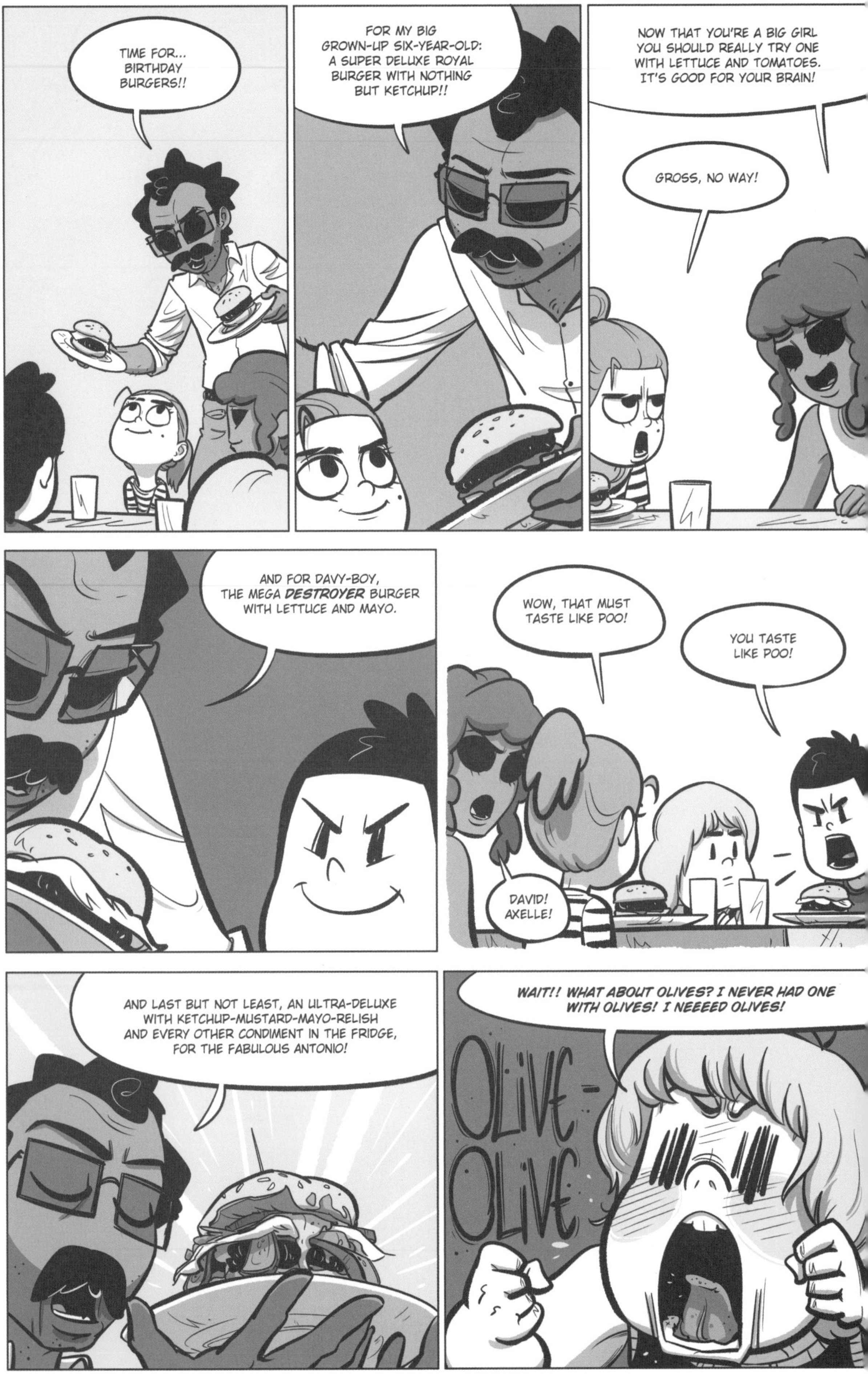
TIME FOR... BIRTHDAY BURGERS!!
FOR MY BIG GROWN-UP SIX-YEAR-OLD: A SUPER DELUXE ROYAL BURGER WITH NOTHING BUT KETCHUP!!
NOW THAT YOU'RE A BIG GIRL YOU SHOULD REALLY TRY ONE WITH LETTUCE AND TOMATOES. IT'S GOOD FOR YOUR BRAIN!
GROSS, NO WAY!
AND FOR DAVY-BOY, THE MEGA *DESTROYER* BURGER WITH LETTUCE AND MAYO.
WOW, THAT MUST TASTE LIKE POO!
YOU TASTE LIKE POO!
DAVID! AXELLE!
AND LAST BUT NOT LEAST, AN ULTRA-DELUXE WITH KETCHUP-MUSTARD-MAYO-RELISH AND EVERY OTHER CONDIMENT IN THE FRIDGE, FOR THE FABULOUS ANTONIO!
WAIT!! WHAT ABOUT OLIVES? I NEVER HAD ONE WITH OLIVES! I NEEEED OLIVES!
OLIVE-OLIVE

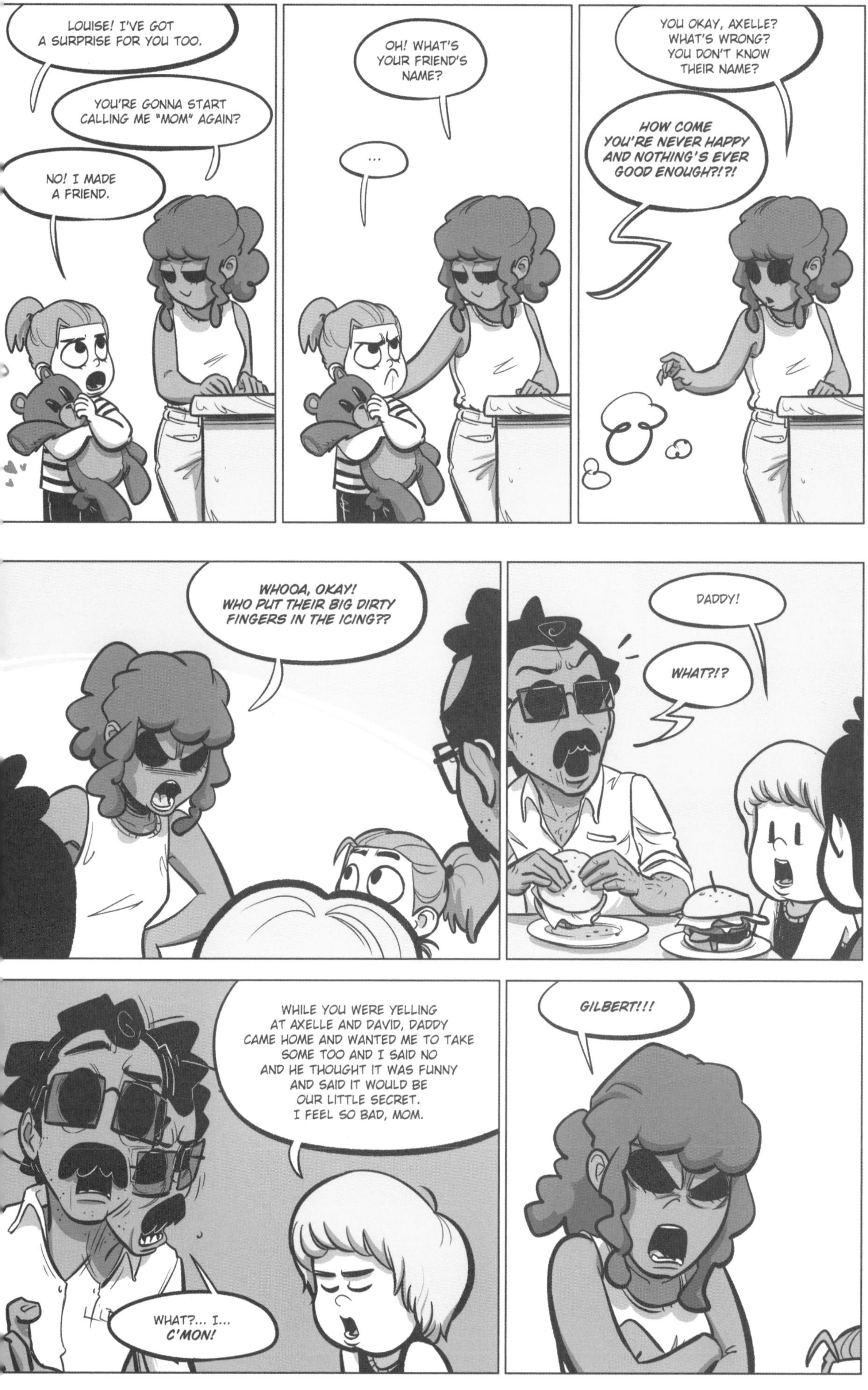
LOUISE! I'VE GOT A SURPRISE FOR YOU TOO.
YOU'RE GONNA START CALLING ME "MOM" AGAIN?
NO! I MADE A FRIEND.
OH! WHAT'S YOUR FRIEND'S NAME?
...
YOU OKAY, AXELLE? WHAT'S WRONG? YOU DON'T KNOW THEIR NAME?
HOW COME YOU'RE NEVER HAPPY AND NOTHING'S EVER GOOD ENOUGH?!?!
WHOOA, OKAY! WHO PUT THEIR BIG DIRTY FINGERS IN THE ICING??
DADDY!
WHAT?!?
WHILE YOU WERE YELLING AT AXELLE AND DAVID, DADDY CAME HOME AND WANTED ME TO TAKE SOME TOO AND I SAID NO AND HE THOUGHT IT WAS FUNNY AND SAID IT WOULD BE OUR LITTLE SECRET. I FEEL SO BAD, MOM.
WHAT?... I... C'MON!
GILBERT!!!

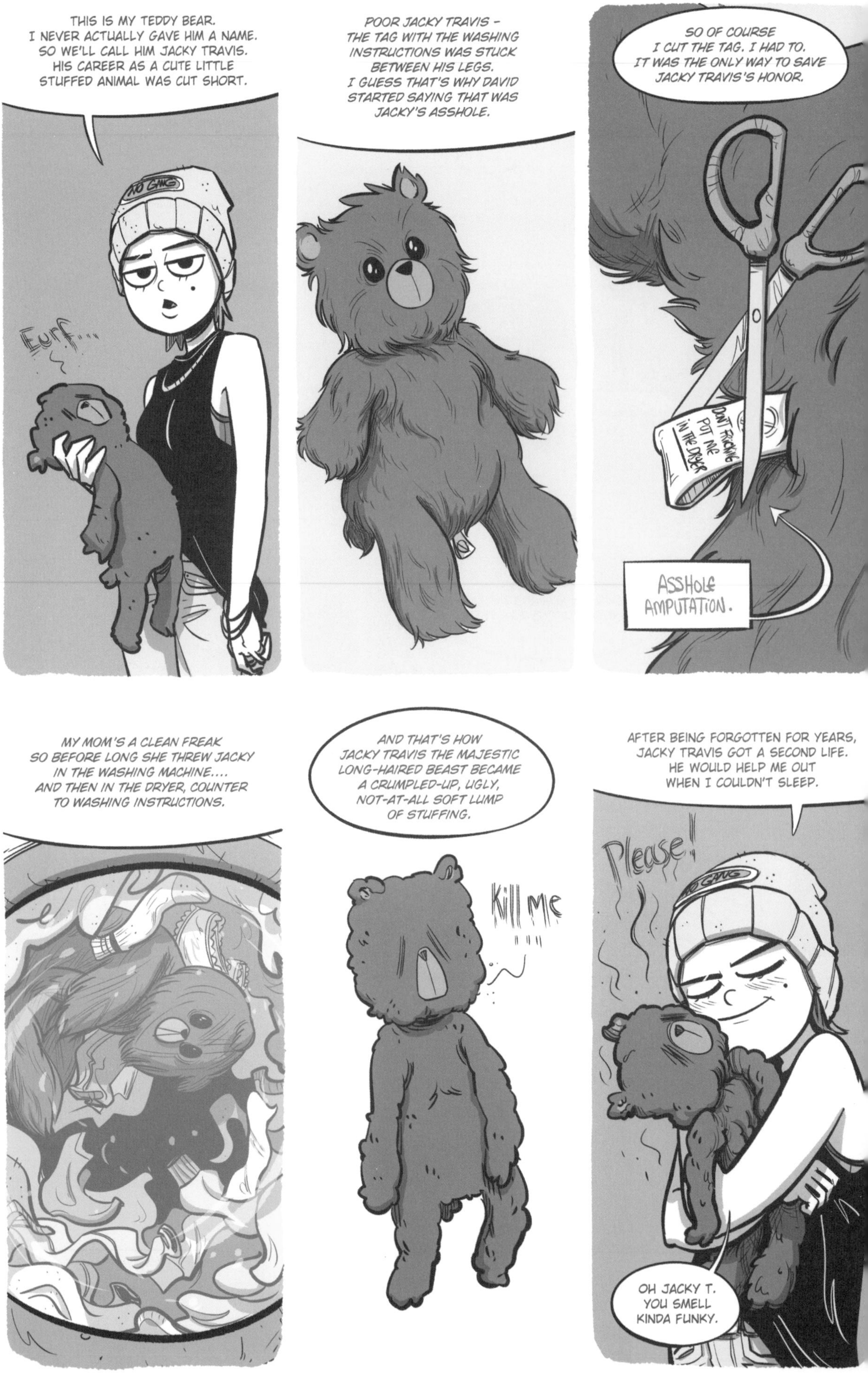
THIS IS MY TEDDY BEAR. I NEVER ACTUALLY GAVE HIM A NAME. SO WE'LL CALL HIM JACKY TRAVIS. HIS CAREER AS A CUTE LITTLE STUFFED ANIMAL WAS CUT SHORT.
NO GANG
EURF...
POOR JACKY TRAVIS - THE TAG WITH THE WASHING INSTRUCTIONS WAS STUCK BETWEEN HIS LEGS. I GUESS THAT'S WHY DAVID STARTED SAYING THAT WAS JACKY'S ASSHOLE.
SO OF COURSE I CUT THE TAG. I HAD TO. IT WAS THE ONLY WAY TO SAVE JACKY TRAVIS'S HONOR.
DON'T FRICKING PUT ME IN THE DRYER
ASSHOLE AMPUTATION.
MY MOM'S A CLEAN FREAK SO BEFORE LONG SHE THREW JACKY IN THE WASHING MACHINE.... AND THEN IN THE DRYER, COUNTER TO WASHING INSTRUCTIONS.
AND THAT'S HOW JACKY TRAVIS THE MAJESTIC LONG-HAIRED BEAST BECAME A CRUMPLED-UP, UGLY, NOT-AT-ALL SOFT LUMP OF STUFFING.
Kill me
AFTER BEING FORGOTTEN FOR YEARS, JACKY TRAVIS GOT A SECOND LIFE. HE WOULD HELP ME OUT WHEN I COULDN'T SLEEP.
Please!
NO GANG
OH JACKY T. YOU SMELL KINDA FUNKY.

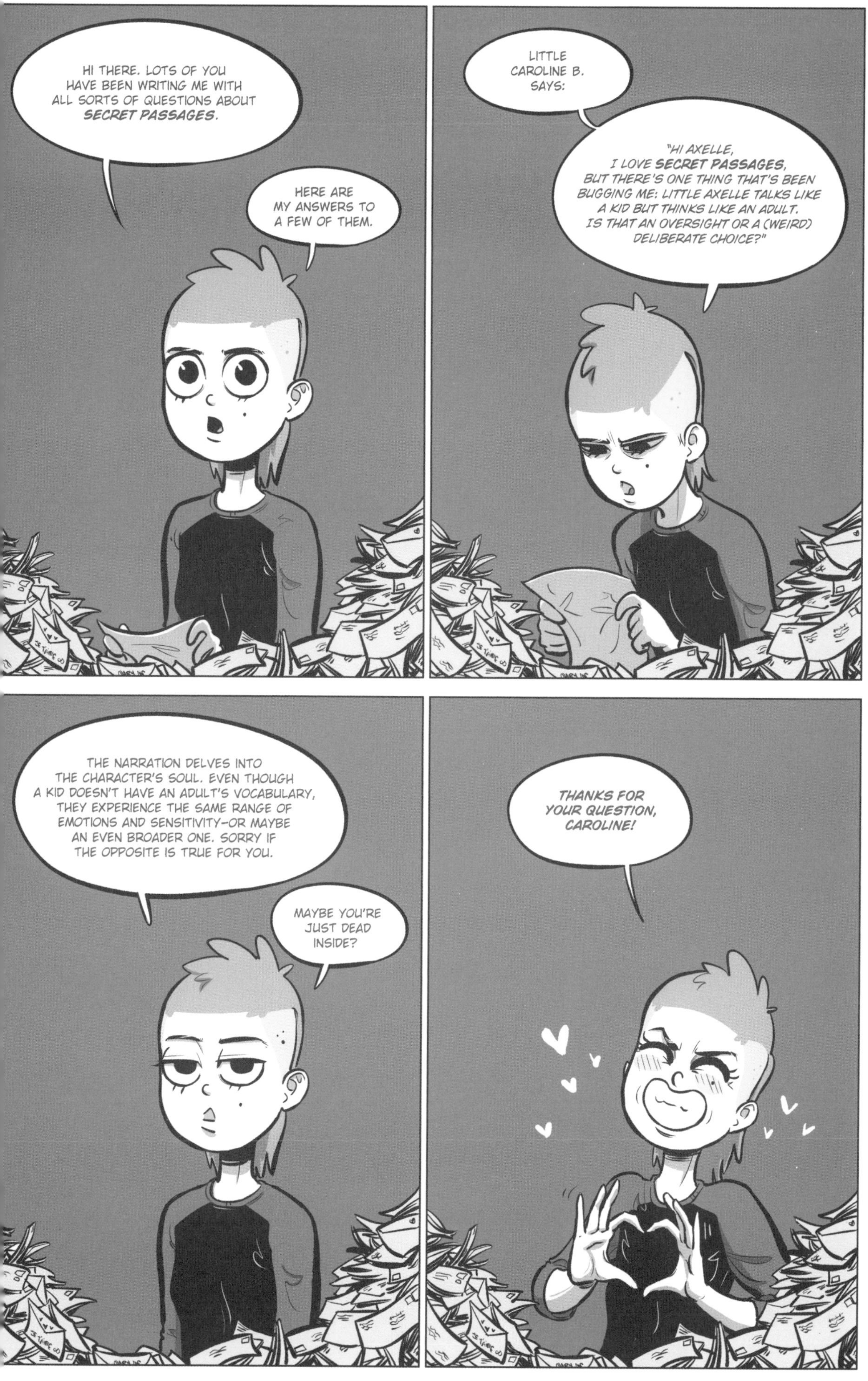
HI THERE. LOTS OF YOU HAVE BEEN WRITING ME WITH ALL SORTS OF QUESTIONS ABOUT SECRET PASSAGES.
HERE ARE MY ANSWERS TO A FEW OF THEM.
LITTLE CAROLINE B. SAYS:
"HI AXELLE, I LOVE SECRET PASSAGES, BUT THERE'S ONE THING THAT'S BEEN BUGGING ME: LITTLE AXELLE TALKS LIKE A KID BUT THINKS LIKE AN ADULT. IS THAT AN OVERSIGHT OR A (WEIRD) DELIBERATE CHOICE?"
THE NARRATION DELVES INTO THE CHARACTER'S SOUL. EVEN THOUGH A KID DOESN'T HAVE AN ADULT'S VOCABULARY, THEY EXPERIENCE THE SAME RANGE OF EMOTIONS AND SENSITIVITY—OR MAYBE AN EVEN BROADER ONE. SORRY IF THE OPPOSITE IS TRUE FOR YOU.
MAYBE YOU'RE JUST DEAD INSIDE?
THANKS FOR YOUR QUESTION, CAROLINE!

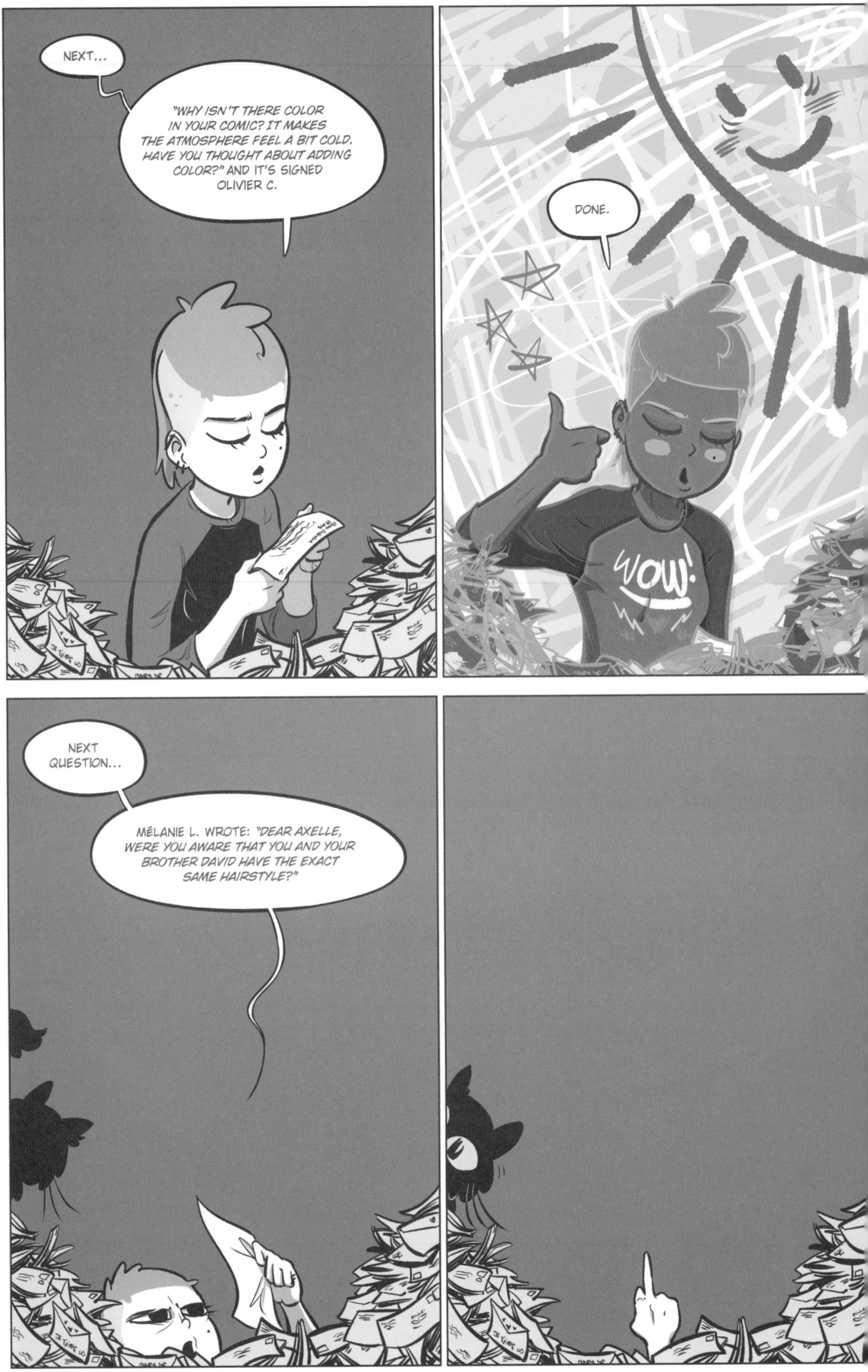
NEXT...
"WHY ISN'T THERE COLOR IN YOUR COMIC? IT MAKES THE ATMOSPHERE FEEL A BIT COLD. HAVE YOU THOUGHT ABOUT ADDING COLOR?" AND IT'S SIGNED OLIVIER C.
DONE.
WOW!
NEXT QUESTION...
MÉLANIE L. WROTE: "DEAR AXELLE, WERE YOU AWARE THAT YOU AND YOUR BROTHER DAVID HAVE THE EXACT SAME HAIRSTYLE?"

CHAPTER III

HALLOWEEN AND THE RIGHT AMOUNT OF BLOOD

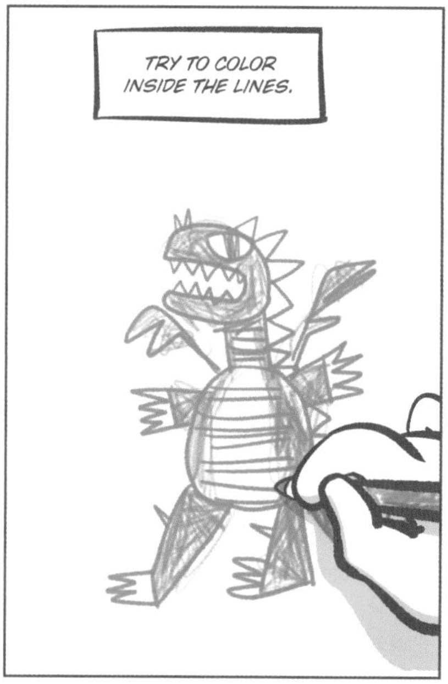
TRY TO COLOR
INSIDE THE LINES.

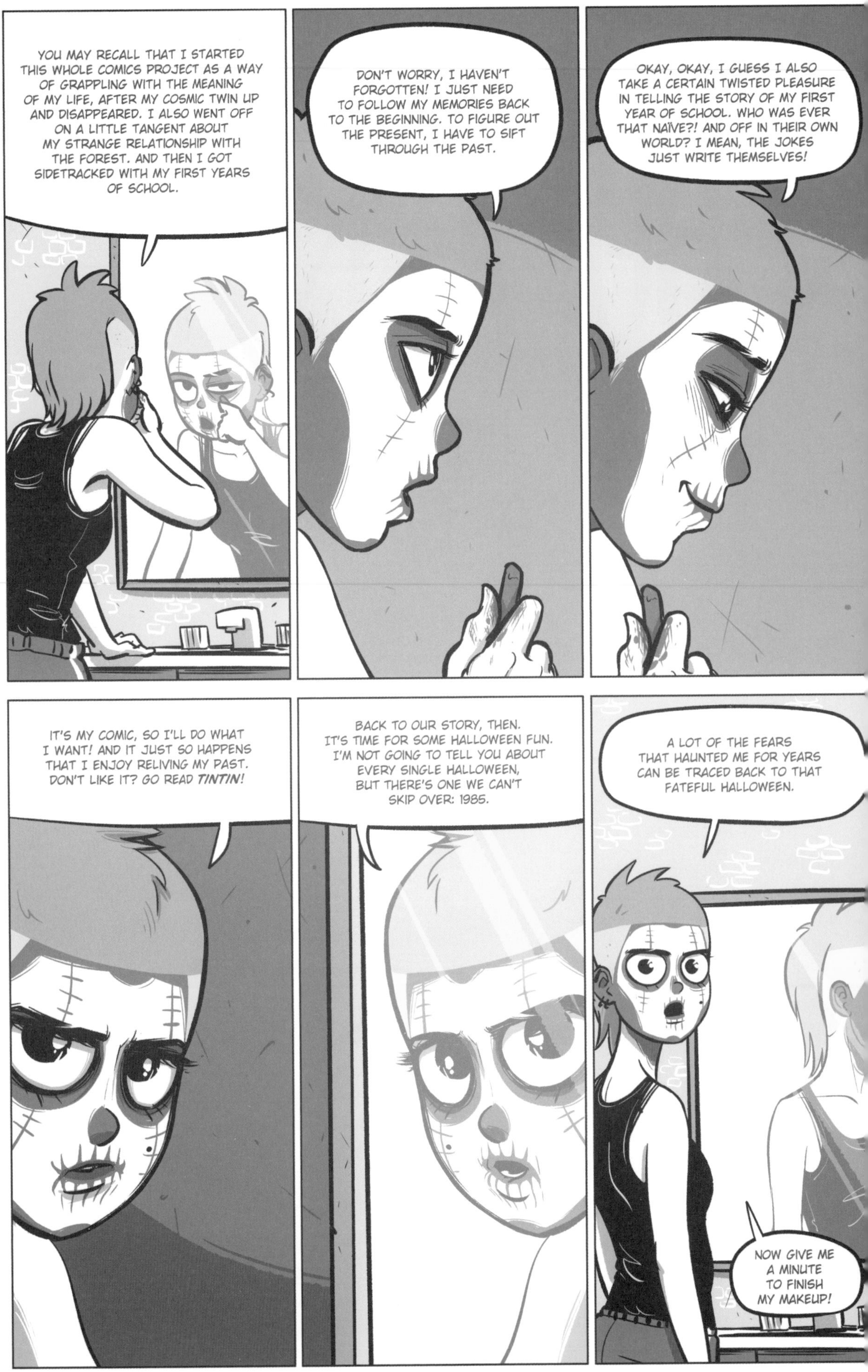
YOU MAY RECALL THAT I STARTED THIS WHOLE COMICS PROJECT AS A WAY OF GRAPPLING WITH THE MEANING OF MY LIFE, AFTER MY COSMIC TWIN UP AND DISAPPEARED. I ALSO WENT OFF ON A LITTLE TANGENT ABOUT MY STRANGE RELATIONSHIP WITH THE FOREST. AND THEN I GOT SIDETRACKED WITH MY FIRST YEARS OF SCHOOL.
DON'T WORRY, I HAVEN'T FORGOTTEN! I JUST NEED TO FOLLOW MY MEMORIES BACK TO THE BEGINNING. TO FIGURE OUT THE PRESENT, I HAVE TO SIFT THROUGH THE PAST.
OKAY, OKAY, I GUESS I ALSO TAKE A CERTAIN TWISTED PLEASURE IN TELLING THE STORY OF MY FIRST YEAR OF SCHOOL. WHO WAS EVER THAT NAÏVE?! AND OFF IN THEIR OWN WORLD? I MEAN, THE JOKES JUST WRITE THEMSELVES!
IT'S MY COMIC, SO I'LL DO WHAT I WANT! AND IT JUST SO HAPPENS THAT I ENJOY RELIVING MY PAST. DON'T LIKE IT? GO READ *TINTIN*!
BACK TO OUR STORY, THEN. IT'S TIME FOR SOME HALLOWEEN FUN. I'M NOT GOING TO TELL YOU ABOUT EVERY SINGLE HALLOWEEN, BUT THERE'S ONE WE CAN'T SKIP OVER: 1985.
A LOT OF THE FEARS THAT HAUNTED ME FOR YEARS CAN BE TRACED BACK TO THAT FATEFUL HALLOWEEN.
NOW GIVE ME A MINUTE TO FINISH MY MAKEUP!

ALMOST HALLOWEEN

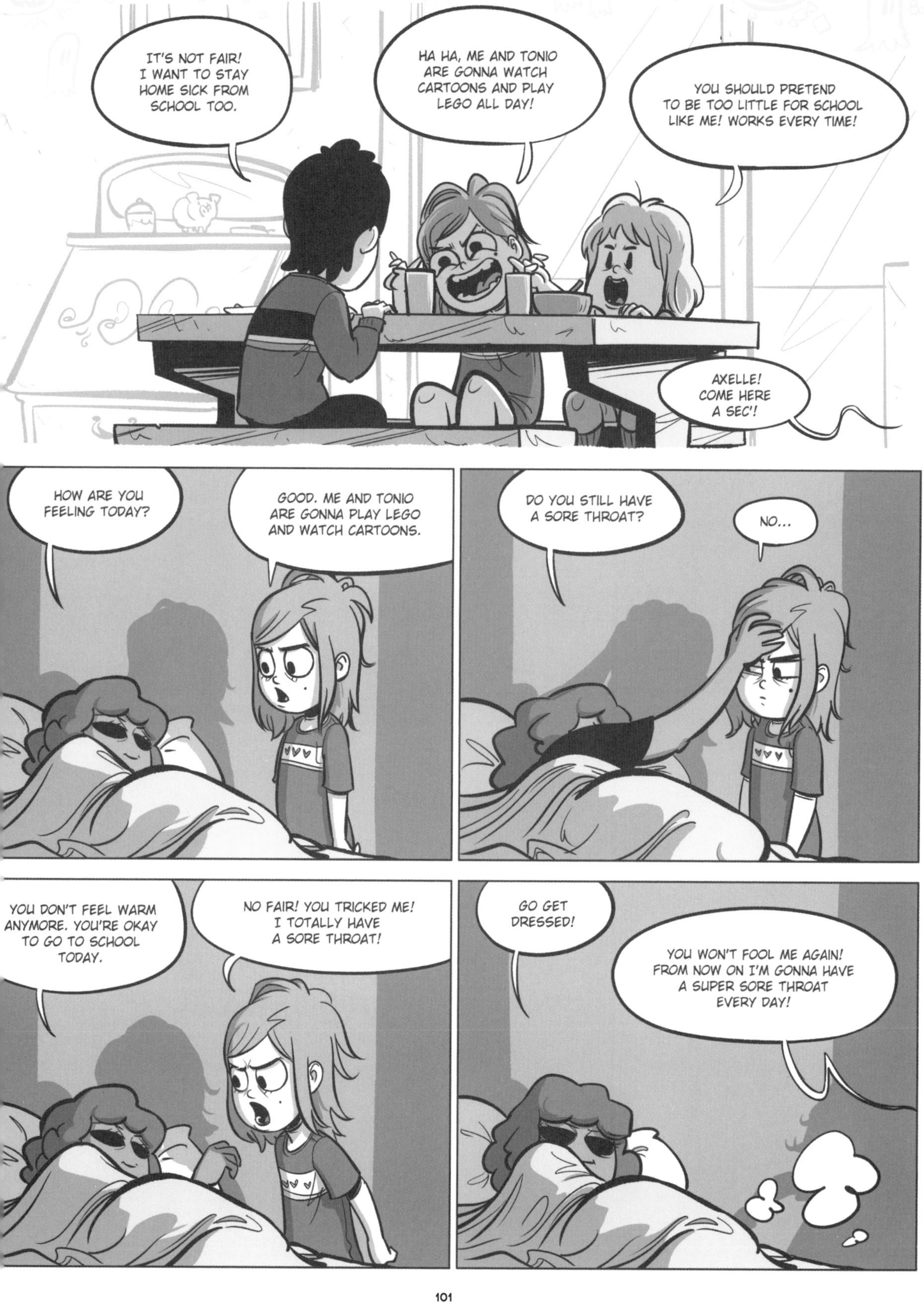

IT'S NOT FAIR! I WANT TO STAY HOME SICK FROM SCHOOL TOO.
HA HA, ME AND TONIO ARE GONNA WATCH CARTOONS AND PLAY LEGO ALL DAY!
YOU SHOULD PRETEND TO BE TOO LITTLE FOR SCHOOL LIKE ME! WORKS EVERY TIME!
AXELLE! COME HERE A SEC'!
HOW ARE YOU FEELING TODAY?
GOOD. ME AND TONIO ARE GONNA PLAY LEGO AND WATCH CARTOONS.
DO YOU STILL HAVE A SORE THROAT?
NO...
YOU DON'T FEEL WARM ANYMORE. YOU'RE OKAY TO GO TO SCHOOL TODAY.
NO FAIR! YOU TRICKED ME! I TOTALLY HAVE A SORE THROAT!
GO GET DRESSED!
YOU WON'T FOOL ME AGAIN! FROM NOW ON I'M GONNA HAVE A SUPER SORE THROAT EVERY DAY!

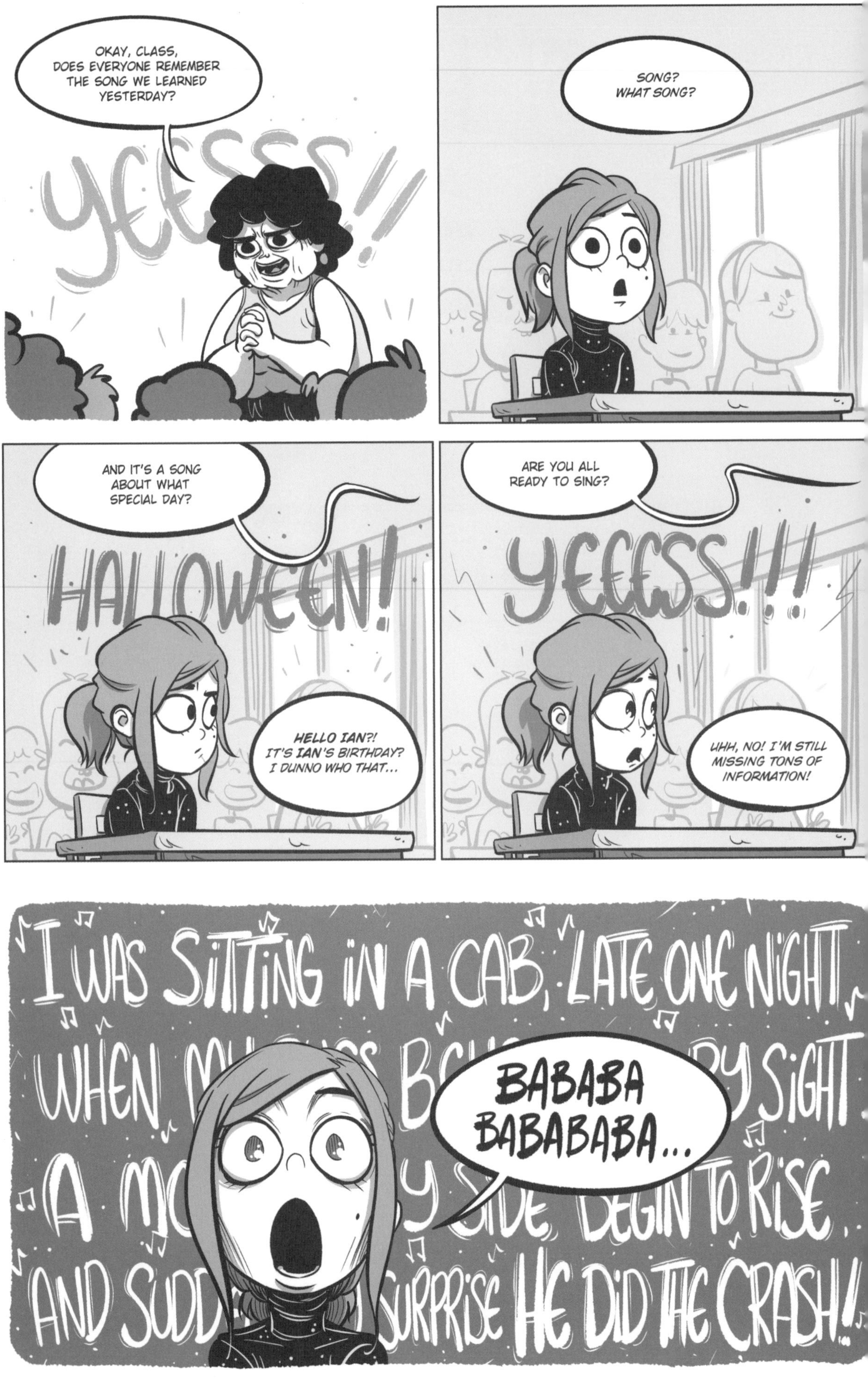
OKAY, CLASS, DOES EVERYONE REMEMBER THE SONG WE LEARNED YESTERDAY?
YEESSS!!
SONG? WHAT SONG?
AND IT'S A SONG ABOUT WHAT SPECIAL DAY?
HALLOWEEN!
HELLO IAN?! IT'S IAN'S BIRTHDAY? I DUNNO WHO THAT...
ARE YOU ALL READY TO SING?
YEEESS!!!
UHH, NO! I'M STILL MISSING TONS OF INFORMATION!
I WAS SITTING IN A CAB, LATE ONE NIGHT
WHEN
SIGHT
A
BEGIN TO RISE
AND
SURPRISE HE DID THE CRASH!!
BABABA BABABABA...

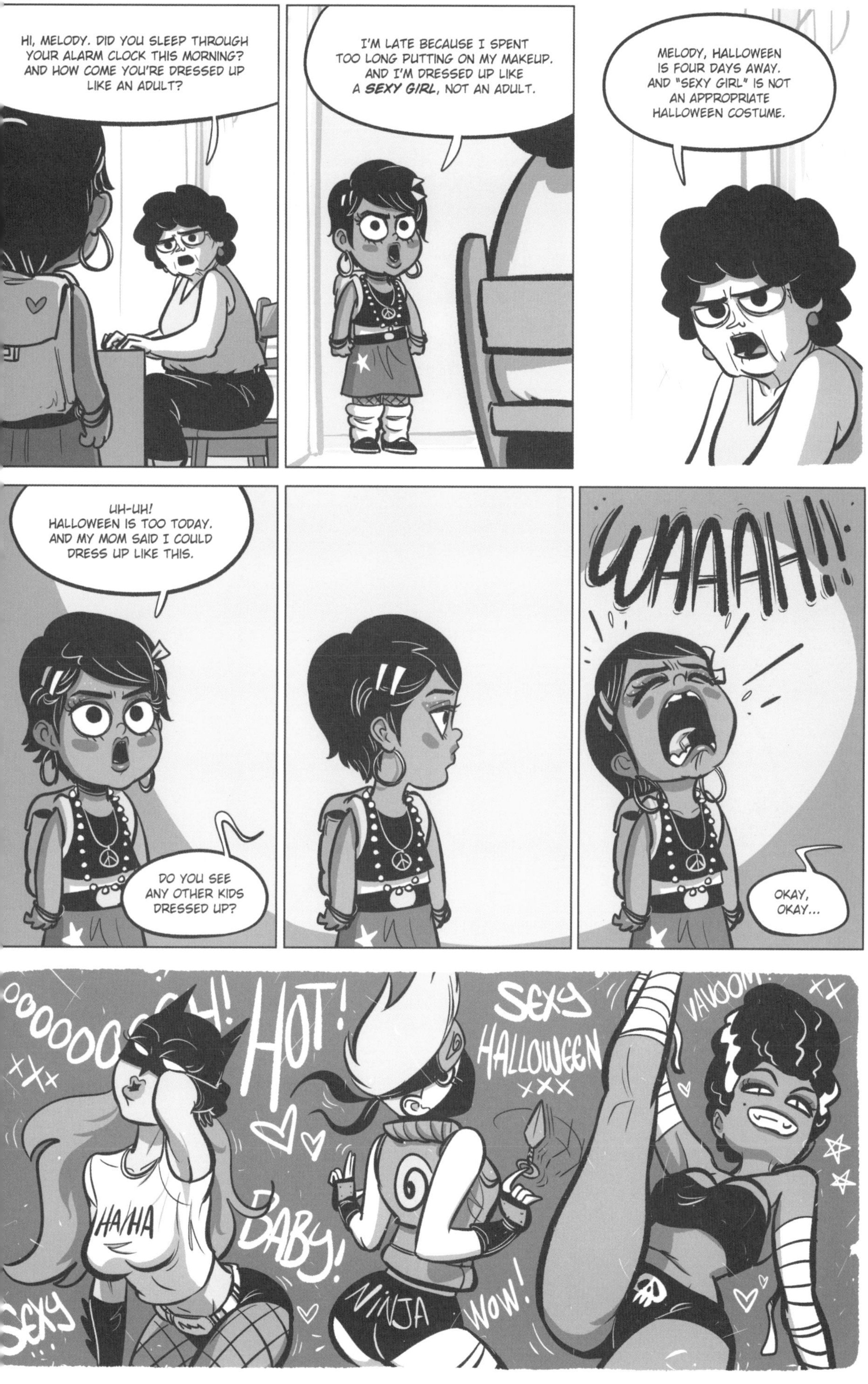
HI, MELODY. DID YOU SLEEP THROUGH YOUR ALARM CLOCK THIS MORNING? AND HOW COME YOU'RE DRESSED UP LIKE AN ADULT?
I'M LATE BECAUSE I SPENT TOO LONG PUTTING ON MY MAKEUP. AND I'M DRESSED UP LIKE A SEXY GIRL, NOT AN ADULT.
MELODY, HALLOWEEN IS FOUR DAYS AWAY. AND "SEXY GIRL" IS NOT AN APPROPRIATE HALLOWEEN COSTUME.
UH-UH! HALLOWEEN IS TOO TODAY. AND MY MOM SAID I COULD DRESS UP LIKE THIS.
DO YOU SEE ANY OTHER KIDS DRESSED UP?
WAAAH!!
OKAY, OKAY...
OOOOOOOH!
HOT!
SEXY HALLOWEEN
VAVOOM!
HA/HA
BABY!
SEXY
NINJA
WOW!

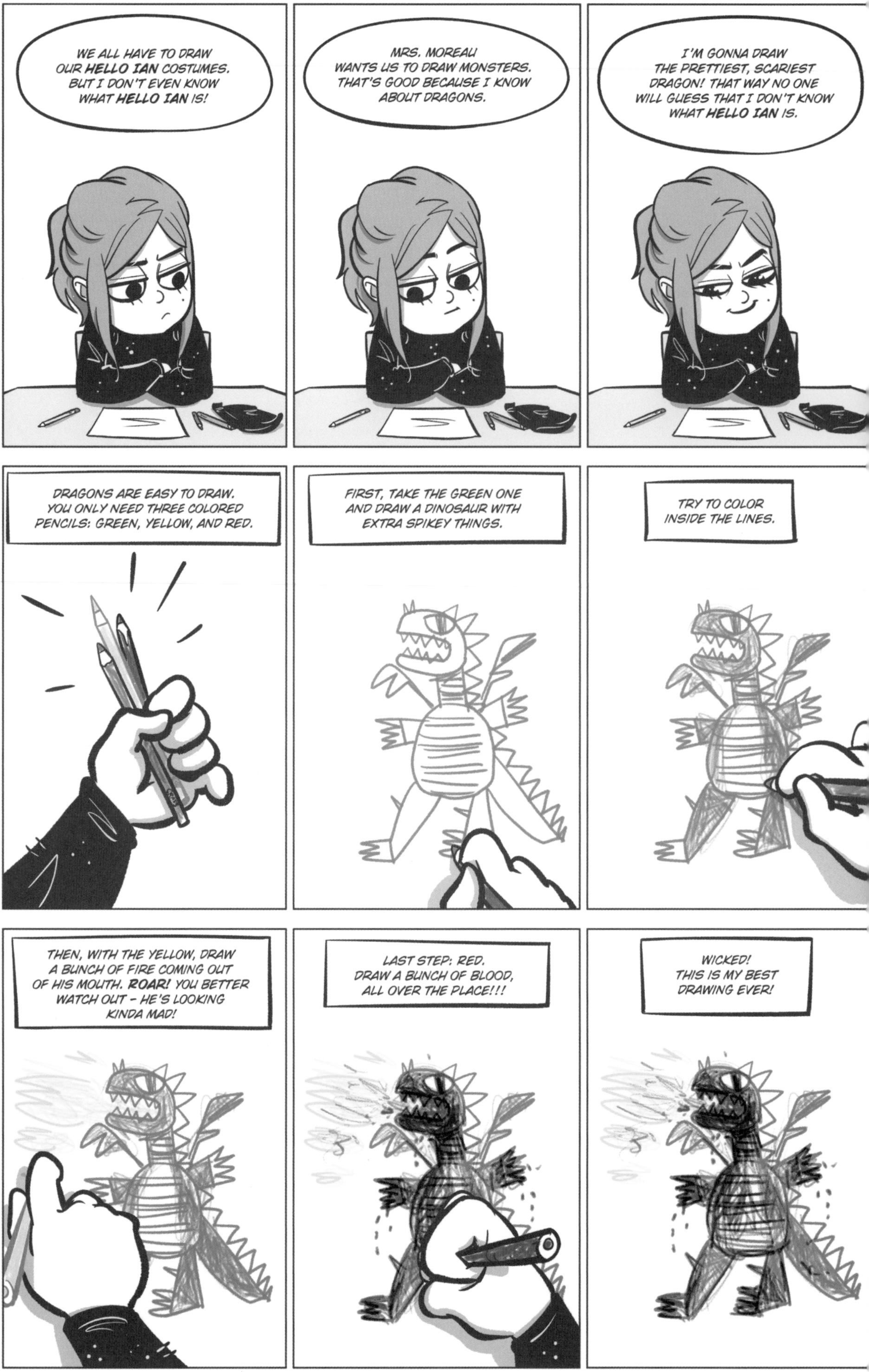
WE ALL HAVE TO DRAW OUR HELLO IAN COSTUMES. BUT I DON'T EVEN KNOW WHAT HELLO IAN IS!
MRS. MOREAU WANTS US TO DRAW MONSTERS. THAT'S GOOD BECAUSE I KNOW ABOUT DRAGONS.
I'M GONNA DRAW THE PRETTIEST, SCARIEST DRAGON! THAT WAY NO ONE WILL GUESS THAT I DON'T KNOW WHAT HELLO IAN IS.
DRAGONS ARE EASY TO DRAW. YOU ONLY NEED THREE COLORED PENCILS: GREEN, YELLOW, AND RED.
FIRST, TAKE THE GREEN ONE AND DRAW A DINOSAUR WITH EXTRA SPIKEY THINGS.
TRY TO COLOR INSIDE THE LINES.
THEN, WITH THE YELLOW, DRAW A BUNCH OF FIRE COMING OUT OF HIS MOUTH. ROAR! YOU BETTER WATCH OUT - HE'S LOOKING KINDA MAD!
LAST STEP: RED. DRAW A BUNCH OF BLOOD, ALL OVER THE PLACE!!!
WICKED! THIS IS MY BEST DRAWING EVER!

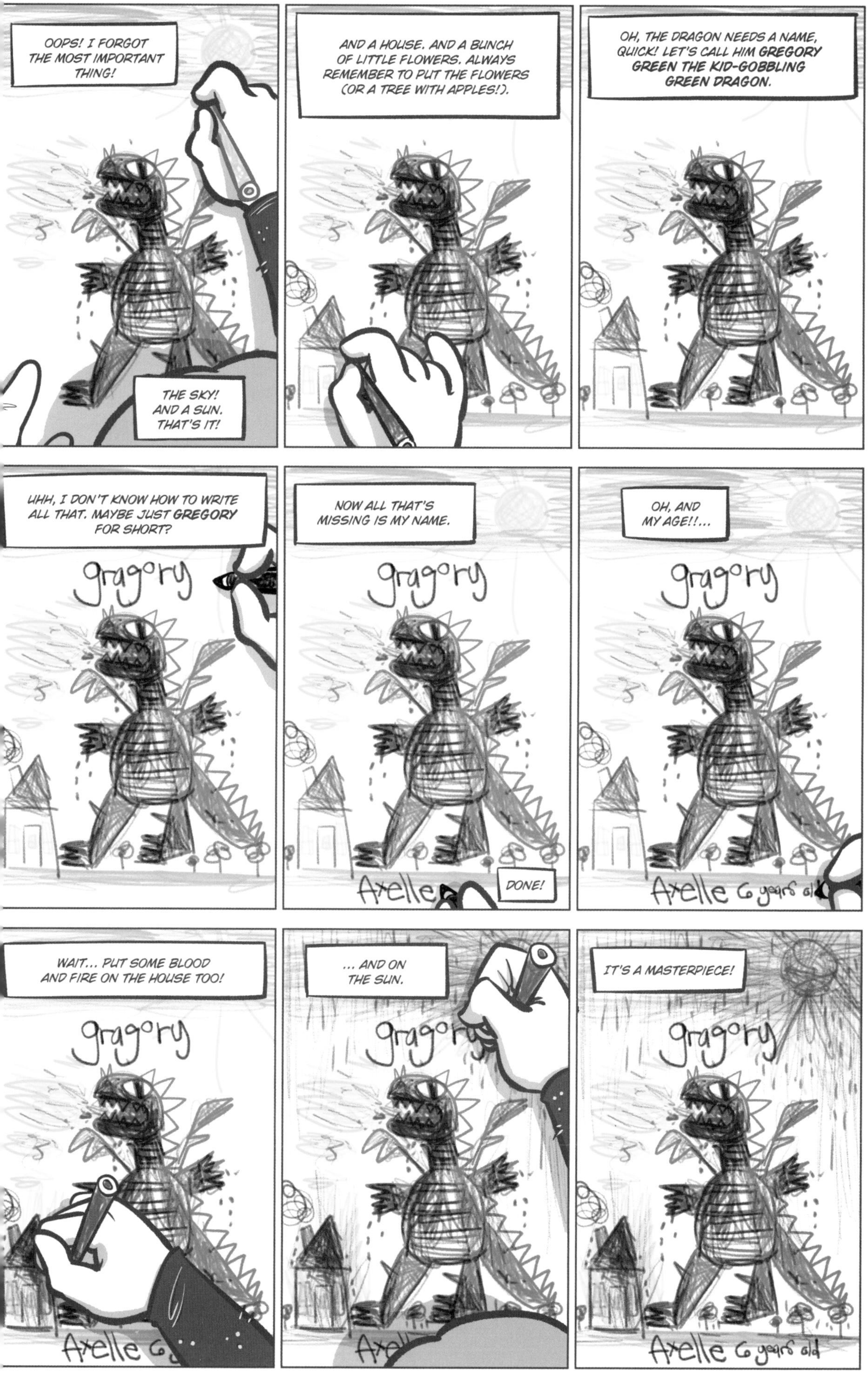
OOPS! I FORGOT THE MOST IMPORTANT THING!
THE SKY! AND A SUN. THAT'S IT!
AND A HOUSE. AND A BUNCH OF LITTLE FLOWERS. ALWAYS REMEMBER TO PUT THE FLOWERS (OR A TREE WITH APPLES!).
OH, THE DRAGON NEEDS A NAME, QUICK! LET'S CALL HIM **GREGORY GREEN THE KID-GOBBLING GREEN DRAGON**.
UHH, I DON'T KNOW HOW TO WRITE ALL THAT. MAYBE JUST **GREGORY** FOR SHORT?
gragory
NOW ALL THAT'S MISSING IS MY NAME.
gragory
Axelle
DONE!
OH, AND MY AGE!!...
gragory
Axelle 6 years old
WAIT... PUT SOME BLOOD AND FIRE ON THE HOUSE TOO!
gragory
... AND ON THE SUN.
IT'S A MASTERPIECE!
gragory
Axelle 6 years old

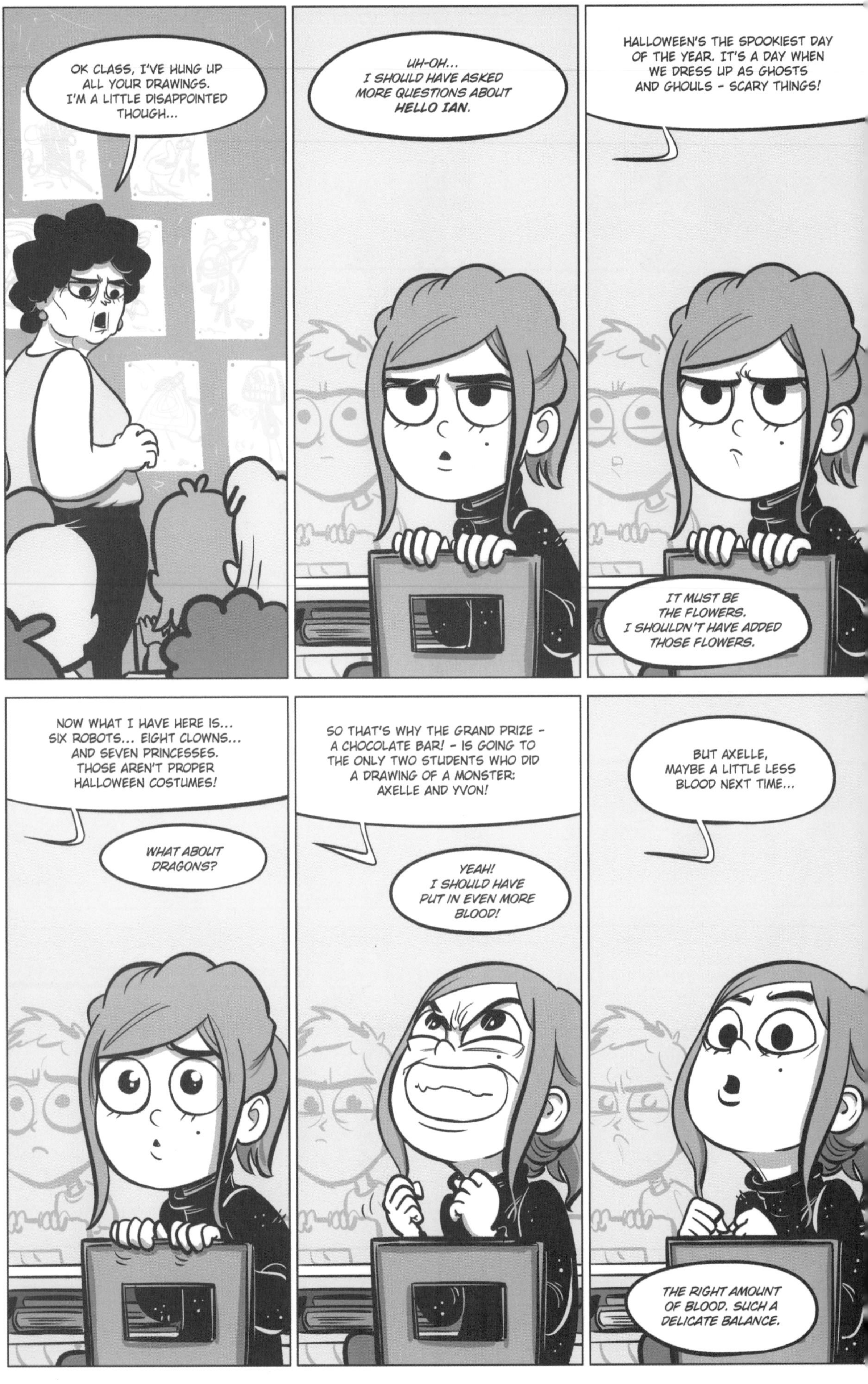
OK CLASS, I'VE HUNG UP ALL YOUR DRAWINGS. I'M A LITTLE DISAPPOINTED THOUGH...
UH-OH... I SHOULD HAVE ASKED MORE QUESTIONS ABOUT HELLO IAN.
HALLOWEEN'S THE SPOOKIEST DAY OF THE YEAR. IT'S A DAY WHEN WE DRESS UP AS GHOSTS AND GHOULS - SCARY THINGS!
IT MUST BE THE FLOWERS. I SHOULDN'T HAVE ADDED THOSE FLOWERS.
NOW WHAT I HAVE HERE IS... SIX ROBOTS... EIGHT CLOWNS... AND SEVEN PRINCESSES. THOSE AREN'T PROPER HALLOWEEN COSTUMES!
WHAT ABOUT DRAGONS?
SO THAT'S WHY THE GRAND PRIZE - A CHOCOLATE BAR! - IS GOING TO THE ONLY TWO STUDENTS WHO DID A DRAWING OF A MONSTER: AXELLE AND YVON!
YEAH! I SHOULD HAVE PUT IN EVEN MORE BLOOD!
BUT AXELLE, MAYBE A LITTLE LESS BLOOD NEXT TIME...
THE RIGHT AMOUNT OF BLOOD. SUCH A DELICATE BALANCE.

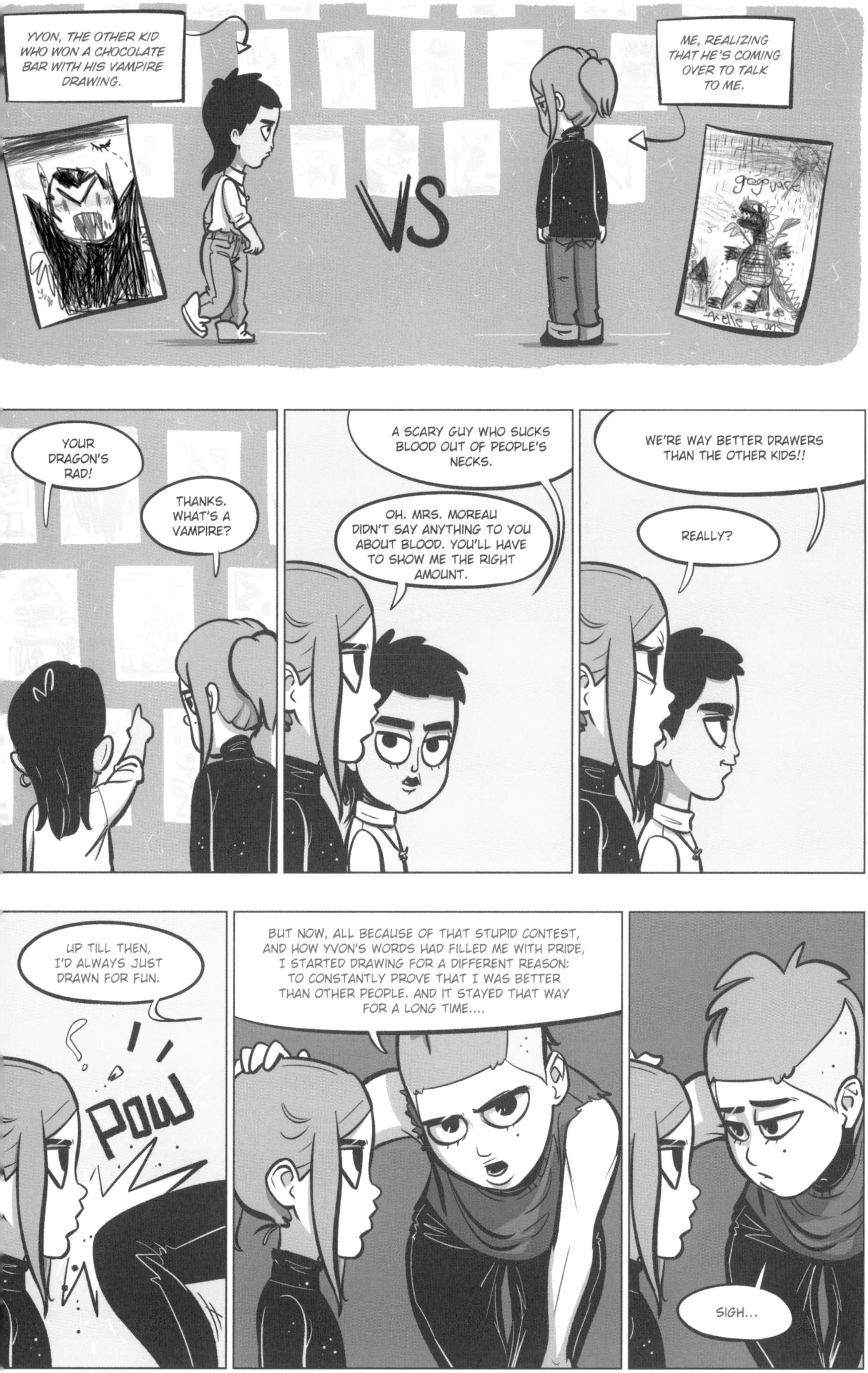
YVON, THE OTHER KID WHO WON A CHOCOLATE BAR WITH HIS VAMPIRE DRAWING.
VS
ME, REALIZING THAT HE'S COMING OVER TO TALK TO ME.
YOUR DRAGON'S RAD!
THANKS. WHAT'S A VAMPIRE?
A SCARY GUY WHO SUCKS BLOOD OUT OF PEOPLE'S NECKS.
OH. MRS. MOREAU DIDN'T SAY ANYTHING TO YOU ABOUT BLOOD. YOU'LL HAVE TO SHOW ME THE RIGHT AMOUNT.
WE'RE WAY BETTER DRAWERS THAN THE OTHER KIDS!!
REALLY?
UP TILL THEN, I'D ALWAYS JUST DRAWN FOR FUN.
POW
BUT NOW, ALL BECAUSE OF THAT STUPID CONTEST, AND HOW YVON'S WORDS HAD FILLED ME WITH PRIDE, I STARTED DRAWING FOR A DIFFERENT REASON: TO CONSTANTLY PROVE THAT I WAS BETTER THAN OTHER PEOPLE. AND IT STAYED THAT WAY FOR A LONG TIME....
SIGH...

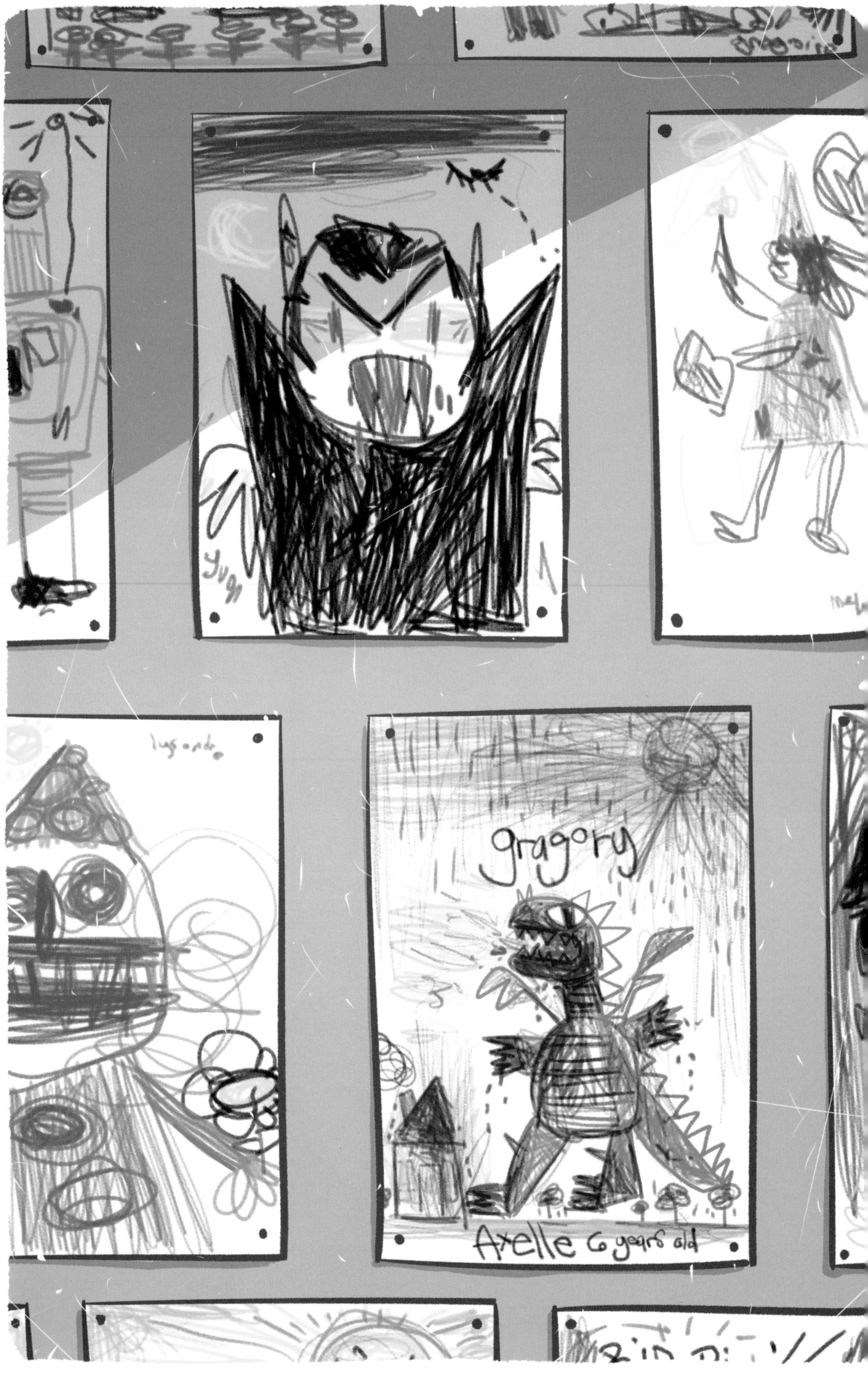
gragory
Axelle 6 years old

HEY DAVID, YOU NERVOUS ABOUT GOING UP ON STAGE?

I DUNNO. MAYBE A LITTLE?

HEY, ISN'T THAT YOUR SISTER UP FRONT? THE ONE WHO'S A FOOT TALLER THAN THE WHOLE CLASS?

YEAH.

IT LOOKS LIKE SHE'S SINGING A DIFFERENT SONG THAN EVERYONE ELSE.

♪ I WAS SITTING IN ...NE NIGHT ♪

BABABABABA!!

WHEN MY EYES ...

A MONSTER AND SUDDEN

HE DID

DING BING BONG CLING CLONG

HEY, YOU, LOOK! IT'S MY BIG BROTHER.

MY NAME'S YVON.

AND THAT'S THE NEIGHBOR GIRL WHO I CAN'T UNDERSTAND WHEN SHE TALKS!

I'S GONNA TELL Y'ALL THE STORY OF THE GHOST WITHA EYES THAT PEE BLOOD! SEEYA, ONE DAY - NOT TWO DAYS, MIND YA - THERE WAS A LIIIITTLE BOY WHO NEVER STOPPED RUNNING ROUND, DAY 'N NIGHT.

SHE TALKS JUST LIKE MY GRAMPA...

DOES YOUR GRAMPA DRIVE A BUS, VON?

"Y-VON," AND NO.

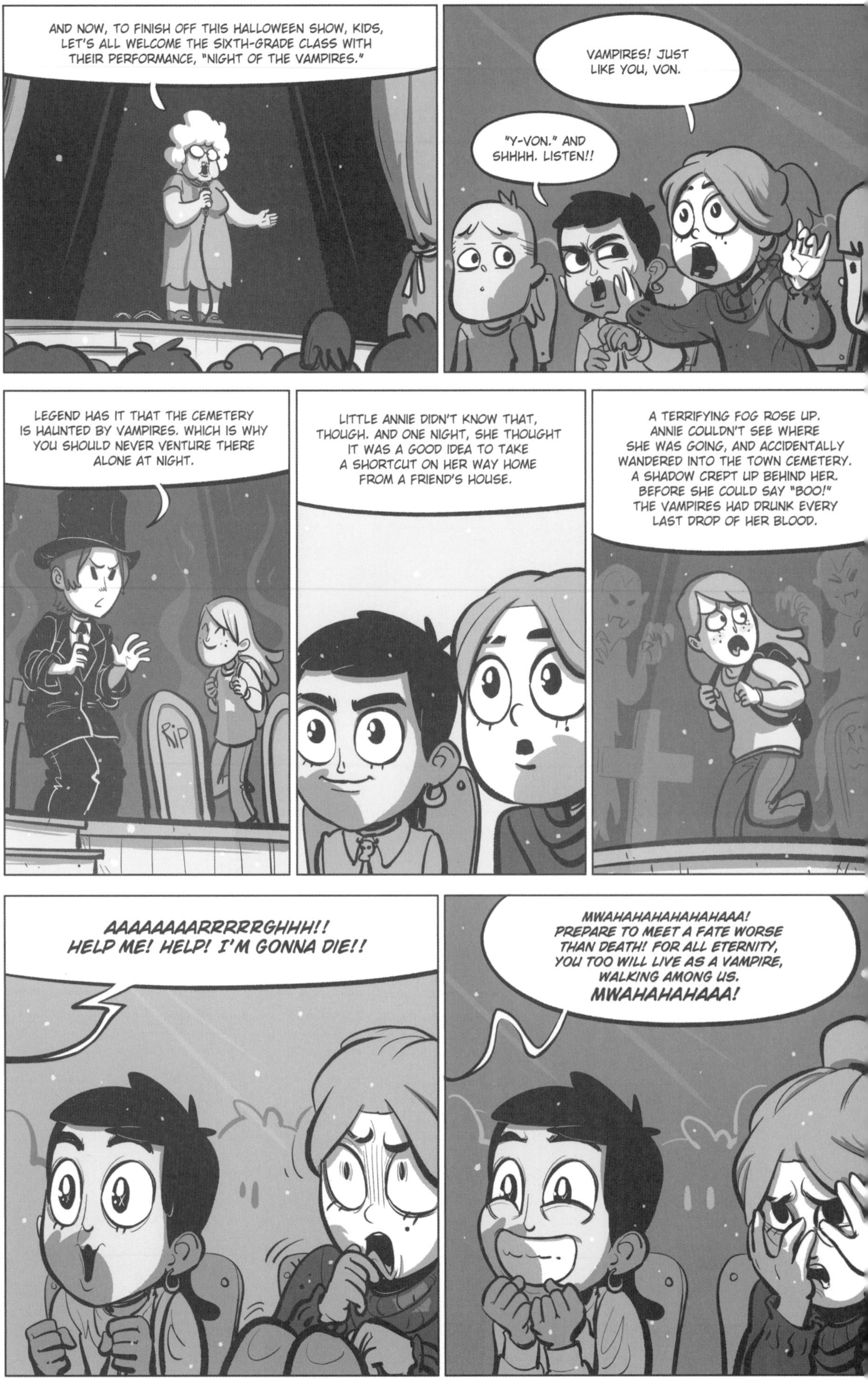

AND NOW, TO FINISH OFF THIS HALLOWEEN SHOW, KIDS, LET'S ALL WELCOME THE SIXTH-GRADE CLASS WITH THEIR PERFORMANCE, "NIGHT OF THE VAMPIRES."
VAMPIRES! JUST LIKE YOU, VON.
"Y-VON." AND SHHHH. LISTEN!!
LEGEND HAS IT THAT THE CEMETERY IS HAUNTED BY VAMPIRES. WHICH IS WHY YOU SHOULD NEVER VENTURE THERE ALONE AT NIGHT.
RIP
LITTLE ANNIE DIDN'T KNOW THAT, THOUGH. AND ONE NIGHT, SHE THOUGHT IT WAS A GOOD IDEA TO TAKE A SHORTCUT ON HER WAY HOME FROM A FRIEND'S HOUSE.
A TERRIFYING FOG ROSE UP. ANNIE COULDN'T SEE WHERE SHE WAS GOING, AND ACCIDENTALLY WANDERED INTO THE TOWN CEMETERY. A SHADOW CREPT UP BEHIND HER. BEFORE SHE COULD SAY "BOO!" THE VAMPIRES HAD DRUNK EVERY LAST DROP OF HER BLOOD.
AAAAAAAARRRRRGHHH!! HELP ME! HELP! I'M GONNA DIE!!
MWAHAHAHAHAHAHAAA! PREPARE TO MEET A FATE WORSE THAN DEATH! FOR ALL ETERNITY, YOU TOO WILL LIVE AS A VAMPIRE, WALKING AMONG US. MWAHAHAHAAA!

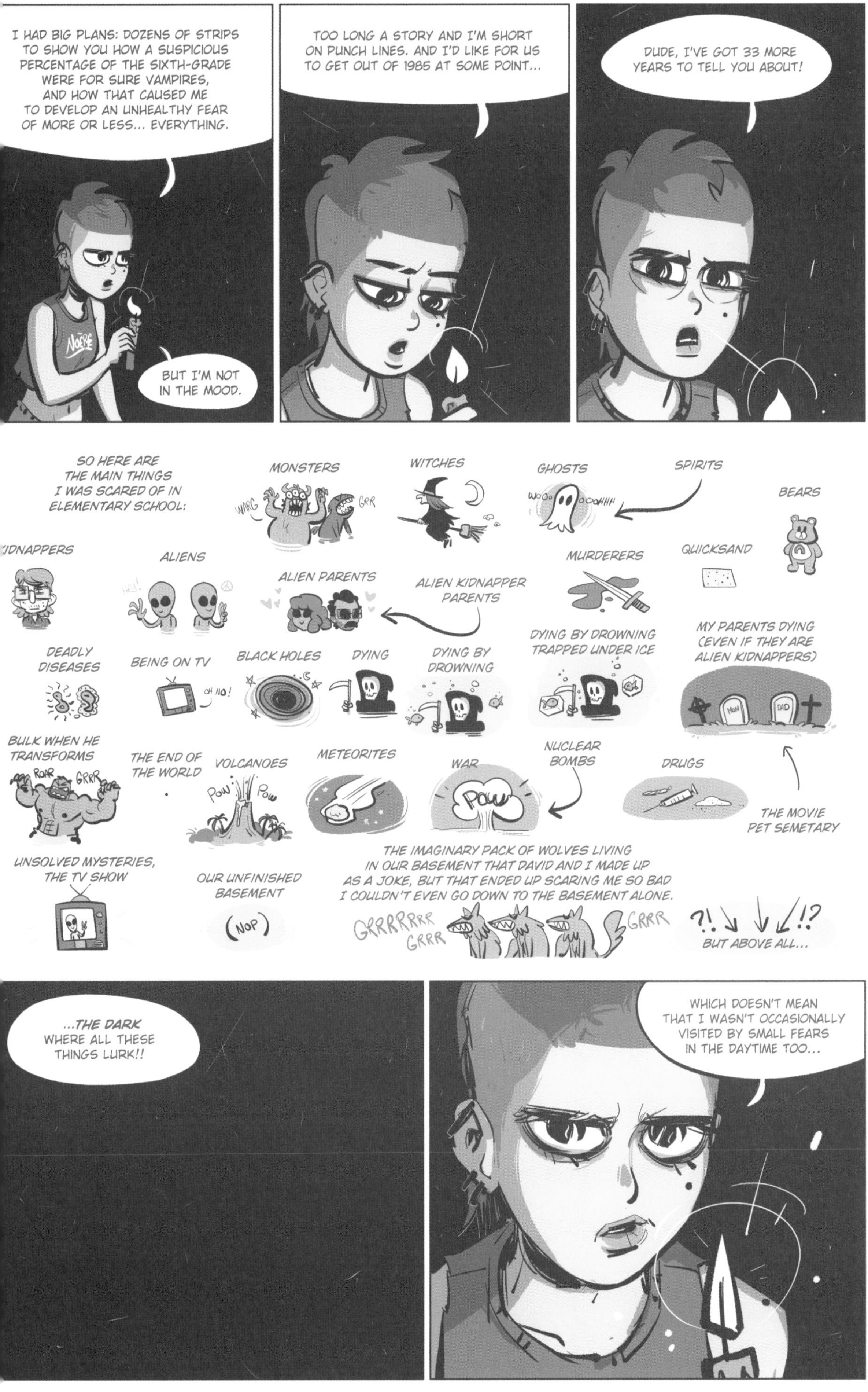

I HAD BIG PLANS: DOZENS OF STRIPS TO SHOW YOU HOW A SUSPICIOUS PERCENTAGE OF THE SIXTH-GRADE WERE FOR SURE VAMPIRES, AND HOW THAT CAUSED ME TO DEVELOP AN UNHEALTHY FEAR OF MORE OR LESS... EVERYTHING.
NOËRE
BUT I'M NOT IN THE MOOD.
TOO LONG A STORY AND I'M SHORT ON PUNCH LINES. AND I'D LIKE FOR US TO GET OUT OF 1985 AT SOME POINT...
DUDE, I'VE GOT 33 MORE YEARS TO TELL YOU ABOUT!
SO HERE ARE THE MAIN THINGS I WAS SCARED OF IN ELEMENTARY SCHOOL:
MONSTERS
WARG
GRR
WITCHES
GHOSTS
WOOO
OOOHHH
SPIRITS
BEARS
IDNAPPERS
ALIENS
HEY!
ALIEN PARENTS
ALIEN KIDNAPPER PARENTS
MURDERERS
QUICKSAND
DEADLY DISEASES
BEING ON TV
OH NO!
BLACK HOLES
DYING
DYING BY DROWNING
DYING BY DROWNING TRAPPED UNDER ICE
MY PARENTS DYING (EVEN IF THEY ARE ALIEN KIDNAPPERS)
MOM
DAD
BULK WHEN HE TRANSFORMS
ROAR
GRRR
THE END OF THE WORLD
VOLCANOES
POW
POW
METEORITES
WAR
POW
NUCLEAR BOMBS
DRUGS
THE MOVIE PET SEMETARY
UNSOLVED MYSTERIES, THE TV SHOW
OUR UNFINISHED BASEMENT
(NOP)
THE IMAGINARY PACK OF WOLVES LIVING IN OUR BASEMENT THAT DAVID AND I MADE UP AS A JOKE, BUT THAT ENDED UP SCARING ME SO BAD I COULDN'T EVEN GO DOWN TO THE BASEMENT ALONE.
GRRRRRRR
GRRR
GRRR
?!
!?
BUT ABOVE ALL...
...THE DARK WHERE ALL THESE THINGS LURK!!
WHICH DOESN'T MEAN THAT I WASN'T OCCASIONALLY VISITED BY SMALL FEARS IN THE DAYTIME TOO...

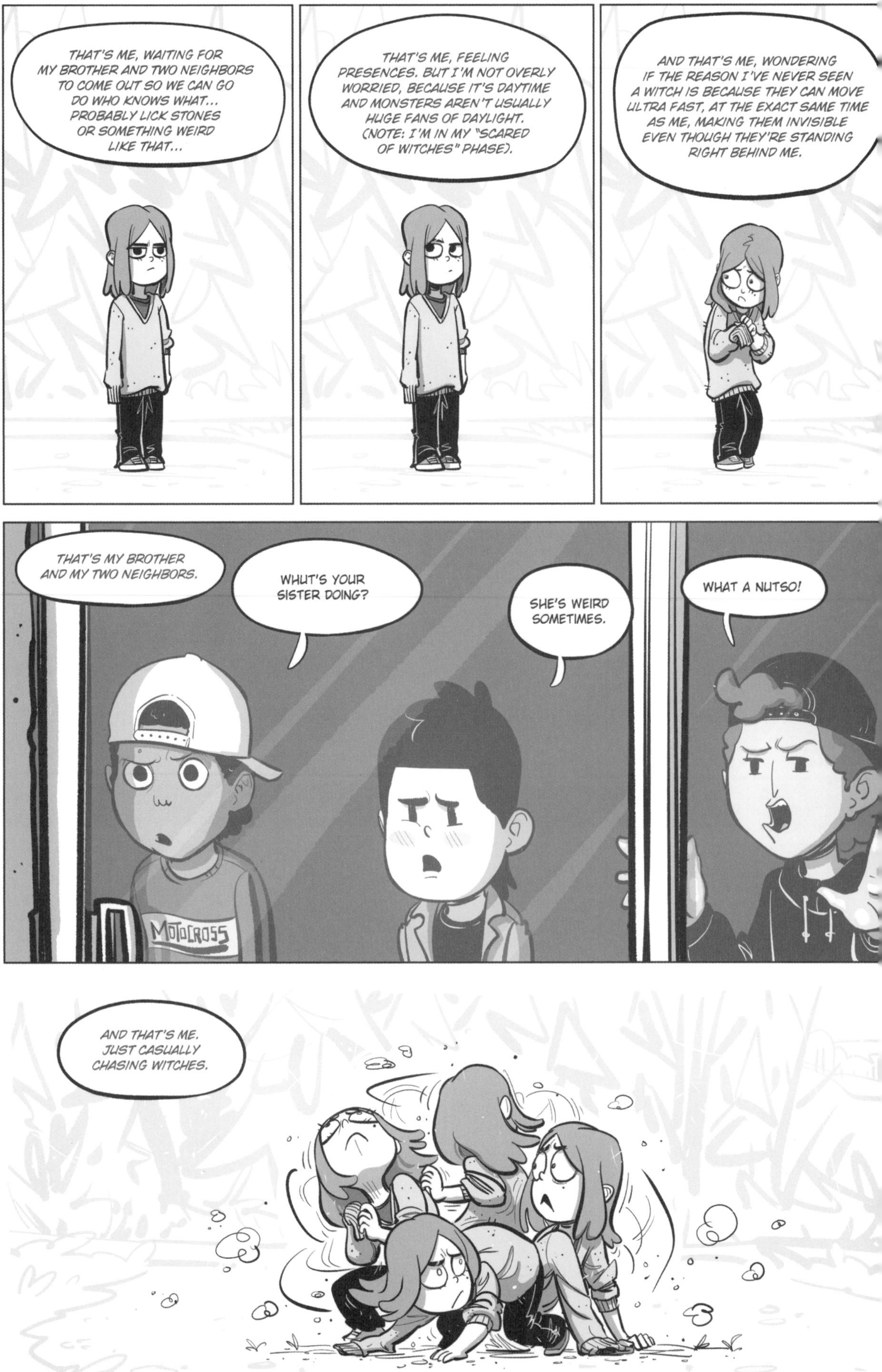
THAT'S ME, WAITING FOR MY BROTHER AND TWO NEIGHBORS TO COME OUT SO WE CAN GO DO WHO KNOWS WHAT... PROBABLY LICK STONES OR SOMETHING WEIRD LIKE THAT...
THAT'S ME, FEELING PRESENCES. BUT I'M NOT OVERLY WORRIED, BECAUSE IT'S DAYTIME AND MONSTERS AREN'T USUALLY HUGE FANS OF DAYLIGHT. (NOTE: I'M IN MY "SCARED OF WITCHES" PHASE).
AND THAT'S ME, WONDERING IF THE REASON I'VE NEVER SEEN A WITCH IS BECAUSE THEY CAN MOVE ULTRA FAST, AT THE EXACT SAME TIME AS ME, MAKING THEM INVISIBLE EVEN THOUGH THEY'RE STANDING RIGHT BEHIND ME.
THAT'S MY BROTHER AND MY TWO NEIGHBORS.
WHUT'S YOUR SISTER DOING?
SHE'S WEIRD SOMETIMES.
WHAT A NUTSO!
MOTOCROSS
AND THAT'S ME. JUST CASUALLY CHASING WITCHES.

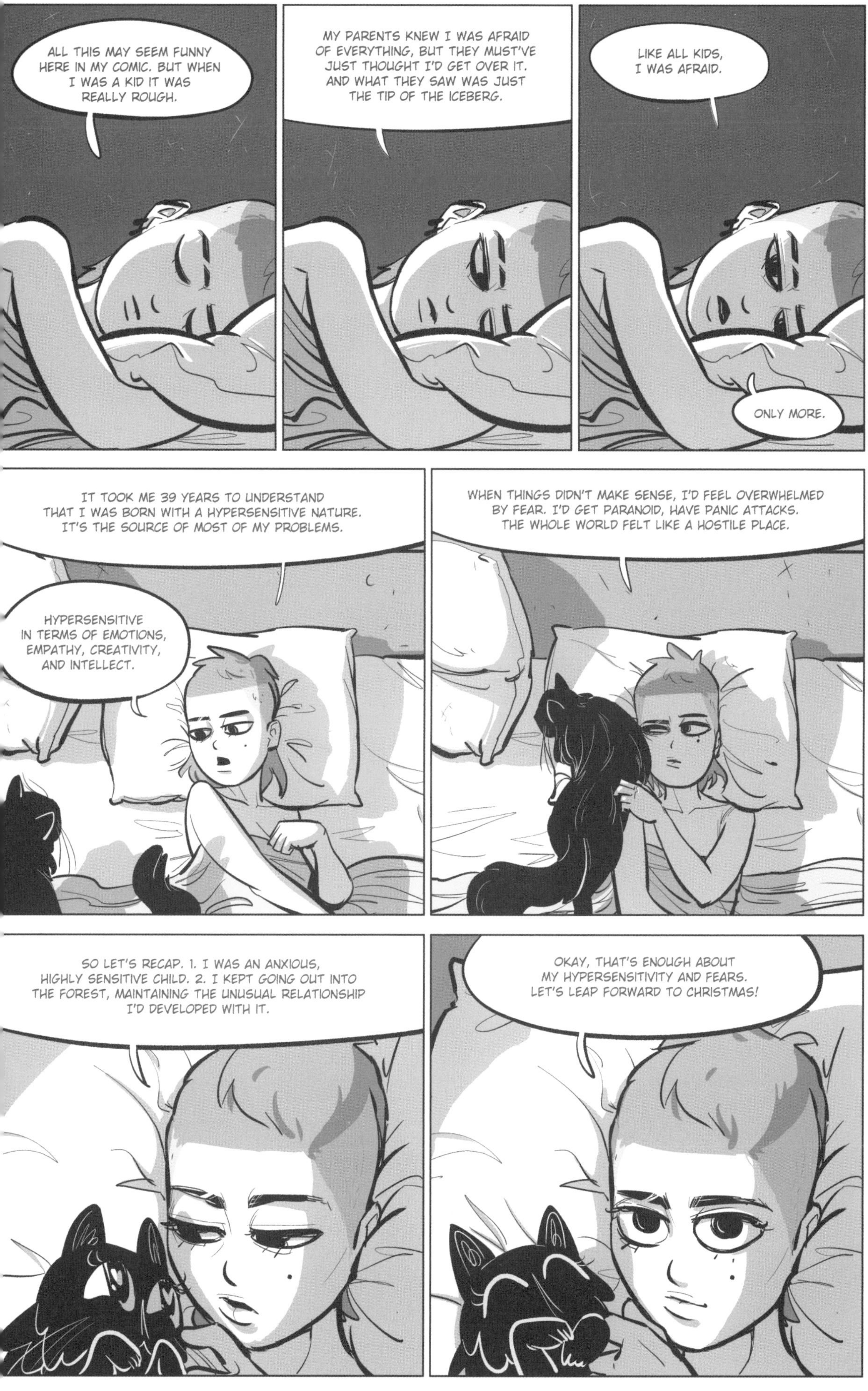
ALL THIS MAY SEEM FUNNY HERE IN MY COMIC. BUT WHEN I WAS A KID IT WAS REALLY ROUGH.
MY PARENTS KNEW I WAS AFRAID OF EVERYTHING, BUT THEY MUST'VE JUST THOUGHT I'D GET OVER IT. AND WHAT THEY SAW WAS JUST THE TIP OF THE ICEBERG.
LIKE ALL KIDS, I WAS AFRAID.
ONLY MORE.
IT TOOK ME 39 YEARS TO UNDERSTAND THAT I WAS BORN WITH A HYPERSENSITIVE NATURE. IT'S THE SOURCE OF MOST OF MY PROBLEMS.
HYPERSENSITIVE IN TERMS OF EMOTIONS, EMPATHY, CREATIVITY, AND INTELLECT.
WHEN THINGS DIDN'T MAKE SENSE, I'D FEEL OVERWHELMED BY FEAR. I'D GET PARANOID, HAVE PANIC ATTACKS. THE WHOLE WORLD FELT LIKE A HOSTILE PLACE.
SO LET'S RECAP. 1. I WAS AN ANXIOUS, HIGHLY SENSITIVE CHILD. 2. I KEPT GOING OUT INTO THE FOREST, MAINTAINING THE UNUSUAL RELATIONSHIP I'D DEVELOPED WITH IT.
OKAY, THAT'S ENOUGH ABOUT MY HYPERSENSITIVITY AND FEARS. LET'S LEAP FORWARD TO CHRISTMAS!

CHAPTER IV

THE CHRISTMAS CATALOG

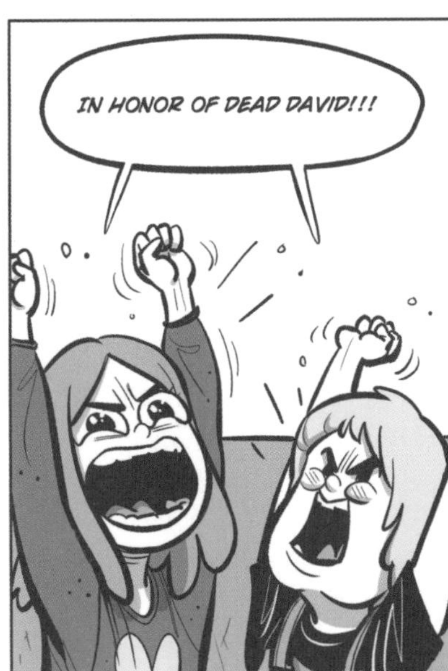
IN HONOR OF DEAD DAVID!!!

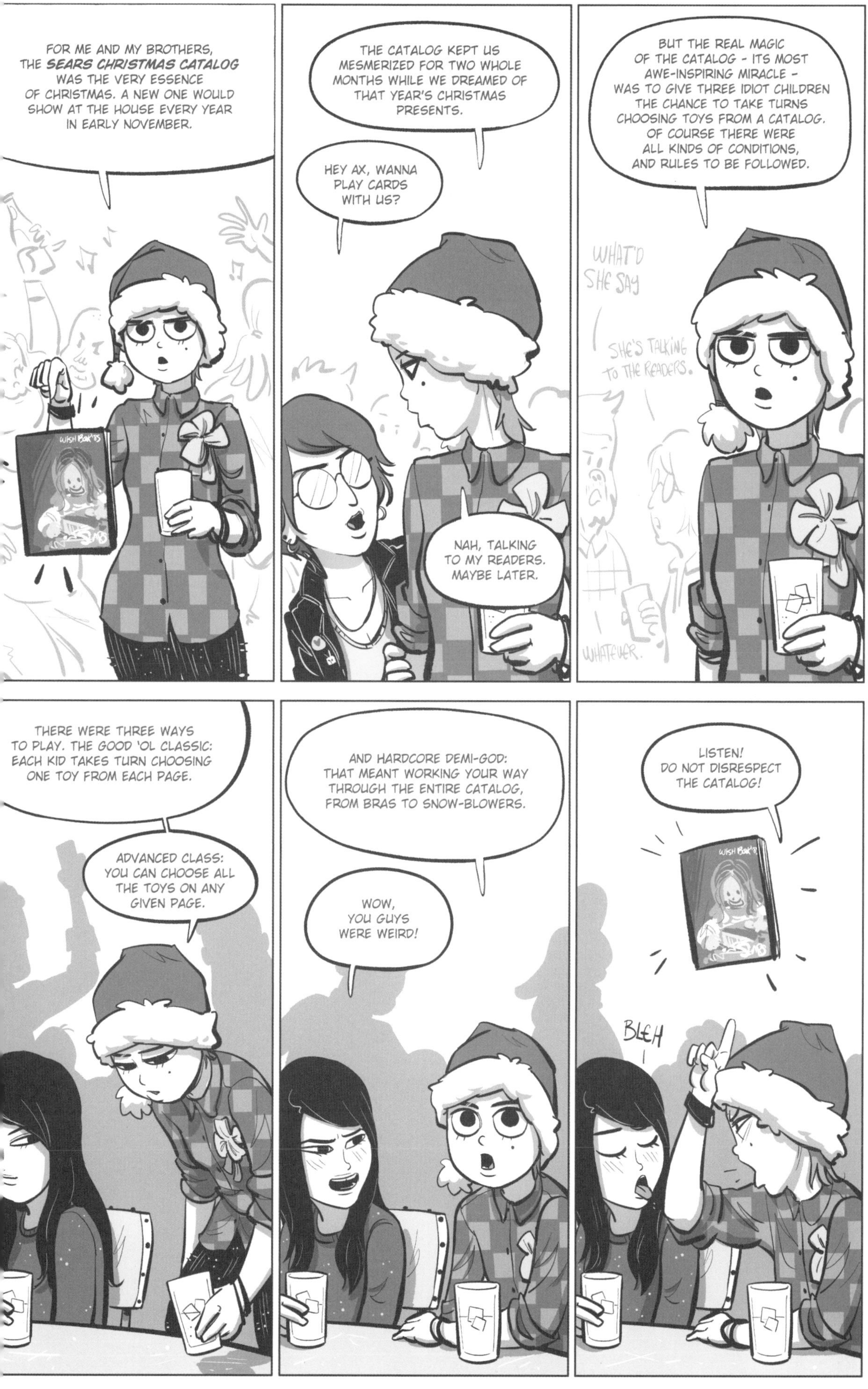
FOR ME AND MY BROTHERS, THE SEARS CHRISTMAS CATALOG WAS THE VERY ESSENCE OF CHRISTMAS. A NEW ONE WOULD SHOW AT THE HOUSE EVERY YEAR IN EARLY NOVEMBER.
THE CATALOG KEPT US MESMERIZED FOR TWO WHOLE MONTHS WHILE WE DREAMED OF THAT YEAR'S CHRISTMAS PRESENTS.
HEY AX, WANNA PLAY CARDS WITH US?
NAH, TALKING TO MY READERS. MAYBE LATER.
BUT THE REAL MAGIC OF THE CATALOG - ITS MOST AWE-INSPIRING MIRACLE - WAS TO GIVE THREE IDIOT CHILDREN THE CHANCE TO TAKE TURNS CHOOSING TOYS FROM A CATALOG. OF COURSE THERE WERE ALL KINDS OF CONDITIONS, AND RULES TO BE FOLLOWED.
WHAT'D SHE SAY
SHE'S TALKING TO THE READERS.
WHATEVER.
THERE WERE THREE WAYS TO PLAY. THE GOOD 'OL CLASSIC: EACH KID TAKES TURN CHOOSING ONE TOY FROM EACH PAGE.
ADVANCED CLASS: YOU CAN CHOOSE ALL THE TOYS ON ANY GIVEN PAGE.
AND HARDCORE DEMI-GOD: THAT MEANT WORKING YOUR WAY THROUGH THE ENTIRE CATALOG, FROM BRAS TO SNOW-BLOWERS.
WOW, YOU GUYS WERE WEIRD!
LISTEN! DO NOT DISRESPECT THE CATALOG!
BLEH

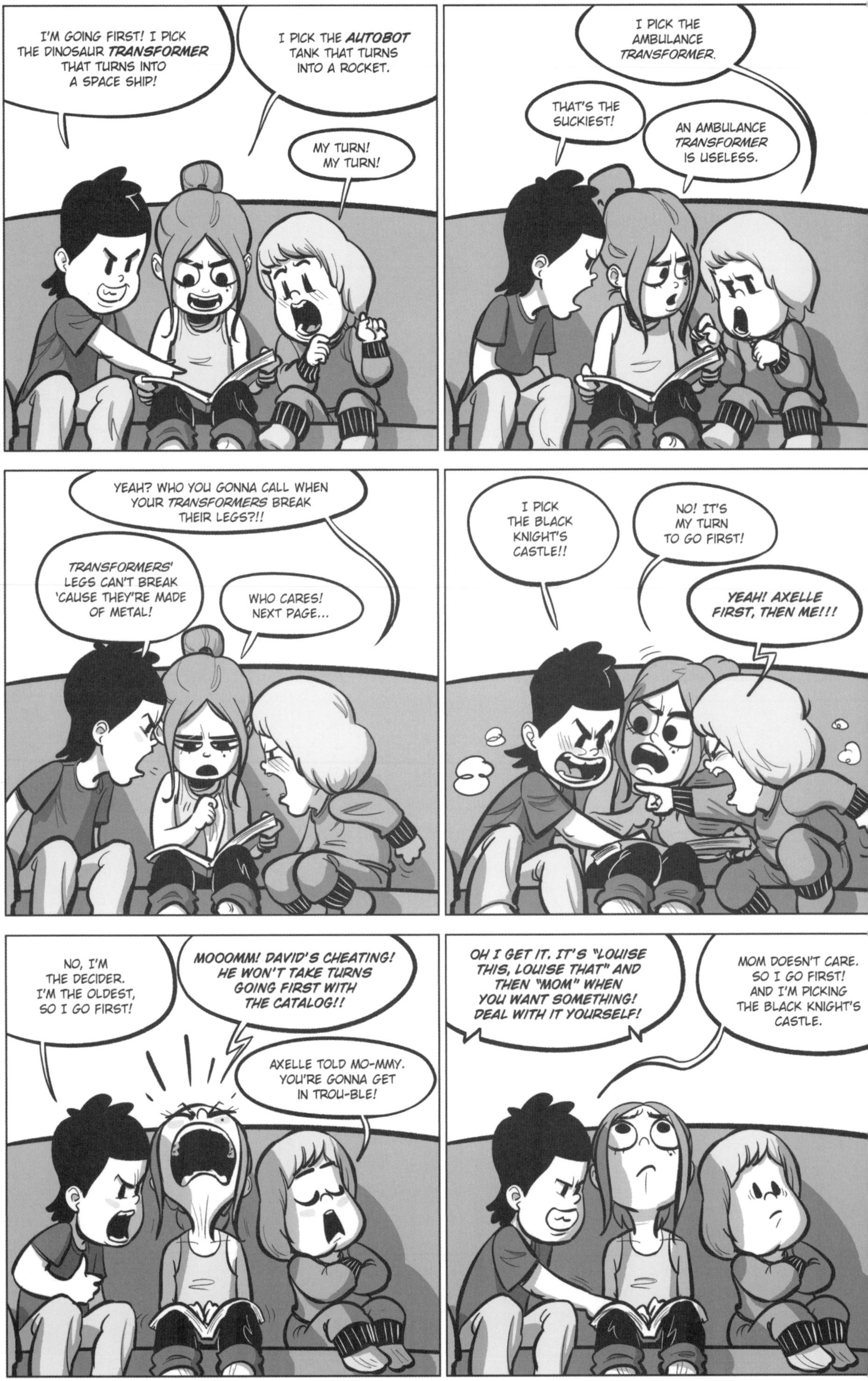
I'M GOING FIRST! I PICK THE DINOSAUR TRANSFORMER THAT TURNS INTO A SPACE SHIP!
I PICK THE AUTOBOT TANK THAT TURNS INTO A ROCKET.
MY TURN! MY TURN!
I PICK THE AMBULANCE TRANSFORMER.
THAT'S THE SUCKIEST!
AN AMBULANCE TRANSFORMER IS USELESS.
YEAH? WHO YOU GONNA CALL WHEN YOUR TRANSFORMERS BREAK THEIR LEGS?!!
TRANSFORMERS' LEGS CAN'T BREAK 'CAUSE THEY'RE MADE OF METAL!
WHO CARES! NEXT PAGE...
I PICK THE BLACK KNIGHT'S CASTLE!!
NO! IT'S MY TURN TO GO FIRST!
YEAH! AXELLE FIRST, THEN ME!!!
NO, I'M THE DECIDER. I'M THE OLDEST, SO I GO FIRST!
MOOOMM! DAVID'S CHEATING! HE WON'T TAKE TURNS GOING FIRST WITH THE CATALOG!!
AXELLE TOLD MO-MMY. YOU'RE GONNA GET IN TROU-BLE!
OH I GET IT. IT'S "LOUISE THIS, LOUISE THAT" AND THEN "MOM" WHEN YOU WANT SOMETHING! DEAL WITH IT YOURSELF!
MOM DOESN'T CARE. SO I GO FIRST! AND I'M PICKING THE BLACK KNIGHT'S CASTLE.

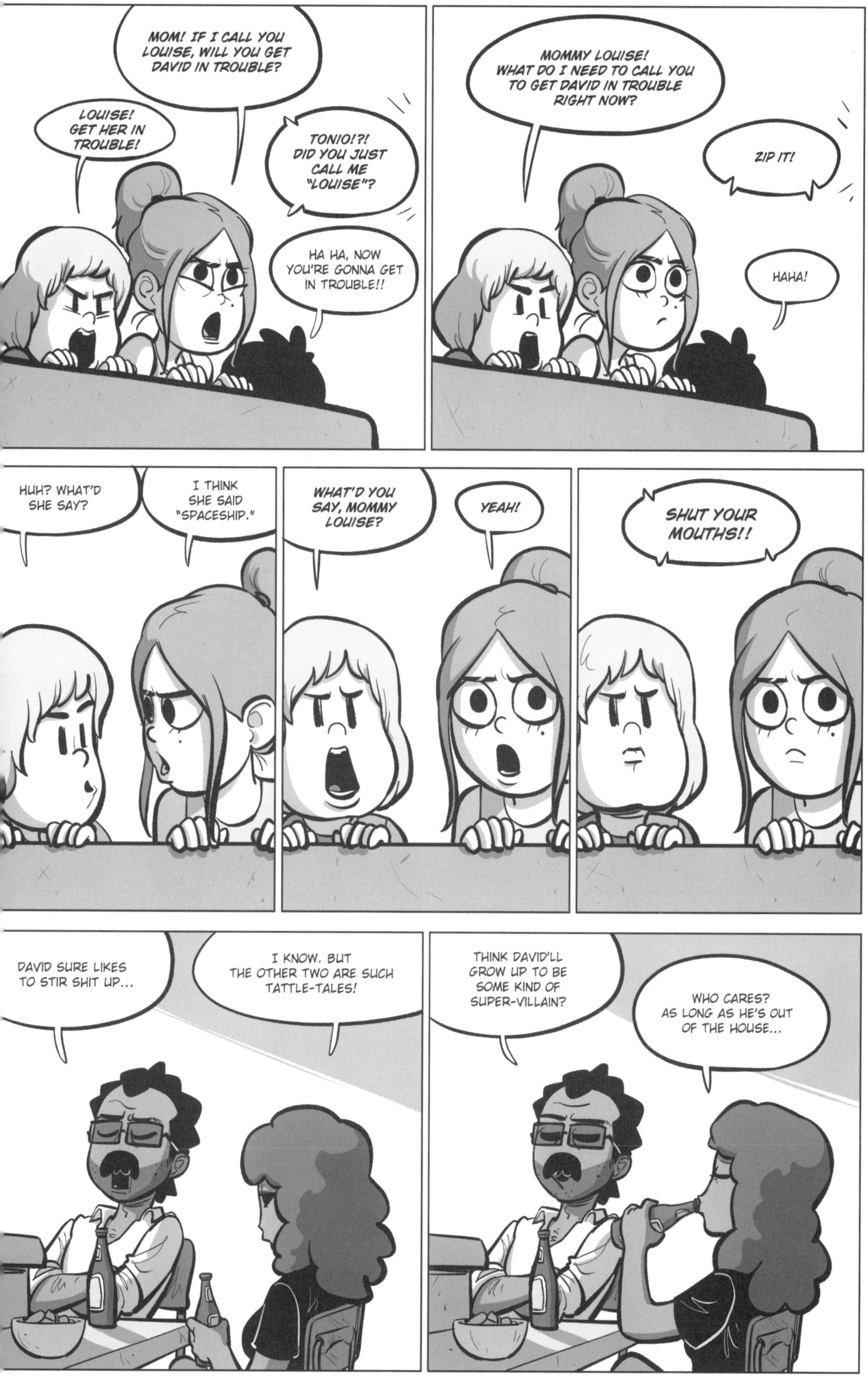
MOM! IF I CALL YOU LOUISE, WILL YOU GET DAVID IN TROUBLE?
LOUISE! GET HER IN TROUBLE!
TONIO!?! DID YOU JUST CALL ME "LOUISE"?
HA HA, NOW YOU'RE GONNA GET IN TROUBLE!!
MOMMY LOUISE! WHAT DO I NEED TO CALL YOU TO GET DAVID IN TROUBLE RIGHT NOW?
ZIP IT!
HAHA!
HUH? WHAT'D SHE SAY?
I THINK SHE SAID "SPACESHIP."
WHAT'D YOU SAY, MOMMY LOUISE?
YEAH!
SHUT YOUR MOUTHS!!
DAVID SURE LIKES TO STIR SHIT UP...
I KNOW. BUT THE OTHER TWO ARE SUCH TATTLE-TALES!
THINK DAVID'LL GROW UP TO BE SOME KIND OF SUPER-VILLAIN?
WHO CARES? AS LONG AS HE'S OUT OF THE HOUSE...

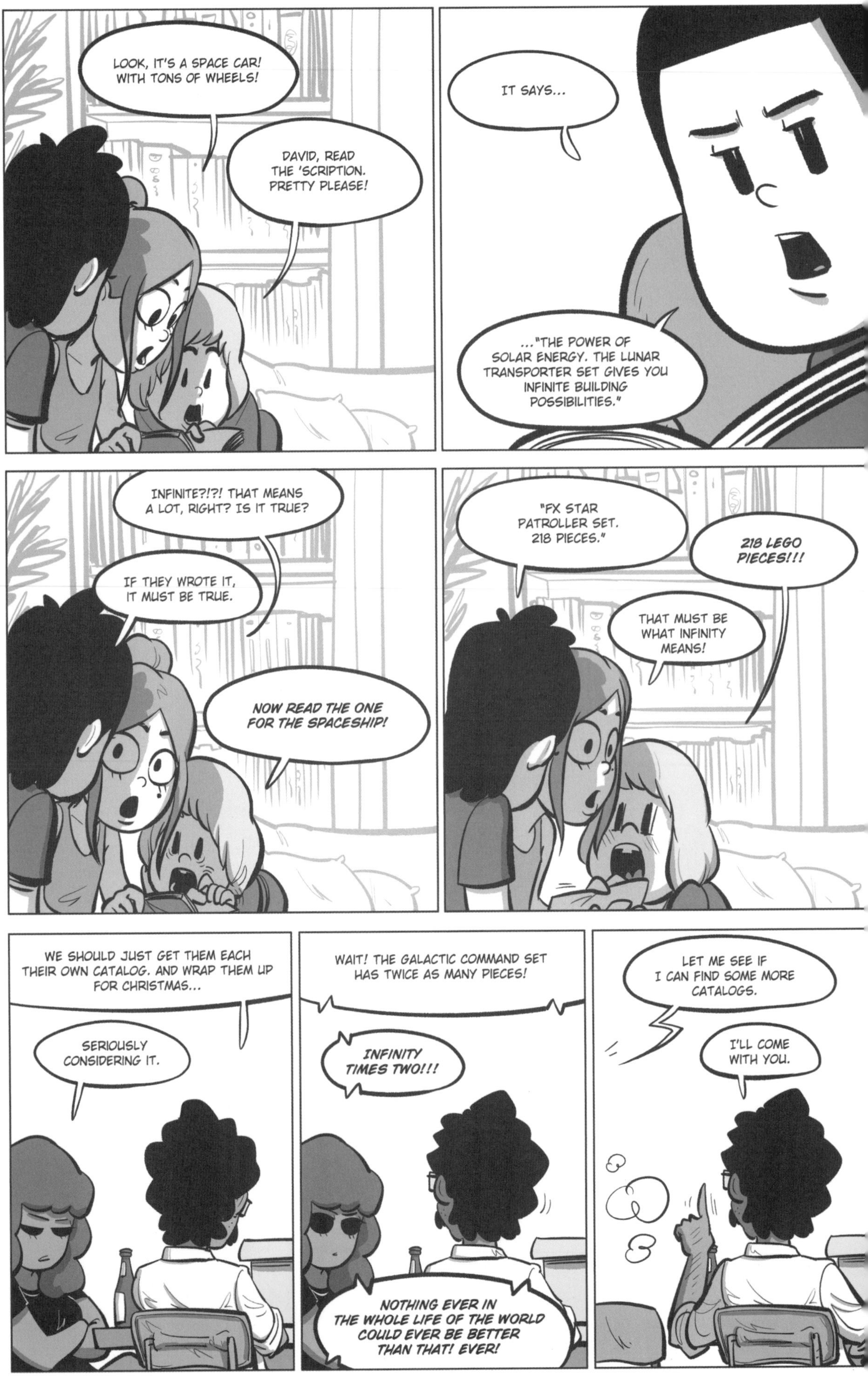
LOOK, IT'S A SPACE CAR! WITH TONS OF WHEELS!
DAVID, READ THE 'SCRIPTION. PRETTY PLEASE!
IT SAYS...
..."THE POWER OF SOLAR ENERGY. THE LUNAR TRANSPORTER SET GIVES YOU INFINITE BUILDING POSSIBILITIES."
INFINITE?!?! THAT MEANS A LOT, RIGHT? IS IT TRUE?
IF THEY WROTE IT, IT MUST BE TRUE.
NOW READ THE ONE FOR THE SPACESHIP!
"FX STAR PATROLLER SET. 218 PIECES."
218 LEGO PIECES!!!
THAT MUST BE WHAT INFINITY MEANS!
WE SHOULD JUST GET THEM EACH THEIR OWN CATALOG. AND WRAP THEM UP FOR CHRISTMAS...
SERIOUSLY CONSIDERING IT.
WAIT! THE GALACTIC COMMAND SET HAS TWICE AS MANY PIECES!
INFINITY TIMES TWO!!!
NOTHING EVER IN THE WHOLE LIFE OF THE WORLD COULD EVER BE BETTER THAN THAT! EVER!
LET ME SEE IF I CAN FIND SOME MORE CATALOGS.
I'LL COME WITH YOU.

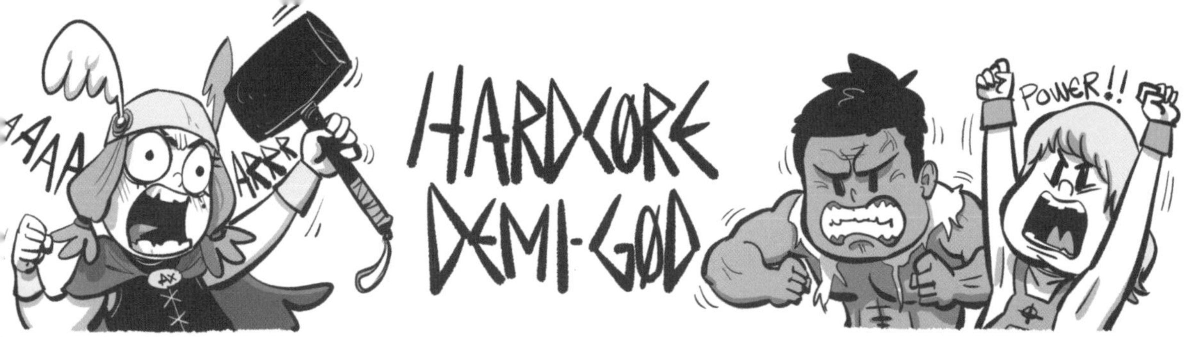
AAAA
ARRR
HARDCORE DEMI-GOD
POWER!!

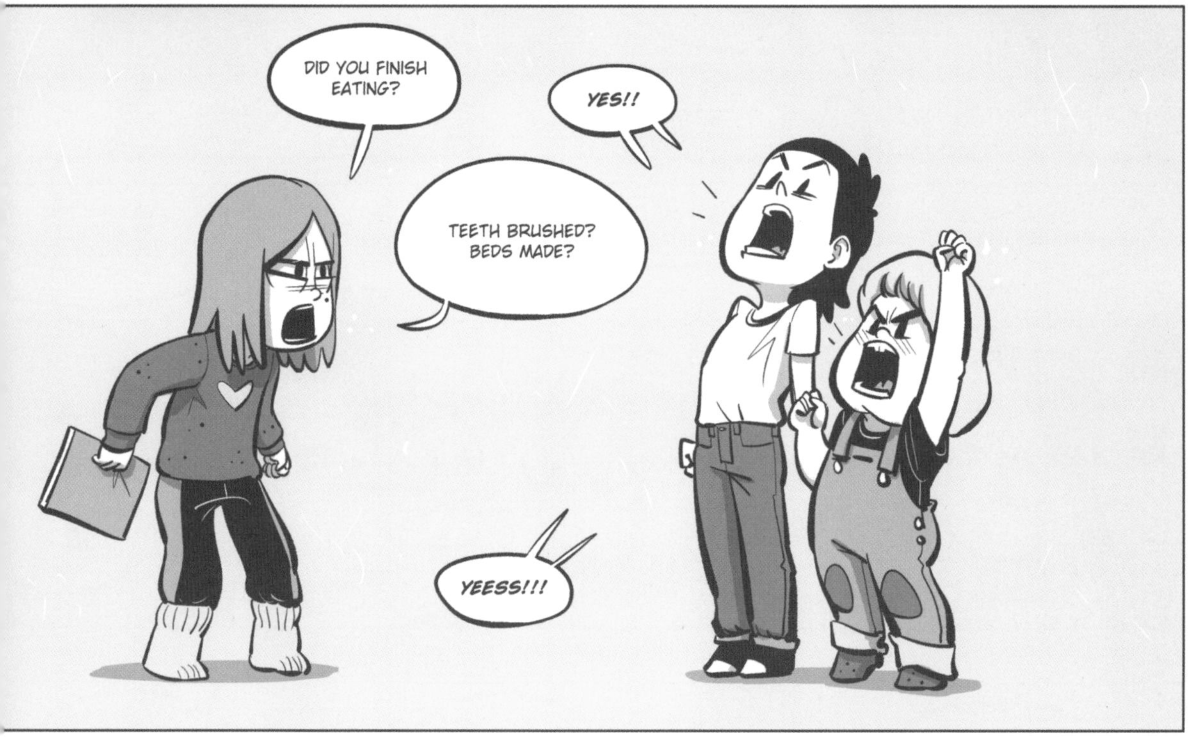
DID YOU FINISH EATING?
YES!!
TEETH BRUSHED? BEDS MADE?
YEESS!!!

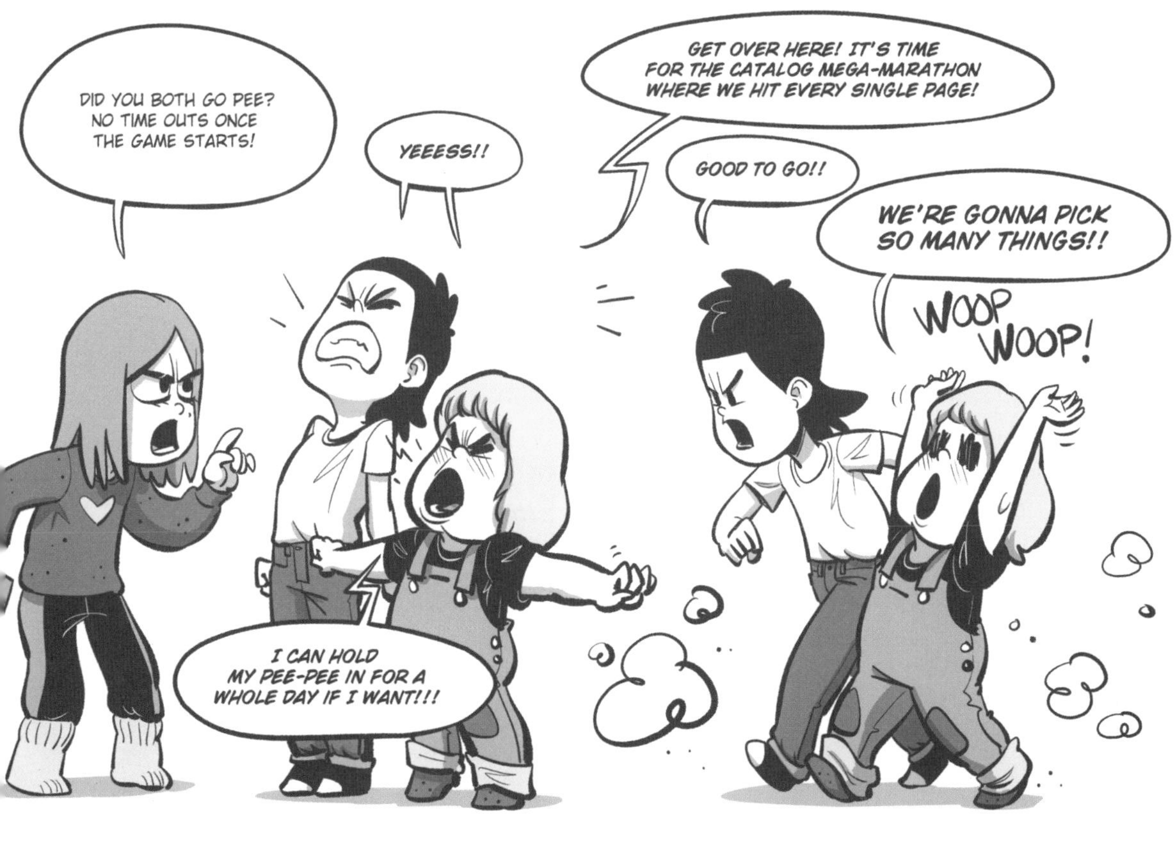
DID YOU BOTH GO PEE? NO TIME OUTS ONCE THE GAME STARTS!
YEEESS!!
I CAN HOLD MY PEE-PEE IN FOR A WHOLE DAY IF I WANT!!!
GET OVER HERE! IT'S TIME FOR THE CATALOG MEGA-MARATHON WHERE WE HIT EVERY SINGLE PAGE!
GOOD TO GO!!
WE'RE GONNA PICK SO MANY THINGS!!
WOOP WOOP!

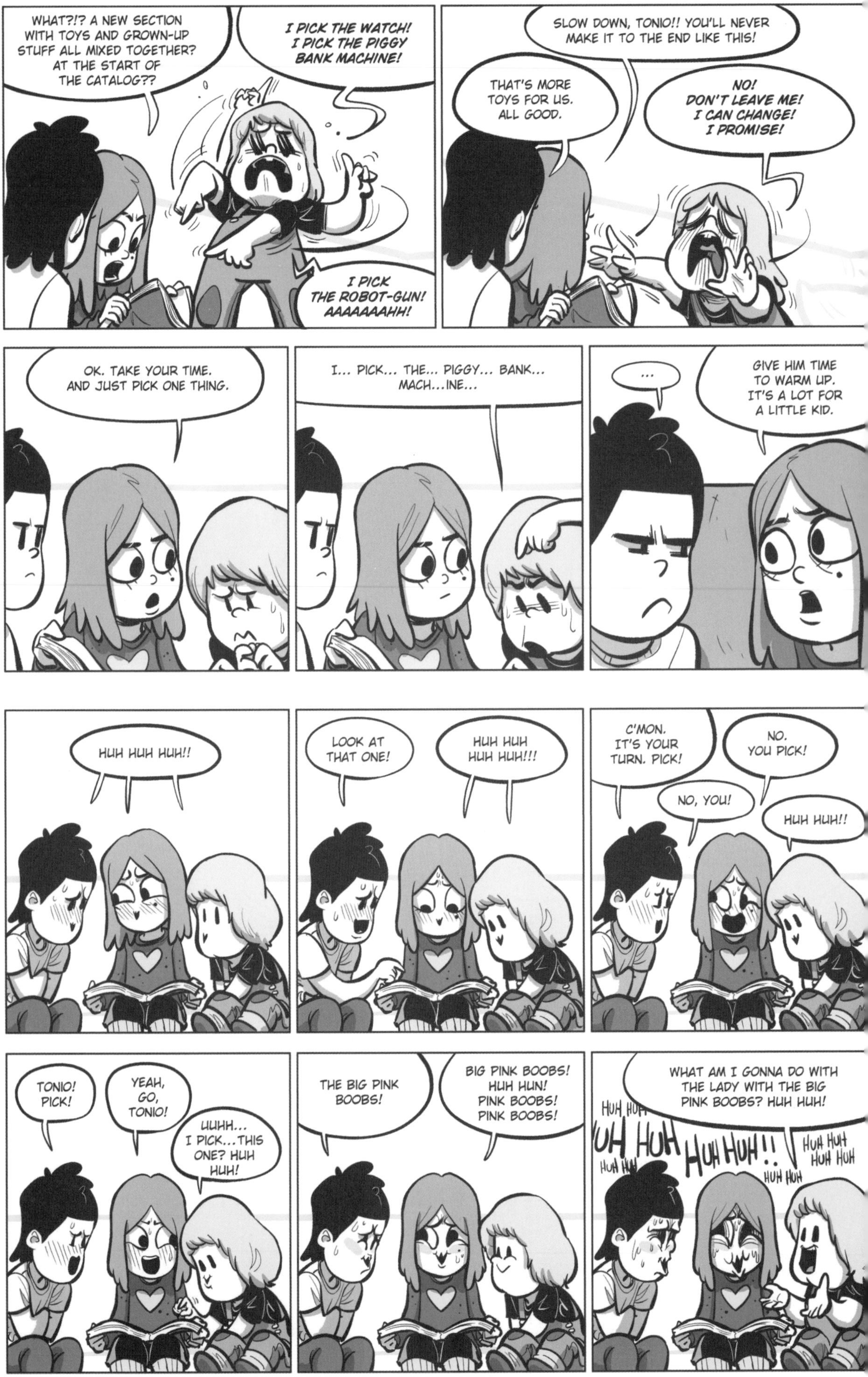
WHAT?!? A NEW SECTION WITH TOYS AND GROWN-UP STUFF ALL MIXED TOGETHER? AT THE START OF THE CATALOG??
I PICK THE WATCH! I PICK THE PIGGY BANK MACHINE!
I PICK THE ROBOT-GUN! AAAAAAAHH!
SLOW DOWN, TONIO!! YOU'LL NEVER MAKE IT TO THE END LIKE THIS!
THAT'S MORE TOYS FOR US. ALL GOOD.
NO! DON'T LEAVE ME! I CAN CHANGE! I PROMISE!
OK. TAKE YOUR TIME. AND JUST PICK ONE THING.
I... PICK... THE... PIGGY... BANK... MACH...INE...
...
GIVE HIM TIME TO WARM UP. IT'S A LOT FOR A LITTLE KID.
HUH HUH HUH!!
LOOK AT THAT ONE!
HUH HUH HUH HUH!!!
C'MON. IT'S YOUR TURN. PICK!
NO. YOU PICK!
NO, YOU!
HUH HUH!!
TONIO! PICK!
YEAH, GO, TONIO!
UUHH... I PICK...THIS ONE? HUH HUH!
THE BIG PINK BOOBS!
BIG PINK BOOBS! HUH HUH! PINK BOOBS! PINK BOOBS!
WHAT AM I GONNA DO WITH THE LADY WITH THE BIG PINK BOOBS? HUH HUH!
HUH HUH
HUH HUH
HUH HUH
HUH HUH!!
HUH HUH
HUH HUH HUH HUH

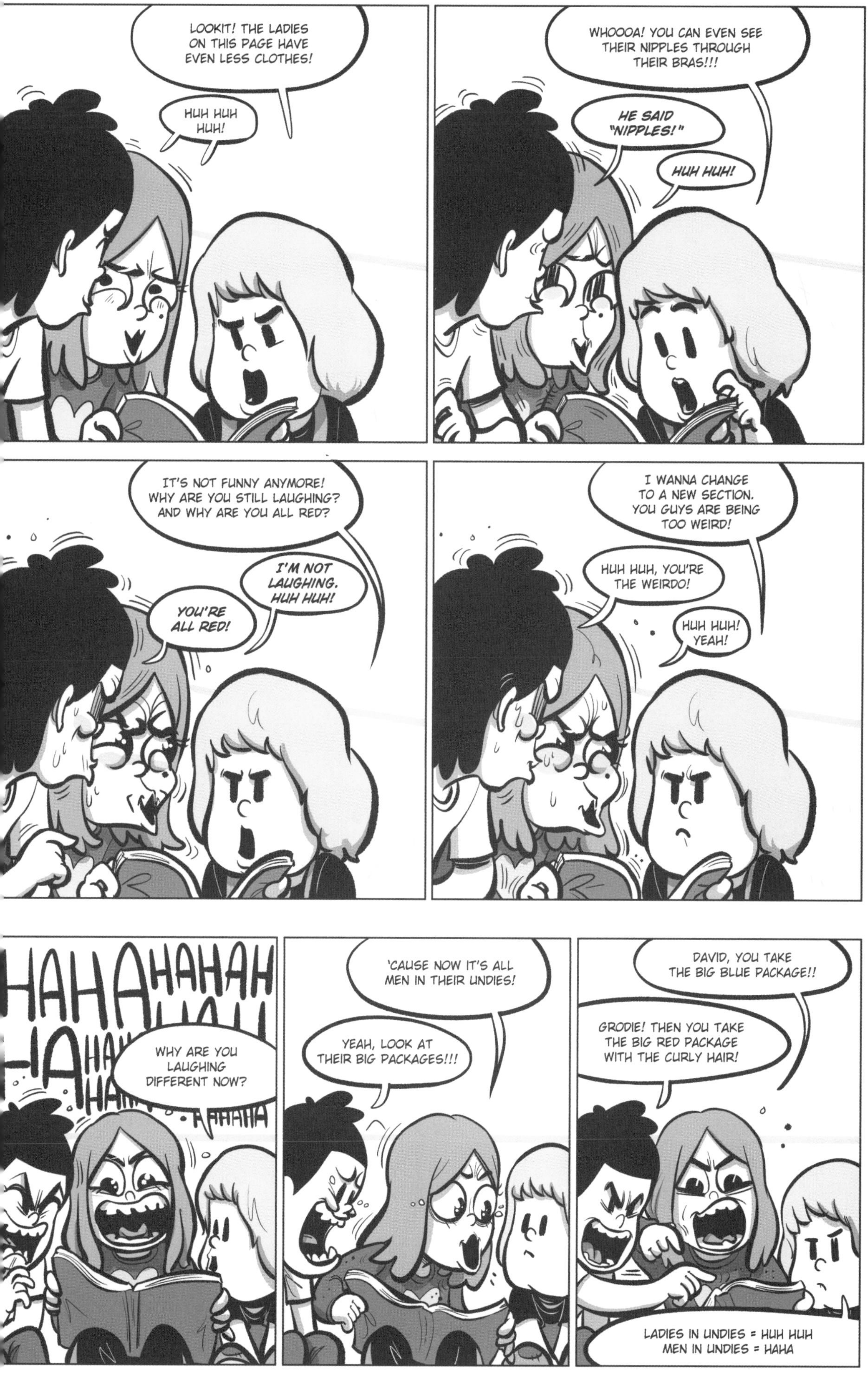
LOOKIT! THE LADIES ON THIS PAGE HAVE EVEN LESS CLOTHES!
HUH HUH HUH!
WHOOOA! YOU CAN EVEN SEE THEIR NIPPLES THROUGH THEIR BRAS!!!
HE SAID "NIPPLES!"
HUH HUH!
IT'S NOT FUNNY ANYMORE! WHY ARE YOU STILL LAUGHING? AND WHY ARE YOU ALL RED?
I'M NOT LAUGHING. HUH HUH!
YOU'RE ALL RED!
I WANNA CHANGE TO A NEW SECTION. YOU GUYS ARE BEING TOO WEIRD!
HUH HUH, YOU'RE THE WEIRDO!
HUH HUH! YEAH!
HAHAHAHAH
HAHAHAHAHAHAHAHA
WHY ARE YOU LAUGHING DIFFERENT NOW?
'CAUSE NOW IT'S ALL MEN IN THEIR UNDIES!
YEAH, LOOK AT THEIR BIG PACKAGES!!!
DAVID, YOU TAKE THE BIG BLUE PACKAGE!!
GRODIE! THEN YOU TAKE THE BIG RED PACKAGE WITH THE CURLY HAIR!
LADIES IN UNDIES = HUH HUH
MEN IN UNDIES = HAHA

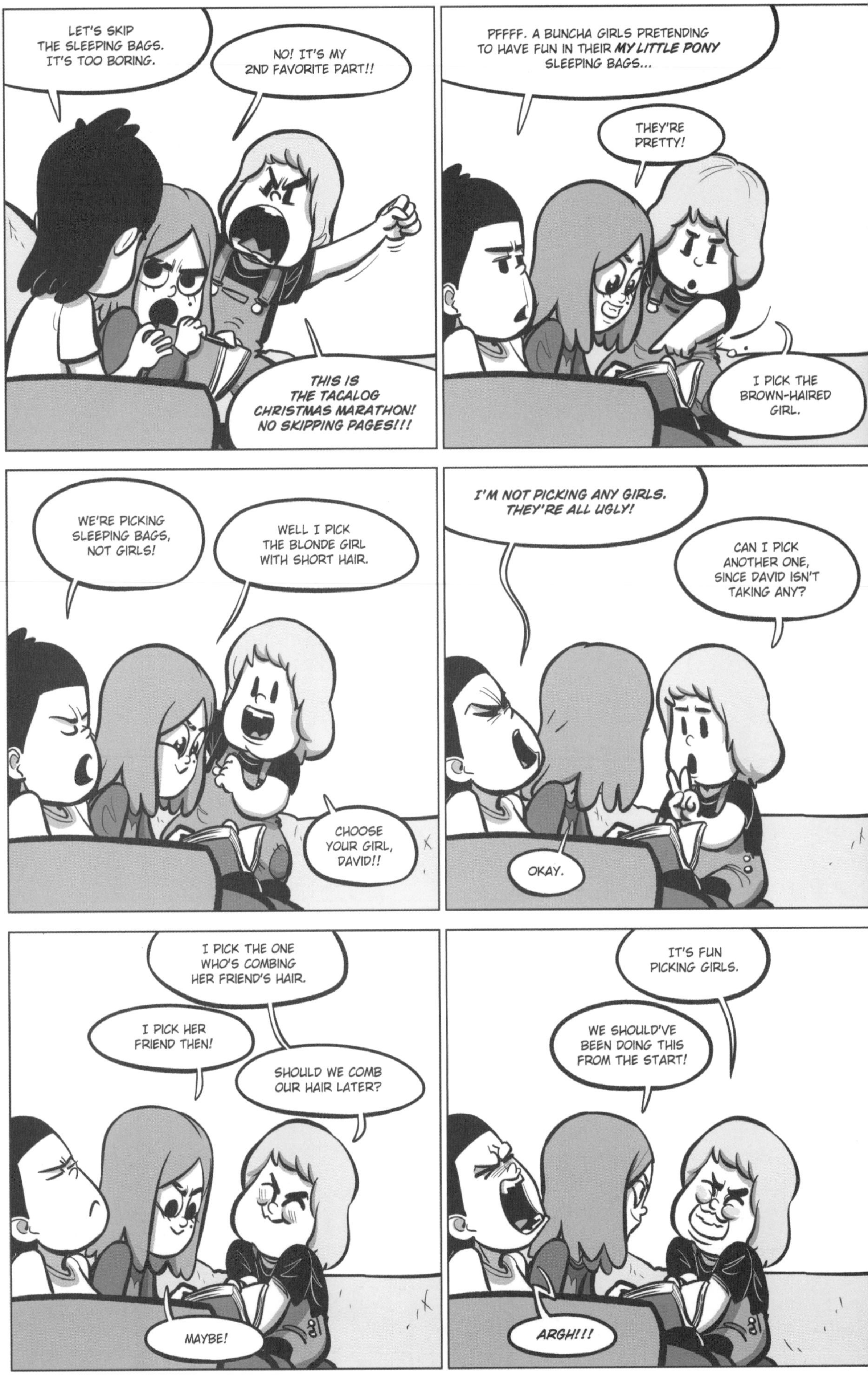
LET'S SKIP THE SLEEPING BAGS. IT'S TOO BORING.
NO! IT'S MY 2ND FAVORITE PART!!
THIS IS THE TACALOG CHRISTMAS MARATHON! NO SKIPPING PAGES!!!
PFFFF. A BUNCHA GIRLS PRETENDING TO HAVE FUN IN THEIR MY LITTLE PONY SLEEPING BAGS...
THEY'RE PRETTY!
I PICK THE BROWN-HAIRED GIRL.
WE'RE PICKING SLEEPING BAGS, NOT GIRLS!
WELL I PICK THE BLONDE GIRL WITH SHORT HAIR.
CHOOSE YOUR GIRL, DAVID!!
I'M NOT PICKING ANY GIRLS. THEY'RE ALL UGLY!
CAN I PICK ANOTHER ONE, SINCE DAVID ISN'T TAKING ANY?
OKAY.
I PICK THE ONE WHO'S COMBING HER FRIEND'S HAIR.
I PICK HER FRIEND THEN!
SHOULD WE COMB OUR HAIR LATER?
MAYBE!
IT'S FUN PICKING GIRLS.
WE SHOULD'VE BEEN DOING THIS FROM THE START!
ARGH!!!

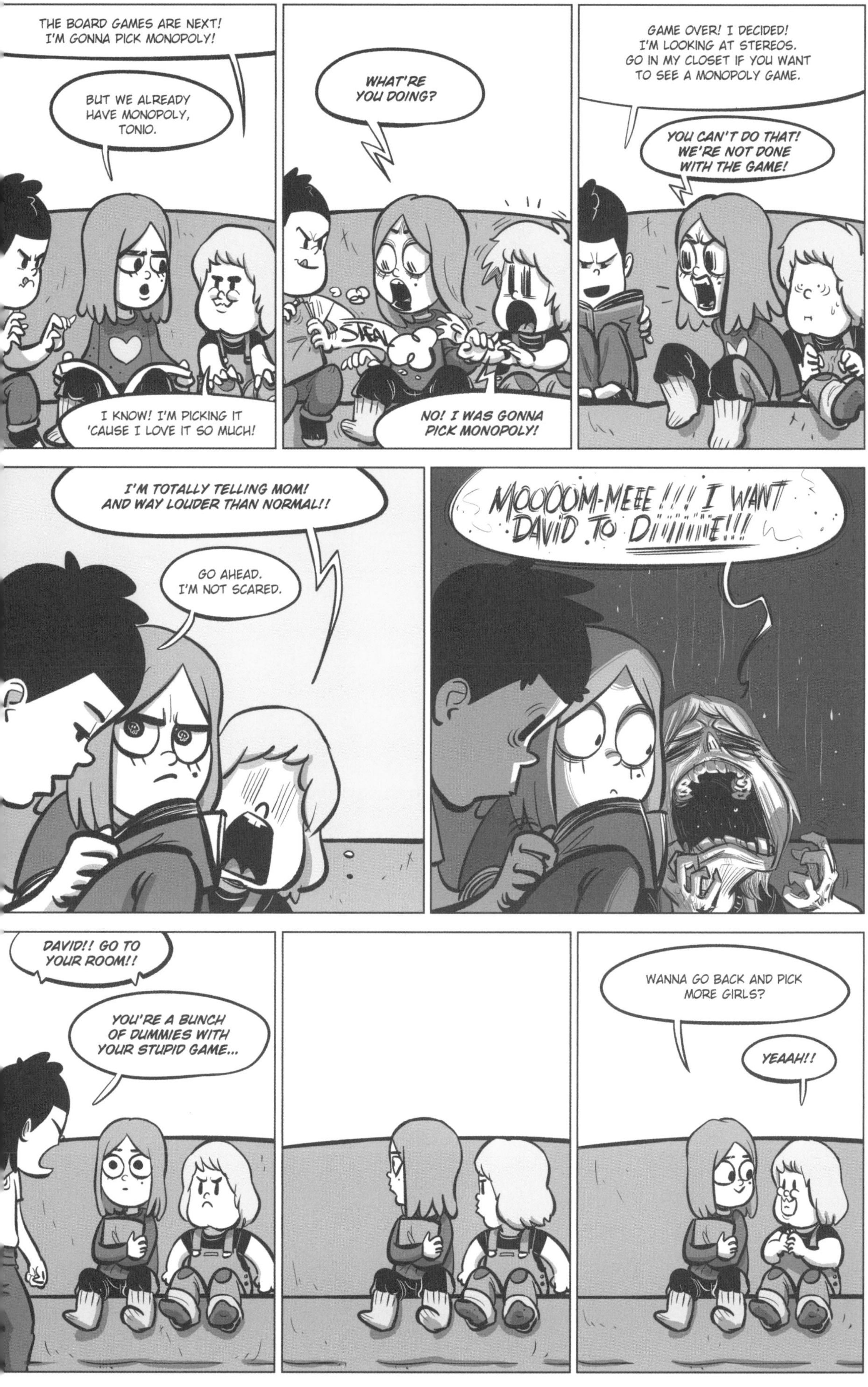
THE BOARD GAMES ARE NEXT! I'M GONNA PICK MONOPOLY!
BUT WE ALREADY HAVE MONOPOLY, TONIO.
I KNOW! I'M PICKING IT 'CAUSE I LOVE IT SO MUCH!
WHAT'RE YOU DOING?
STEAL
NO! I WAS GONNA PICK MONOPOLY!
GAME OVER! I DECIDED! I'M LOOKING AT STEREOS. GO IN MY CLOSET IF YOU WANT TO SEE A MONOPOLY GAME.
YOU CAN'T DO THAT! WE'RE NOT DONE WITH THE GAME!
I'M TOTALLY TELLING MOM! AND WAY LOUDER THAN NORMAL!!
GO AHEAD. I'M NOT SCARED.
MOOOOM-MEEE!!! I WANT DAVID TO DIIIIIIE!!!
DAVID!! GO TO YOUR ROOM!!
YOU'RE A BUNCH OF DUMMIES WITH YOUR STUPID GAME...
WANNA GO BACK AND PICK MORE GIRLS?
YEAAH!!

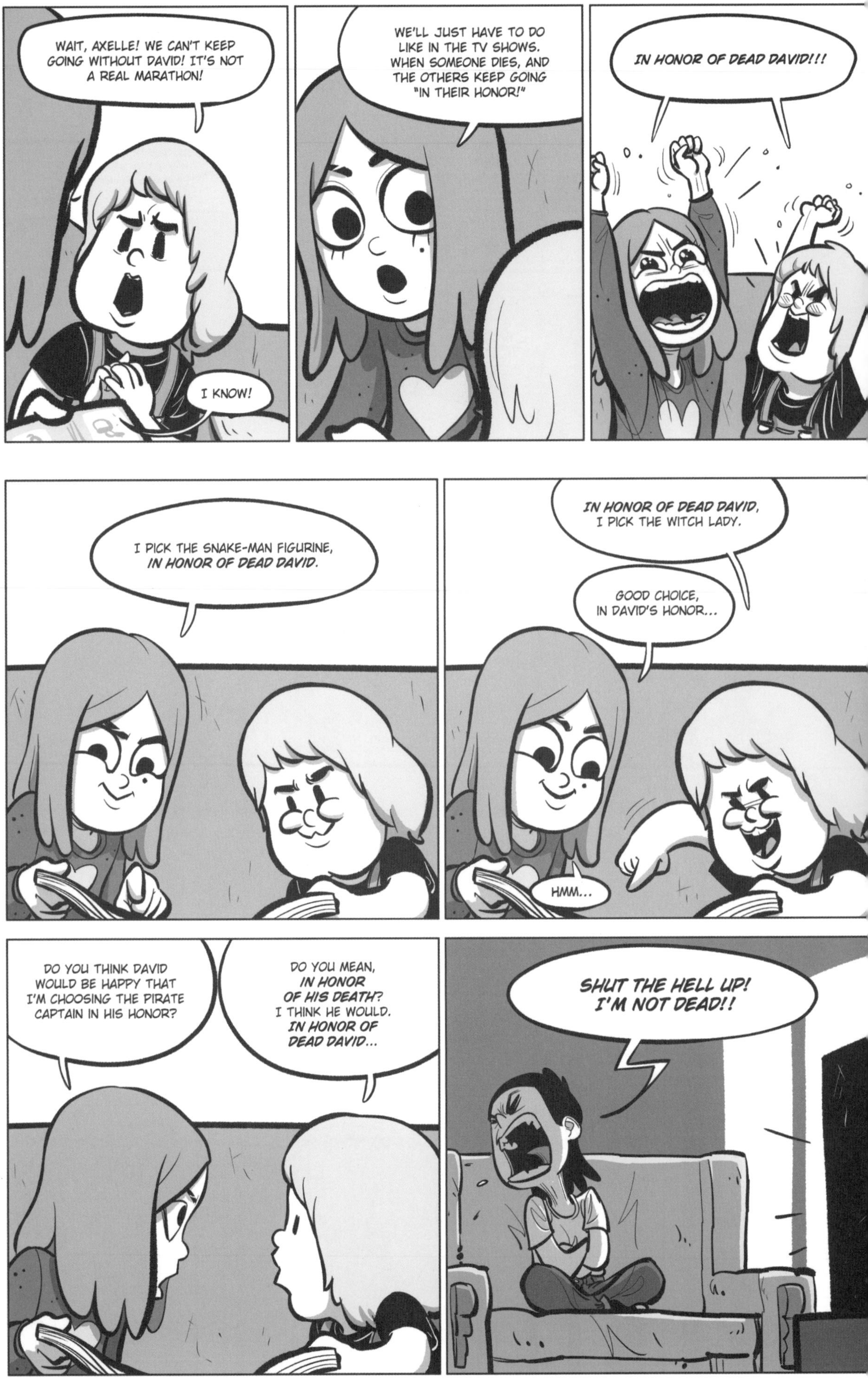
WAIT, AXELLE! WE CAN'T KEEP GOING WITHOUT DAVID! IT'S NOT A REAL MARATHON!
I KNOW!
WE'LL JUST HAVE TO DO LIKE IN THE TV SHOWS. WHEN SOMEONE DIES, AND THE OTHERS KEEP GOING "IN THEIR HONOR!"
IN HONOR OF DEAD DAVID!!!
I PICK THE SNAKE-MAN FIGURINE, IN HONOR OF DEAD DAVID.
IN HONOR OF DEAD DAVID, I PICK THE WITCH LADY.
GOOD CHOICE, IN DAVID'S HONOR...
HMM...
DO YOU THINK DAVID WOULD BE HAPPY THAT I'M CHOOSING THE PIRATE CAPTAIN IN HIS HONOR?
DO YOU MEAN, IN HONOR OF HIS DEATH? I THINK HE WOULD. IN HONOR OF DEAD DAVID...
SHUT THE HELL UP! I'M NOT DEAD!!

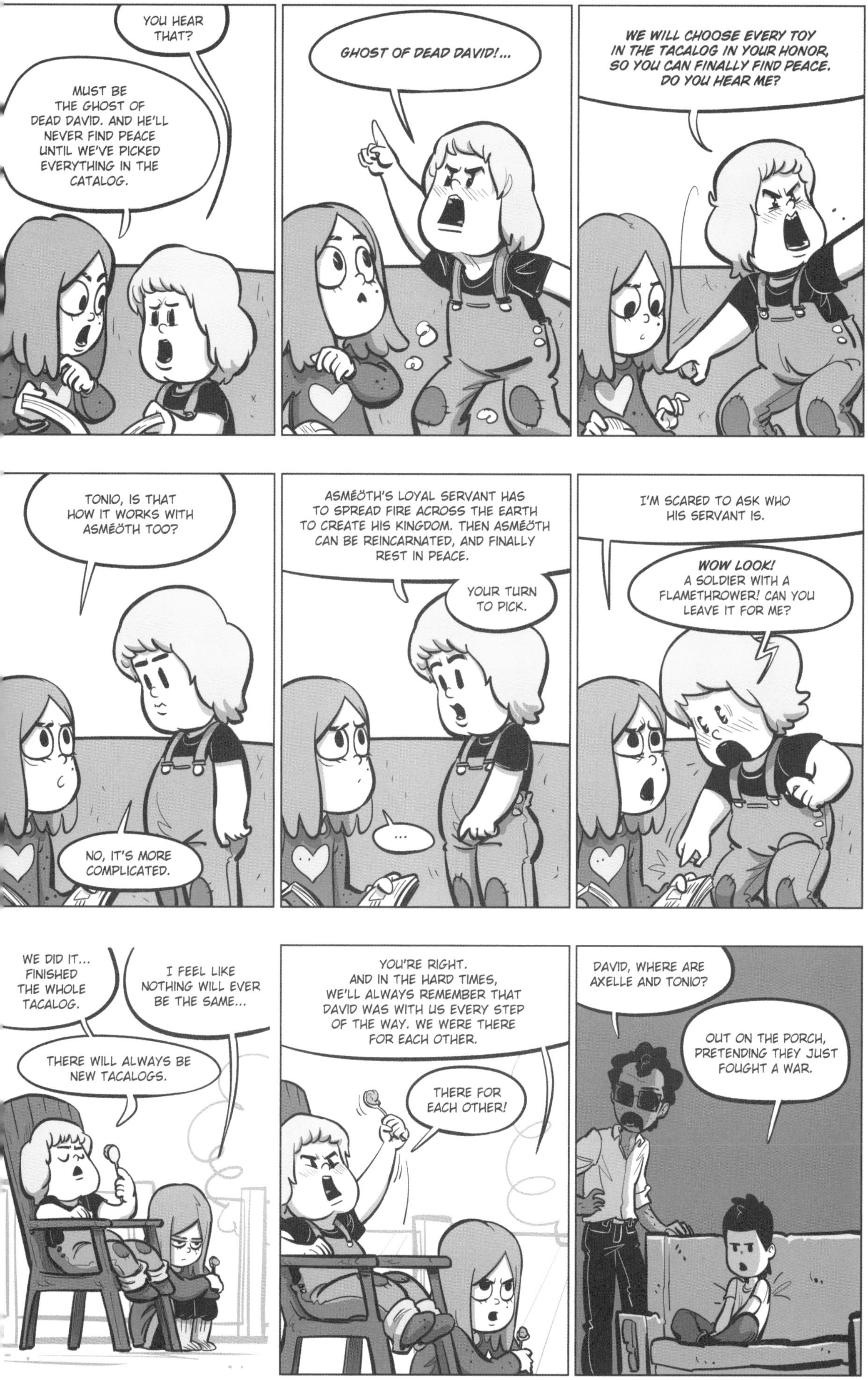
YOU HEAR THAT?
MUST BE THE GHOST OF DEAD DAVID. AND HE'LL NEVER FIND PEACE UNTIL WE'VE PICKED EVERYTHING IN THE CATALOG.
GHOST OF DEAD DAVID!...
WE WILL CHOOSE EVERY TOY IN THE TACALOG IN YOUR HONOR, SO YOU CAN FINALLY FIND PEACE. DO YOU HEAR ME?
TONIO, IS THAT HOW IT WORKS WITH ASMÉÖTH TOO?
NO, IT'S MORE COMPLICATED.
ASMÉÖTH'S LOYAL SERVANT HAS TO SPREAD FIRE ACROSS THE EARTH TO CREATE HIS KINGDOM. THEN ASMÉÖTH CAN BE REINCARNATED, AND FINALLY REST IN PEACE.
YOUR TURN TO PICK.
...
I'M SCARED TO ASK WHO HIS SERVANT IS.
WOW LOOK! A SOLDIER WITH A FLAMETHROWER! CAN YOU LEAVE IT FOR ME?
WE DID IT... FINISHED THE WHOLE TACALOG.
I FEEL LIKE NOTHING WILL EVER BE THE SAME...
THERE WILL ALWAYS BE NEW TACALOGS.
YOU'RE RIGHT. AND IN THE HARD TIMES, WE'LL ALWAYS REMEMBER THAT DAVID WAS WITH US EVERY STEP OF THE WAY. WE WERE THERE FOR EACH OTHER.
THERE FOR EACH OTHER!
DAVID, WHERE ARE AXELLE AND TONIO?
OUT ON THE PORCH, PRETENDING THEY JUST FOUGHT A WAR.

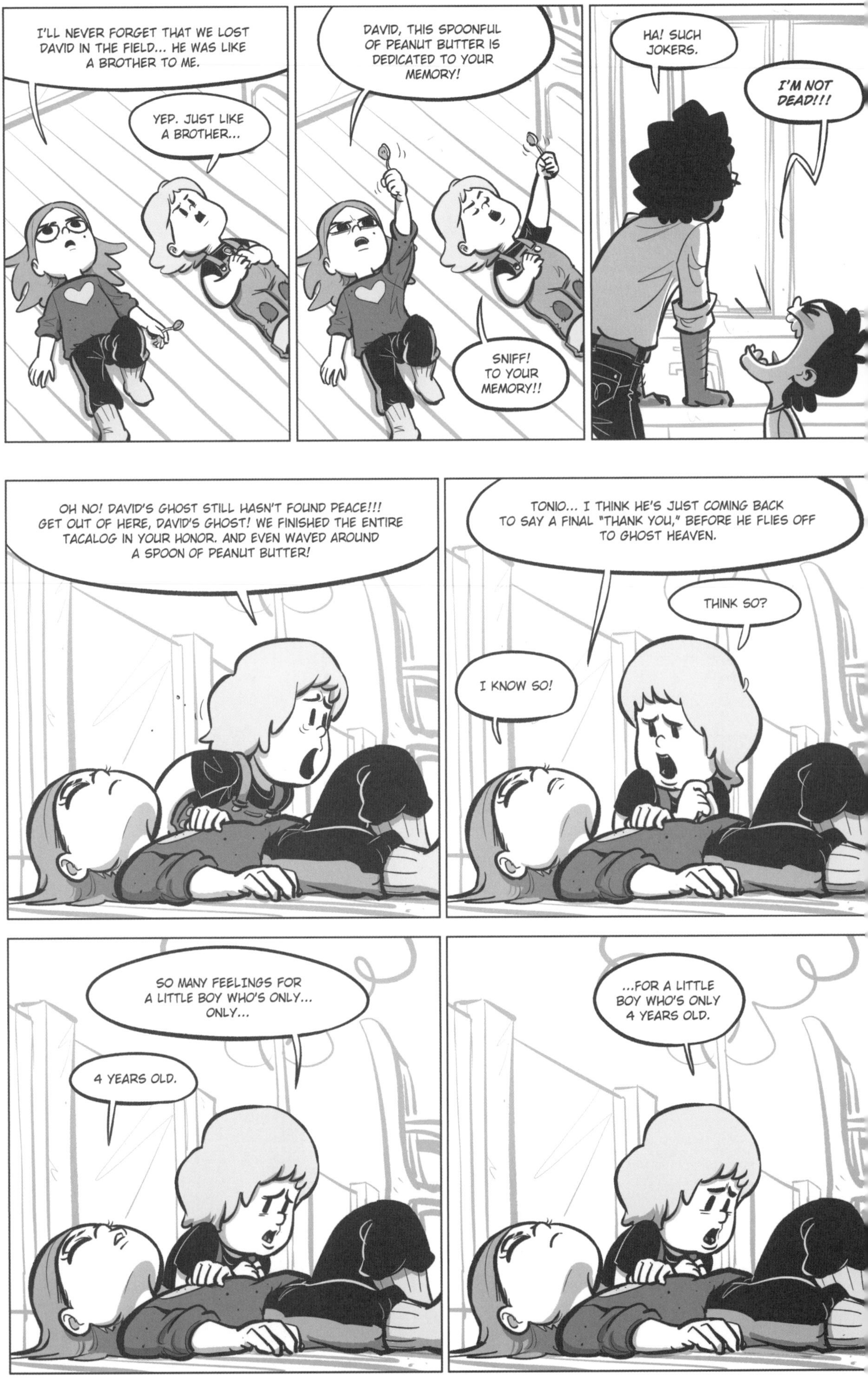
I'LL NEVER FORGET THAT WE LOST DAVID IN THE FIELD... HE WAS LIKE A BROTHER TO ME.
YEP. JUST LIKE A BROTHER...
DAVID, THIS SPOONFUL OF PEANUT BUTTER IS DEDICATED TO YOUR MEMORY!
SNIFF! TO YOUR MEMORY!!
HA! SUCH JOKERS.
I'M NOT DEAD!!!
OH NO! DAVID'S GHOST STILL HASN'T FOUND PEACE!!! GET OUT OF HERE, DAVID'S GHOST! WE FINISHED THE ENTIRE TACALOG IN YOUR HONOR. AND EVEN WAVED AROUND A SPOON OF PEANUT BUTTER!
TONIO... I THINK HE'S JUST COMING BACK TO SAY A FINAL "THANK YOU," BEFORE HE FLIES OFF TO GHOST HEAVEN.
THINK SO?
I KNOW SO!
SO MANY FEELINGS FOR A LITTLE BOY WHO'S ONLY... ONLY...
4 YEARS OLD.
...FOR A LITTLE BOY WHO'S ONLY 4 YEARS OLD.

CHAPTER V

CHRISTMAS HOLIDAYS. DECEMBER 27, '85

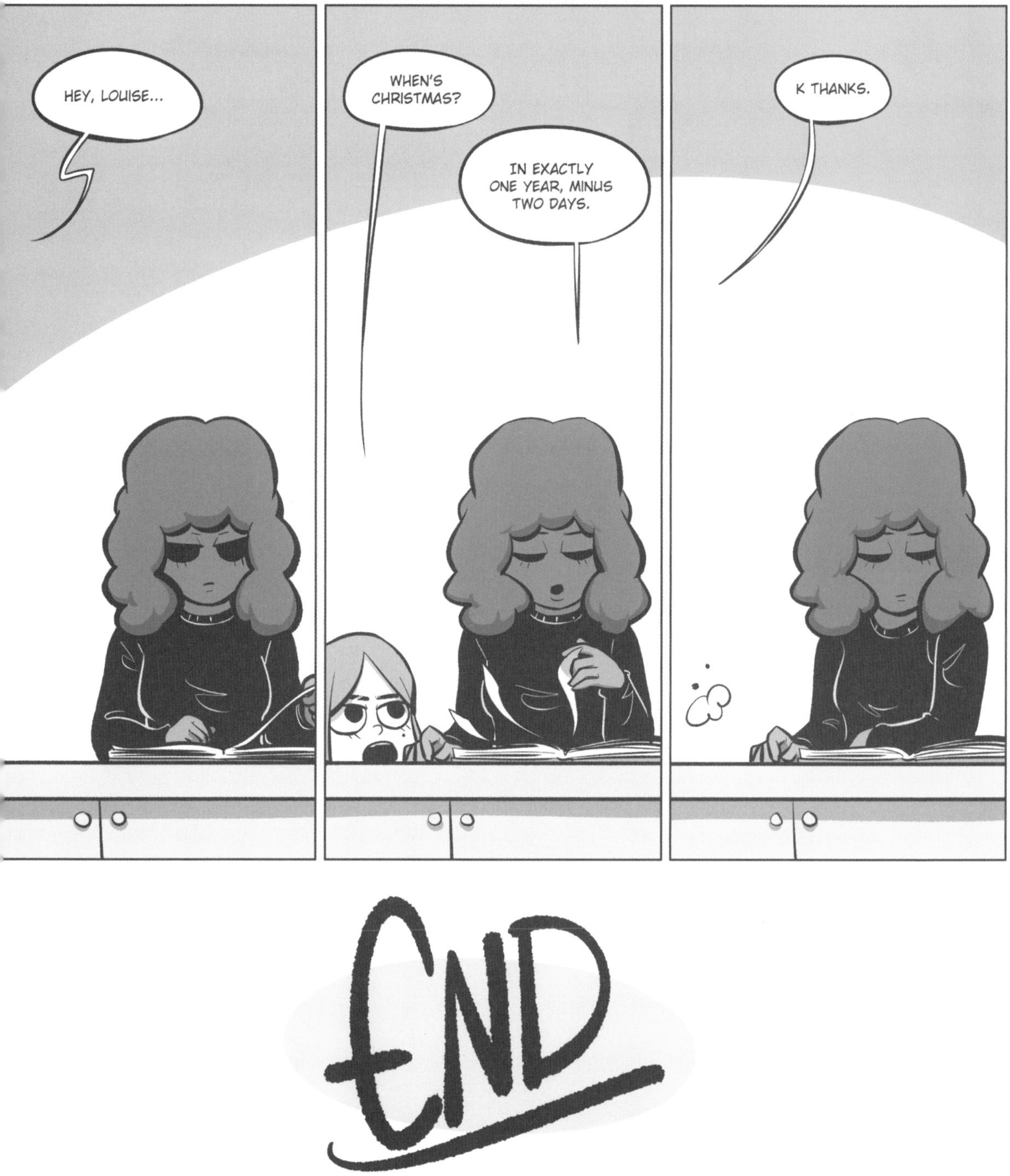
HEY, LOUISE...
WHEN'S CHRISTMAS?
IN EXACTLY ONE YEAR, MINUS TWO DAYS.
K THANKS.

END

CHAPITRE VI

1986, THE FORGOTTEN PART.
AND THE NOT-SO FORGOTTEN PART.

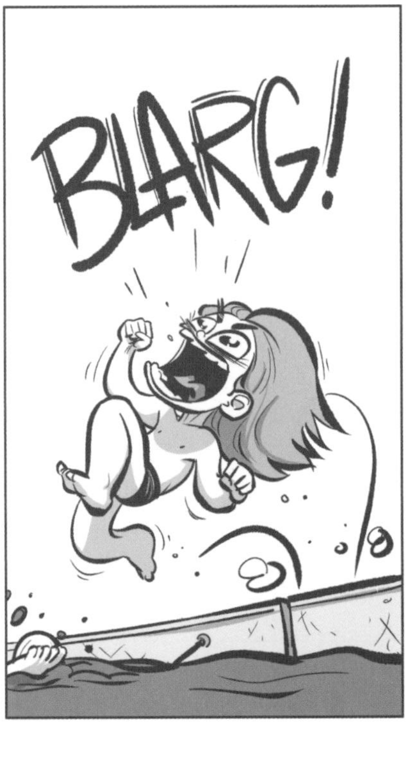
BLARG!

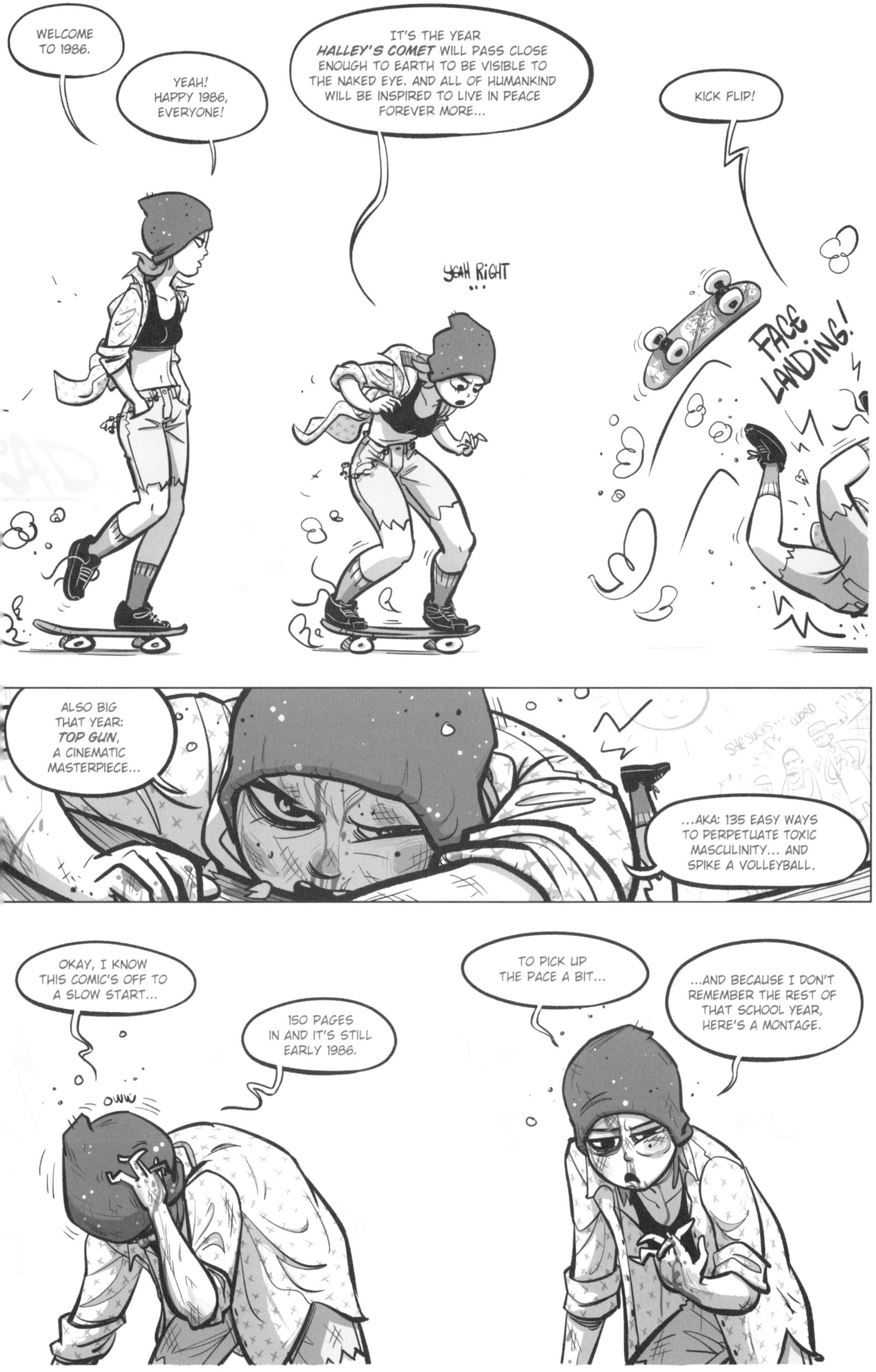
WELCOME TO 1986.
YEAH! HAPPY 1986, EVERYONE!
IT'S THE YEAR **HALLEY'S COMET** WILL PASS CLOSE ENOUGH TO EARTH TO BE VISIBLE TO THE NAKED EYE. AND ALL OF HUMANKIND WILL BE INSPIRED TO LIVE IN PEACE FOREVER MORE...
YEAH RIGHT ...
KICK FLIP!
FACE LANDING!
ALSO BIG THAT YEAR: ***TOP GUN***, A CINEMATIC MASTERPIECE...
...AKA: 135 EASY WAYS TO PERPETUATE TOXIC MASCULINITY... AND SPIKE A VOLLEYBALL.
OKAY, I KNOW THIS COMIC'S OFF TO A SLOW START...
150 PAGES IN AND IT'S STILL EARLY 1986.
OWW
TO PICK UP THE PACE A BIT...
...AND BECAUSE I DON'T REMEMBER THE REST OF THAT SCHOOL YEAR, HERE'S A MONTAGE.

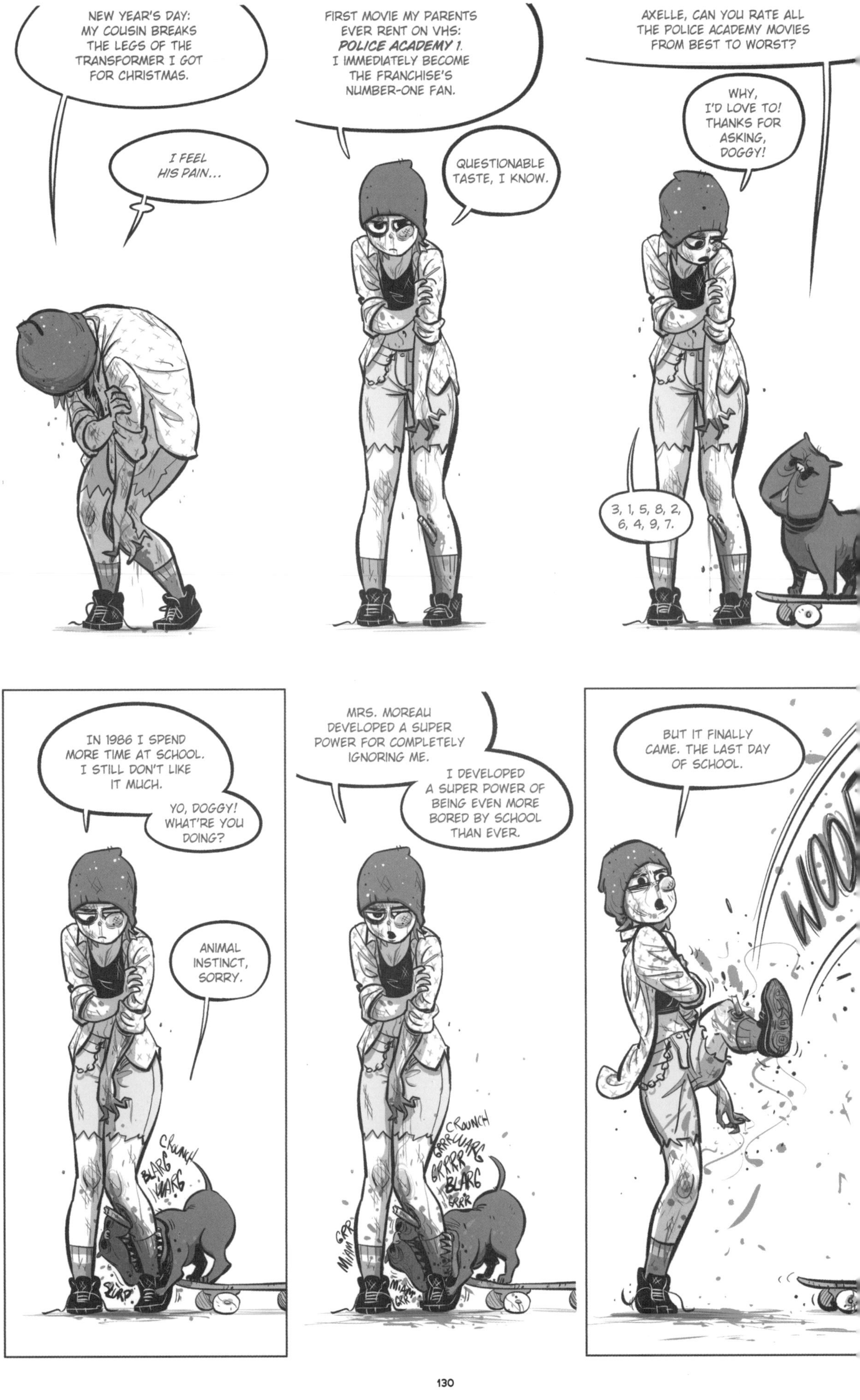
NEW YEAR'S DAY: MY COUSIN BREAKS THE LEGS OF THE TRANSFORMER I GOT FOR CHRISTMAS.
I FEEL HIS PAIN...
FIRST MOVIE MY PARENTS EVER RENT ON VHS: ***POLICE ACADEMY 1***. I IMMEDIATELY BECOME THE FRANCHISE'S NUMBER-ONE FAN.
QUESTIONABLE TASTE, I KNOW.
AXELLE, CAN YOU RATE ALL THE POLICE ACADEMY MOVIES FROM BEST TO WORST?
WHY, I'D LOVE TO! THANKS FOR ASKING, DOGGY!
3, 1, 5, 8, 2, 6, 4, 9, 7.
IN 1986 I SPEND MORE TIME AT SCHOOL. I STILL DON'T LIKE IT MUCH.
YO, DOGGY! WHAT'RE YOU DOING?
ANIMAL INSTINCT, SORRY.
CRUNCH
BLARG
WARG
SLURP
MRS. MOREAU DEVELOPED A SUPER POWER FOR COMPLETELY IGNORING ME.
I DEVELOPED A SUPER POWER OF BEING EVEN MORE BORED BY SCHOOL THAN EVER.
CRUNCH
BLARG
BUT IT FINALLY CAME. THE LAST DAY OF SCHOOL.

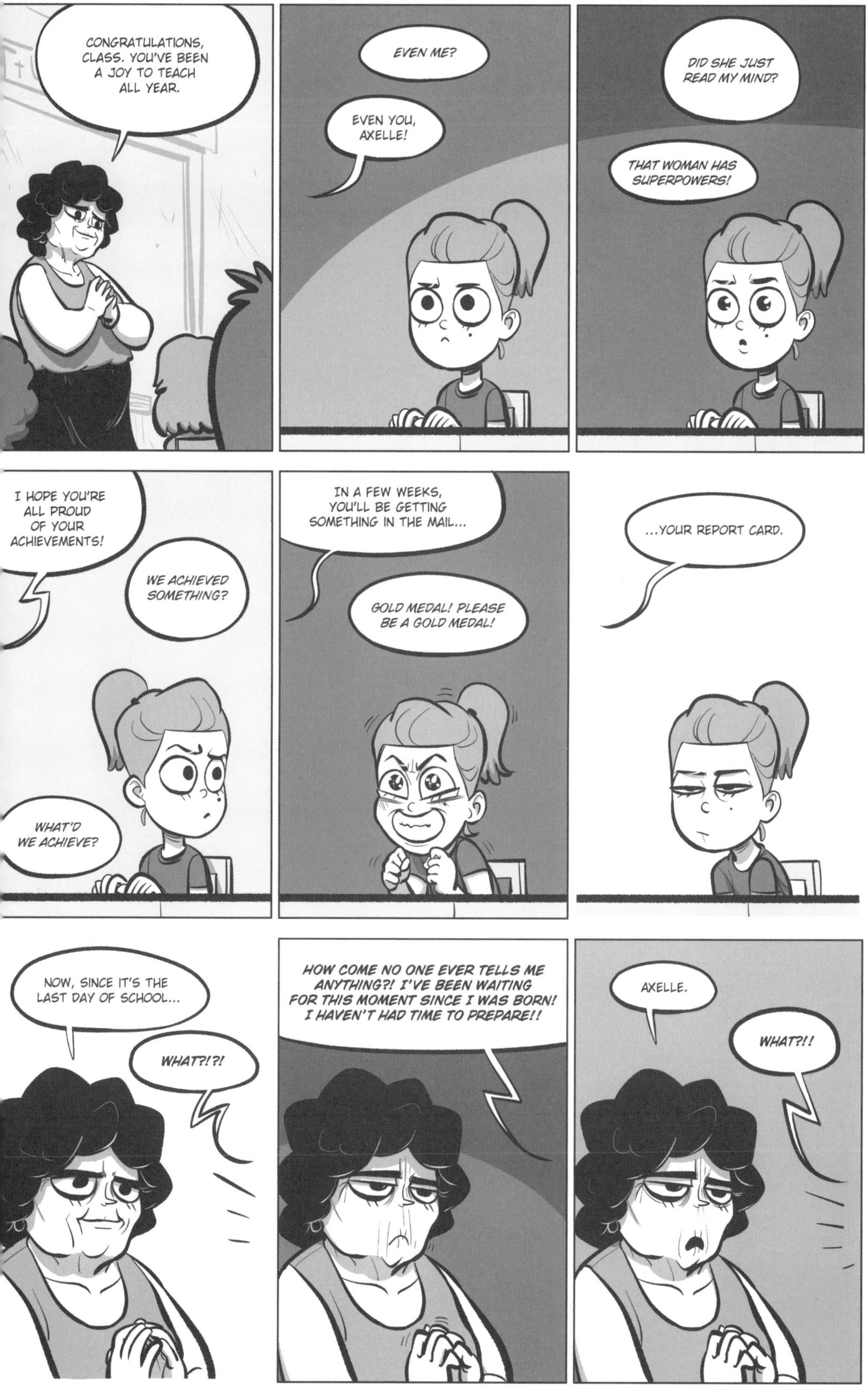
CONGRATULATIONS, CLASS. YOU'VE BEEN A JOY TO TEACH ALL YEAR.
EVEN ME?
EVEN YOU, AXELLE!
DID SHE JUST READ MY MIND?
THAT WOMAN HAS SUPERPOWERS!
I HOPE YOU'RE ALL PROUD OF YOUR ACHIEVEMENTS!
WE ACHIEVED SOMETHING?
WHAT'D WE ACHIEVE?
IN A FEW WEEKS, YOU'LL BE GETTING SOMETHING IN THE MAIL...
GOLD MEDAL! PLEASE BE A GOLD MEDAL!
...YOUR REPORT CARD.
NOW, SINCE IT'S THE LAST DAY OF SCHOOL...
WHAT?!?!
HOW COME NO ONE EVER TELLS ME ANYTHING?! I'VE BEEN WAITING FOR THIS MOMENT SINCE I WAS BORN! I HAVEN'T HAD TIME TO PREPARE!!
AXELLE.
WHAT?!!

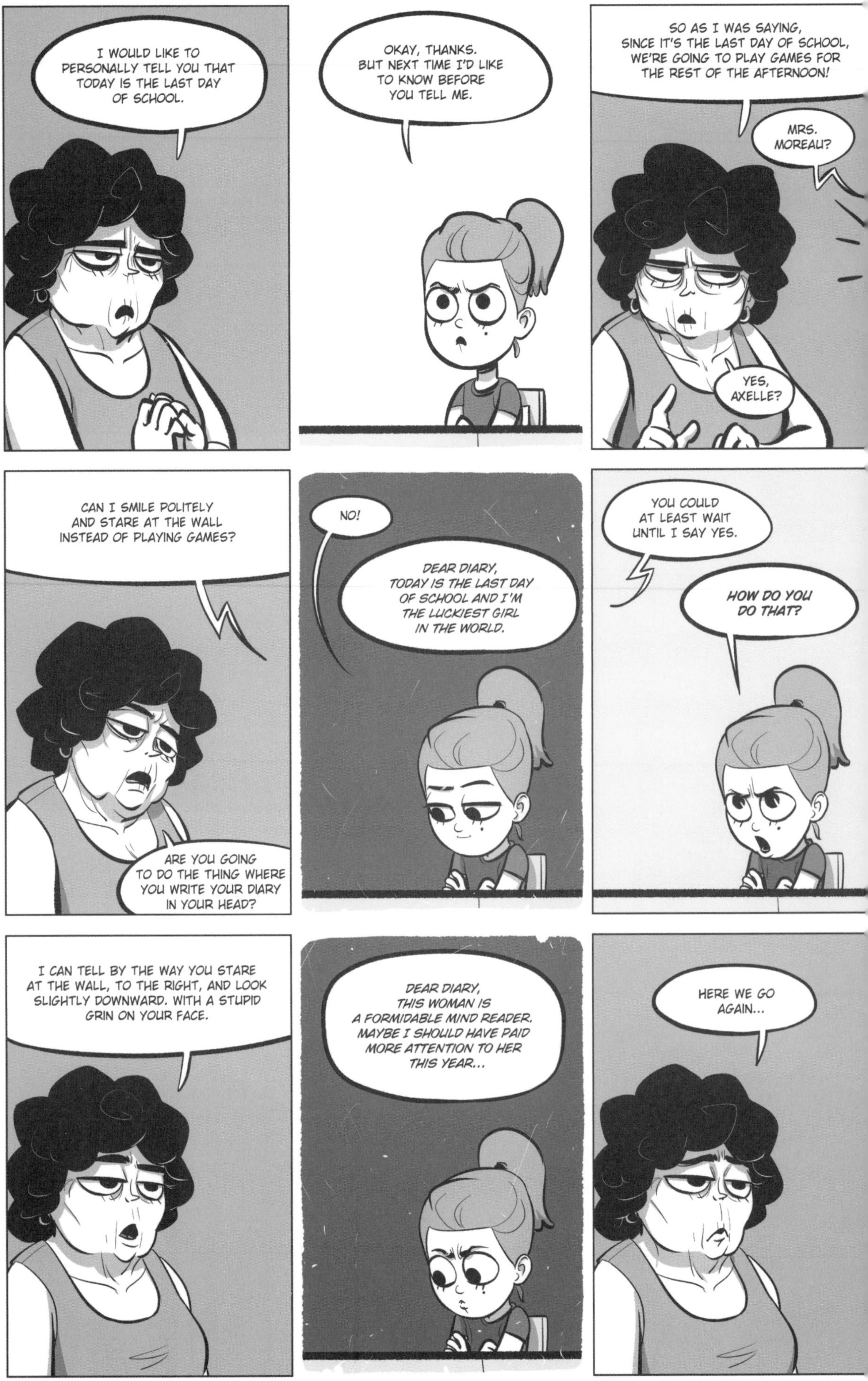
I WOULD LIKE TO PERSONALLY TELL YOU THAT TODAY IS THE LAST DAY OF SCHOOL.
OKAY, THANKS. BUT NEXT TIME I'D LIKE TO KNOW BEFORE YOU TELL ME.
SO AS I WAS SAYING, SINCE IT'S THE LAST DAY OF SCHOOL, WE'RE GOING TO PLAY GAMES FOR THE REST OF THE AFTERNOON!
MRS. MOREAU?
YES, AXELLE?
CAN I SMILE POLITELY AND STARE AT THE WALL INSTEAD OF PLAYING GAMES?
ARE YOU GOING TO DO THE THING WHERE YOU WRITE YOUR DIARY IN YOUR HEAD?
NO!
DEAR DIARY, TODAY IS THE LAST DAY OF SCHOOL AND I'M THE LUCKIEST GIRL IN THE WORLD.
YOU COULD AT LEAST WAIT UNTIL I SAY YES.
HOW DO YOU DO THAT?
I CAN TELL BY THE WAY YOU STARE AT THE WALL, TO THE RIGHT, AND LOOK SLIGHTLY DOWNWARD. WITH A STUPID GRIN ON YOUR FACE.
DEAR DIARY, THIS WOMAN IS A FORMIDABLE MIND READER. MAYBE I SHOULD HAVE PAID MORE ATTENTION TO HER THIS YEAR...
HERE WE GO AGAIN...

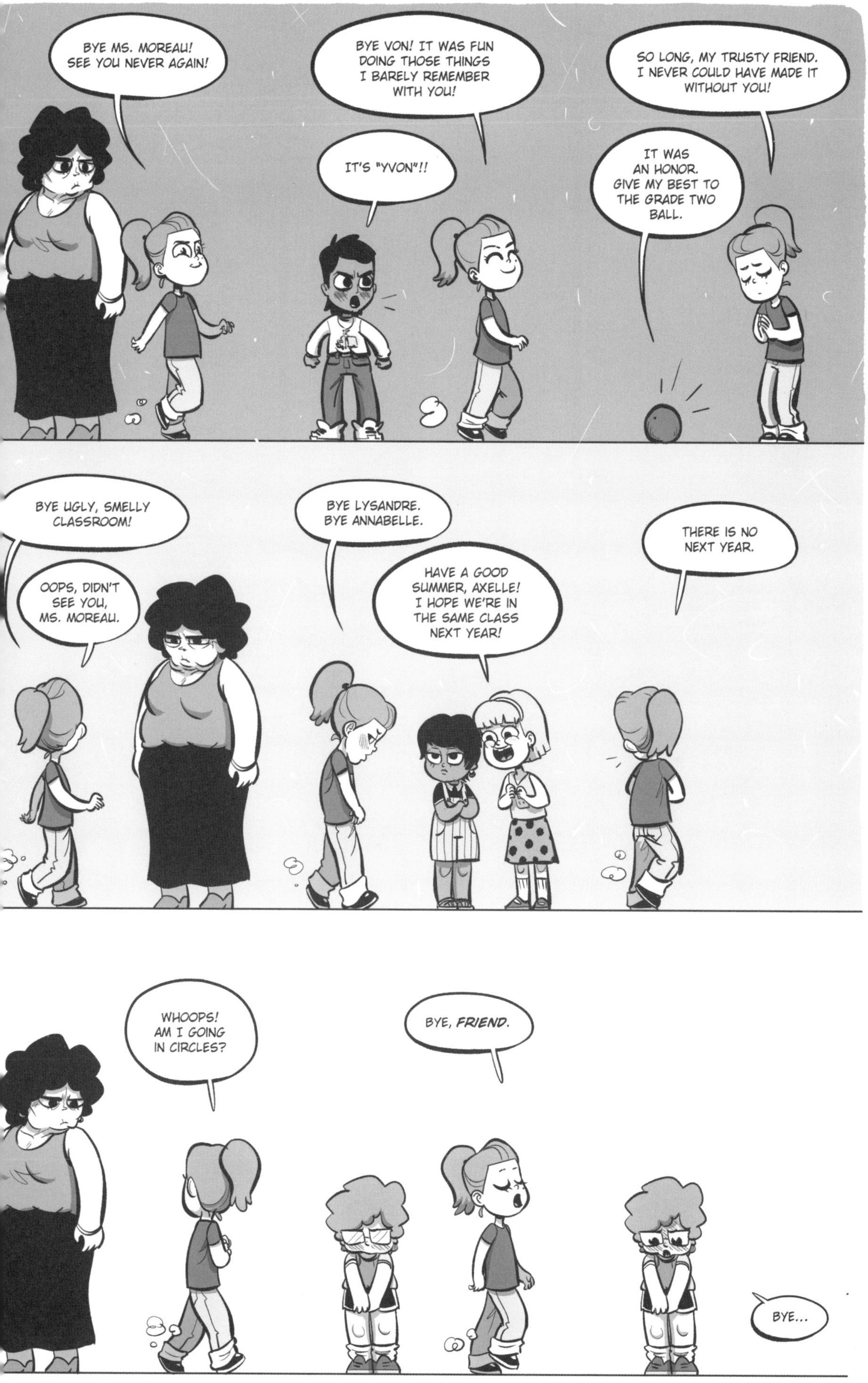

BYE MS. MOREAU! SEE YOU NEVER AGAIN!
BYE VON! IT WAS FUN DOING THOSE THINGS I BARELY REMEMBER WITH YOU!
IT'S "YVON"!!
SO LONG, MY TRUSTY FRIEND. I NEVER COULD HAVE MADE IT WITHOUT YOU!
IT WAS AN HONOR. GIVE MY BEST TO THE GRADE TWO BALL.
BYE UGLY, SMELLY CLASSROOM!
OOPS, DIDN'T SEE YOU, MS. MOREAU.
BYE LYSANDRE. BYE ANNABELLE.
HAVE A GOOD SUMMER, AXELLE! I HOPE WE'RE IN THE SAME CLASS NEXT YEAR!
THERE IS NO NEXT YEAR.
WHOOPS! AM I GOING IN CIRCLES?
BYE, *FRIEND*.
BYE...

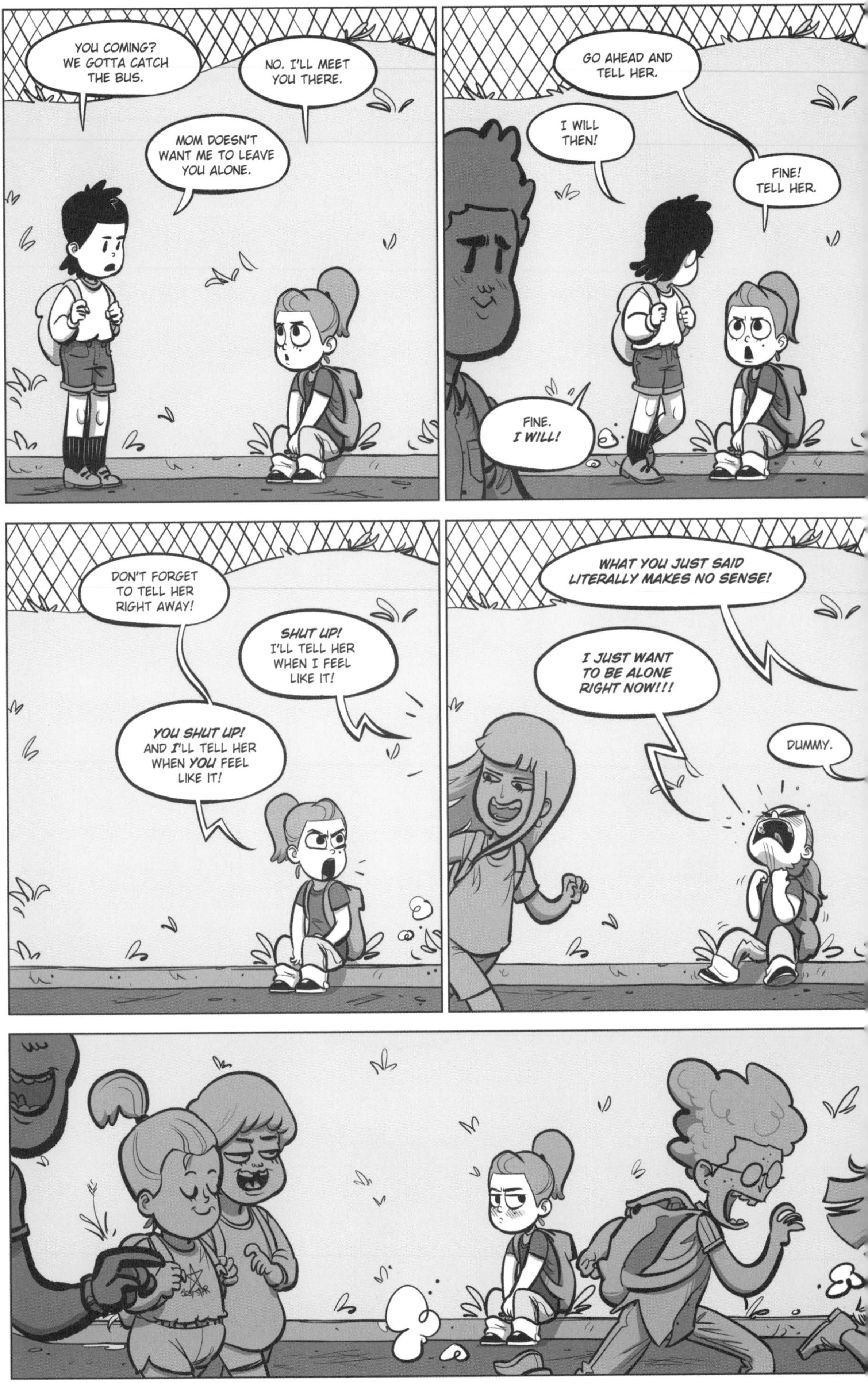
YOU COMING? WE GOTTA CATCH THE BUS.
NO. I'LL MEET YOU THERE.
MOM DOESN'T WANT ME TO LEAVE YOU ALONE.
GO AHEAD AND TELL HER.
I WILL THEN!
FINE! TELL HER.
FINE. *I WILL!*
DON'T FORGET TO TELL HER RIGHT AWAY!
SHUT UP! I'LL TELL HER WHEN I FEEL LIKE IT!
YOU SHUT UP! AND *I'LL* TELL HER WHEN *YOU* FEEL LIKE IT!
WHAT YOU JUST SAID LITERALLY MAKES NO SENSE!
I JUST WANT TO BE ALONE RIGHT NOW!!!
DUMMY.

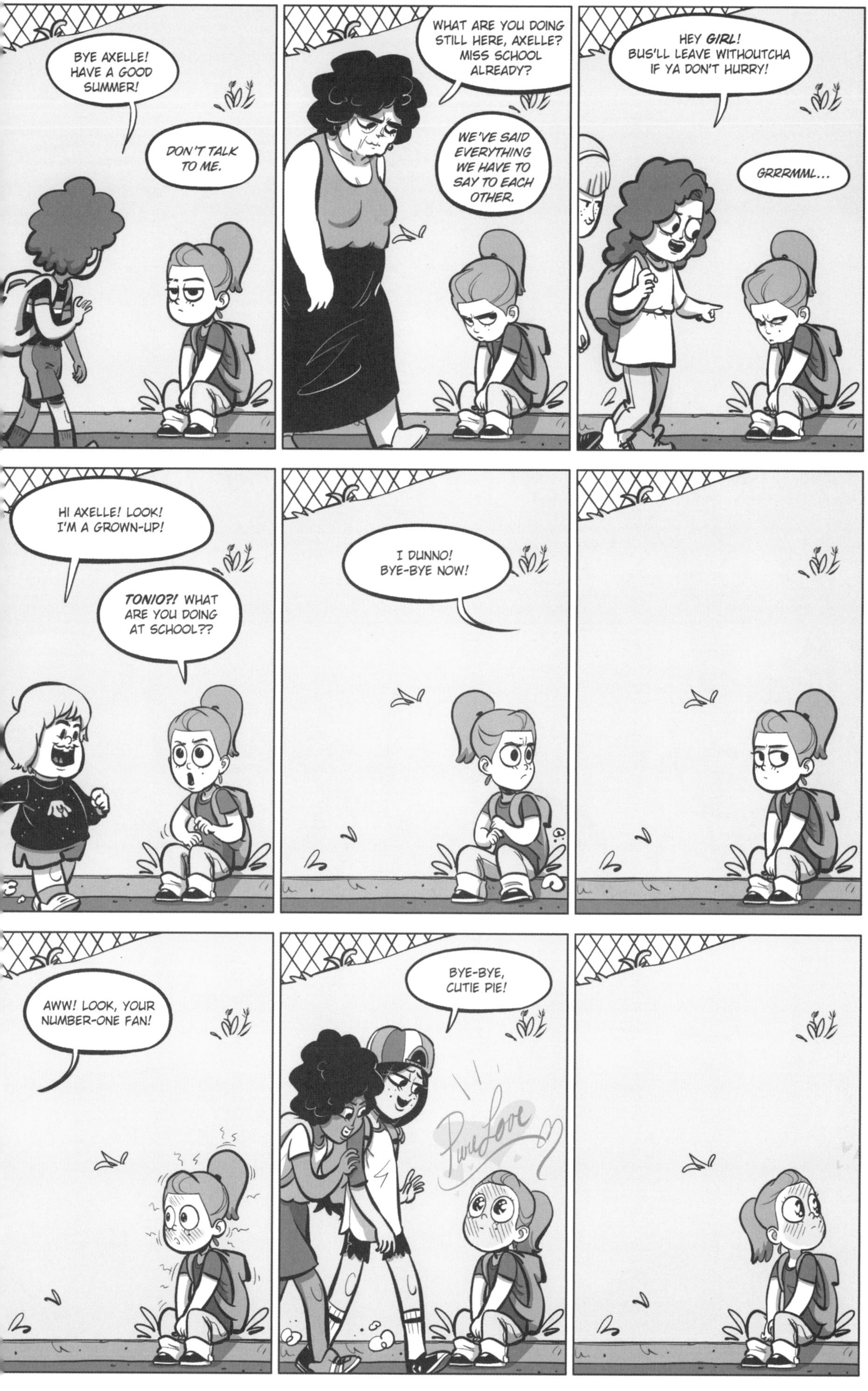

BYE AXELLE! HAVE A GOOD SUMMER!
DON'T TALK TO ME.
WHAT ARE YOU DOING STILL HERE, AXELLE? MISS SCHOOL ALREADY?
WE'VE SAID EVERYTHING WE HAVE TO SAY TO EACH OTHER.
HEY GIRL! BUS'LL LEAVE WITHOUTCHA IF YA DON'T HURRY!
GRRRMML...
HI AXELLE! LOOK! I'M A GROWN-UP!
TONIO?! WHAT ARE YOU DOING AT SCHOOL??
I DUNNO! BYE-BYE NOW!
AWW! LOOK, YOUR NUMBER-ONE FAN!
BYE-BYE, CUTIE PIE!
Pure Love

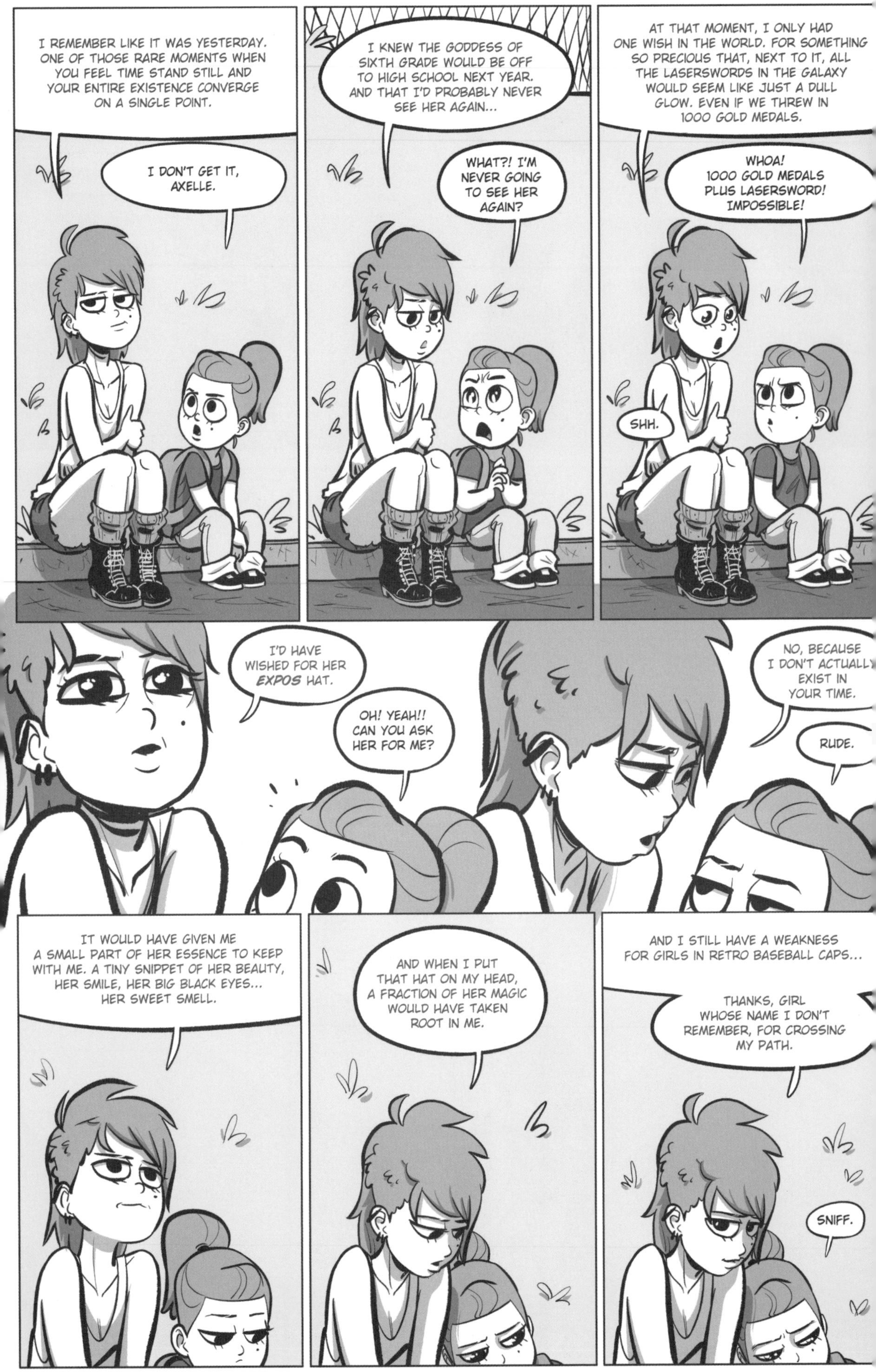
I REMEMBER LIKE IT WAS YESTERDAY. ONE OF THOSE RARE MOMENTS WHEN YOU FEEL TIME STAND STILL AND YOUR ENTIRE EXISTENCE CONVERGE ON A SINGLE POINT.
I DON'T GET IT, AXELLE.
I KNEW THE GODDESS OF SIXTH GRADE WOULD BE OFF TO HIGH SCHOOL NEXT YEAR. AND THAT I'D PROBABLY NEVER SEE HER AGAIN...
WHAT?! I'M NEVER GOING TO SEE HER AGAIN?
AT THAT MOMENT, I ONLY HAD ONE WISH IN THE WORLD. FOR SOMETHING SO PRECIOUS THAT, NEXT TO IT, ALL THE LASERSWORDS IN THE GALAXY WOULD SEEM LIKE JUST A DULL GLOW. EVEN IF WE THREW IN 1000 GOLD MEDALS.
WHOA! 1000 GOLD MEDALS PLUS LASERSWORD! IMPOSSIBLE!
SHH.
I'D HAVE WISHED FOR HER *EXPOS* HAT.
OH! YEAH!! CAN YOU ASK HER FOR ME?
NO, BECAUSE I DON'T ACTUALLY EXIST IN YOUR TIME.
RUDE.
IT WOULD HAVE GIVEN ME A SMALL PART OF HER ESSENCE TO KEEP WITH ME. A TINY SNIPPET OF HER BEAUTY, HER SMILE, HER BIG BLACK EYES... HER SWEET SMELL.
AND WHEN I PUT THAT HAT ON MY HEAD, A FRACTION OF HER MAGIC WOULD HAVE TAKEN ROOT IN ME.
AND I STILL HAVE A WEAKNESS FOR GIRLS IN RETRO BASEBALL CAPS...
THANKS, GIRL WHOSE NAME I DON'T REMEMBER, FOR CROSSING MY PATH.
SNIFF.

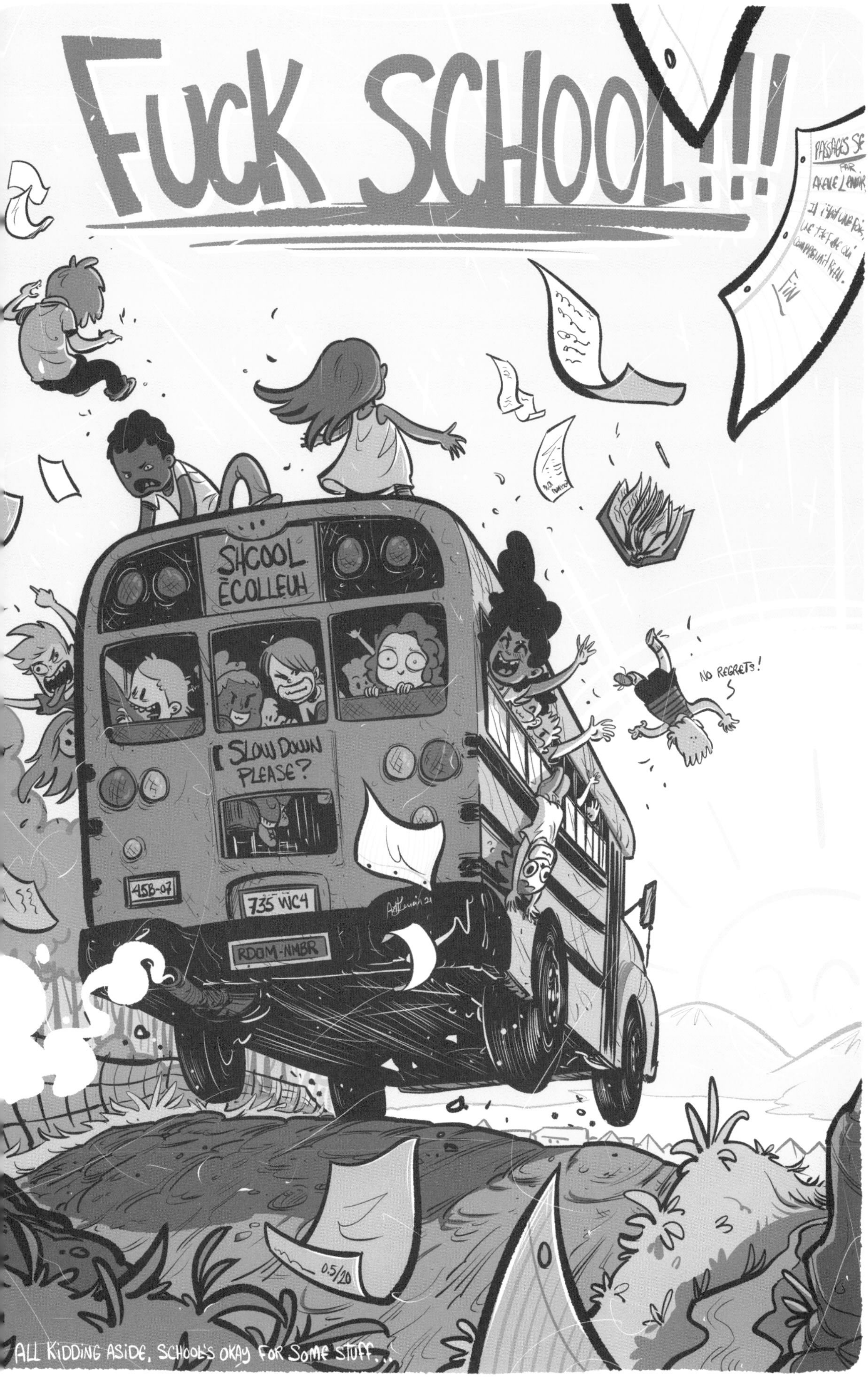
FUCK SCHOOL!!!
SHCOOL ÉCOLLEUH
SLOW DOWN PLEASE?
NO REGRETS!
45B-07
735 WC4
RDOM-NMBR
0.5/20
ALL KIDDING ASIDE, SCHOOL'S OKAY FOR SOME STUFF...

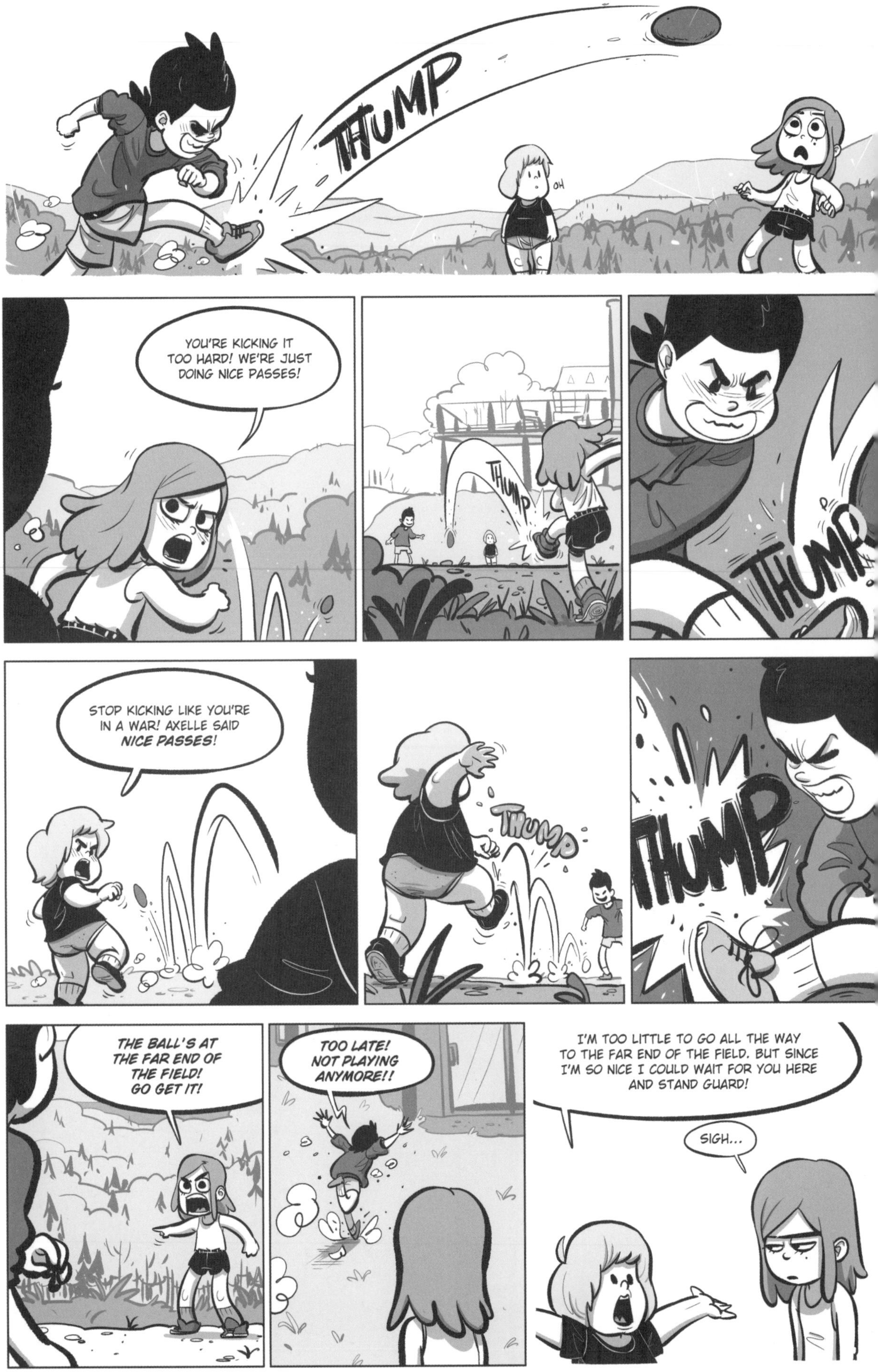
THUMP
OH
YOU'RE KICKING IT TOO HARD! WE'RE JUST DOING NICE PASSES!
THUMP
THUMP
STOP KICKING LIKE YOU'RE IN A WAR! AXELLE SAID NICE PASSES!
THUMP
THUMP
THE BALL'S AT THE FAR END OF THE FIELD! GO GET IT!
TOO LATE! NOT PLAYING ANYMORE!!
I'M TOO LITTLE TO GO ALL THE WAY TO THE FAR END OF THE FIELD. BUT SINCE I'M SO NICE I COULD WAIT FOR YOU HERE AND STAND GUARD!
SIGH...

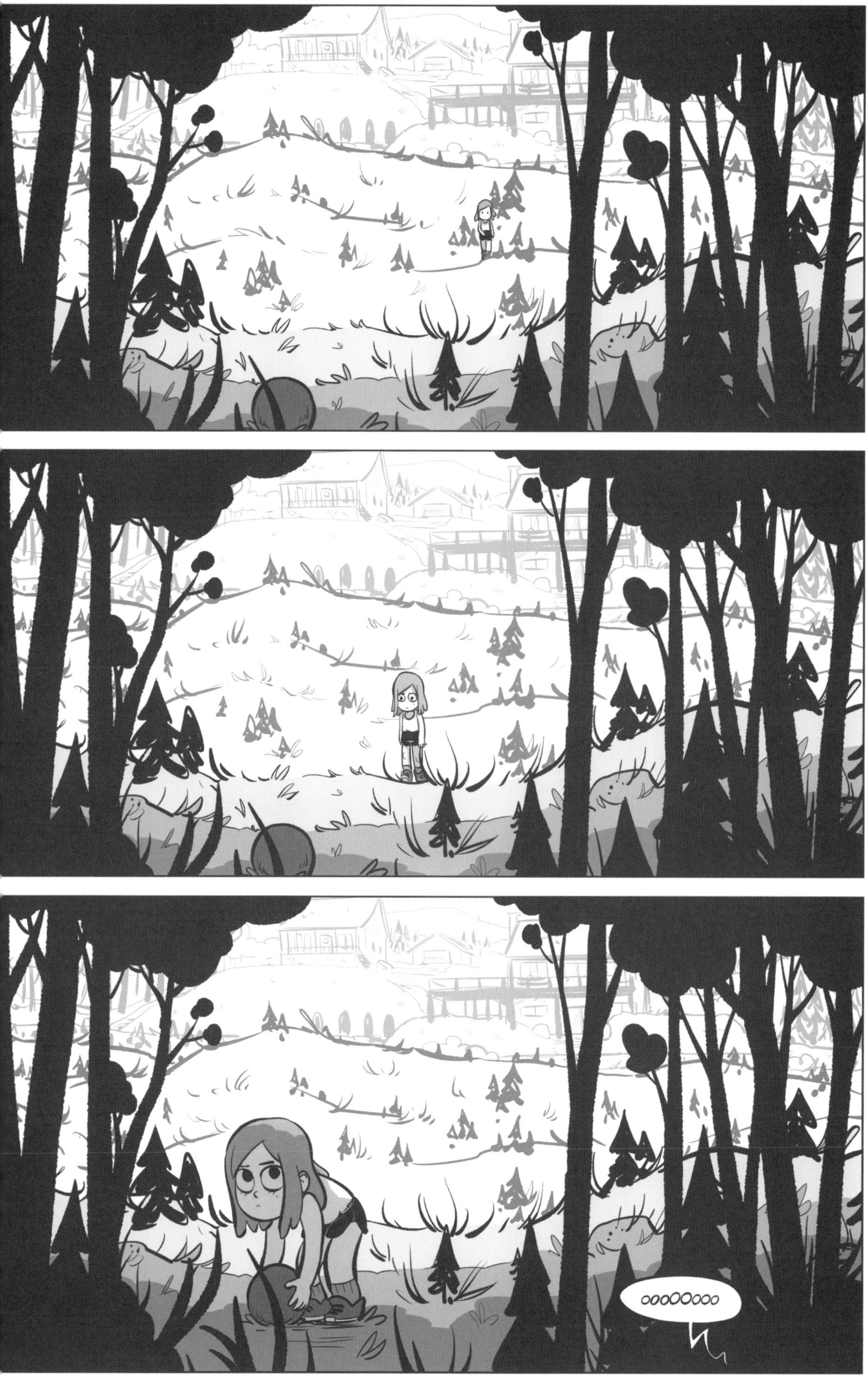
oooOOooo

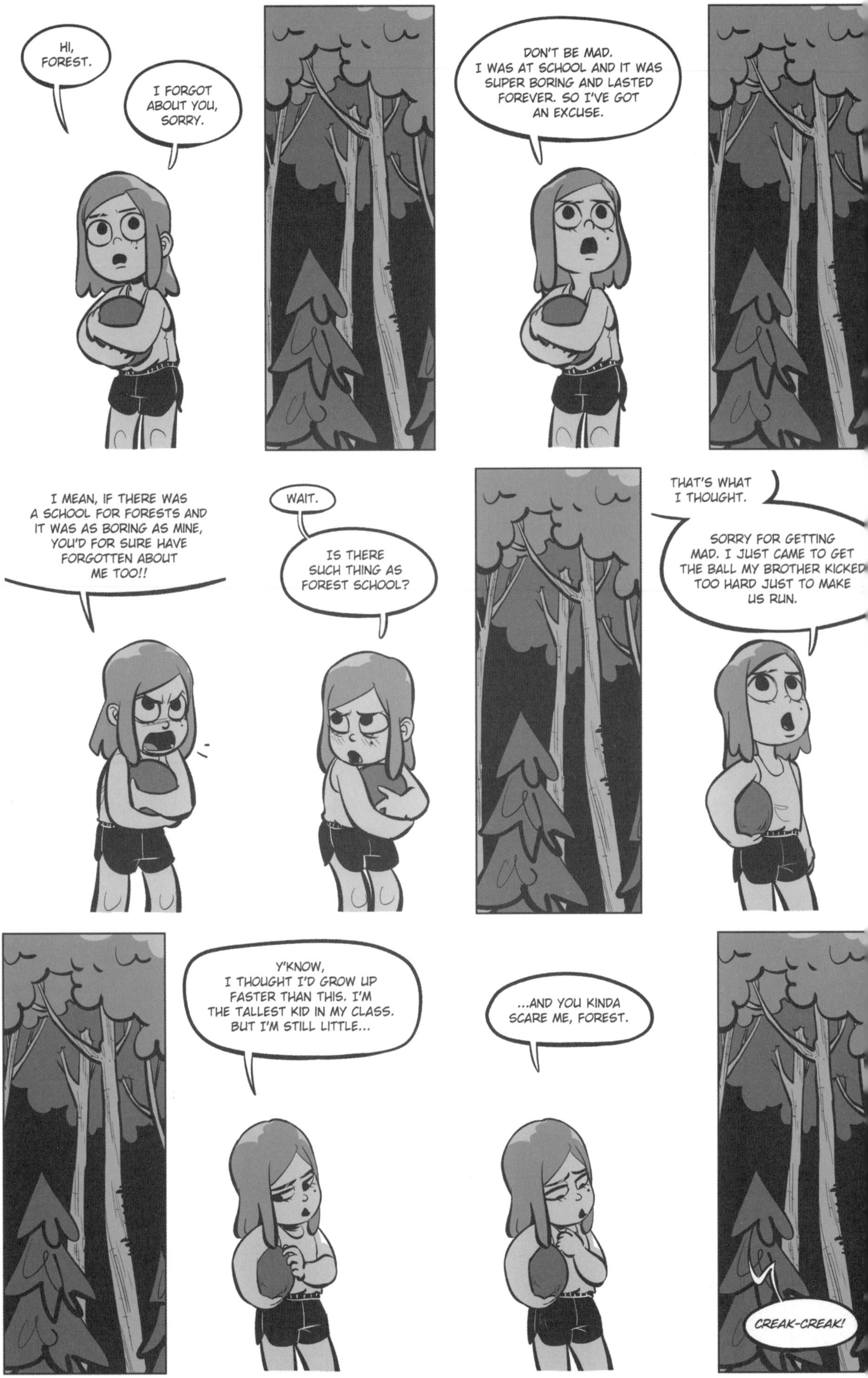
HI, FOREST.
I FORGOT ABOUT YOU, SORRY.
DON'T BE MAD. I WAS AT SCHOOL AND IT WAS SUPER BORING AND LASTED FOREVER. SO I'VE GOT AN EXCUSE.
I MEAN, IF THERE WAS A SCHOOL FOR FORESTS AND IT WAS AS BORING AS MINE, YOU'D FOR SURE HAVE FORGOTTEN ABOUT ME TOO!!
WAIT.
IS THERE SUCH THING AS FOREST SCHOOL?
THAT'S WHAT I THOUGHT.
SORRY FOR GETTING MAD. I JUST CAME TO GET THE BALL MY BROTHER KICKED TOO HARD JUST TO MAKE US RUN.
Y'KNOW, I THOUGHT I'D GROW UP FASTER THAN THIS. I'M THE TALLEST KID IN MY CLASS. BUT I'M STILL LITTLE...
...AND YOU KINDA SCARE ME, FOREST.
CREAK-CREAK!

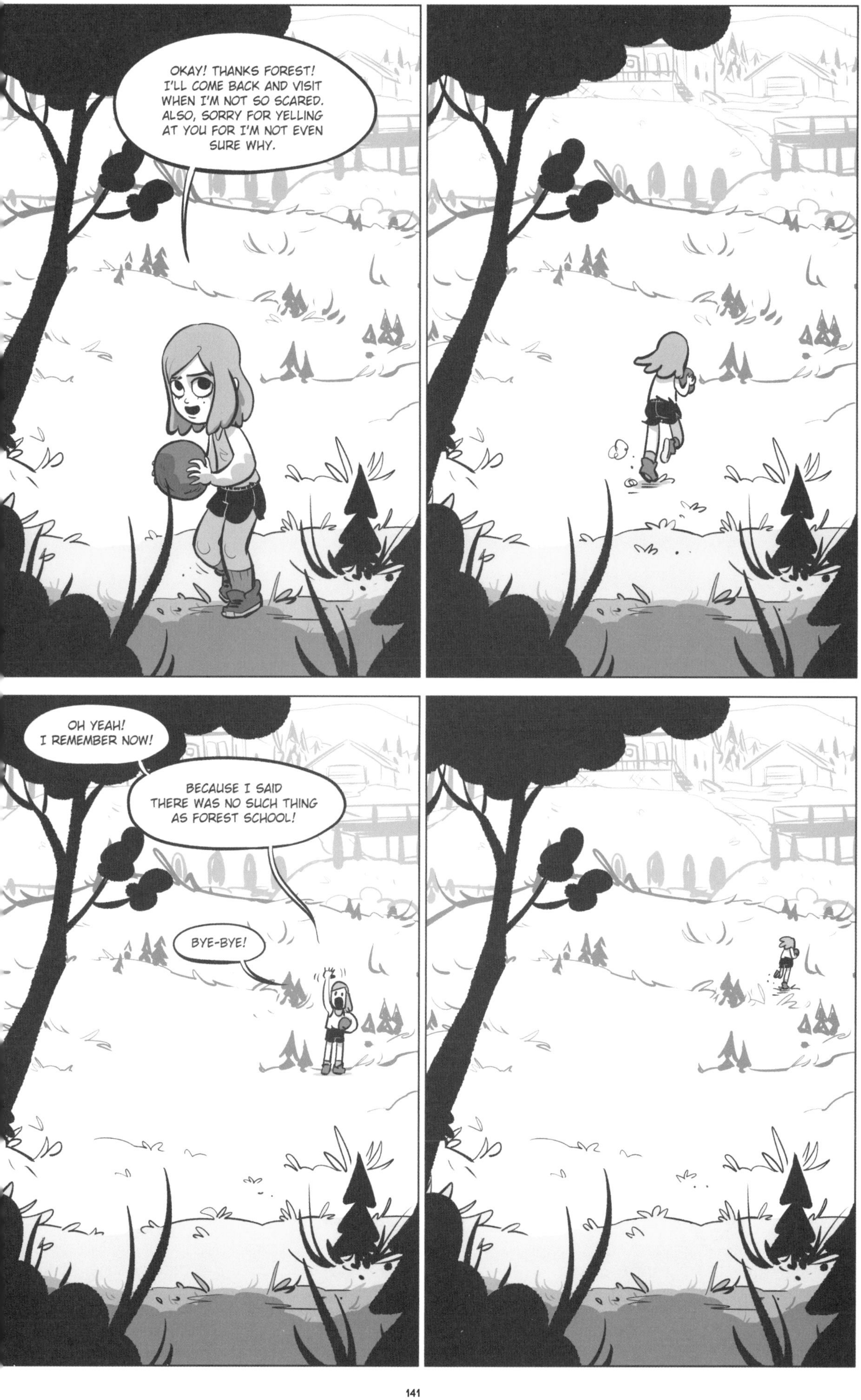
OKAY! THANKS FOREST! I'LL COME BACK AND VISIT WHEN I'M NOT SO SCARED. ALSO, SORRY FOR YELLING AT YOU FOR I'M NOT EVEN SURE WHY.
OH YEAH! I REMEMBER NOW!
BECAUSE I SAID THERE WAS NO SUCH THING AS FOREST SCHOOL!
BYE-BYE!

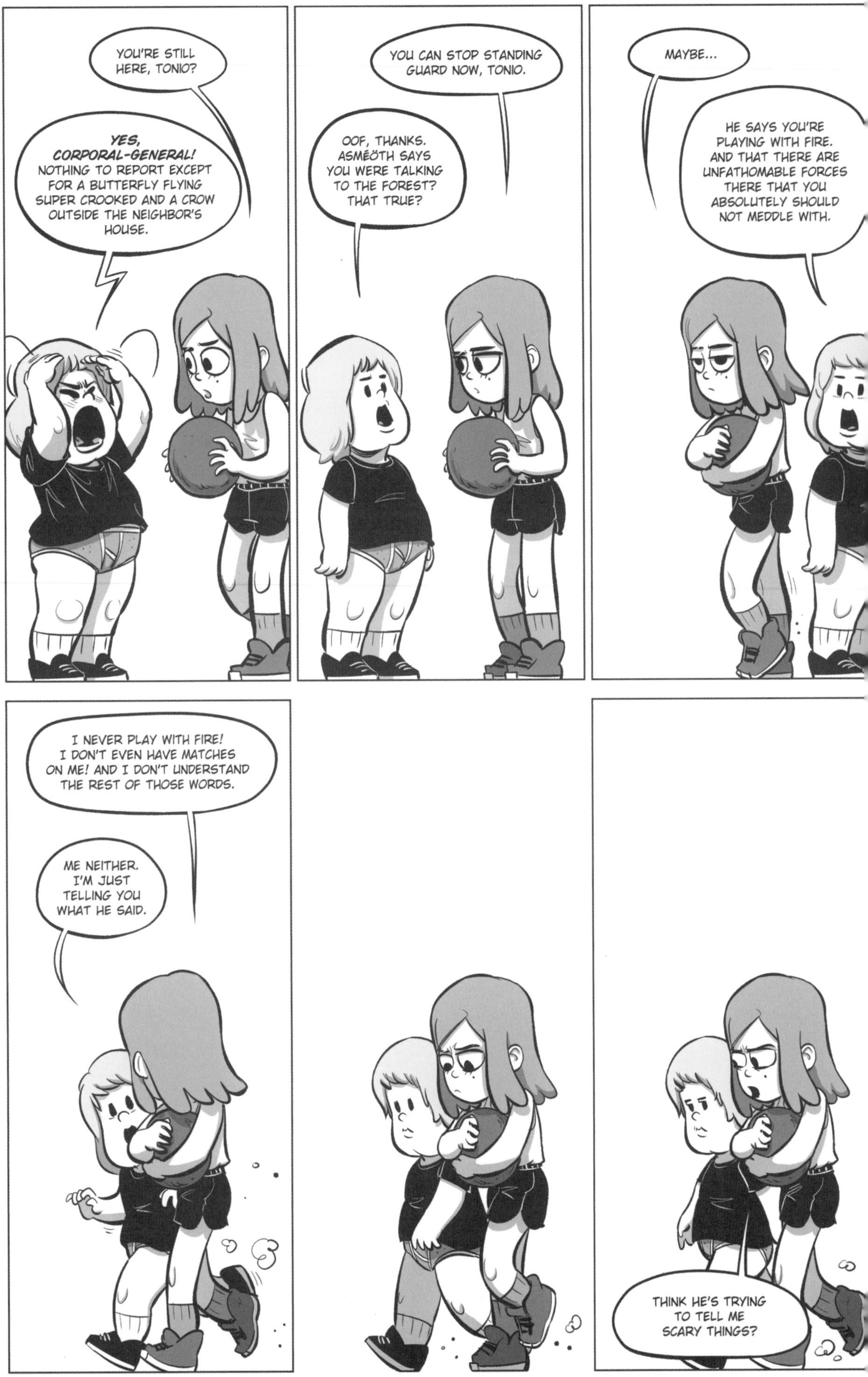
YOU'RE STILL HERE, TONIO?
YES, CORPORAL-GENERAL! NOTHING TO REPORT EXCEPT FOR A BUTTERFLY FLYING SUPER CROOKED AND A CROW OUTSIDE THE NEIGHBOR'S HOUSE.
YOU CAN STOP STANDING GUARD NOW, TONIO.
OOF, THANKS. ASMÉÖTH SAYS YOU WERE TALKING TO THE FOREST? THAT TRUE?
MAYBE...
HE SAYS YOU'RE PLAYING WITH FIRE. AND THAT THERE ARE UNFATHOMABLE FORCES THERE THAT YOU ABSOLUTELY SHOULD NOT MEDDLE WITH.
I NEVER PLAY WITH FIRE! I DON'T EVEN HAVE MATCHES ON ME! AND I DON'T UNDERSTAND THE REST OF THOSE WORDS.
ME NEITHER. I'M JUST TELLING YOU WHAT HE SAID.
THINK HE'S TRYING TO TELL ME SCARY THINGS?

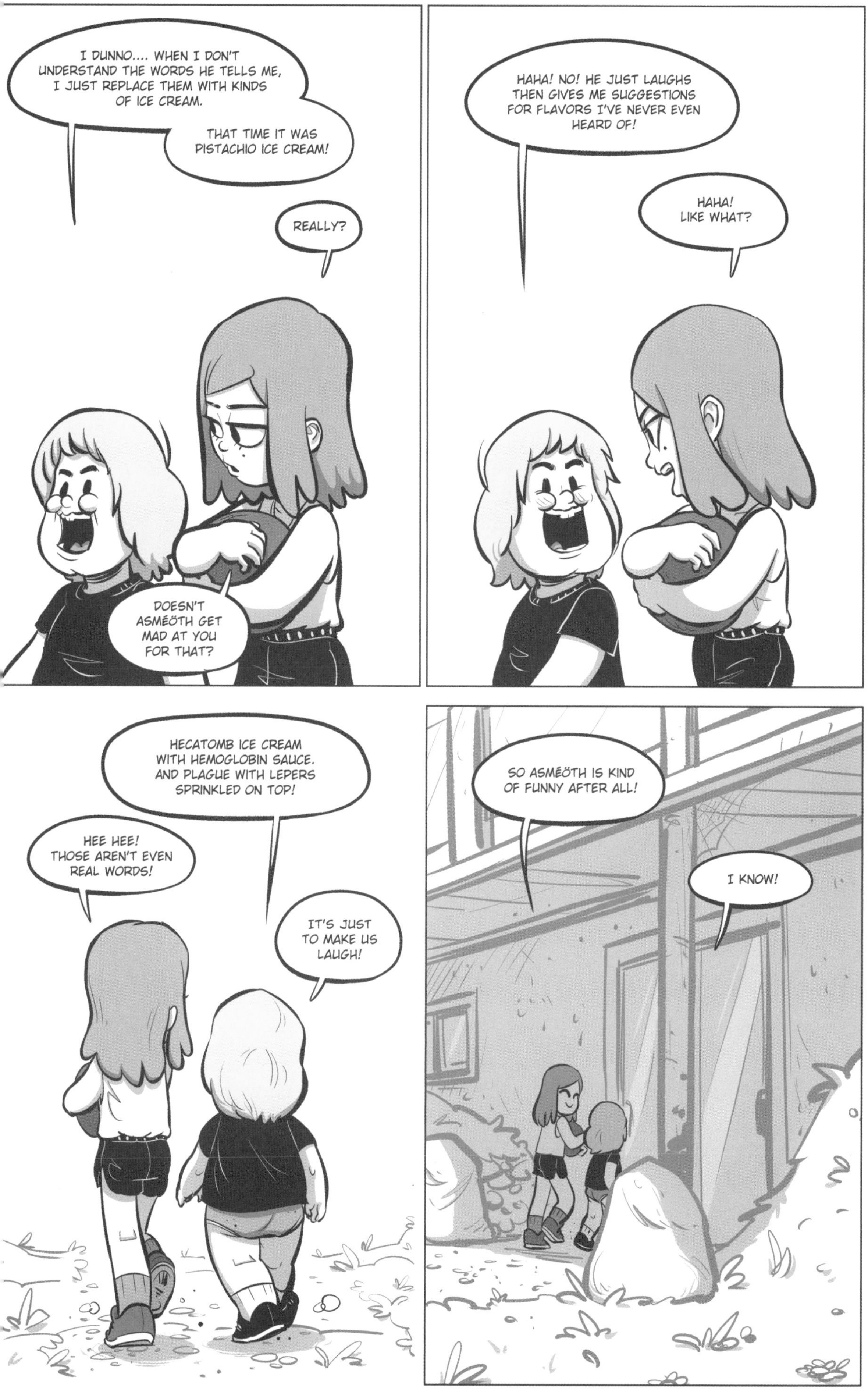
I DUNNO.... WHEN I DON'T UNDERSTAND THE WORDS HE TELLS ME, I JUST REPLACE THEM WITH KINDS OF ICE CREAM.
THAT TIME IT WAS PISTACHIO ICE CREAM!
REALLY?
DOESN'T ASMÉÖTH GET MAD AT YOU FOR THAT?
HAHA! NO! HE JUST LAUGHS THEN GIVES ME SUGGESTIONS FOR FLAVORS I'VE NEVER EVEN HEARD OF!
HAHA! LIKE WHAT?
HECATOMB ICE CREAM WITH HEMOGLOBIN SAUCE. AND PLAGUE WITH LEPERS SPRINKLED ON TOP!
HEE HEE! THOSE AREN'T EVEN REAL WORDS!
IT'S JUST TO MAKE US LAUGH!
SO ASMÉÖTH IS KIND OF FUNNY AFTER ALL!
I KNOW!

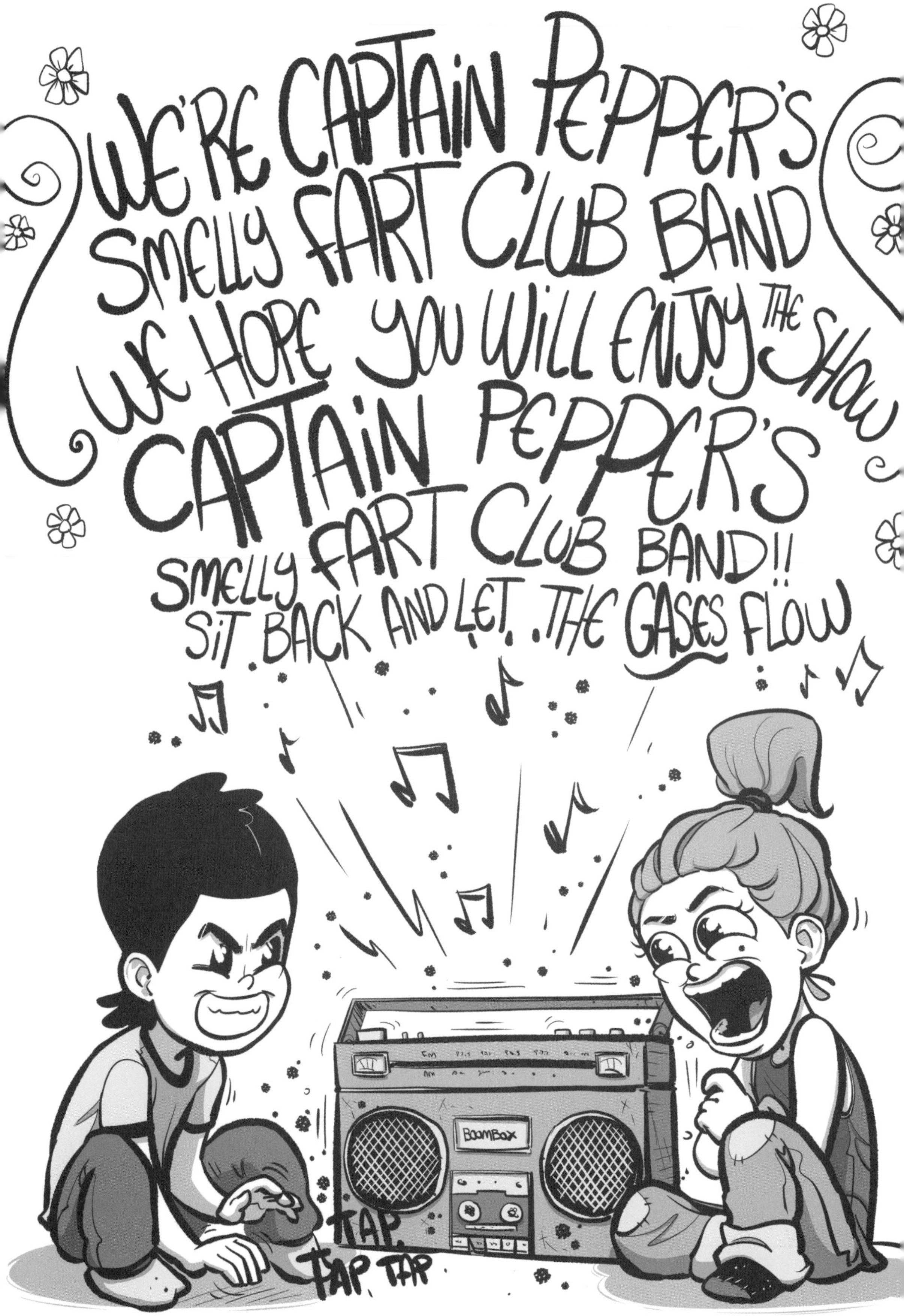
WE'RE CAPTAIN PEPPER'S
SMELLY FART CLUB BAND
WE HOPE YOU WILL ENJOY THE SHOW
CAPTAIN PEPPER'S
SMELLY FART CLUB BAND!!
SIT BACK AND LET. .THE GASES FLOW
BoomBox
TAP, TAP, TAP

SUMMER, 1986. DAVID AND I
ARE OBSESSED WITH CAPTAIN PEPPER.

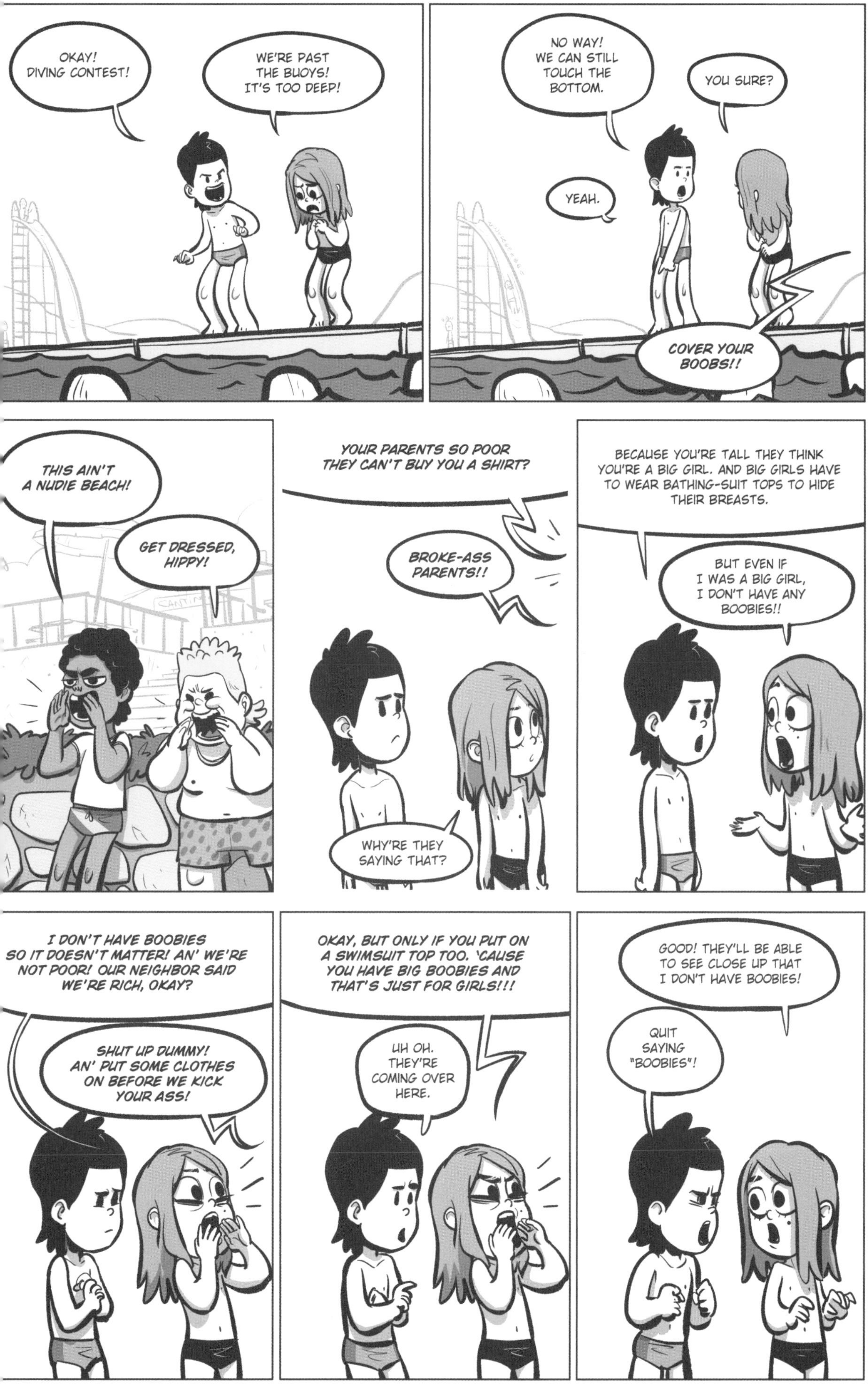
OKAY! DIVING CONTEST!
WE'RE PAST THE BUOYS! IT'S TOO DEEP!
NO WAY! WE CAN STILL TOUCH THE BOTTOM.
YOU SURE?
YEAH.
COVER YOUR BOOBS!!
THIS AIN'T A NUDIE BEACH!
GET DRESSED, HIPPY!
YOUR PARENTS SO POOR THEY CAN'T BUY YOU A SHIRT?
BROKE-ASS PARENTS!!
WHY'RE THEY SAYING THAT?
BECAUSE YOU'RE TALL THEY THINK YOU'RE A BIG GIRL. AND BIG GIRLS HAVE TO WEAR BATHING-SUIT TOPS TO HIDE THEIR BREASTS.
BUT EVEN IF I WAS A BIG GIRL, I DON'T HAVE ANY BOOBIES!!
I DON'T HAVE BOOBIES SO IT DOESN'T MATTER! AN' WE'RE NOT POOR! OUR NEIGHBOR SAID WE'RE RICH, OKAY?
SHUT UP DUMMY! AN' PUT SOME CLOTHES ON BEFORE WE KICK YOUR ASS!
OKAY, BUT ONLY IF YOU PUT ON A SWIMSUIT TOP TOO. 'CAUSE YOU HAVE BIG BOOBIES AND THAT'S JUST FOR GIRLS!!!
UH OH. THEY'RE COMING OVER HERE.
GOOD! THEY'LL BE ABLE TO SEE CLOSE UP THAT I DON'T HAVE BOOBIES!
QUIT SAYING "BOOBIES"!

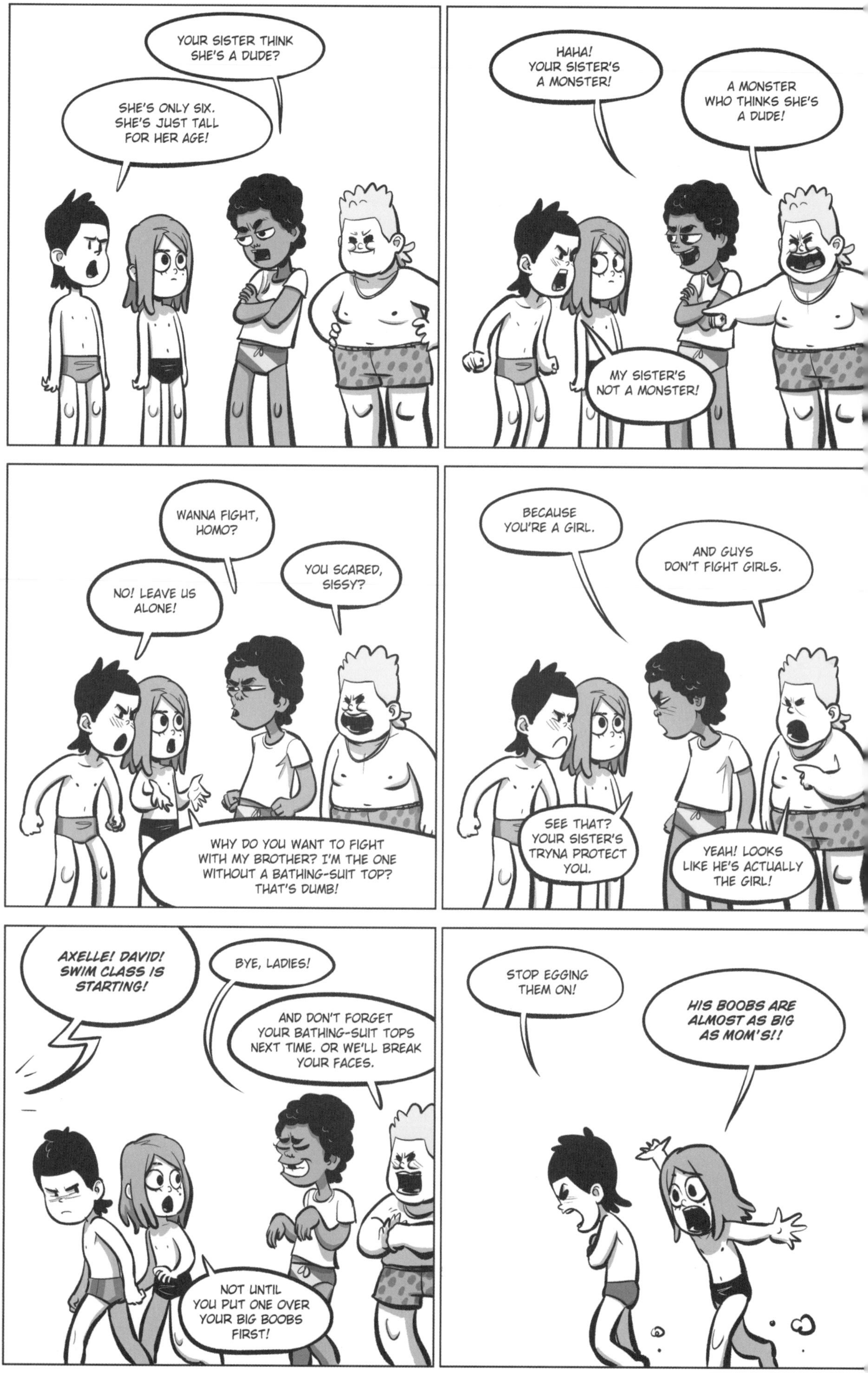
YOUR SISTER THINK SHE'S A DUDE?
SHE'S ONLY SIX. SHE'S JUST TALL FOR HER AGE!
HAHA! YOUR SISTER'S A MONSTER!
A MONSTER WHO THINKS SHE'S A DUDE!
MY SISTER'S NOT A MONSTER!
WANNA FIGHT, HOMO?
NO! LEAVE US ALONE!
YOU SCARED, SISSY?
WHY DO YOU WANT TO FIGHT WITH MY BROTHER? I'M THE ONE WITHOUT A BATHING-SUIT TOP? THAT'S DUMB!
BECAUSE YOU'RE A GIRL.
AND GUYS DON'T FIGHT GIRLS.
SEE THAT? YOUR SISTER'S TRYNA PROTECT YOU.
YEAH! LOOKS LIKE HE'S ACTUALLY THE GIRL!
AXELLE! DAVID! SWIM CLASS IS STARTING!
BYE, LADIES!
AND DON'T FORGET YOUR BATHING-SUIT TOPS NEXT TIME. OR WE'LL BREAK YOUR FACES.
NOT UNTIL YOU PUT ONE OVER YOUR BIG BOOBS FIRST!
STOP EGGING THEM ON!
HIS BOOBS ARE ALMOST AS BIG AS MOM'S!!

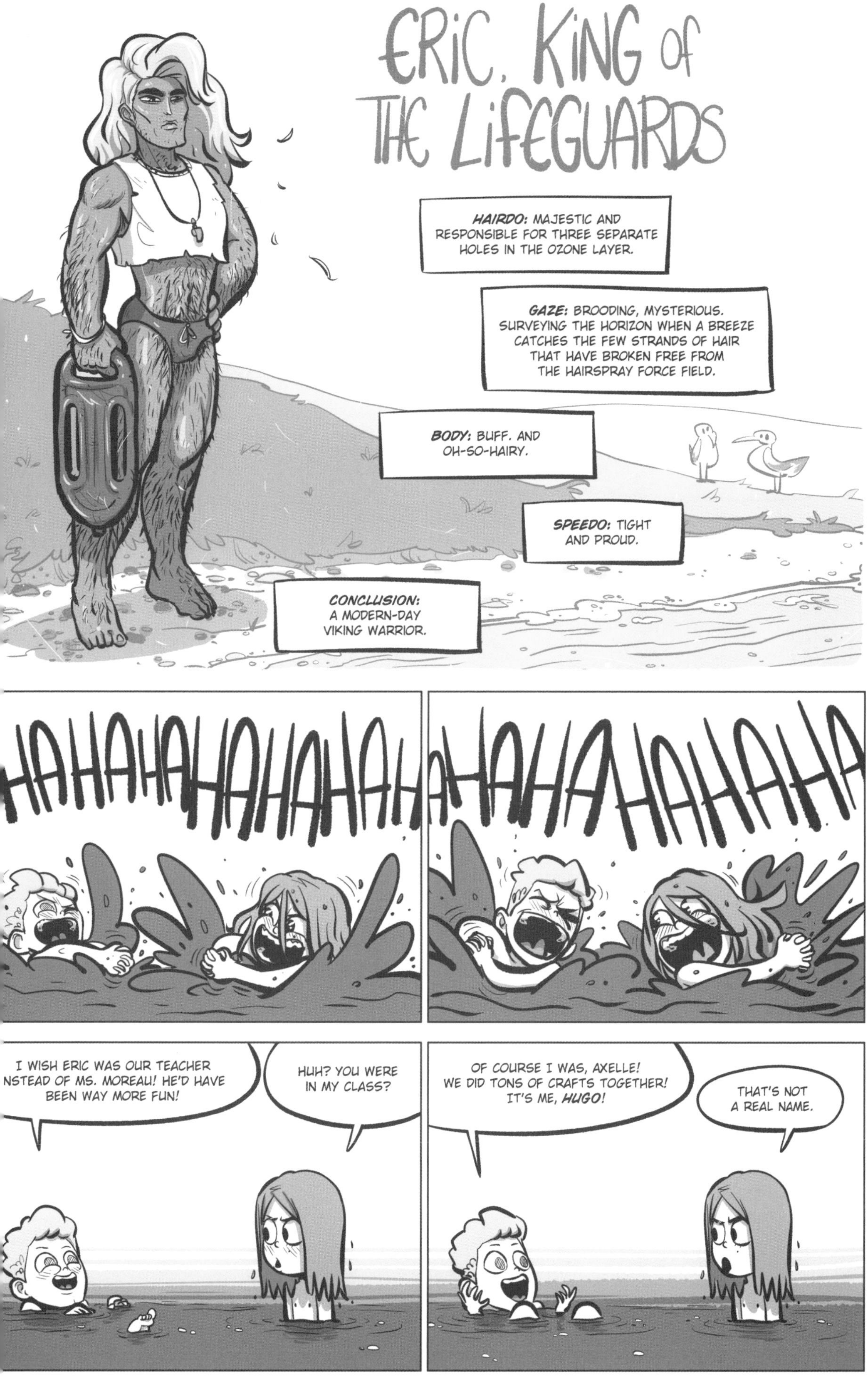
ERIC, KING OF THE LIFEGUARDS
HAIRDO: MAJESTIC AND RESPONSIBLE FOR THREE SEPARATE HOLES IN THE OZONE LAYER.
GAZE: BROODING, MYSTERIOUS. SURVEYING THE HORIZON WHEN A BREEZE CATCHES THE FEW STRANDS OF HAIR THAT HAVE BROKEN FREE FROM THE HAIRSPRAY FORCE FIELD.
BODY: BUFF. AND OH-SO-HAIRY.
SPEEDO: TIGHT AND PROUD.
CONCLUSION: A MODERN-DAY VIKING WARRIOR.
HAHAHAHAHAHAHAHAH
AHAHAHAHAHAHAHA
I WISH ERIC WAS OUR TEACHER NSTEAD OF MS. MOREAU! HE'D HAVE BEEN WAY MORE FUN!
HUH? YOU WERE IN MY CLASS?
OF COURSE I WAS, AXELLE! WE DID TONS OF CRAFTS TOGETHER! IT'S ME, HUGO!
THAT'S NOT A REAL NAME.

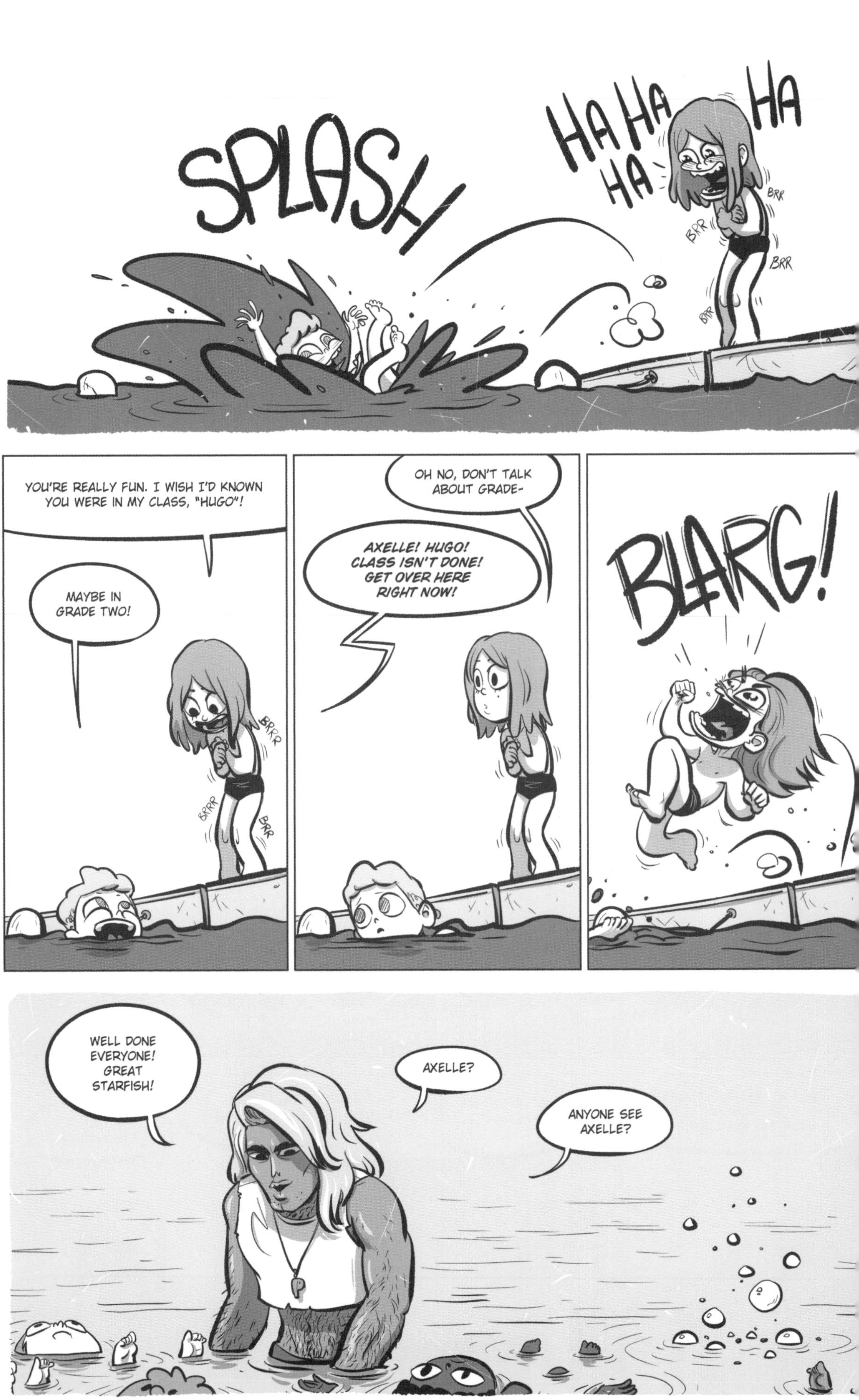
SPLASH
HA HA
HA
HA
BRR
BRR
BRR
BRR
YOU'RE REALLY FUN. I WISH I'D KNOWN YOU WERE IN MY CLASS, "HUGO"!
MAYBE IN GRADE TWO!
BRRR
BRRR
BRR
OH NO, DON'T TALK ABOUT GRADE-
AXELLE! HUGO! CLASS ISN'T DONE! GET OVER HERE RIGHT NOW!
BLARG!
WELL DONE EVERYONE! GREAT STARFISH!
AXELLE?
ANYONE SEE AXELLE?

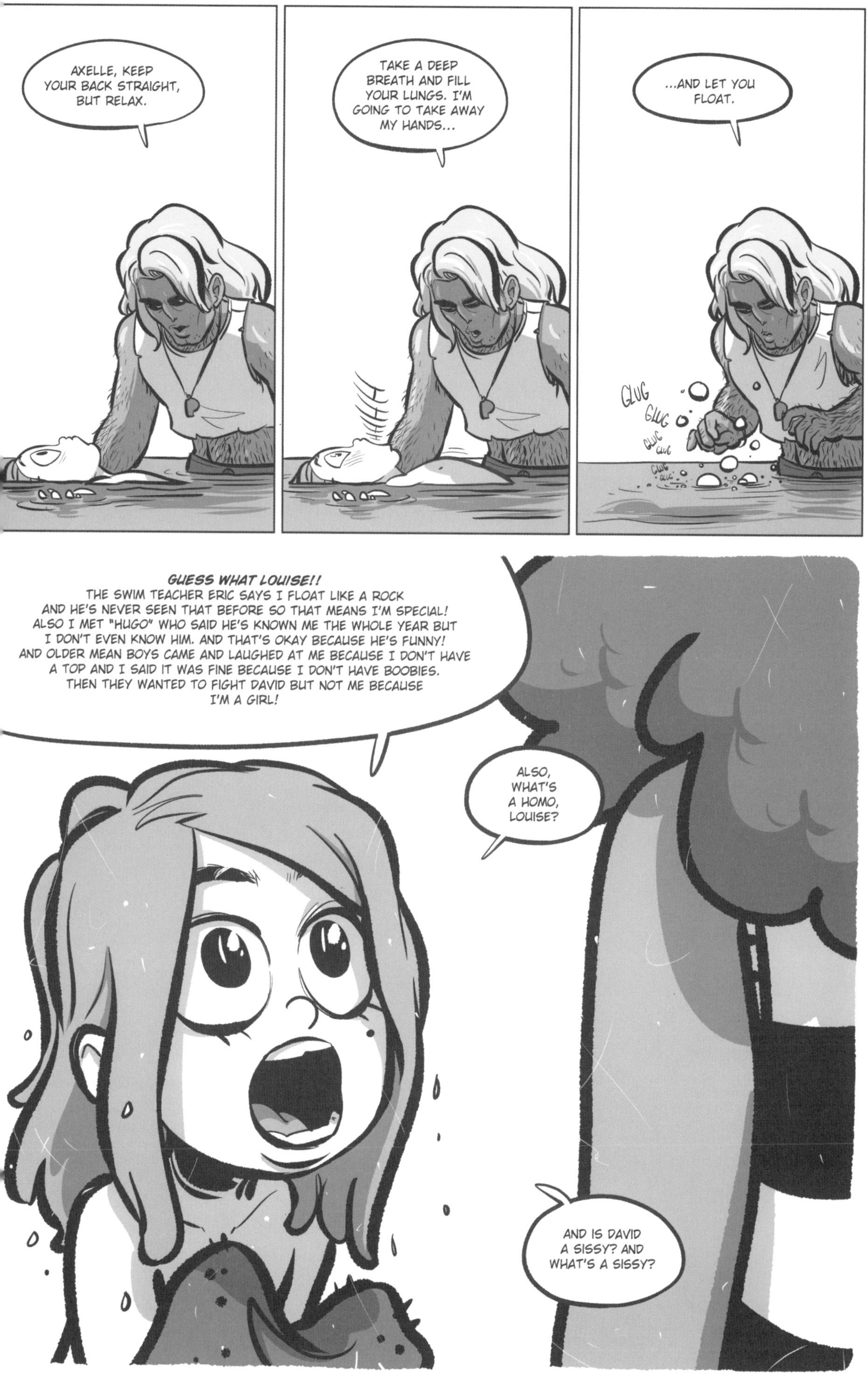
AXELLE, KEEP YOUR BACK STRAIGHT, BUT RELAX.
TAKE A DEEP BREATH AND FILL YOUR LUNGS. I'M GOING TO TAKE AWAY MY HANDS...
...AND LET YOU FLOAT.
GLUG GLUG GLUG GLUG GLUG GLUG
GUESS WHAT LOUISE!! THE SWIM TEACHER ERIC SAYS I FLOAT LIKE A ROCK AND HE'S NEVER SEEN THAT BEFORE SO THAT MEANS I'M SPECIAL! ALSO I MET "HUGO" WHO SAID HE'S KNOWN ME THE WHOLE YEAR BUT I DON'T EVEN KNOW HIM. AND THAT'S OKAY BECAUSE HE'S FUNNY! AND OLDER MEAN BOYS CAME AND LAUGHED AT ME BECAUSE I DON'T HAVE A TOP AND I SAID IT WAS FINE BECAUSE I DON'T HAVE BOOBIES. THEN THEY WANTED TO FIGHT DAVID BUT NOT ME BECAUSE I'M A GIRL!
ALSO, WHAT'S A HOMO, LOUISE?
AND IS DAVID A SISSY? AND WHAT'S A SISSY?

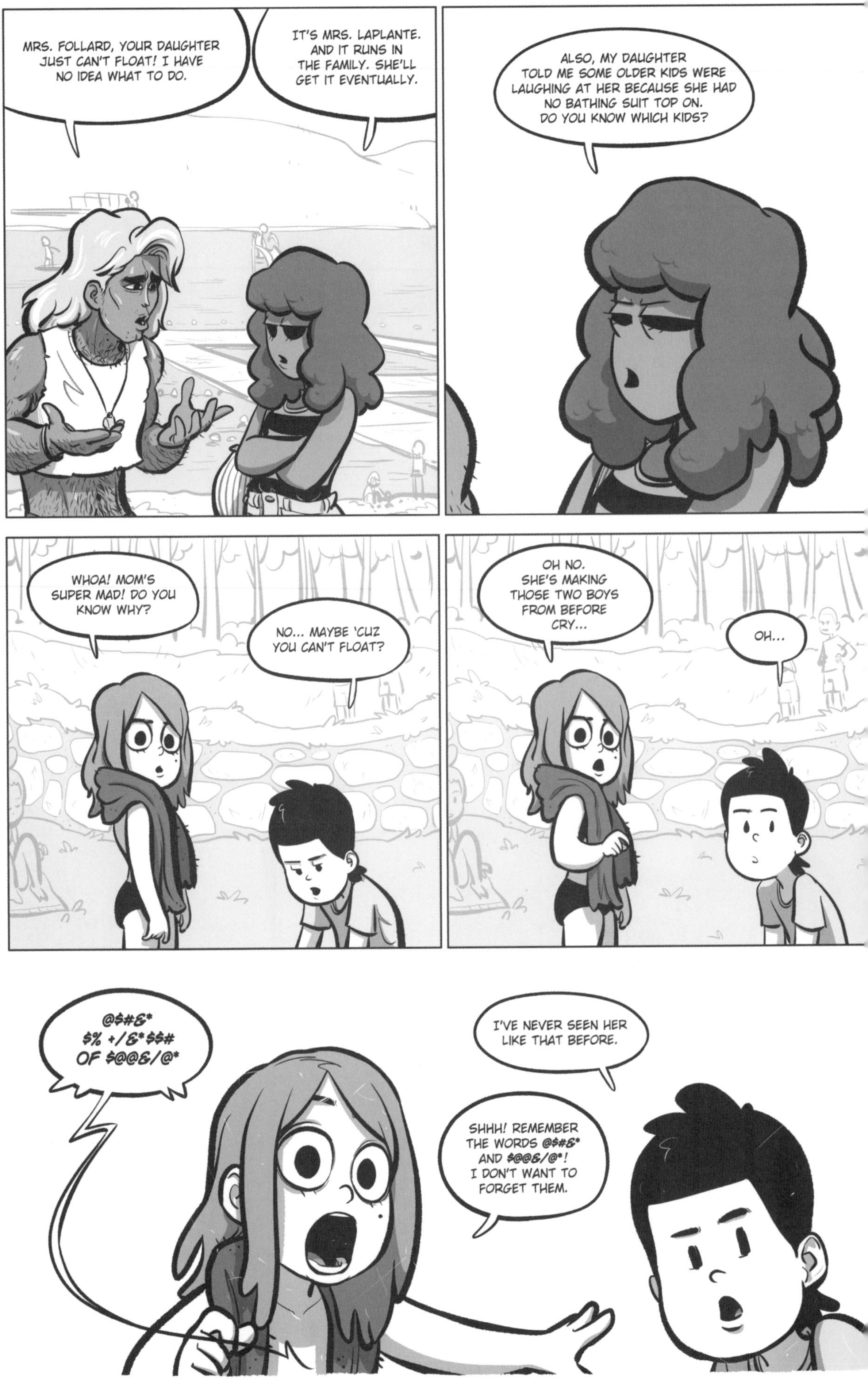

MRS. FOLLARD, YOUR DAUGHTER JUST CAN'T FLOAT! I HAVE NO IDEA WHAT TO DO.
IT'S MRS. LAPLANTE. AND IT RUNS IN THE FAMILY. SHE'LL GET IT EVENTUALLY.
ALSO, MY DAUGHTER TOLD ME SOME OLDER KIDS WERE LAUGHING AT HER BECAUSE SHE HAD NO BATHING SUIT TOP ON. DO YOU KNOW WHICH KIDS?
WHOA! MOM'S SUPER MAD! DO YOU KNOW WHY?
NO... MAYBE 'CUZ YOU CAN'T FLOAT?
OH NO. SHE'S MAKING THOSE TWO BOYS FROM BEFORE CRY...
OH...
@$#&* $% +/&*$$# OF $@@&/@*
I'VE NEVER SEEN HER LIKE THAT BEFORE.
SHHH! REMEMBER THE WORDS @$#&* AND $@@&/@*! I DON'T WANT TO FORGET THEM.

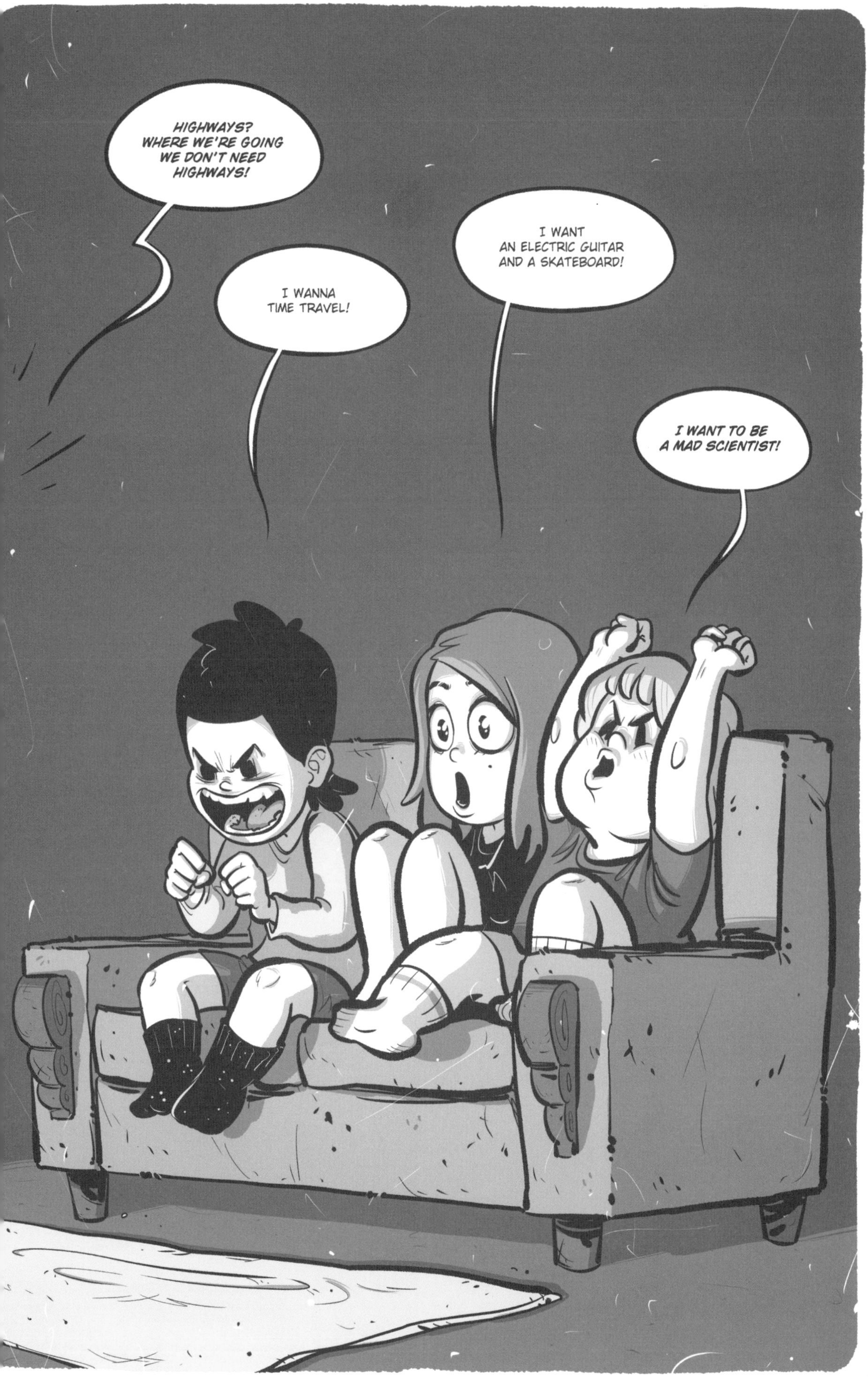
HIGHWAYS? WHERE WE'RE GOING WE DON'T NEED HIGHWAYS!
I WANNA TIME TRAVEL!
I WANT AN ELECTRIC GUITAR AND A SKATEBOARD!
I WANT TO BE A MAD SCIENTIST!

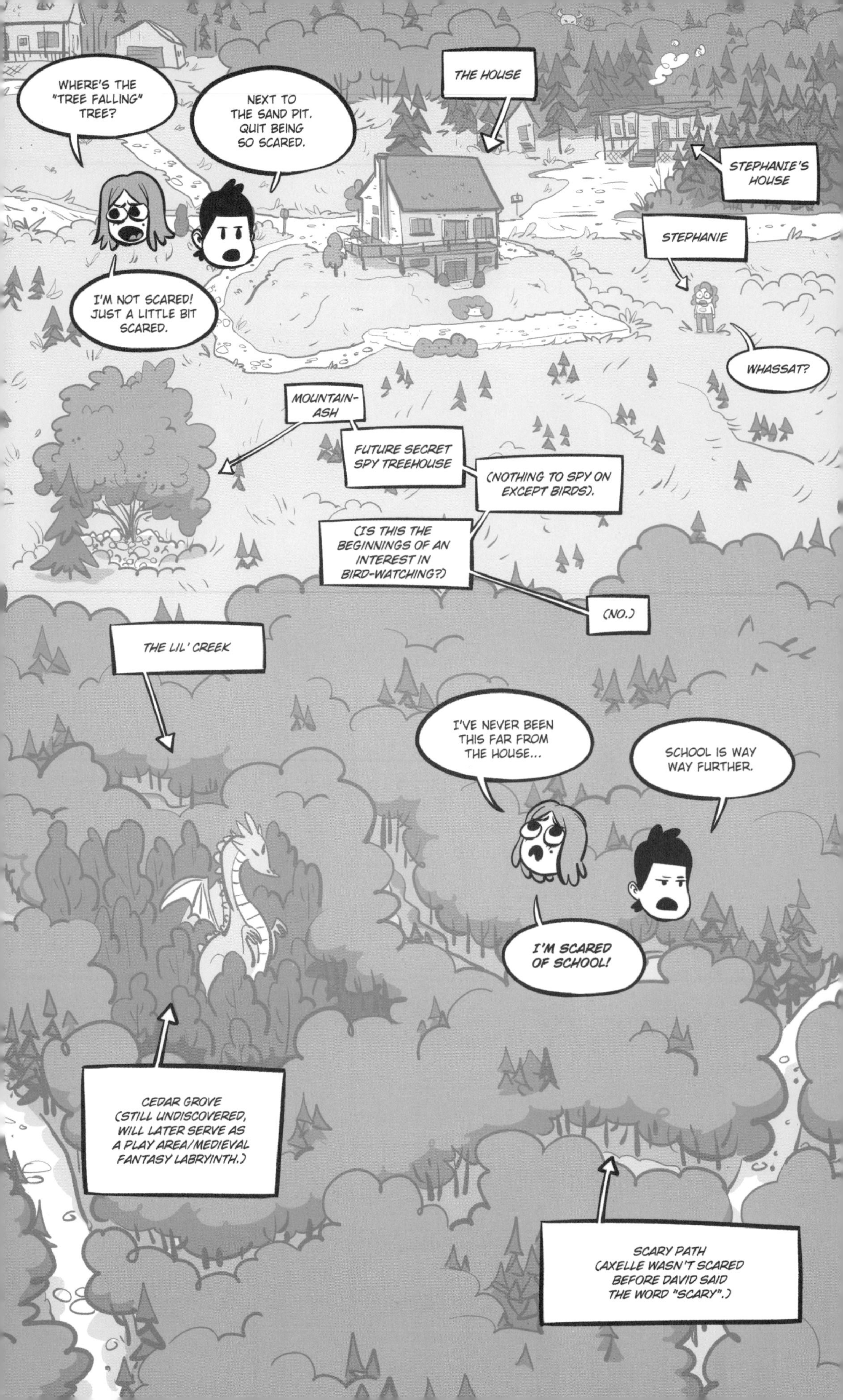
WHERE'S THE "TREE FALLING" TREE?
NEXT TO THE SAND PIT. QUIT BEING SO SCARED.
I'M NOT SCARED! JUST A LITTLE BIT SCARED.
THE HOUSE
STEPHANIE'S HOUSE
STEPHANIE
WHASSAT?
MOUNTAIN-ASH
FUTURE SECRET SPY TREEHOUSE
(NOTHING TO SPY ON EXCEPT BIRDS).
(IS THIS THE BEGINNINGS OF AN INTEREST IN BIRD-WATCHING?)
(NO.)
THE LIL' CREEK
I'VE NEVER BEEN THIS FAR FROM THE HOUSE...
SCHOOL IS WAY WAY FURTHER.
I'M SCARED OF SCHOOL!
CEDAR GROVE (STILL UNDISCOVERED, WILL LATER SERVE AS A PLAY AREA/MEDIEVAL FANTASY LABRYINTH.)
SCARY PATH (AXELLE WASN'T SCARED BEFORE DAVID SAID THE WORD "SCARY".)

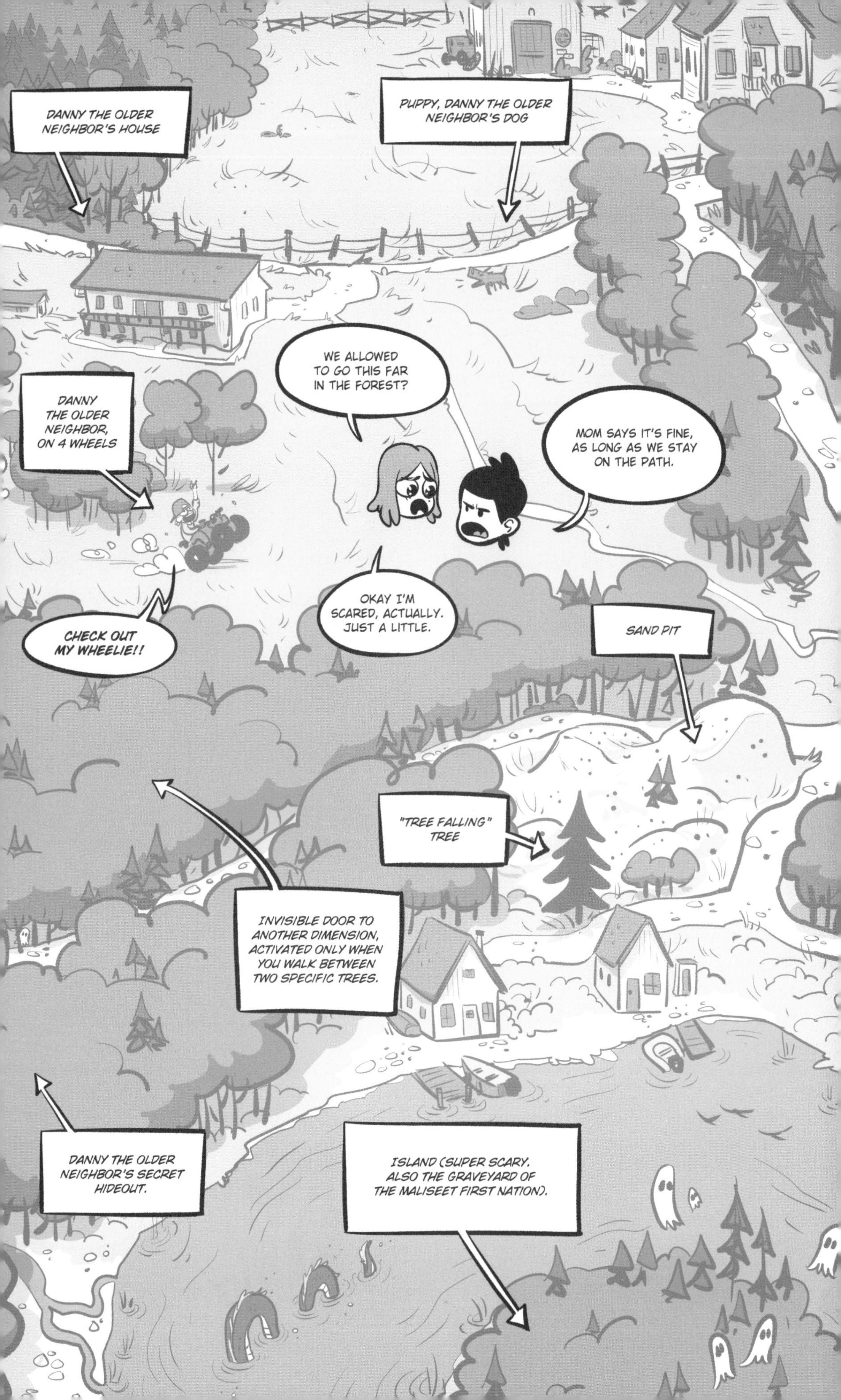
DANNY THE OLDER NEIGHBOR'S HOUSE
PUPPY, DANNY THE OLDER NEIGHBOR'S DOG
WE ALLOWED TO GO THIS FAR IN THE FOREST?
DANNY THE OLDER NEIGHBOR, ON 4 WHEELS
MOM SAYS IT'S FINE, AS LONG AS WE STAY ON THE PATH.
OKAY I'M SCARED, ACTUALLY. JUST A LITTLE.
CHECK OUT MY WHEELIE!!
SAND PIT
"TREE FALLING" TREE
INVISIBLE DOOR TO ANOTHER DIMENSION, ACTIVATED ONLY WHEN YOU WALK BETWEEN TWO SPECIFIC TREES.
DANNY THE OLDER NEIGHBOR'S SECRET HIDEOUT.
ISLAND (SUPER SCARY. ALSO THE GRAVEYARD OF THE MALISEET FIRST NATION).

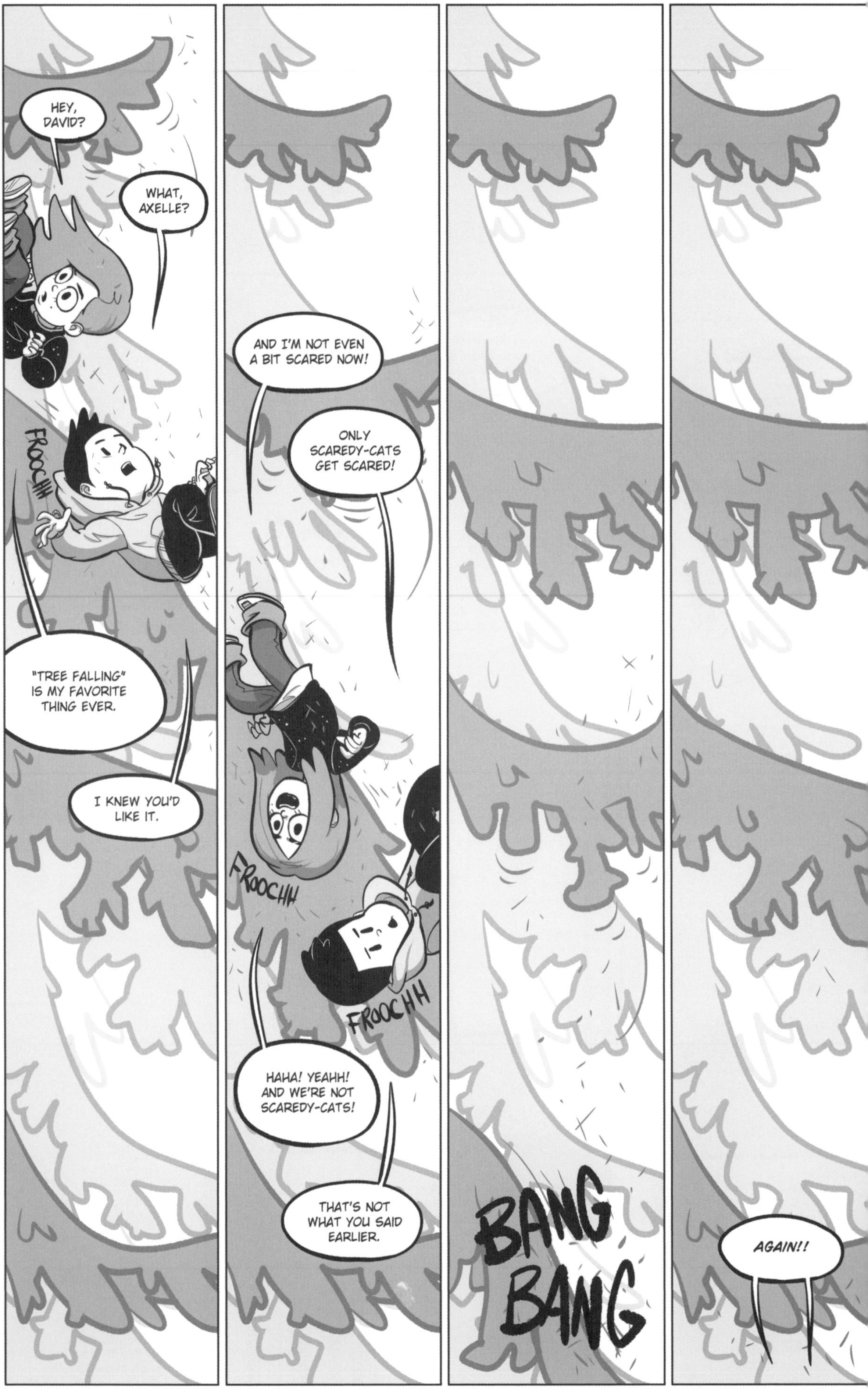
HEY, DAVID?
WHAT, AXELLE?
FROOCHH
"TREE FALLING" IS MY FAVORITE THING EVER.
I KNEW YOU'D LIKE IT.
AND I'M NOT EVEN A BIT SCARED NOW!
ONLY SCAREDY-CATS GET SCARED!
FROOCHH
FROOCHH
HAHA! YEAHH! AND WE'RE NOT SCAREDY-CATS!
THAT'S NOT WHAT YOU SAID EARLIER.
BANG BANG
AGAIN!!

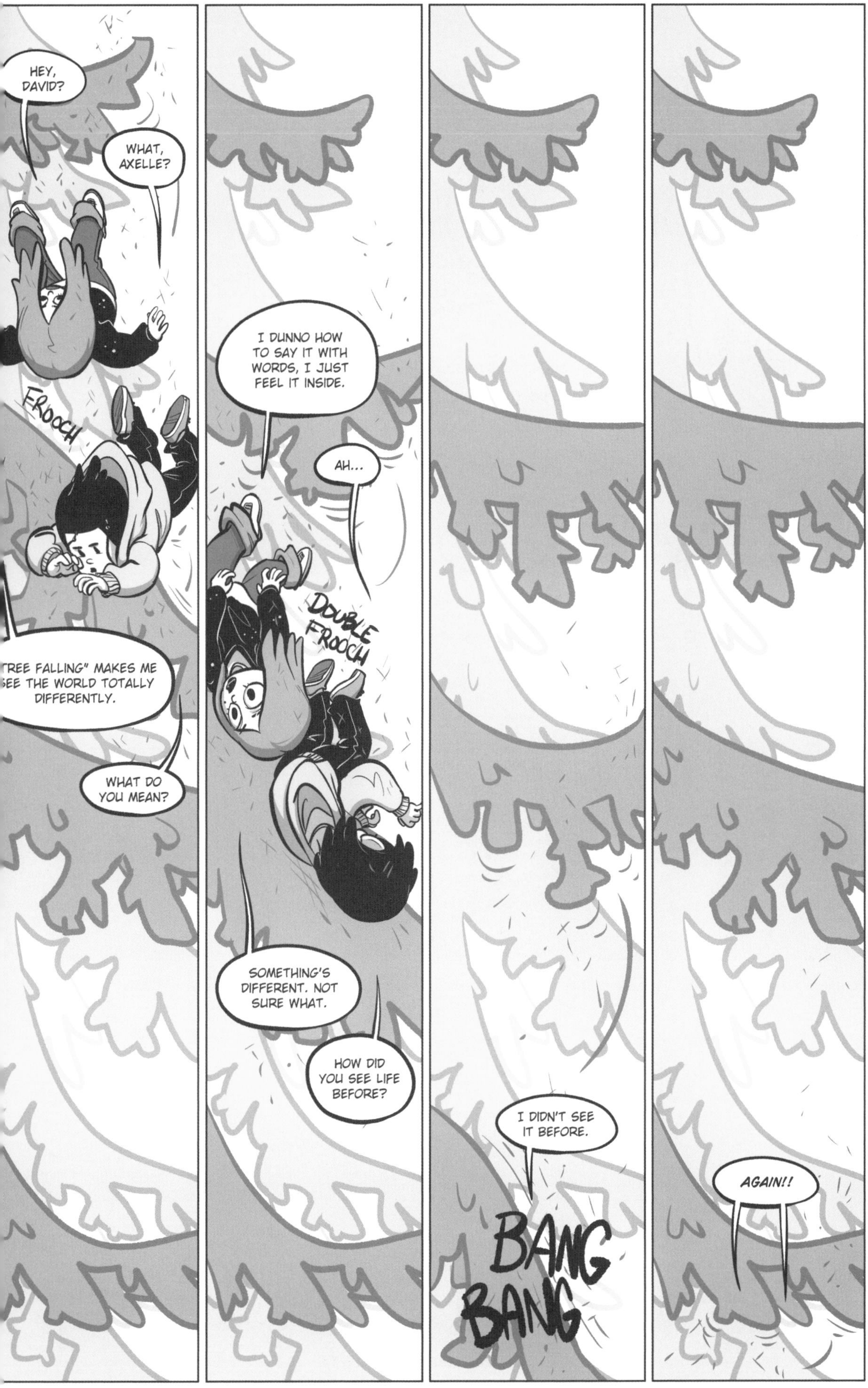
HEY, DAVID?
WHAT, AXELLE?
FROOCH
"TREE FALLING" MAKES ME SEE THE WORLD TOTALLY DIFFERENTLY.
WHAT DO YOU MEAN?
I DUNNO HOW TO SAY IT WITH WORDS, I JUST FEEL IT INSIDE.
AH...
DOUBLE FROOCH
SOMETHING'S DIFFERENT. NOT SURE WHAT.
HOW DID YOU SEE LIFE BEFORE?
I DIDN'T SEE IT BEFORE.
BANG BANG
AGAIN!!

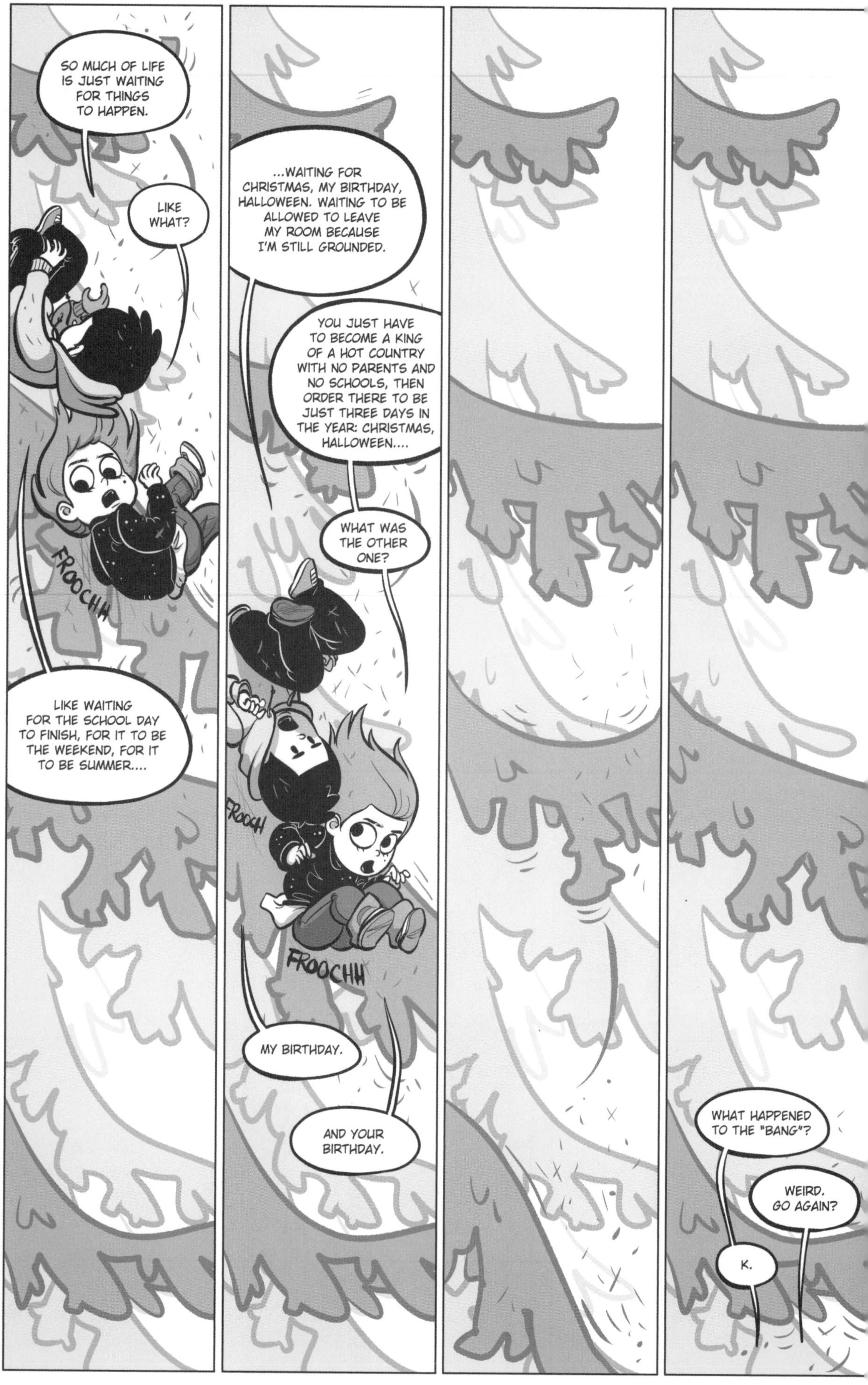
SO MUCH OF LIFE IS JUST WAITING FOR THINGS TO HAPPEN.
LIKE WHAT?
FROOCHH
LIKE WAITING FOR THE SCHOOL DAY TO FINISH, FOR IT TO BE THE WEEKEND, FOR IT TO BE SUMMER....
...WAITING FOR CHRISTMAS, MY BIRTHDAY, HALLOWEEN. WAITING TO BE ALLOWED TO LEAVE MY ROOM BECAUSE I'M STILL GROUNDED.
YOU JUST HAVE TO BECOME A KING OF A HOT COUNTRY WITH NO PARENTS AND NO SCHOOLS, THEN ORDER THERE TO BE JUST THREE DAYS IN THE YEAR: CHRISTMAS, HALLOWEEN....
WHAT WAS THE OTHER ONE?
FROOCH
FROOCHH
MY BIRTHDAY.
AND YOUR BIRTHDAY.
WHAT HAPPENED TO THE "BANG"?
WEIRD. GO AGAIN?
K.

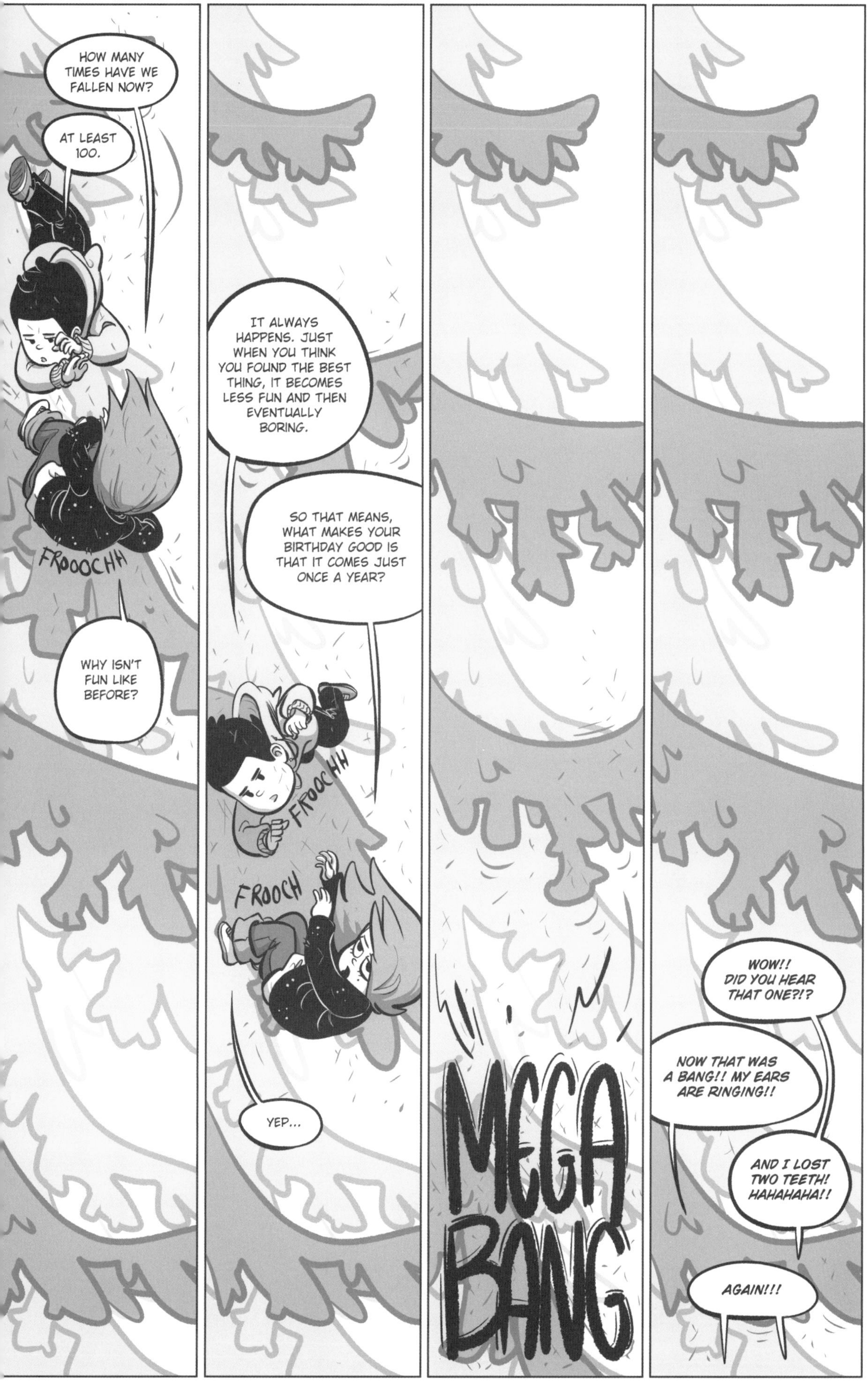
HOW MANY TIMES HAVE WE FALLEN NOW?
AT LEAST 100.
FROOOCHH
WHY ISN'T FUN LIKE BEFORE?
IT ALWAYS HAPPENS. JUST WHEN YOU THINK YOU FOUND THE BEST THING, IT BECOMES LESS FUN AND THEN EVENTUALLY BORING.
SO THAT MEANS, WHAT MAKES YOUR BIRTHDAY GOOD IS THAT IT COMES JUST ONCE A YEAR?
FROOCHH
FROOCH
YEP...
MEGA BANG
WOW!! DID YOU HEAR THAT ONE?!?
NOW THAT WAS A BANG!! MY EARS ARE RINGING!!
AND I LOST TWO TEETH! HAHAHAHA!!
AGAIN!!!

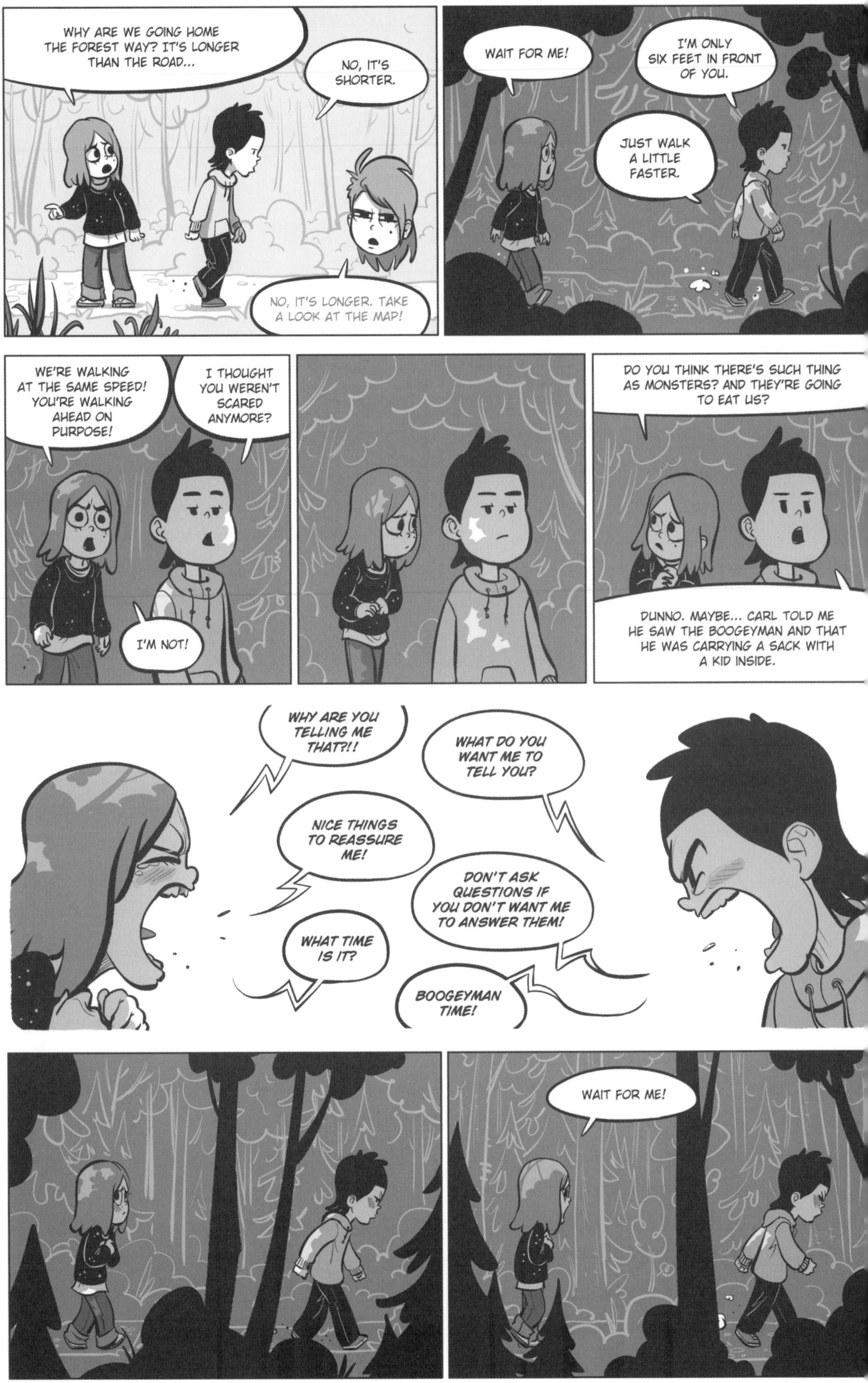
WHY ARE WE GOING HOME THE FOREST WAY? IT'S LONGER THAN THE ROAD...
NO, IT'S SHORTER.
NO, IT'S LONGER. TAKE A LOOK AT THE MAP!
WAIT FOR ME!
I'M ONLY SIX FEET IN FRONT OF YOU.
JUST WALK A LITTLE FASTER.
WE'RE WALKING AT THE SAME SPEED! YOU'RE WALKING AHEAD ON PURPOSE!
I THOUGHT YOU WEREN'T SCARED ANYMORE?
I'M NOT!
DO YOU THINK THERE'S SUCH THING AS MONSTERS? AND THEY'RE GOING TO EAT US?
DUNNO. MAYBE... CARL TOLD ME HE SAW THE BOOGEYMAN AND THAT HE WAS CARRYING A SACK WITH A KID INSIDE.
WHY ARE YOU TELLING ME THAT?!!
WHAT DO YOU WANT ME TO TELL YOU?
NICE THINGS TO REASSURE ME!
DON'T ASK QUESTIONS IF YOU DON'T WANT ME TO ANSWER THEM!
WHAT TIME IS IT?
BOOGEYMAN TIME!
WAIT FOR ME!

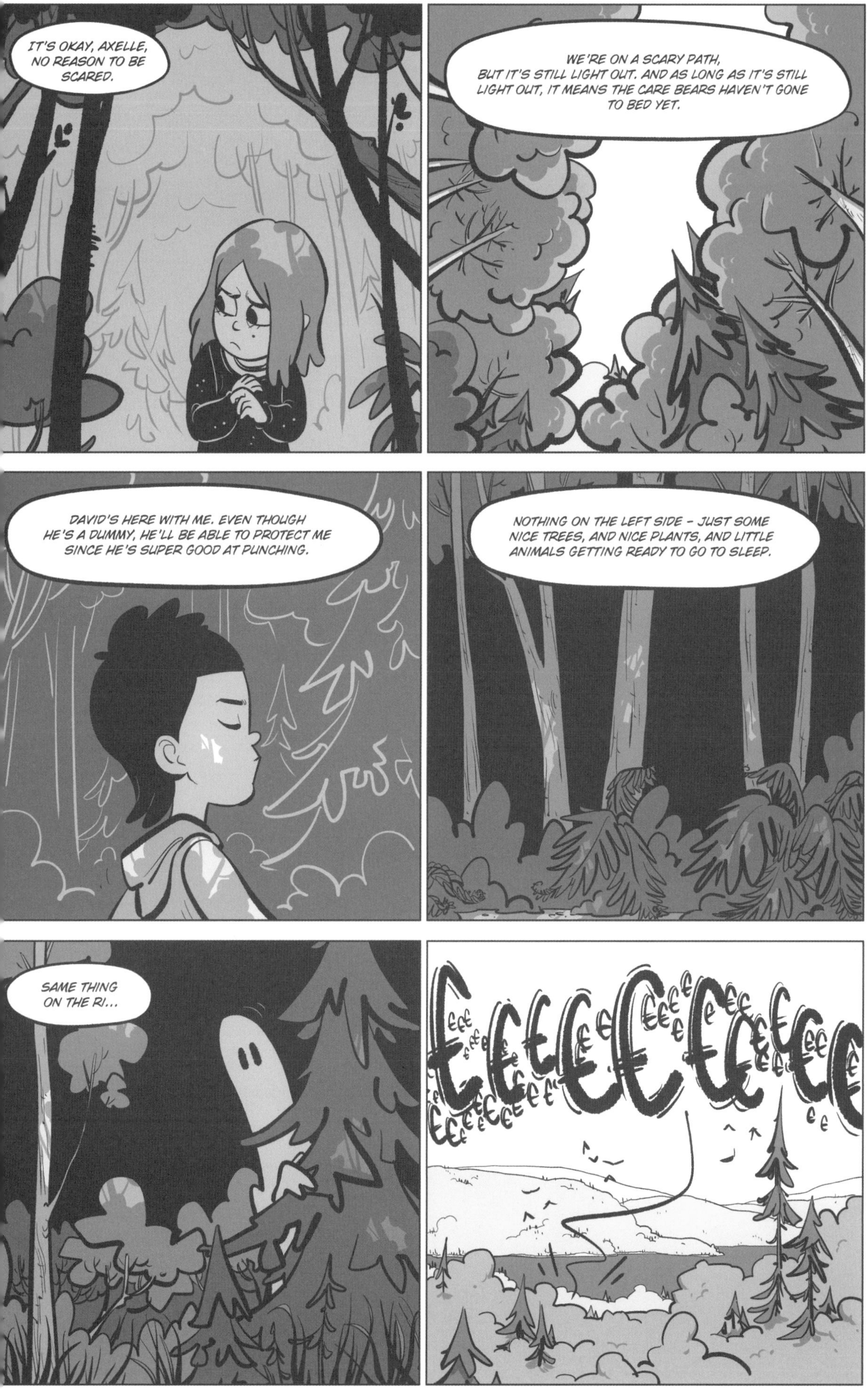
IT'S OKAY, AXELLE, NO REASON TO BE SCARED.
WE'RE ON A SCARY PATH, BUT IT'S STILL LIGHT OUT. AND AS LONG AS IT'S STILL LIGHT OUT, IT MEANS THE CARE BEARS HAVEN'T GONE TO BED YET.
DAVID'S HERE WITH ME. EVEN THOUGH HE'S A DUMMY, HE'LL BE ABLE TO PROTECT ME SINCE HE'S SUPER GOOD AT PUNCHING.
NOTHING ON THE LEFT SIDE - JUST SOME NICE TREES, AND NICE PLANTS, AND LITTLE ANIMALS GETTING READY TO GO TO SLEEP.
SAME THING ON THE RI...

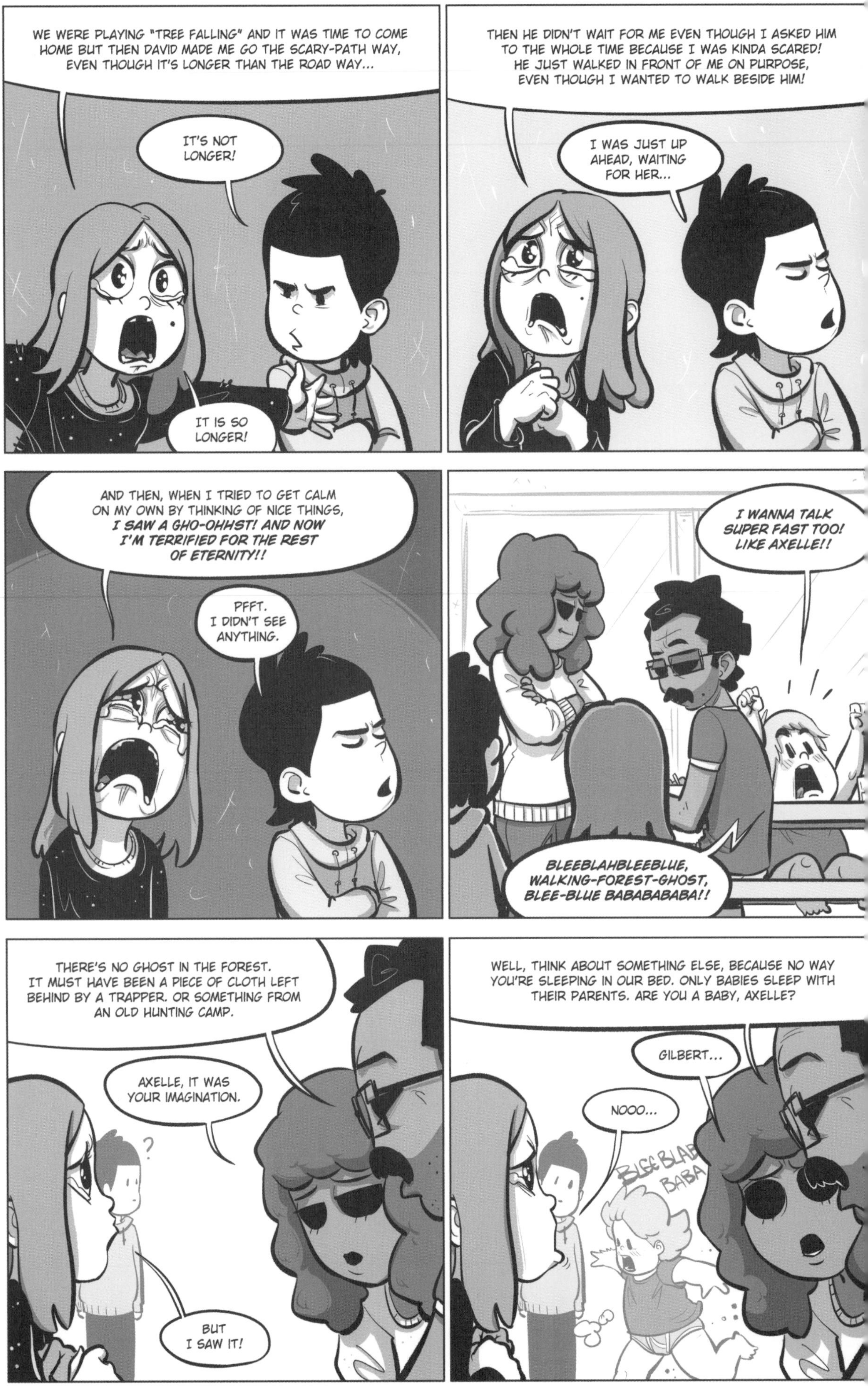
WE WERE PLAYING "TREE FALLING" AND IT WAS TIME TO COME HOME BUT THEN DAVID MADE ME GO THE SCARY-PATH WAY, EVEN THOUGH IT'S LONGER THAN THE ROAD WAY...
IT'S NOT LONGER!
IT IS SO LONGER!
THEN HE DIDN'T WAIT FOR ME EVEN THOUGH I ASKED HIM TO THE WHOLE TIME BECAUSE I WAS KINDA SCARED! HE JUST WALKED IN FRONT OF ME ON PURPOSE, EVEN THOUGH I WANTED TO WALK BESIDE HIM!
I WAS JUST UP AHEAD, WAITING FOR HER...
AND THEN, WHEN I TRIED TO GET CALM ON MY OWN BY THINKING OF NICE THINGS, I SAW A GHO-OHHST! AND NOW I'M TERRIFIED FOR THE REST OF ETERNITY!!
PFFT. I DIDN'T SEE ANYTHING.
I WANNA TALK SUPER FAST TOO! LIKE AXELLE!!
BLEEBLAHBLEEBLUE, WALKING-FOREST-GHOST, BLEE-BLUE BABABABABA!!
THERE'S NO GHOST IN THE FOREST. IT MUST HAVE BEEN A PIECE OF CLOTH LEFT BEHIND BY A TRAPPER. OR SOMETHING FROM AN OLD HUNTING CAMP.
AXELLE, IT WAS YOUR IMAGINATION.
?
BUT I SAW IT!
WELL, THINK ABOUT SOMETHING ELSE, BECAUSE NO WAY YOU'RE SLEEPING IN OUR BED. ONLY BABIES SLEEP WITH THEIR PARENTS. ARE YOU A BABY, AXELLE?
GILBERT...
NOOO...
BLEEBLAB BABA

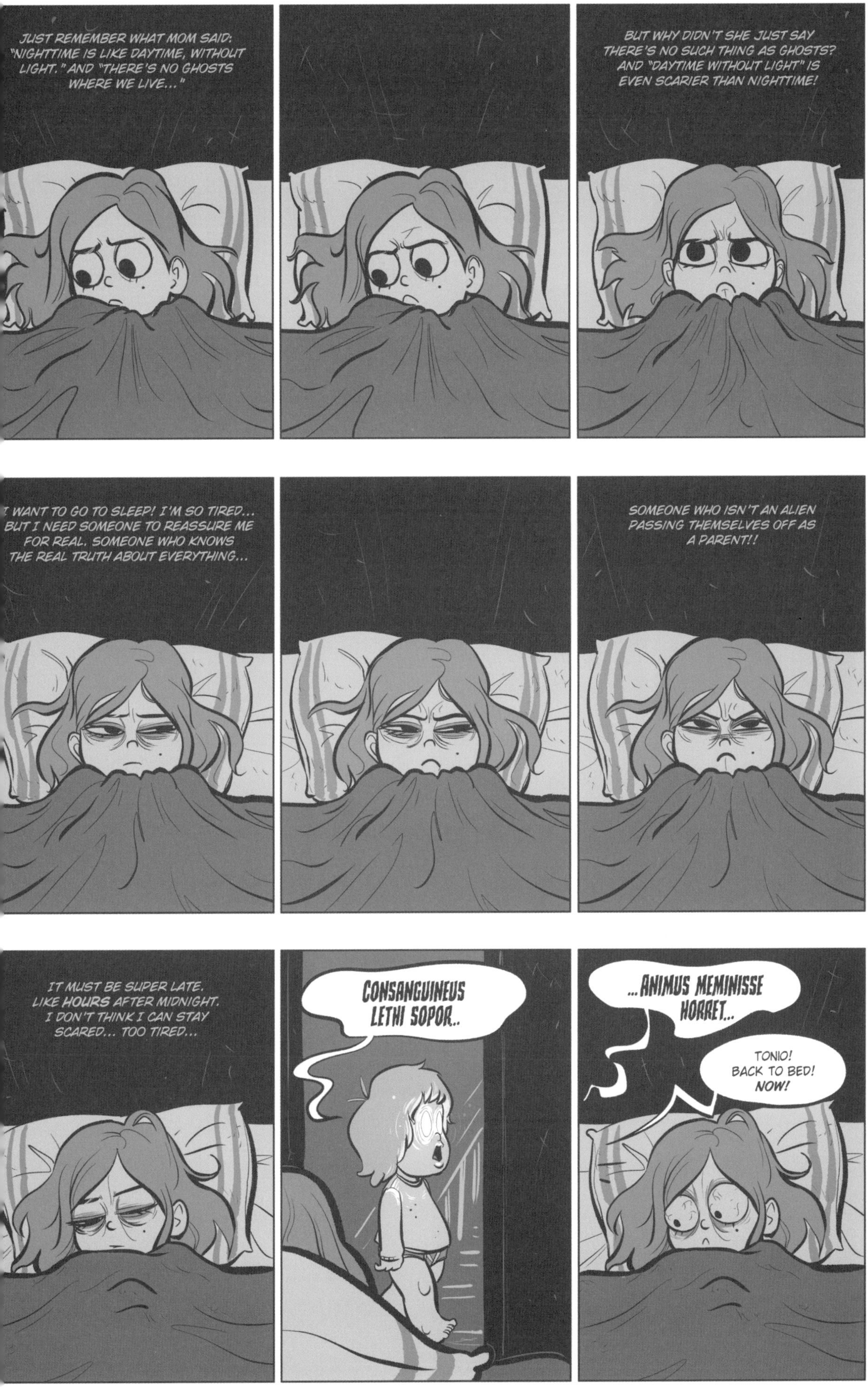
JUST REMEMBER WHAT MOM SAID: "NIGHTTIME IS LIKE DAYTIME, WITHOUT LIGHT." AND "THERE'S NO GHOSTS WHERE WE LIVE..."
BUT WHY DIDN'T SHE JUST SAY THERE'S NO SUCH THING AS GHOSTS? AND "DAYTIME WITHOUT LIGHT" IS EVEN SCARIER THAN NIGHTTIME!
I WANT TO GO TO SLEEP! I'M SO TIRED... BUT I NEED SOMEONE TO REASSURE ME FOR REAL. SOMEONE WHO KNOWS THE REAL TRUTH ABOUT EVERYTHING...
SOMEONE WHO ISN'T AN ALIEN PASSING THEMSELVES OFF AS A PARENT!!
IT MUST BE SUPER LATE. LIKE HOURS AFTER MIDNIGHT. I DON'T THINK I CAN STAY SCARED... TOO TIRED...
CONSANGUINEUS LETHI SOPOR..
...ANIMUS MEMINISSE HORRET...
TONIO! BACK TO BED! NOW!

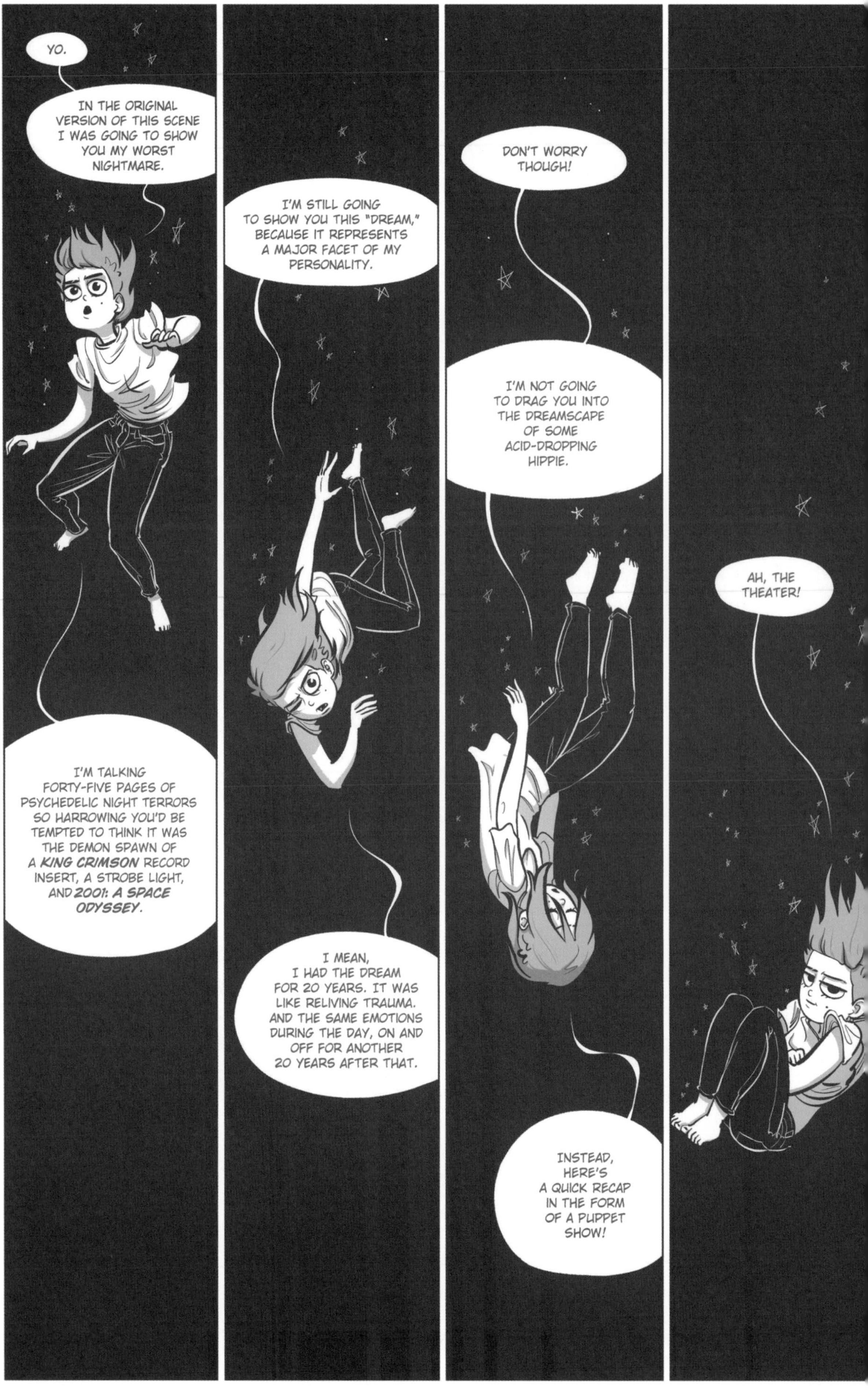
YO.
IN THE ORIGINAL VERSION OF THIS SCENE I WAS GOING TO SHOW YOU MY WORST NIGHTMARE.
I'M TALKING FORTY-FIVE PAGES OF PSYCHEDELIC NIGHT TERRORS SO HARROWING YOU'D BE TEMPTED TO THINK IT WAS THE DEMON SPAWN OF A KING CRIMSON RECORD INSERT, A STROBE LIGHT, AND 2001: A SPACE ODYSSEY.
I'M STILL GOING TO SHOW YOU THIS "DREAM," BECAUSE IT REPRESENTS A MAJOR FACET OF MY PERSONALITY.
I MEAN, I HAD THE DREAM FOR 20 YEARS. IT WAS LIKE RELIVING TRAUMA. AND THE SAME EMOTIONS DURING THE DAY, ON AND OFF FOR ANOTHER 20 YEARS AFTER THAT.
DON'T WORRY THOUGH!
I'M NOT GOING TO DRAG YOU INTO THE DREAMSCAPE OF SOME ACID-DROPPING HIPPIE.
INSTEAD, HERE'S A QUICK RECAP IN THE FORM OF A PUPPET SHOW!
AH, THE THEATER!

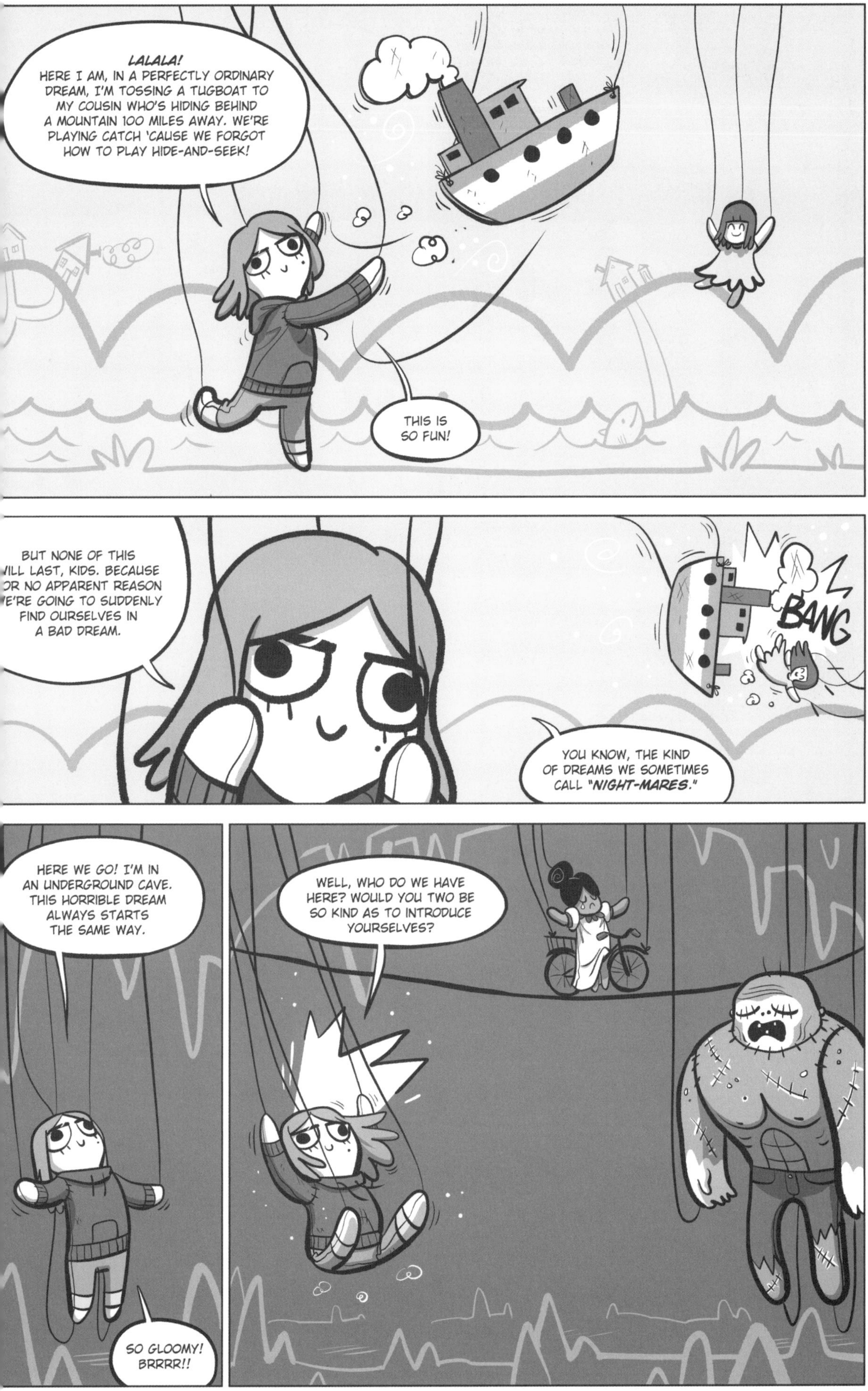
LALALA!
HERE I AM, IN A PERFECTLY ORDINARY DREAM, I'M TOSSING A TUGBOAT TO MY COUSIN WHO'S HIDING BEHIND A MOUNTAIN 100 MILES AWAY. WE'RE PLAYING CATCH 'CAUSE WE FORGOT HOW TO PLAY HIDE-AND-SEEK!
THIS IS SO FUN!
BUT NONE OF THIS WILL LAST, KIDS. BECAUSE FOR NO APPARENT REASON WE'RE GOING TO SUDDENLY FIND OURSELVES IN A BAD DREAM.
BANG
YOU KNOW, THE KIND OF DREAMS WE SOMETIMES CALL "NIGHT-MARES."
HERE WE GO! I'M IN AN UNDERGROUND CAVE. THIS HORRIBLE DREAM ALWAYS STARTS THE SAME WAY.
SO GLOOMY! BRRRR!!
WELL, WHO DO WE HAVE HERE? WOULD YOU TWO BE SO KIND AS TO INTRODUCE YOURSELVES?

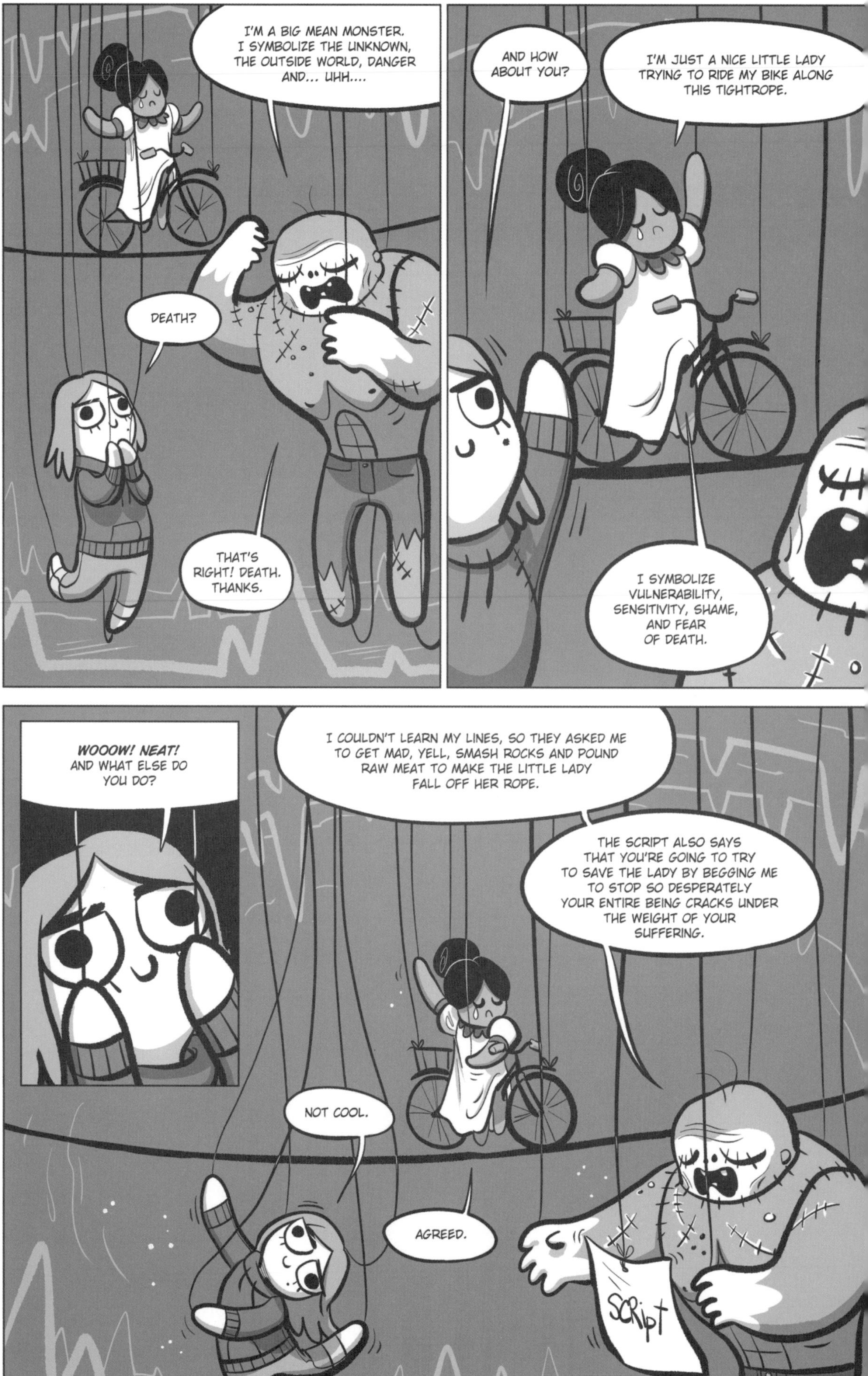
I'M A BIG MEAN MONSTER. I SYMBOLIZE THE UNKNOWN, THE OUTSIDE WORLD, DANGER AND... UHH....
DEATH?
THAT'S RIGHT! DEATH. THANKS.
AND HOW ABOUT YOU?
I'M JUST A NICE LITTLE LADY TRYING TO RIDE MY BIKE ALONG THIS TIGHTROPE.
I SYMBOLIZE VULNERABILITY, SENSITIVITY, SHAME, AND FEAR OF DEATH.
WOOOW! NEAT! AND WHAT ELSE DO YOU DO?
I COULDN'T LEARN MY LINES, SO THEY ASKED ME TO GET MAD, YELL, SMASH ROCKS AND POUND RAW MEAT TO MAKE THE LITTLE LADY FALL OFF HER ROPE.
THE SCRIPT ALSO SAYS THAT YOU'RE GOING TO TRY TO SAVE THE LADY BY BEGGING ME TO STOP SO DESPERATELY YOUR ENTIRE BEING CRACKS UNDER THE WEIGHT OF YOUR SUFFERING.
NOT COOL.
AGREED.
SCRIPT

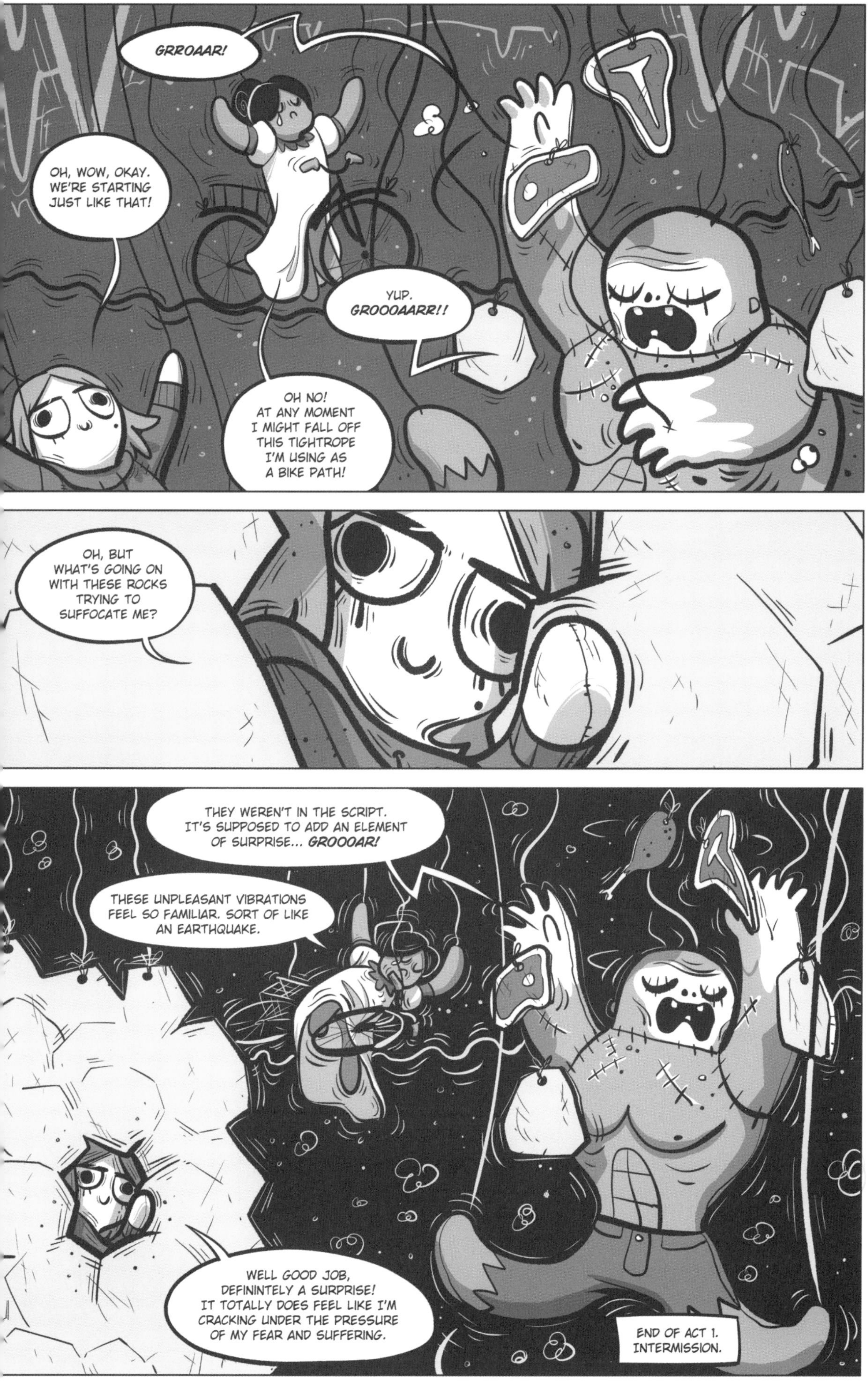
GRROAAR!
OH, WOW, OKAY. WE'RE STARTING JUST LIKE THAT!
YUP. GROOOAARR!!
OH NO! AT ANY MOMENT I MIGHT FALL OFF THIS TIGHTROPE I'M USING AS A BIKE PATH!
OH, BUT WHAT'S GOING ON WITH THESE ROCKS TRYING TO SUFFOCATE ME?
THEY WEREN'T IN THE SCRIPT. IT'S SUPPOSED TO ADD AN ELEMENT OF SURPRISE... GROOOAR!
THESE UNPLEASANT VIBRATIONS FEEL SO FAMILIAR. SORT OF LIKE AN EARTHQUAKE.
WELL GOOD JOB, DEFININTELY A SURPRISE! IT TOTALLY DOES FEEL LIKE I'M CRACKING UNDER THE PRESSURE OF MY FEAR AND SUFFERING.
END OF ACT 1. INTERMISSION.

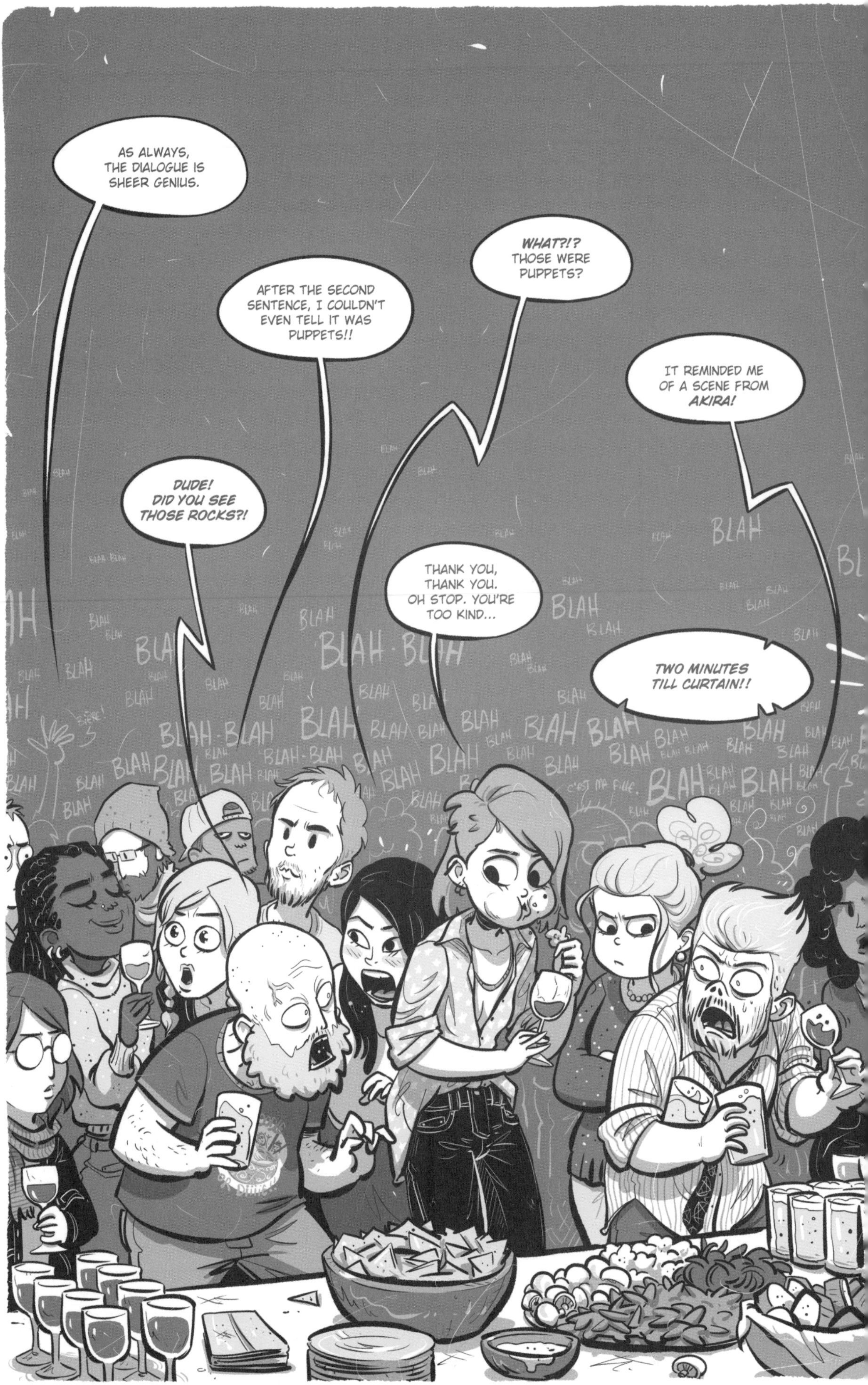
AS ALWAYS, THE DIALOGUE IS SHEER GENIUS.
AFTER THE SECOND SENTENCE, I COULDN'T EVEN TELL IT WAS PUPPETS!!
WHAT?!? THOSE WERE PUPPETS?
IT REMINDED ME OF A SCENE FROM AKIRA!
DUDE! DID YOU SEE THOSE ROCKS?!
THANK YOU, THANK YOU. OH STOP. YOU'RE TOO KIND...
TWO MINUTES TILL CURTAIN!!
BLAH BLAH BLAH-BLAH BLAH BLAH

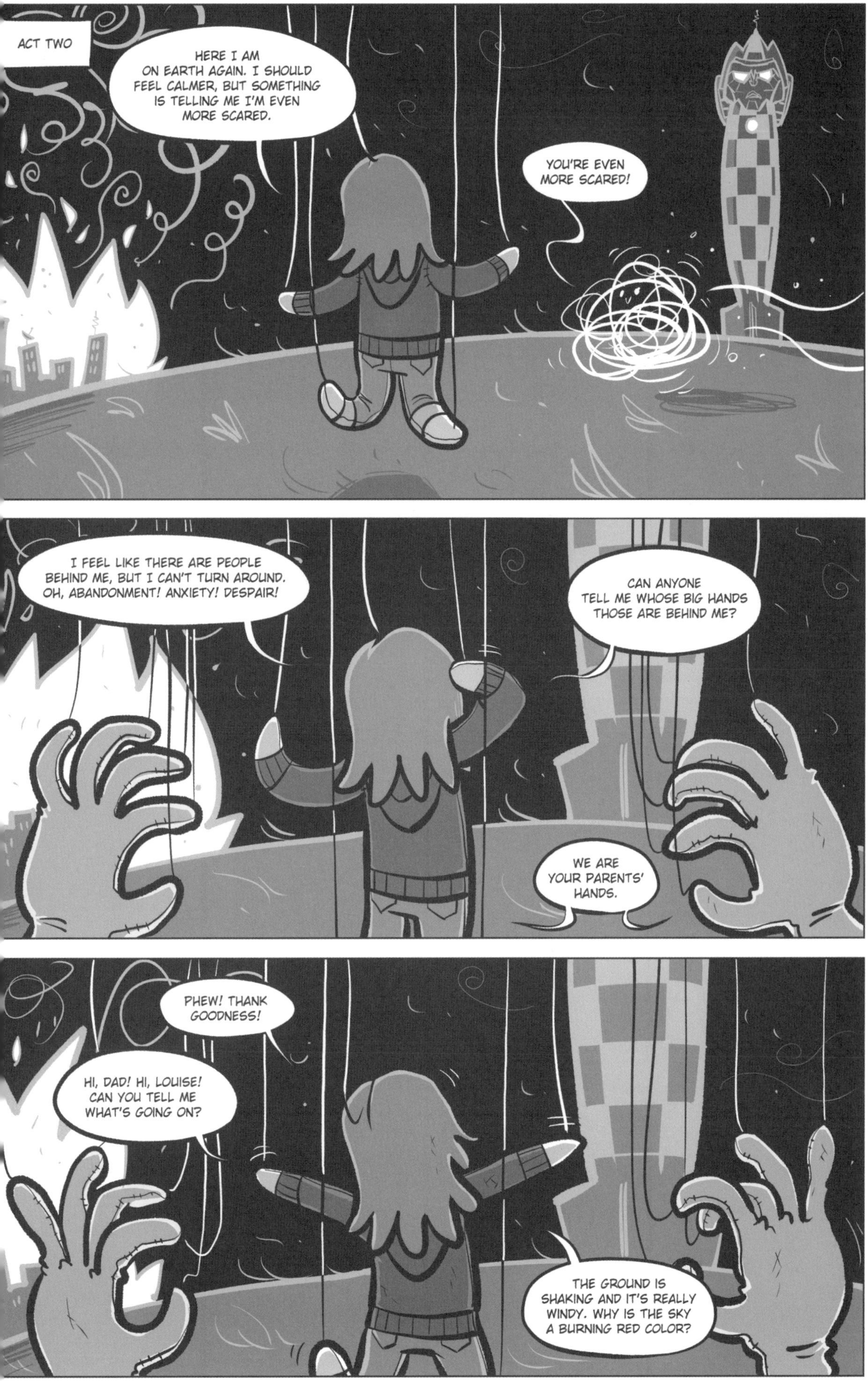
ACT TWO
HERE I AM ON EARTH AGAIN. I SHOULD FEEL CALMER, BUT SOMETHING IS TELLING ME I'M EVEN MORE SCARED.
YOU'RE EVEN MORE SCARED!
I FEEL LIKE THERE ARE PEOPLE BEHIND ME, BUT I CAN'T TURN AROUND. OH, ABANDONMENT! ANXIETY! DESPAIR!
CAN ANYONE TELL ME WHOSE BIG HANDS THOSE ARE BEHIND ME?
WE ARE YOUR PARENTS' HANDS.
PHEW! THANK GOODNESS!
HI, DAD! HI, LOUISE! CAN YOU TELL ME WHAT'S GOING ON?
THE GROUND IS SHAKING AND IT'S REALLY WINDY. WHY IS THE SKY A BURNING RED COLOR?

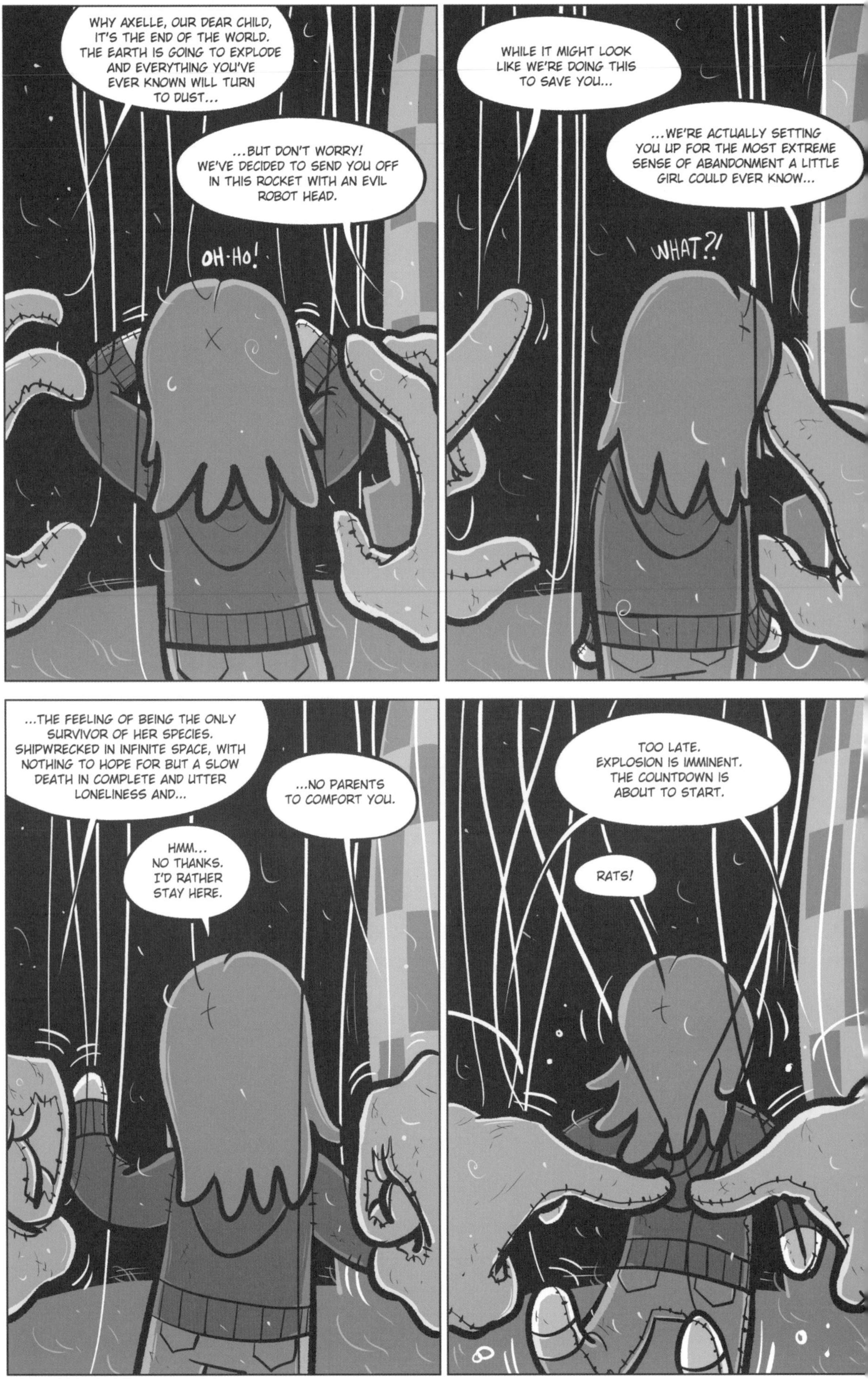
WHY AXELLE, OUR DEAR CHILD, IT'S THE END OF THE WORLD. THE EARTH IS GOING TO EXPLODE AND EVERYTHING YOU'VE EVER KNOWN WILL TURN TO DUST...
...BUT DON'T WORRY! WE'VE DECIDED TO SEND YOU OFF IN THIS ROCKET WITH AN EVIL ROBOT HEAD.
OH-HO!
WHILE IT MIGHT LOOK LIKE WE'RE DOING THIS TO SAVE YOU...
...WE'RE ACTUALLY SETTING YOU UP FOR THE MOST EXTREME SENSE OF ABANDONMENT A LITTLE GIRL COULD EVER KNOW...
WHAT?!
...THE FEELING OF BEING THE ONLY SURVIVOR OF HER SPECIES. SHIPWRECKED IN INFINITE SPACE, WITH NOTHING TO HOPE FOR BUT A SLOW DEATH IN COMPLETE AND UTTER LONELINESS AND...
...NO PARENTS TO COMFORT YOU.
HMM... NO THANKS. I'D RATHER STAY HERE.
TOO LATE. EXPLOSION IS IMMINENT. THE COUNTDOWN IS ABOUT TO START.
RATS!

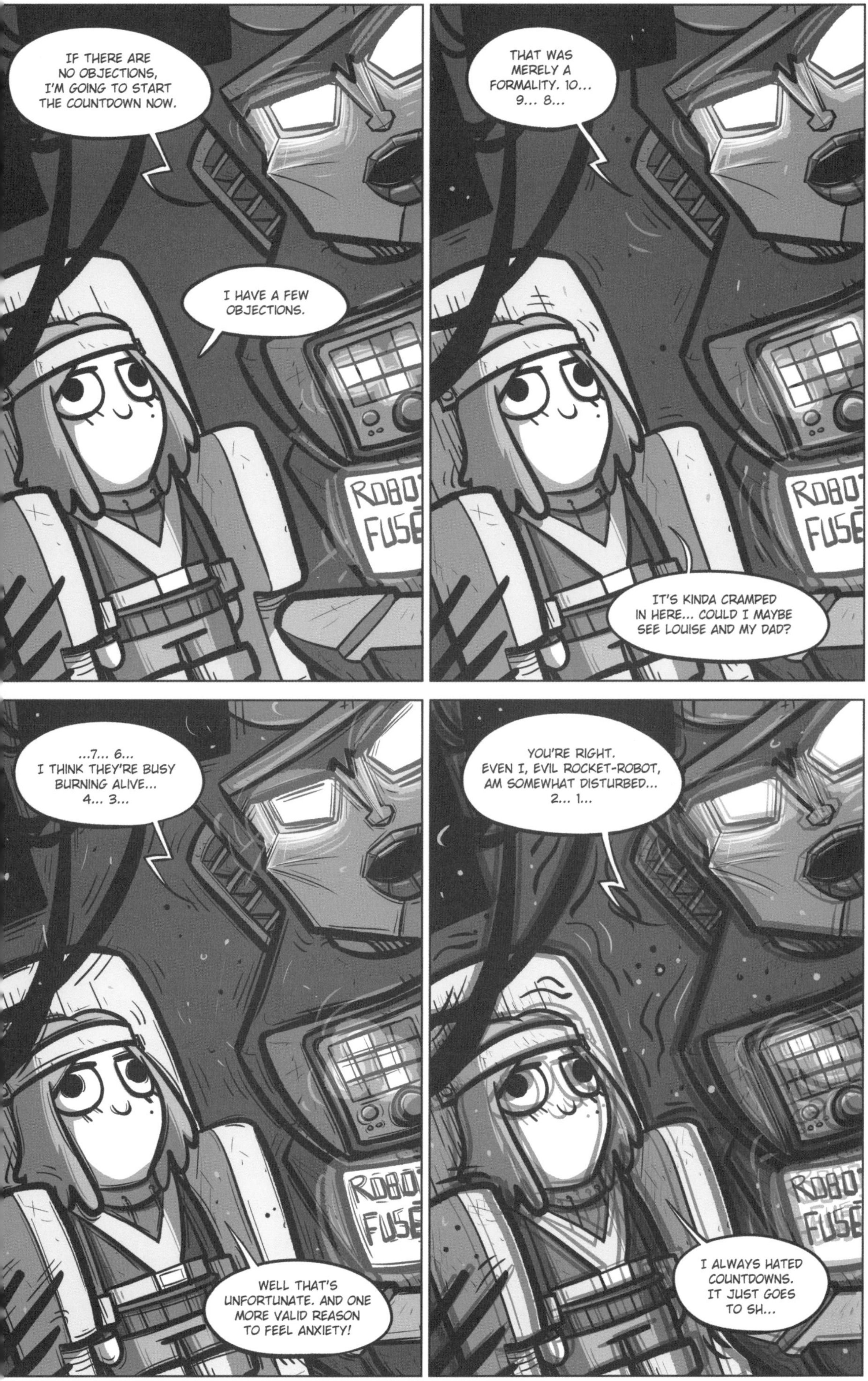
IF THERE ARE NO OBJECTIONS, I'M GOING TO START THE COUNTDOWN NOW.
I HAVE A FEW OBJECTIONS.
THAT WAS MERELY A FORMALITY. 10... 9... 8...
ROBOT FUSE
IT'S KINDA CRAMPED IN HERE... COULD I MAYBE SEE LOUISE AND MY DAD?
...7... 6... I THINK THEY'RE BUSY BURNING ALIVE... 4... 3...
WELL THAT'S UNFORTUNATE. AND ONE MORE VALID REASON TO FEEL ANXIETY!
YOU'RE RIGHT. EVEN I, EVIL ROCKET-ROBOT, AM SOMEWHAT DISTURBED... 2... 1...
I ALWAYS HATED COUNTDOWNS. IT JUST GOES TO SH...

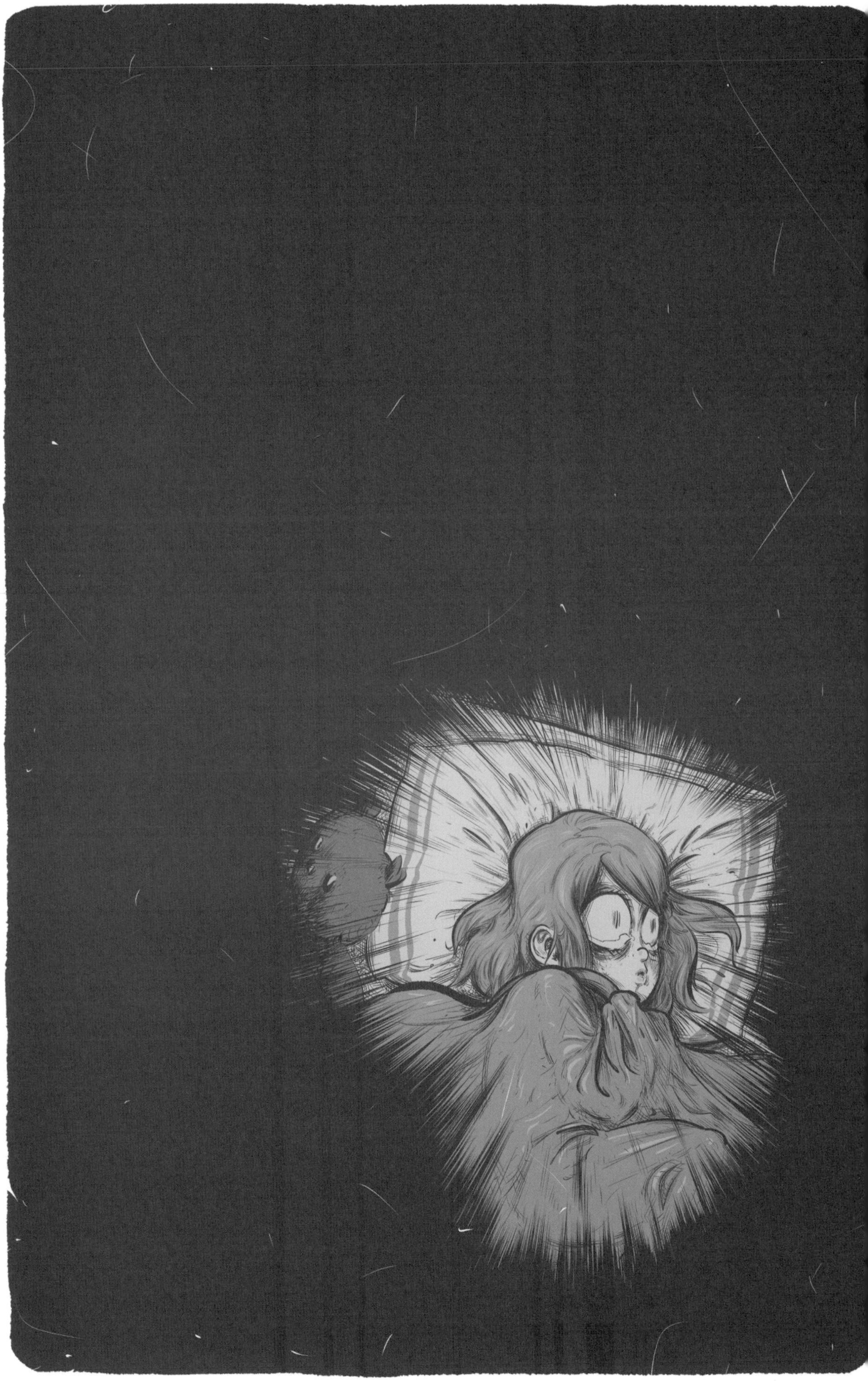

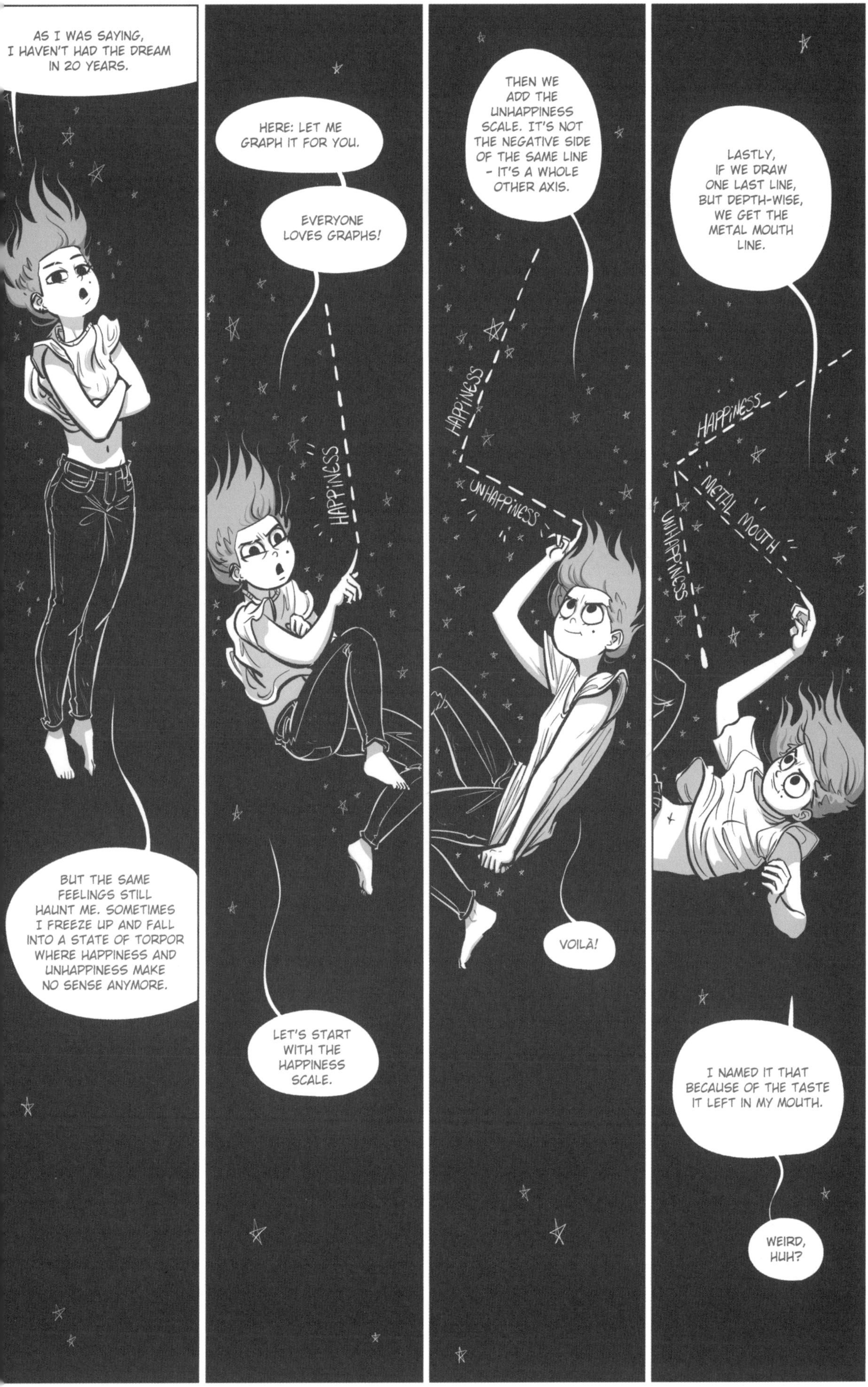
AS I WAS SAYING, I HAVEN'T HAD THE DREAM IN 20 YEARS.
BUT THE SAME FEELINGS STILL HAUNT ME. SOMETIMES I FREEZE UP AND FALL INTO A STATE OF TORPOR WHERE HAPPINESS AND UNHAPPINESS MAKE NO SENSE ANYMORE.
HERE: LET ME GRAPH IT FOR YOU.
EVERYONE LOVES GRAPHS!
HAPPINESS
LET'S START WITH THE HAPPINESS SCALE.
THEN WE ADD THE UNHAPPINESS SCALE. IT'S NOT THE NEGATIVE SIDE OF THE SAME LINE - IT'S A WHOLE OTHER AXIS.
HAPPINESS
UNHAPPINESS
VOILÀ!
LASTLY, IF WE DRAW ONE LAST LINE, BUT DEPTH-WISE, WE GET THE METAL MOUTH LINE.
HAPPINESS
UNHAPPINESS
METAL MOUTH
I NAMED IT THAT BECAUSE OF THE TASTE IT LEFT IN MY MOUTH.
WEIRD, HUH?

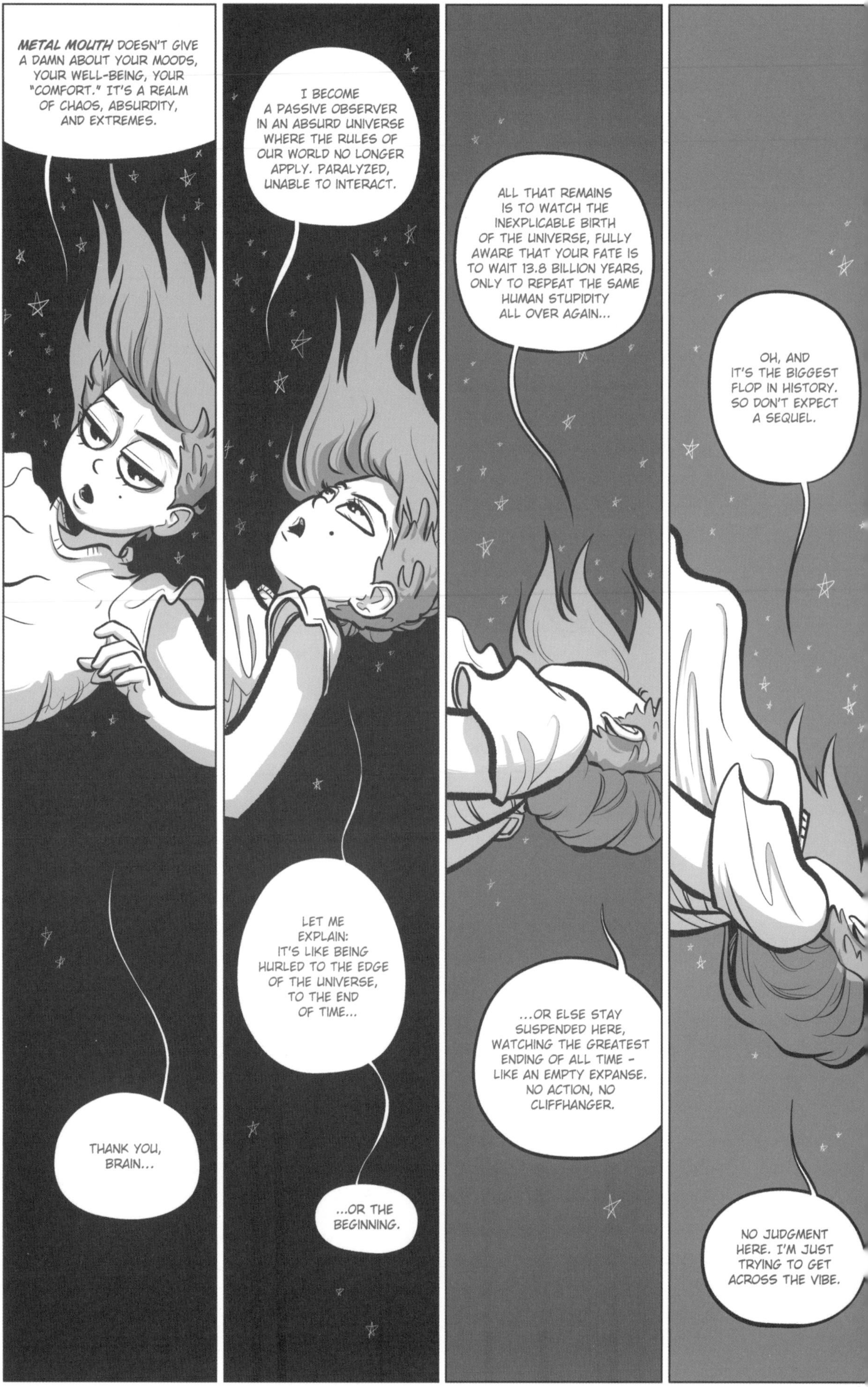
METAL MOUTH DOESN'T GIVE A DAMN ABOUT YOUR MOODS, YOUR WELL-BEING, YOUR "COMFORT." IT'S A REALM OF CHAOS, ABSURDITY, AND EXTREMES.
THANK YOU, BRAIN...
I BECOME A PASSIVE OBSERVER IN AN ABSURD UNIVERSE WHERE THE RULES OF OUR WORLD NO LONGER APPLY. PARALYZED, UNABLE TO INTERACT.
LET ME EXPLAIN: IT'S LIKE BEING HURLED TO THE EDGE OF THE UNIVERSE, TO THE END OF TIME...
...OR THE BEGINNING.
ALL THAT REMAINS IS TO WATCH THE INEXPLICABLE BIRTH OF THE UNIVERSE, FULLY AWARE THAT YOUR FATE IS TO WAIT 13.8 BILLION YEARS, ONLY TO REPEAT THE SAME HUMAN STUPIDITY ALL OVER AGAIN...
...OR ELSE STAY SUSPENDED HERE, WATCHING THE GREATEST ENDING OF ALL TIME - LIKE AN EMPTY EXPANSE. NO ACTION, NO CLIFFHANGER.
OH, AND IT'S THE BIGGEST FLOP IN HISTORY. SO DON'T EXPECT A SEQUEL.
NO JUDGMENT HERE. I'M JUST TRYING TO GET ACROSS THE VIBE.

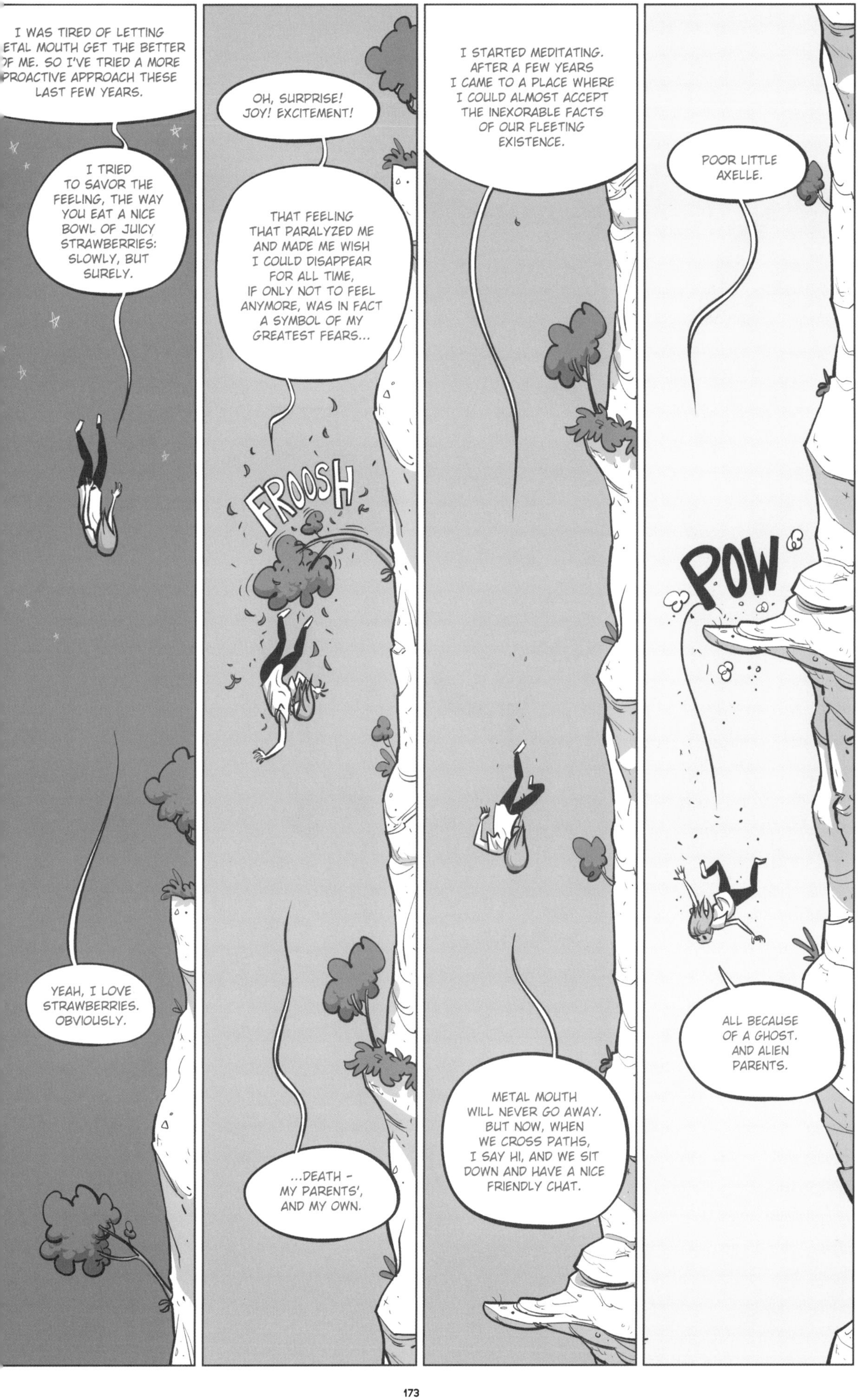
I WAS TIRED OF LETTING METAL MOUTH GET THE BETTER OF ME. SO I'VE TRIED A MORE PROACTIVE APPROACH THESE LAST FEW YEARS.
I TRIED TO SAVOR THE FEELING, THE WAY YOU EAT A NICE BOWL OF JUICY STRAWBERRIES: SLOWLY, BUT SURELY.
YEAH, I LOVE STRAWBERRIES. OBVIOUSLY.
OH, SURPRISE! JOY! EXCITEMENT!
THAT FEELING THAT PARALYZED ME AND MADE ME WISH I COULD DISAPPEAR FOR ALL TIME, IF ONLY NOT TO FEEL ANYMORE, WAS IN FACT A SYMBOL OF MY GREATEST FEARS...
FROOSH
...DEATH - MY PARENTS', AND MY OWN.
I STARTED MEDITATING. AFTER A FEW YEARS I CAME TO A PLACE WHERE I COULD ALMOST ACCEPT THE INEXORABLE FACTS OF OUR FLEETING EXISTENCE.
METAL MOUTH WILL NEVER GO AWAY. BUT NOW, WHEN WE CROSS PATHS, I SAY HI, AND WE SIT DOWN AND HAVE A NICE FRIENDLY CHAT.
POOR LITTLE AXELLE.
POW
ALL BECAUSE OF A GHOST. AND ALIEN PARENTS.

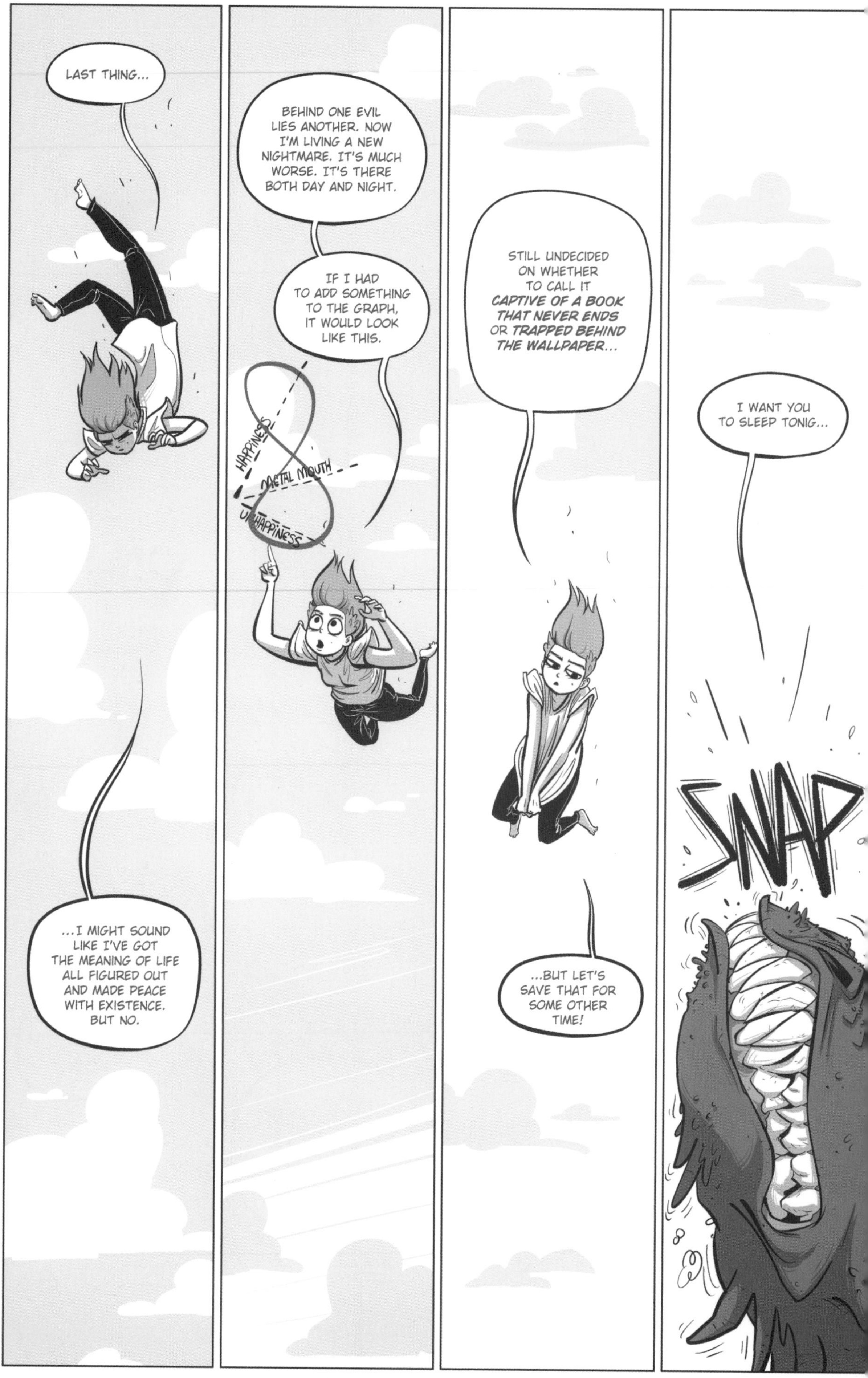
LAST THING...
...I MIGHT SOUND LIKE I'VE GOT THE MEANING OF LIFE ALL FIGURED OUT AND MADE PEACE WITH EXISTENCE. BUT NO.
BEHIND ONE EVIL LIES ANOTHER. NOW I'M LIVING A NEW NIGHTMARE. IT'S MUCH WORSE. IT'S THERE BOTH DAY AND NIGHT.
IF I HAD TO ADD SOMETHING TO THE GRAPH, IT WOULD LOOK LIKE THIS.
HAPPINESS
METAL MOUTH
UNHAPPINESS
STILL UNDECIDED ON WHETHER TO CALL IT CAPTIVE OF A BOOK THAT NEVER ENDS OR TRAPPED BEHIND THE WALLPAPER...
...BUT LET'S SAVE THAT FOR SOME OTHER TIME!
I WANT YOU TO SLEEP TONIG...
SNAP

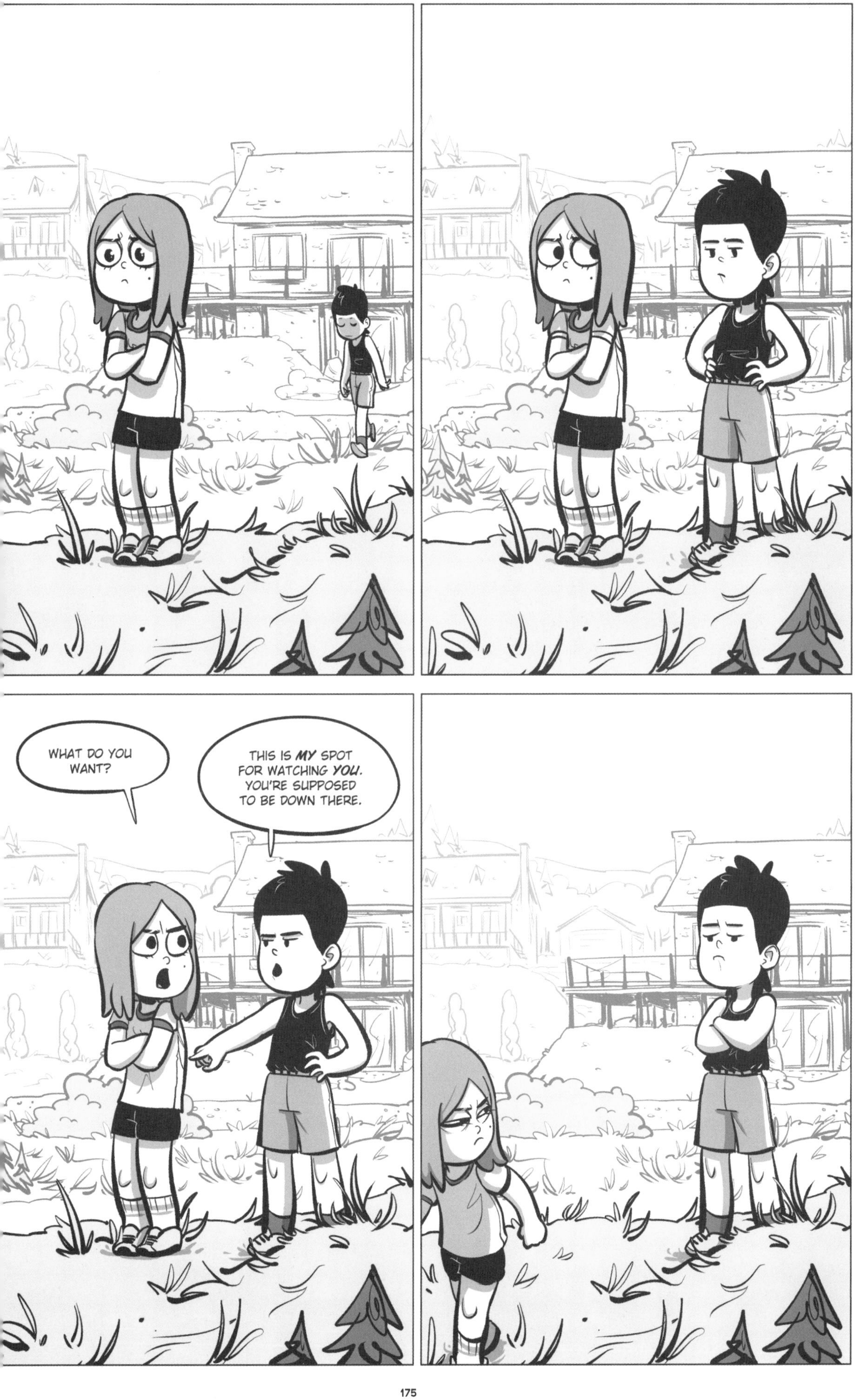
WHAT DO YOU WANT?
THIS IS *MY* SPOT FOR WATCHING *YOU*. YOU'RE SUPPOSED TO BE DOWN THERE.

I DON'T GET WHAT'S GOING ON ANYMORE, FOREST. EVER SINCE THAT TIME I VISITED YOU, AND I THOUGHT I SAW A GHOST IN YOU, IT'S LIKE IT STIRRED STUFF UP INSIDE ME THAT I DIDN'T WANT TO FEEL.

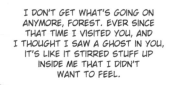

I'M SCARED ALL THE TIME NOW. IT FEELS LIKE SOMETHING'S HOLDING ME PRISONER. AND SOMETIMES IT HURTS WHEN I BREATHE.

I FEEL LIKE I WON'T BE ABLE TO BE WHAT PEOPLE WANT ME TO BE.

IT'S TOO MUCH...

I'M NOT SURE I'M EVER COMING BACK, FOREST. MOM DOESN'T WANT ME DOING THINGS THAT COULD SCARE ME.

I'M SORRY...

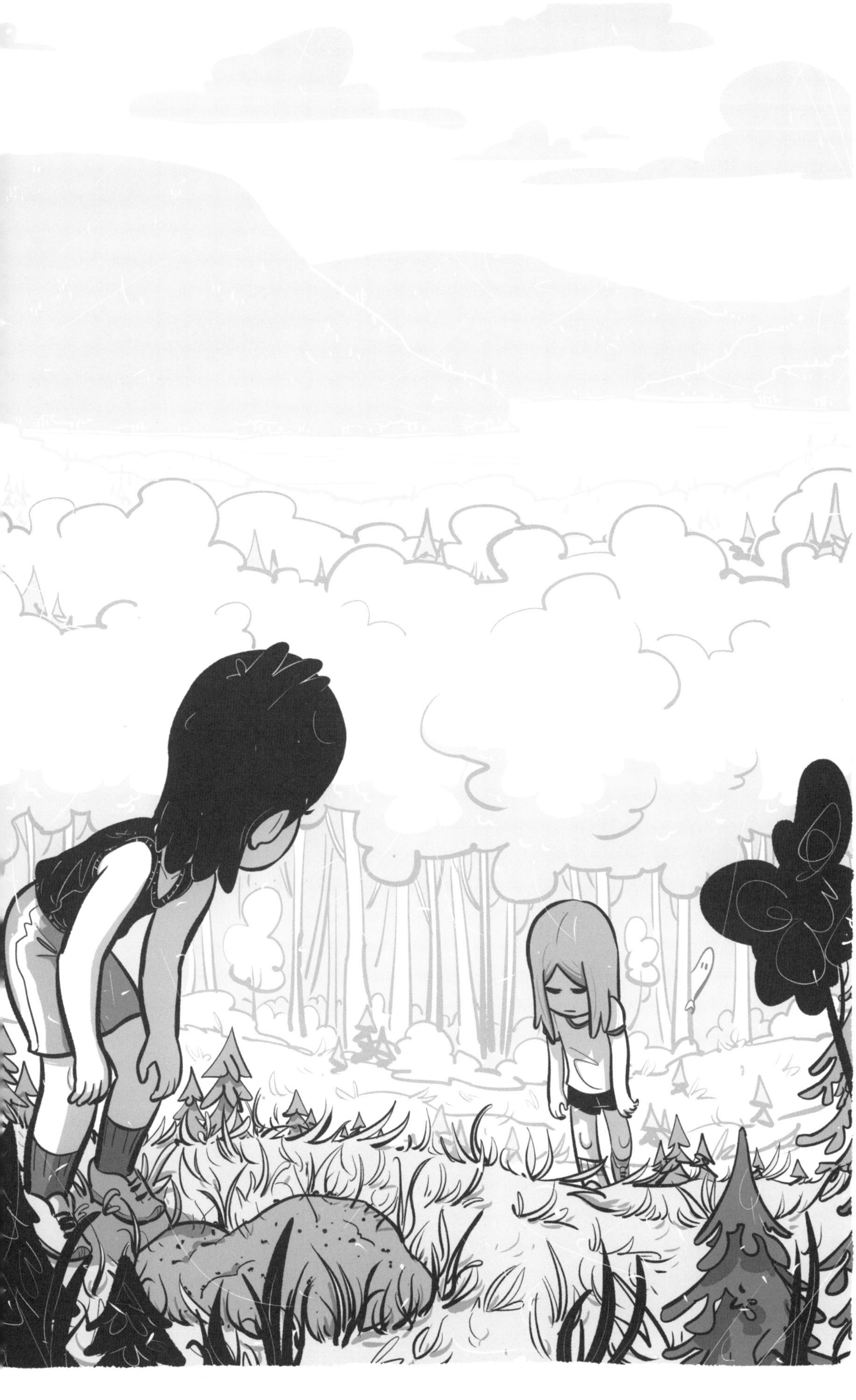

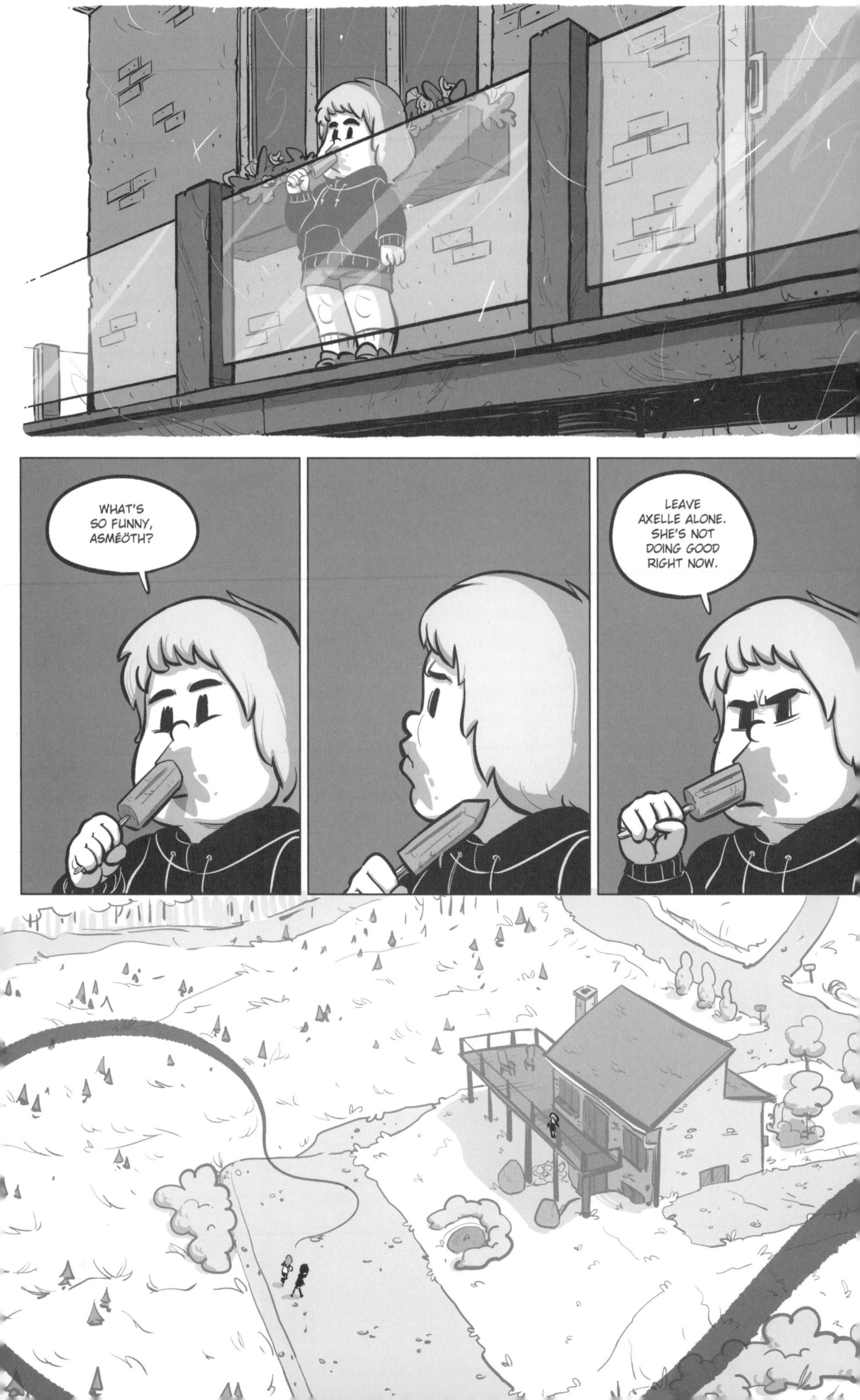
WHAT'S SO FUNNY, ASMÉÖTH?
LEAVE AXELLE ALONE. SHE'S NOT DOING GOOD RIGHT NOW.

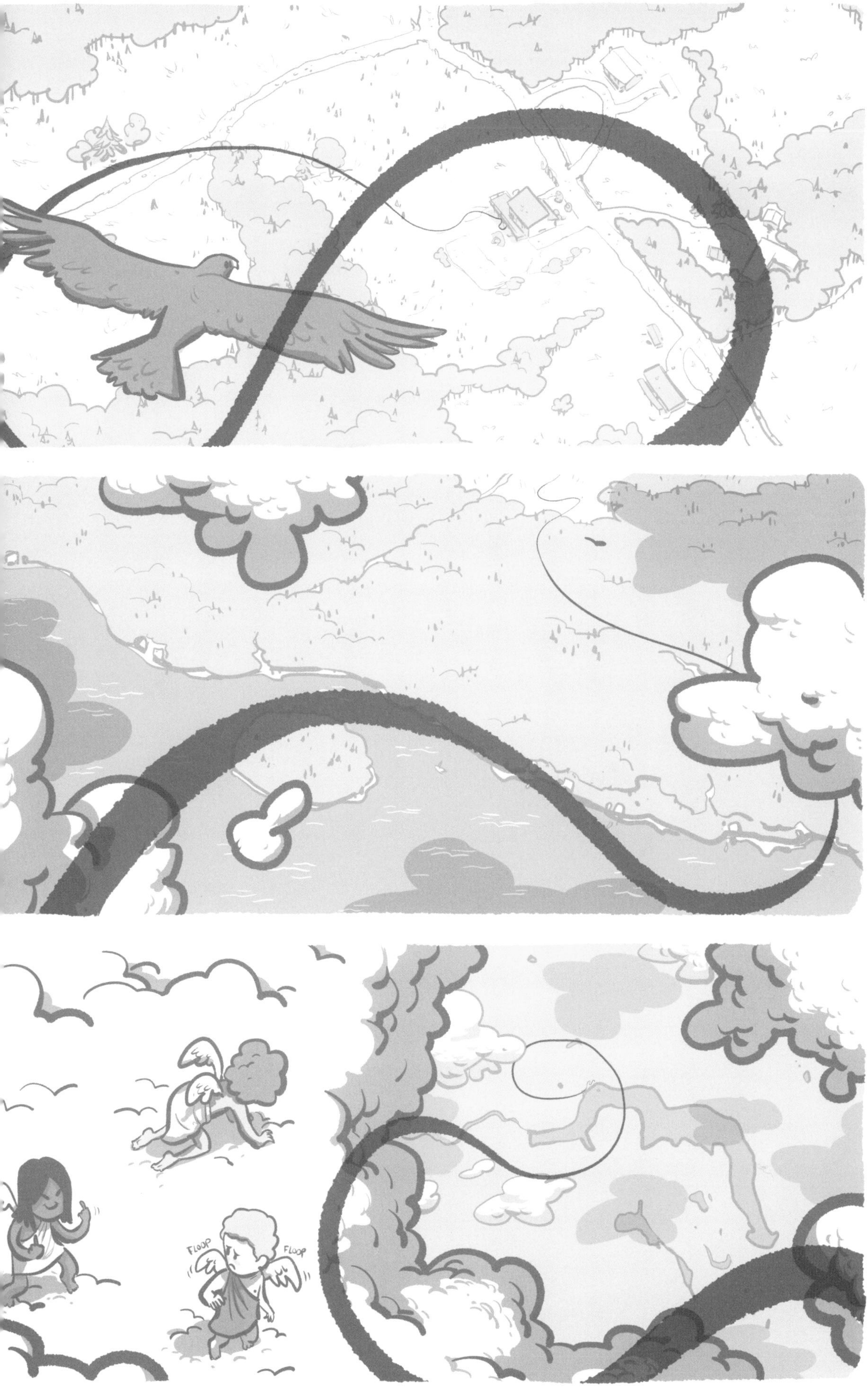
FLOOP
FLOOP

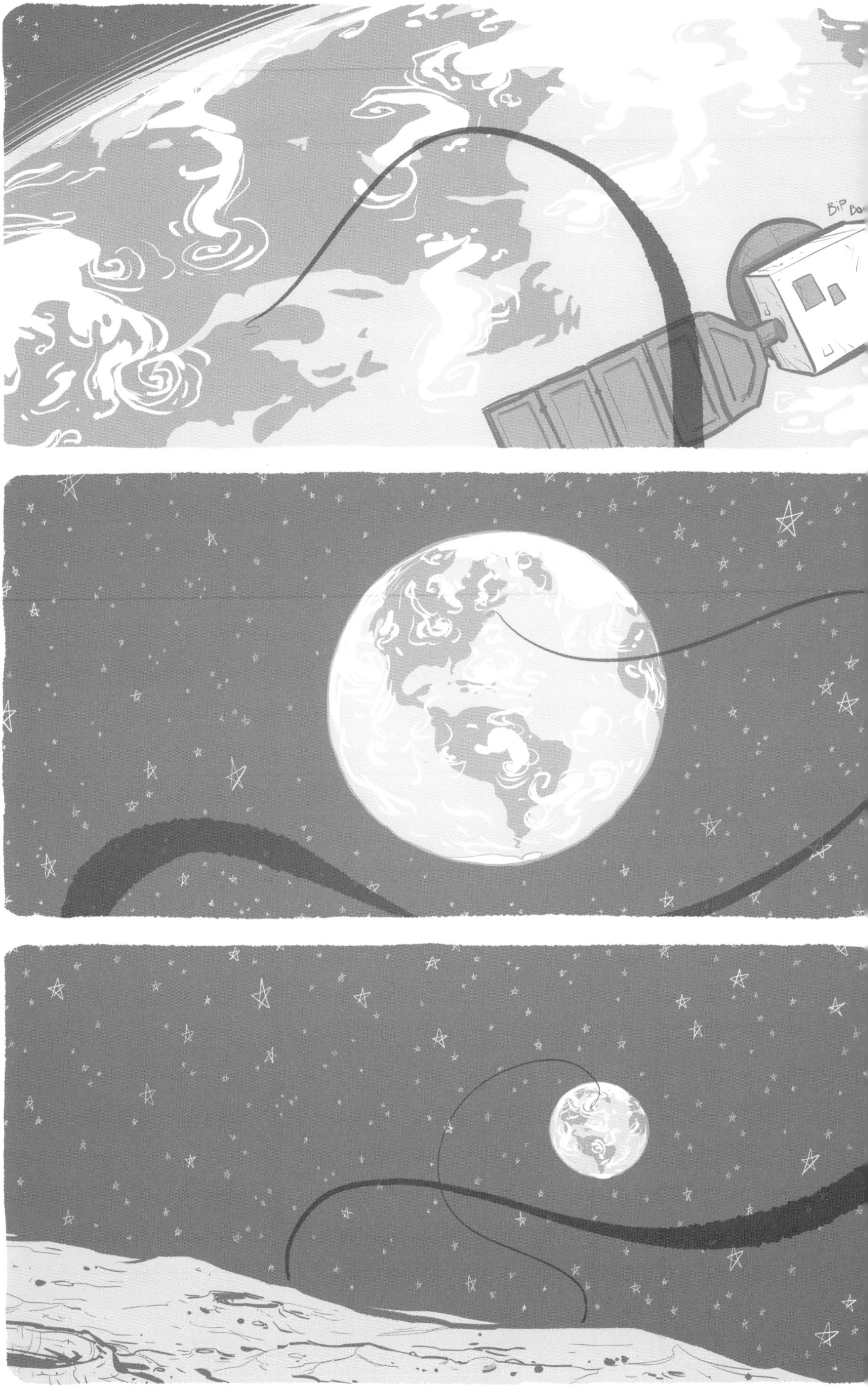
BiP

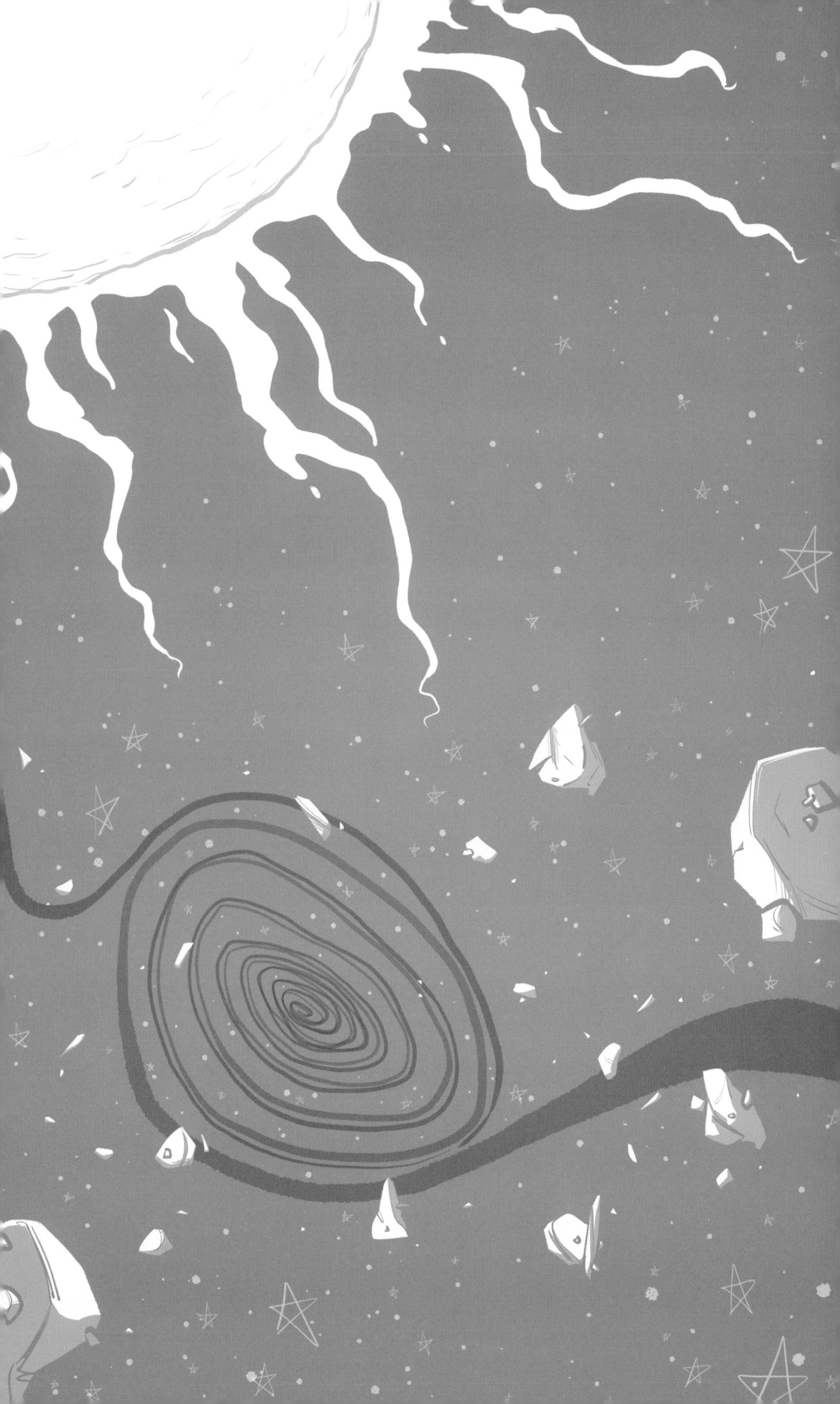

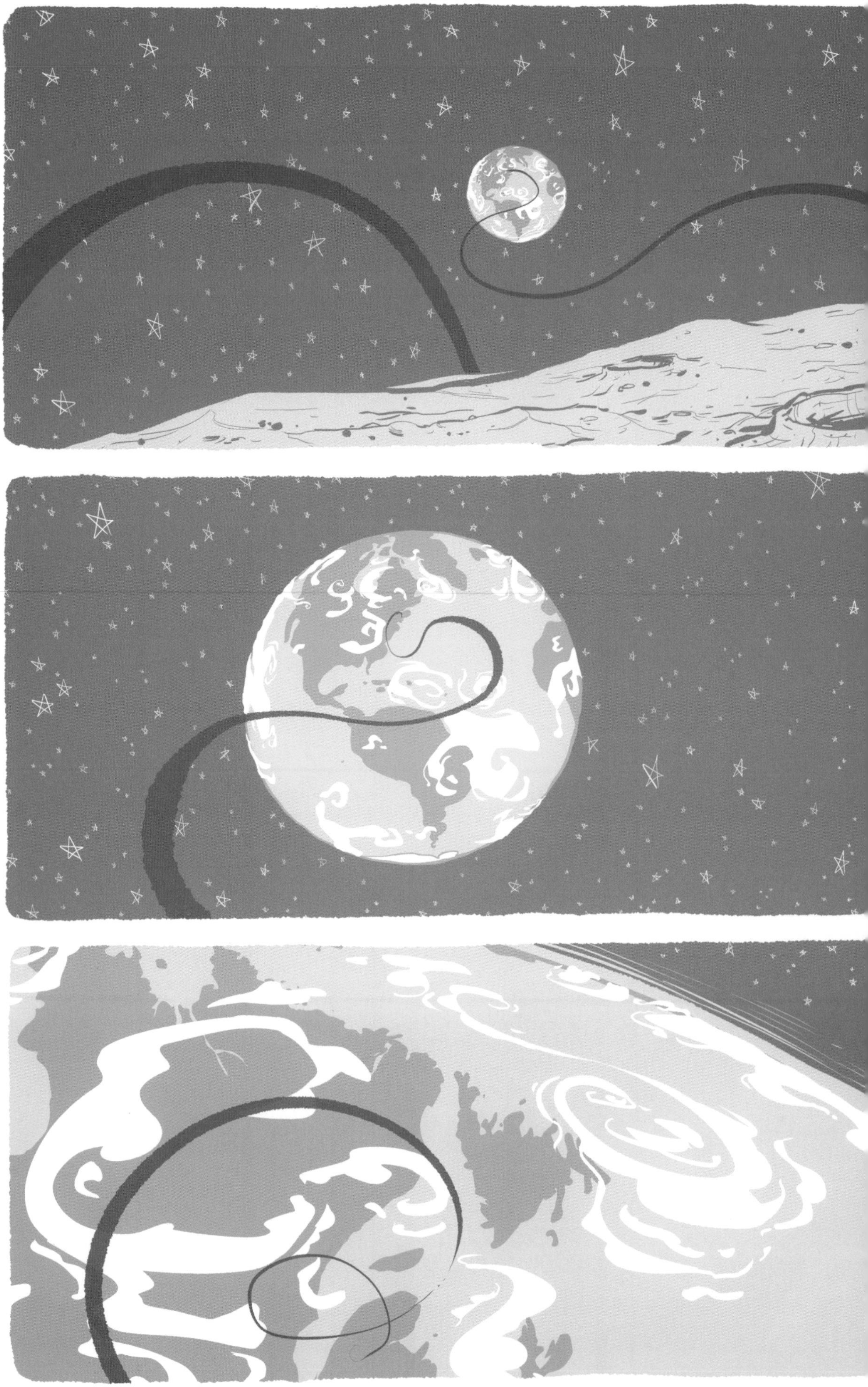

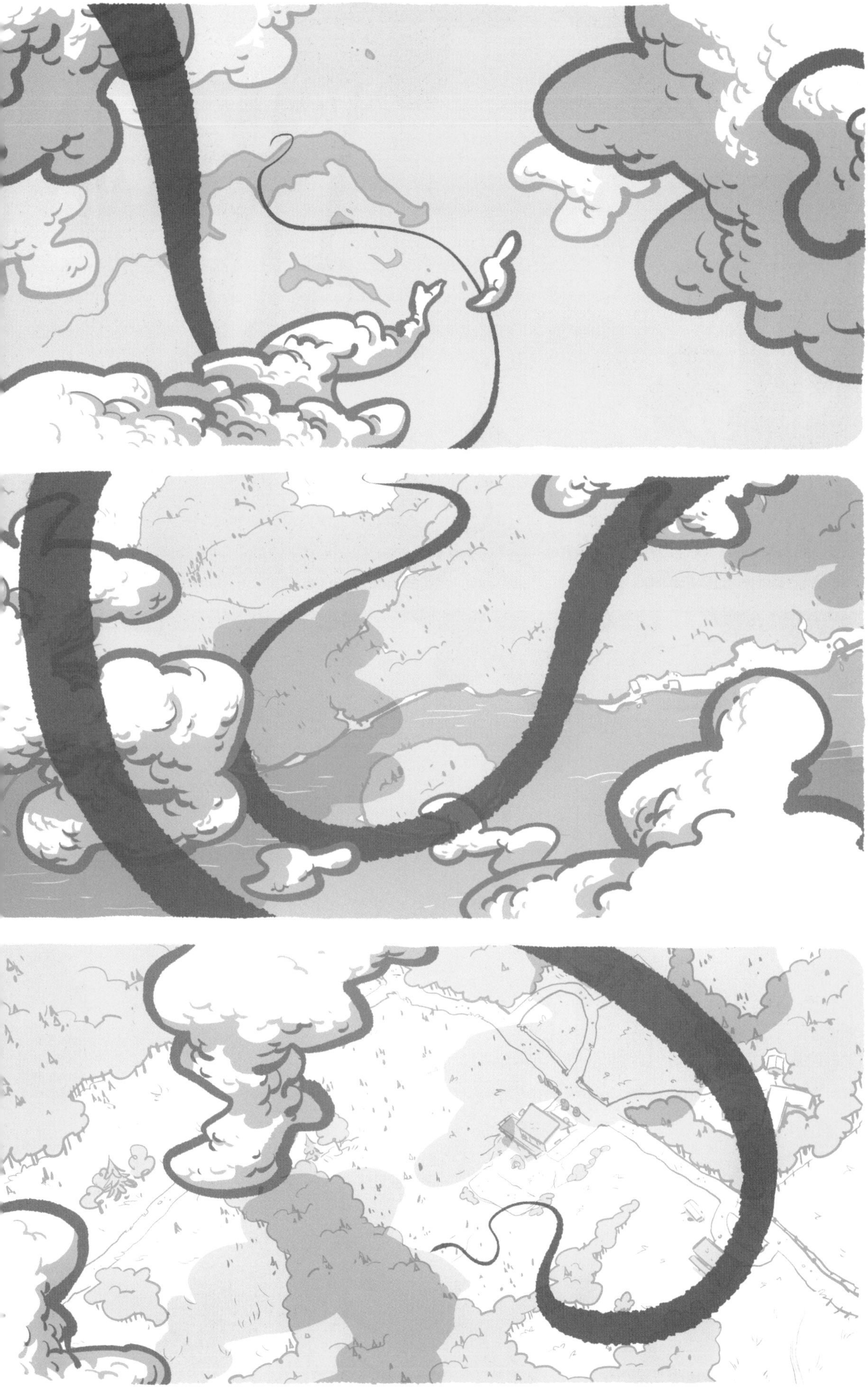

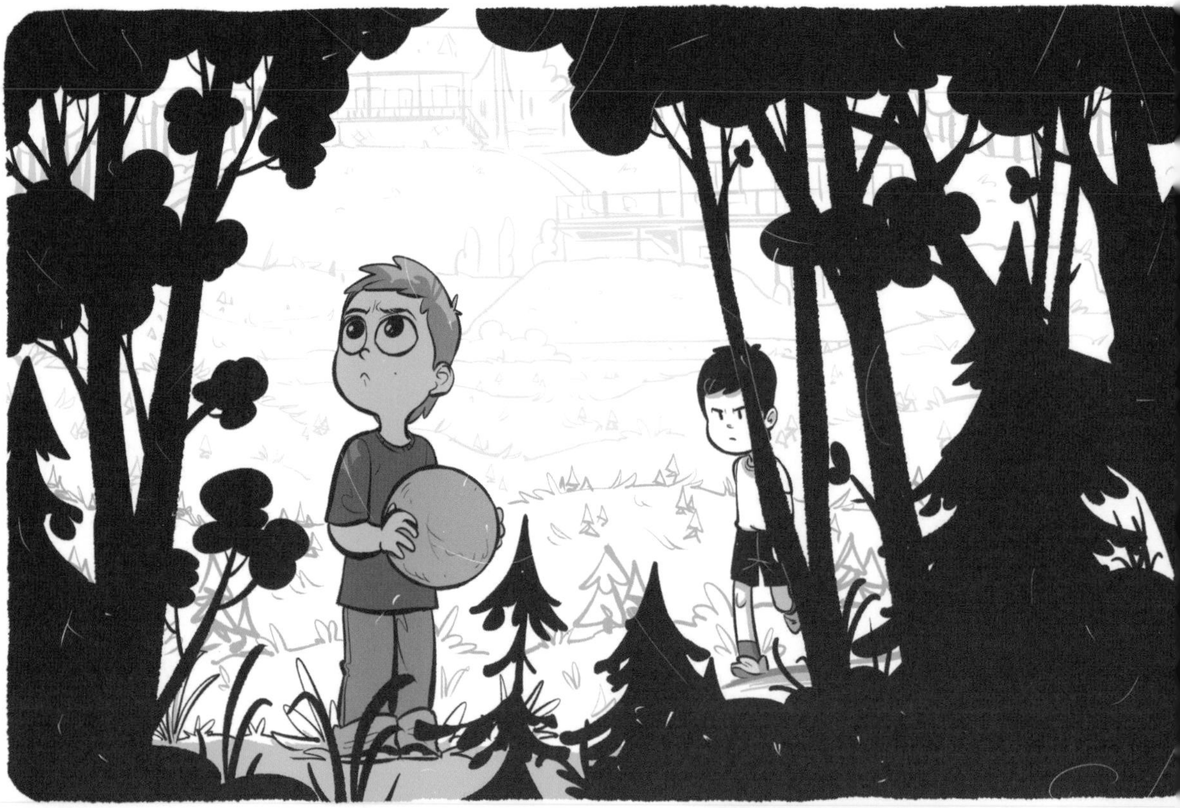
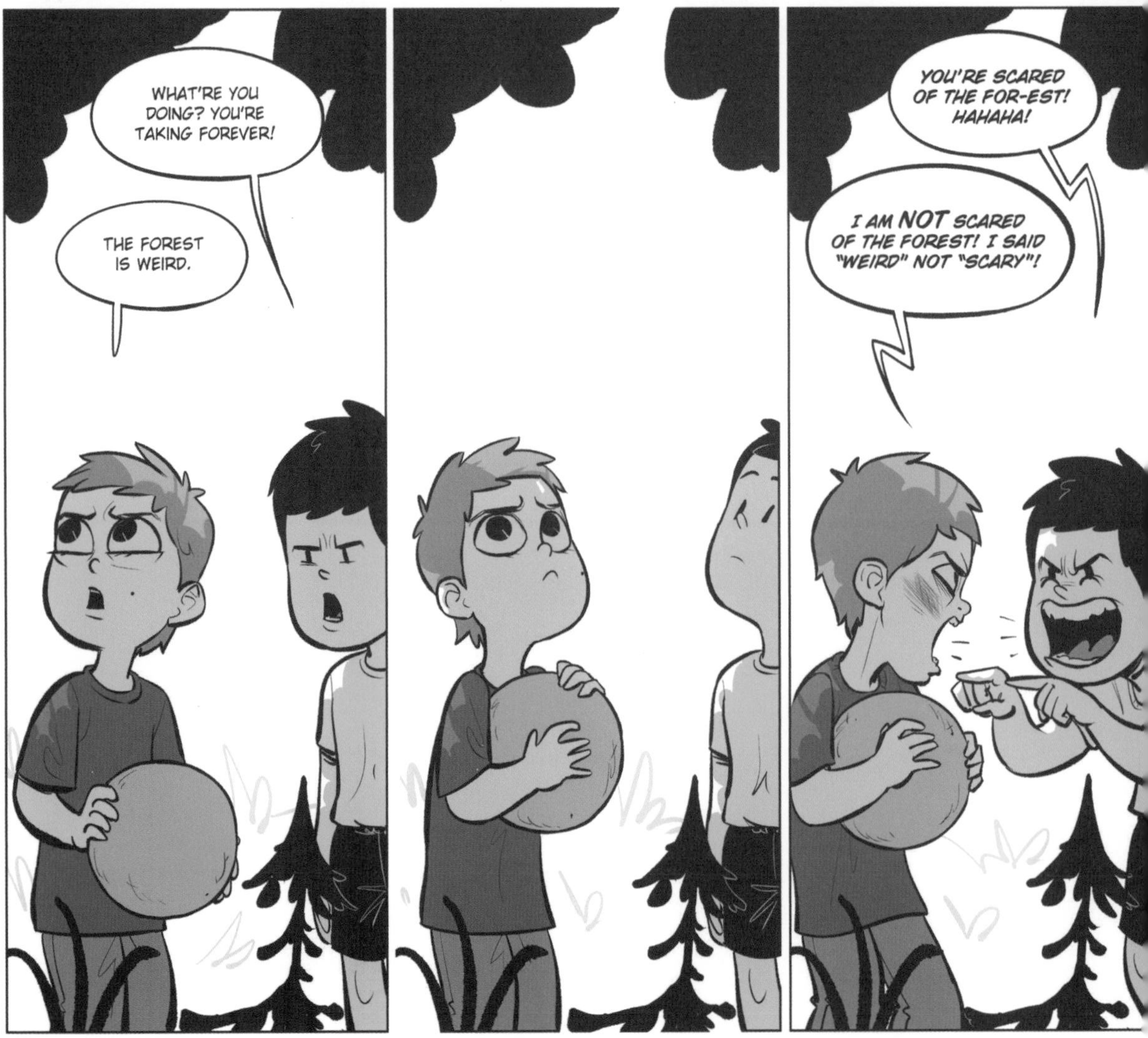
WHAT'RE YOU DOING? YOU'RE TAKING FOREVER!
THE FOREST IS WEIRD.
YOU'RE SCARED OF THE FOR-EST! HAHAHA!
I AM NOT SCARED OF THE FOREST! I SAID "WEIRD" NOT "SCARY"!

ANTOINE, GO TELL YOUR BROTHERS DINNER IS READY.

OKAY.

COME EAT! DINNER'S READY!

NO, GO DOWN THERE AND TELL THEM.

COME EAT!! DINNER'S READY! COME EAT! TIME TO GO IN!!

WHAT HAPPENED? EVERYTHING OKAY?

YEAH, ANTOINE'S JUST GOING TO GET THE BOYS...

RIGHT NOW!! GO WASH YOUR HANDS!! DAD SAYS GET OVER HERE AND EAT!! EAT NOW!! IT'S RE...!! DINNER...ME!!! WE'RE HAVING HAMBURG... AT!!! I'M HUNGRY!!

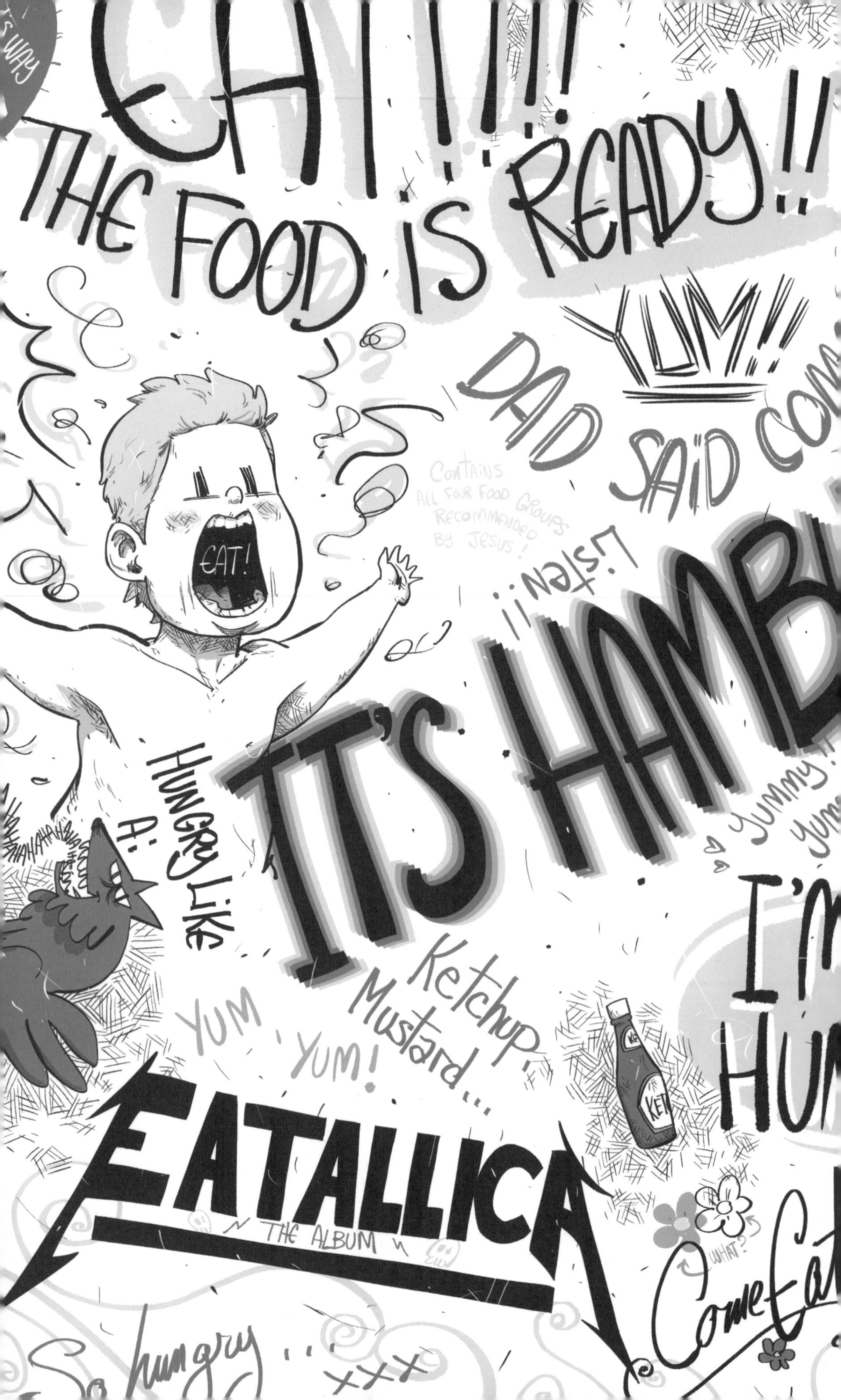
EAT!!!!
THE FOOD IS READY!!
YUM!!
DAD SAID COM
CONTAINS ALL FOUR FOOD GROUPS RECOMMENDED BY JESUS!
EAT!
Listen!!
IT'S HAMB
HUNGRY LIKE A:
Yummy!
Yum
I'M
HUN
Ketchup, Mustard...
YUM
YUM!
EATALLICA
THE ALBUM
WHAT?
Come Eat
So hungry... xxx

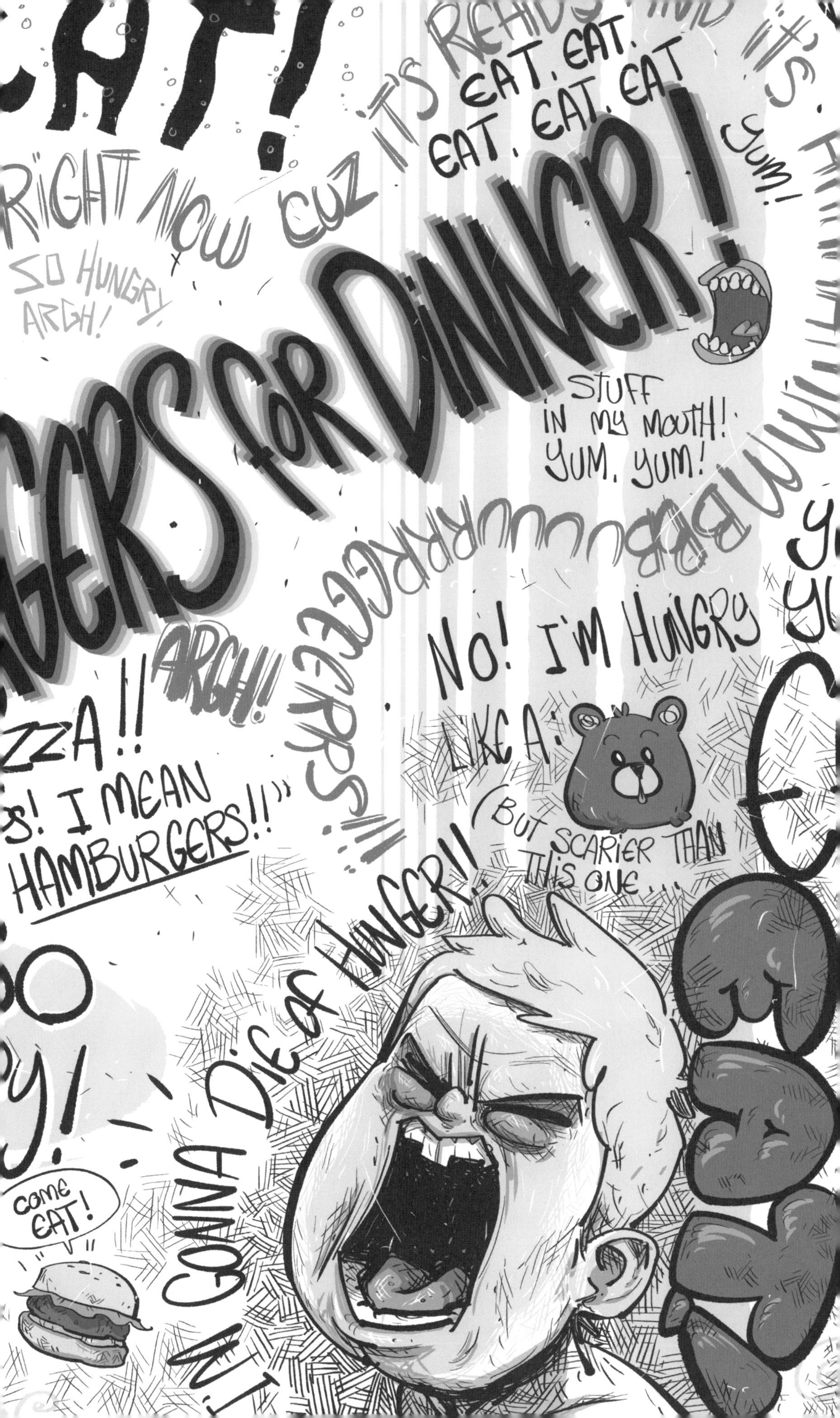
EAT!
RIGHT NOW CUZ IT'S
EAT, EAT, EAT, EAT, EAT
YUM!
SO HUNGRY ARGH!
GERS FOR DINNER!
STUFF IN MY MOUTH! YUM, YUM!
BBBUUURRRGGEERRRS!!
ARGH!
ZZA!!
S! I MEAN HAMBURGERS!!"
NO! I'M HUNGRY LIKE A:
(BUT SCARIER THAN THIS ONE...
DIE OF HUNGER!!
I'M GONNA
COME EAT!

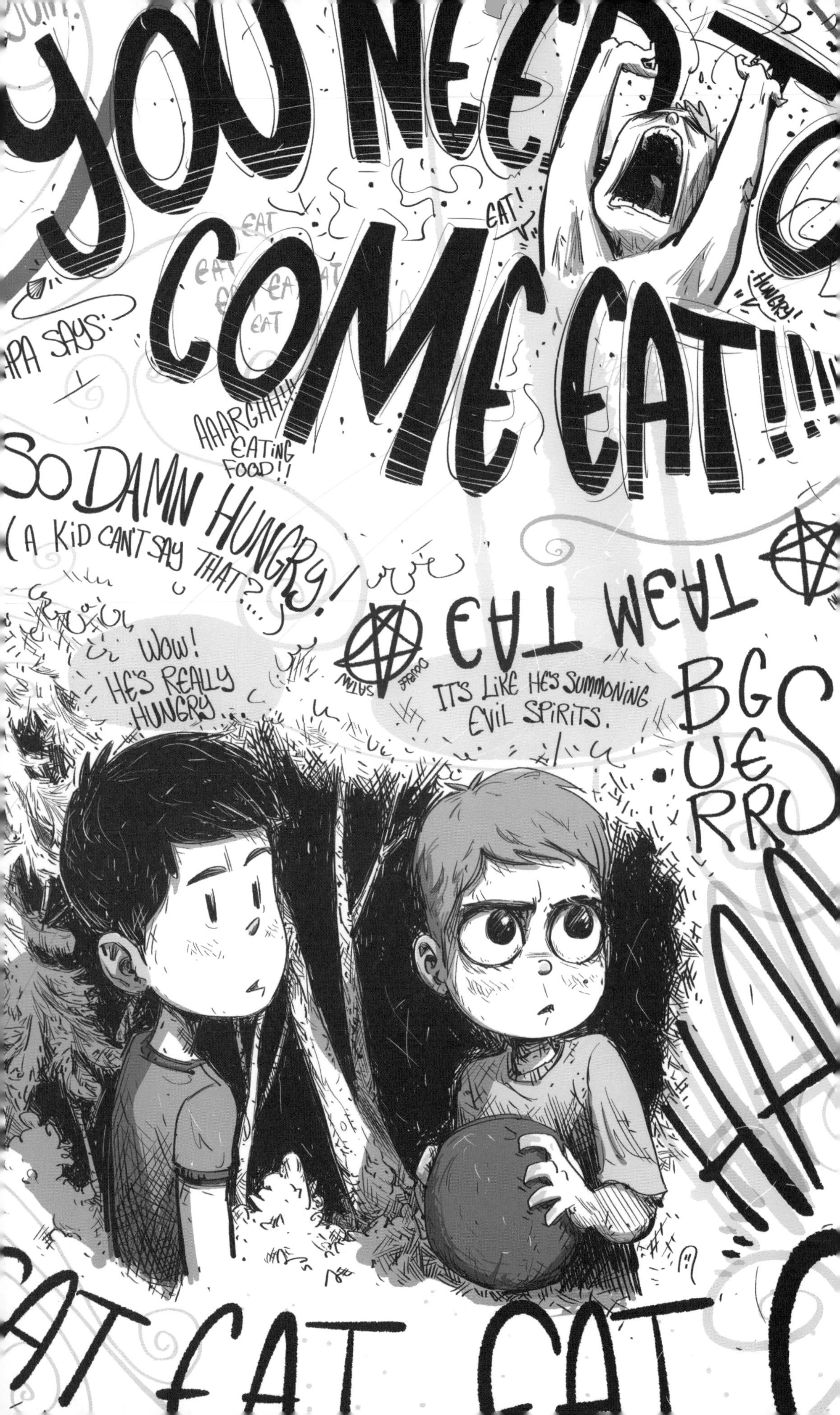

PA SAYS:
COME EAT!!!!
EAT!
HUNGRY!
AAARGHH!! EATING FOOD!!
SO DAMN HUNGRY!
(A KID CAN'T SAY THAT?)
WOW! HE'S REALLY HUNGRY...
IT'S LIKE HE'S SUMMONING EVIL SPIRITS.

...PH SAYS
VORTEX
EAT NOWWWWW!!!
WHAT TIME IS IT?
BURGER TIME!!
I'M CALM.
IT'S READY NOW.
LIED! NOT CALM!! COME EAT!!!
HURRY UP!!
WHOOP!!
SO HUNGRY...
BURGERS
BOO HOO...
BAHAHA
HAHA!
BURBURBURBURBURGEEEERS!!!!
WARG!!!!!

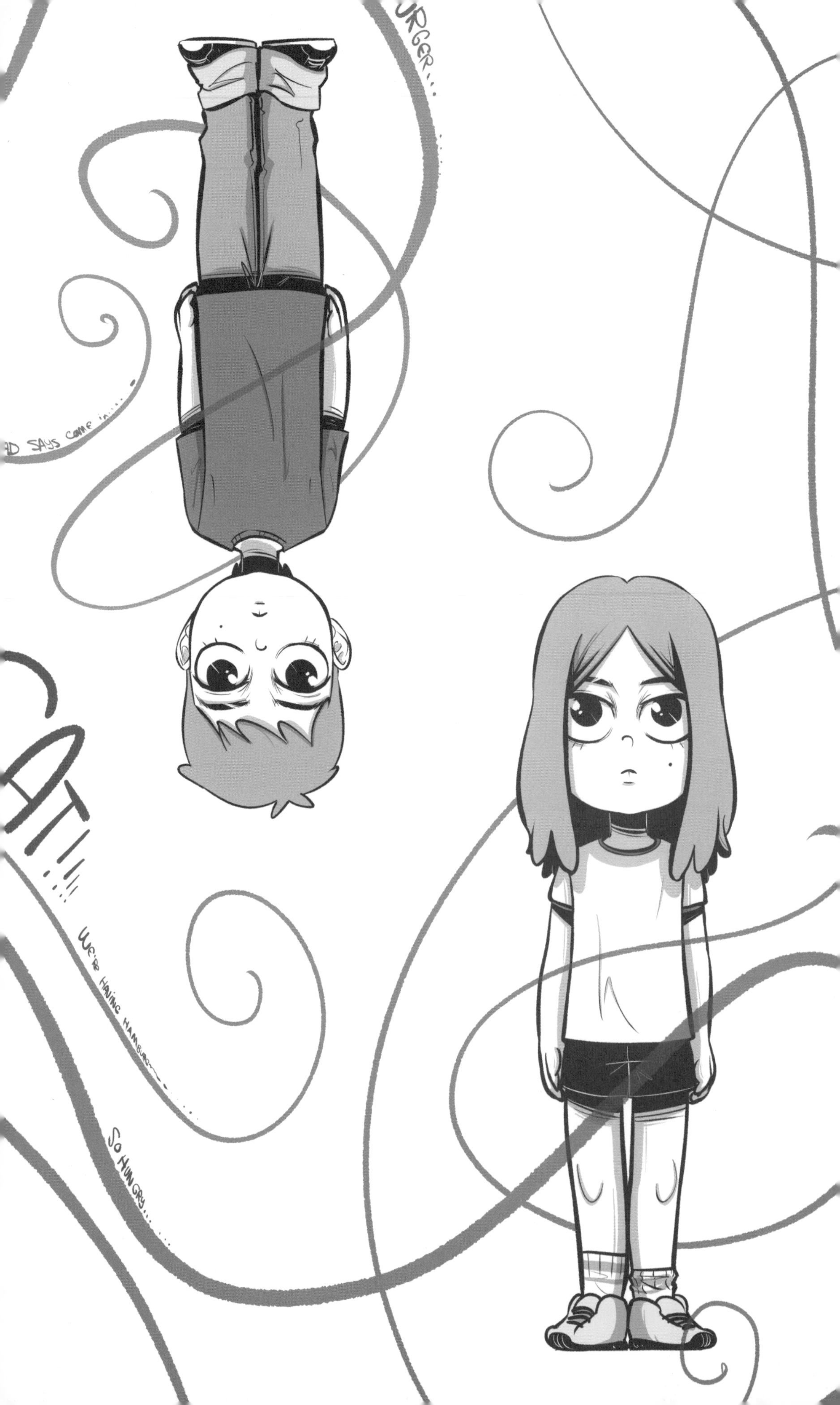
AD SAYS COME IN....
AT!!!
WE'RE HAVING HAMBURG...
URGER...
SO HUNGRY...

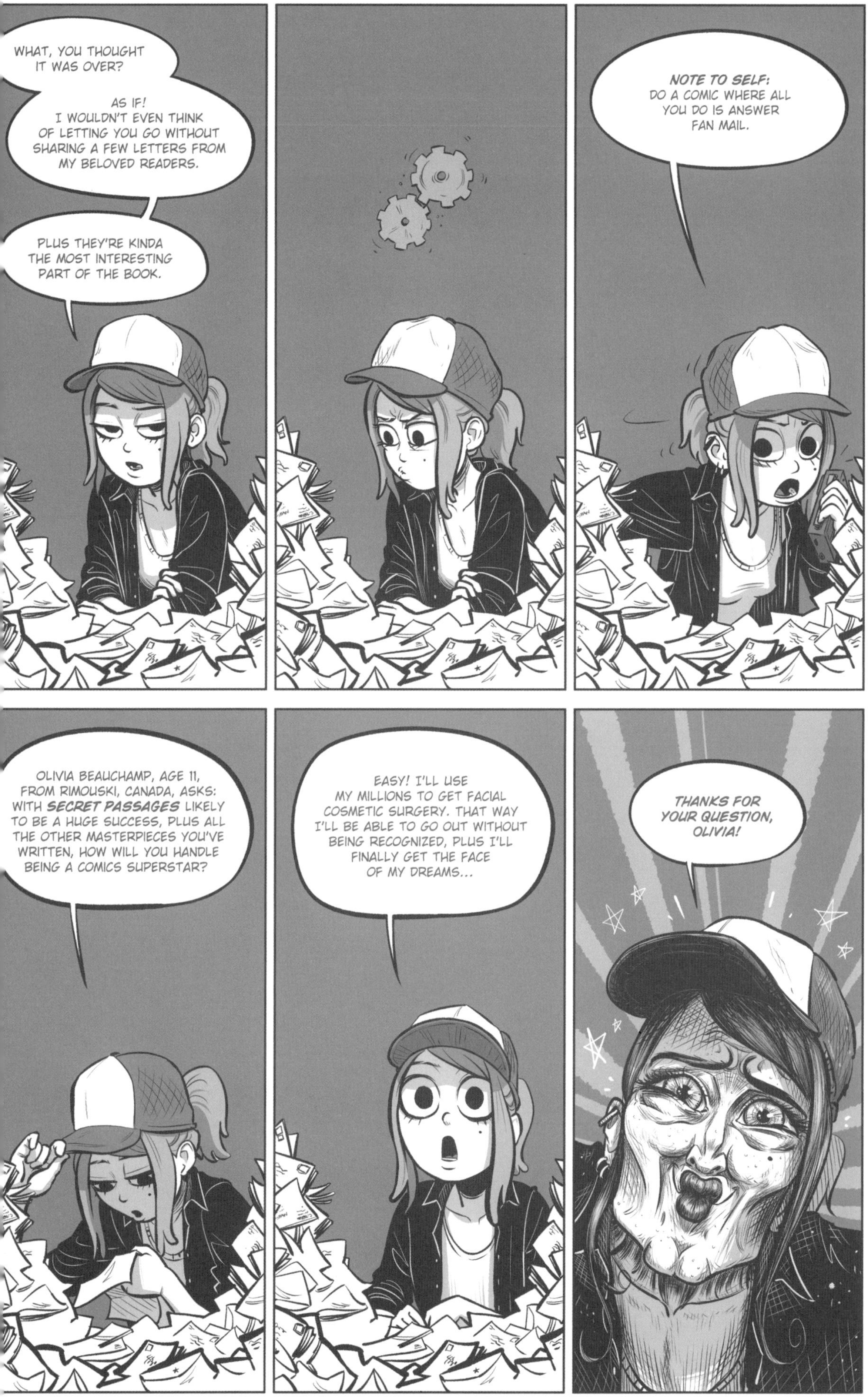
WHAT, YOU THOUGHT IT WAS OVER?
AS IF! I WOULDN'T EVEN THINK OF LETTING YOU GO WITHOUT SHARING A FEW LETTERS FROM MY BELOVED READERS.
PLUS THEY'RE KINDA THE MOST INTERESTING PART OF THE BOOK.
NOTE TO SELF: DO A COMIC WHERE ALL YOU DO IS ANSWER FAN MAIL.
OLIVIA BEAUCHAMP, AGE 11, FROM RIMOUSKI, CANADA, ASKS: WITH SECRET PASSAGES LIKELY TO BE A HUGE SUCCESS, PLUS ALL THE OTHER MASTERPIECES YOU'VE WRITTEN, HOW WILL YOU HANDLE BEING A COMICS SUPERSTAR?
EASY! I'LL USE MY MILLIONS TO GET FACIAL COSMETIC SURGERY. THAT WAY I'LL BE ABLE TO GO OUT WITHOUT BEING RECOGNIZED, PLUS I'LL FINALLY GET THE FACE OF MY DREAMS...
THANKS FOR YOUR QUESTION, OLIVIA!

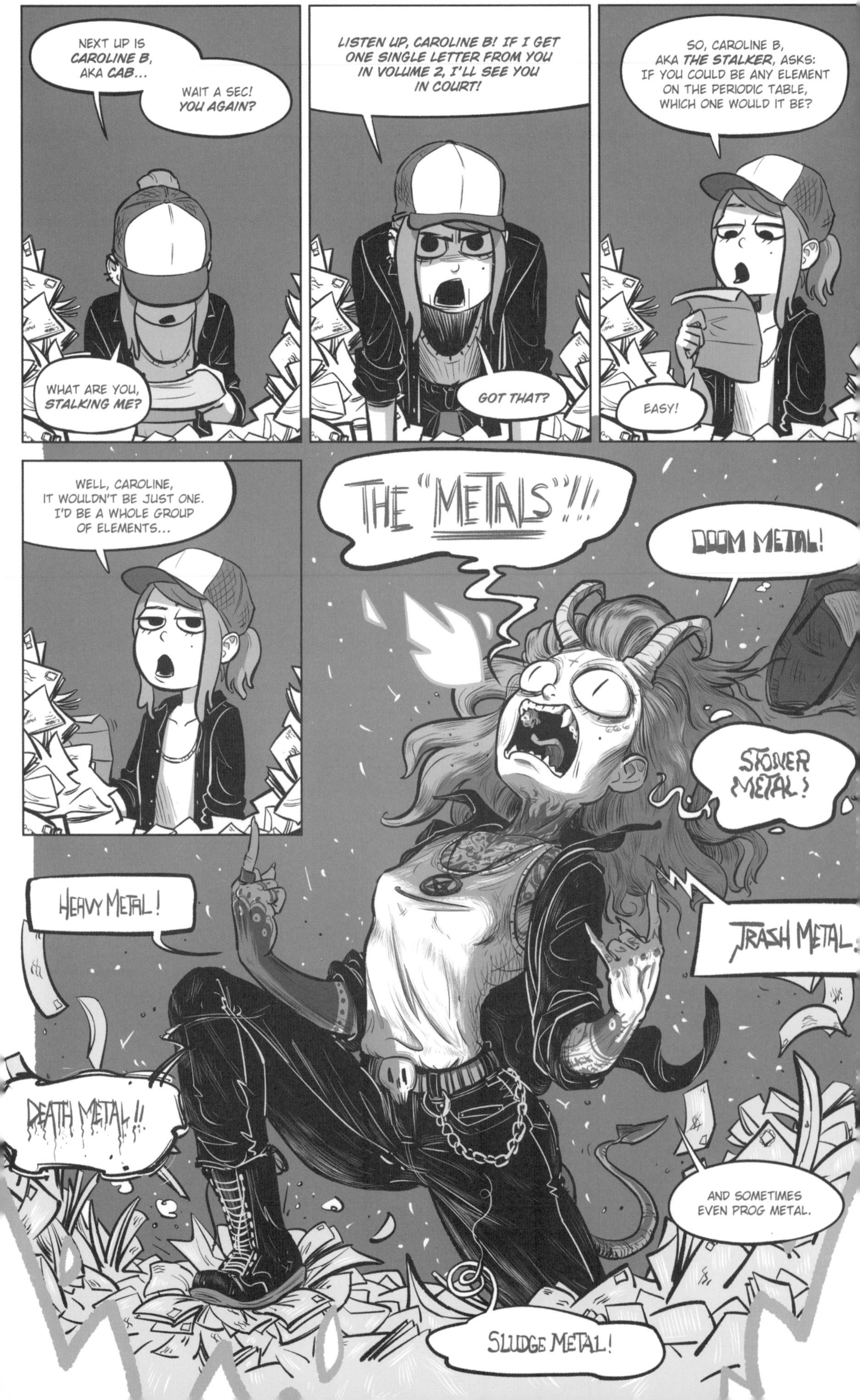

NEXT UP IS CAROLINE B, AKA CAB...
WAIT A SEC! YOU AGAIN?
WHAT ARE YOU, STALKING ME?
LISTEN UP, CAROLINE B! IF I GET ONE SINGLE LETTER FROM YOU IN VOLUME 2, I'LL SEE YOU IN COURT!
GOT THAT?
SO, CAROLINE B, AKA THE STALKER, ASKS: IF YOU COULD BE ANY ELEMENT ON THE PERIODIC TABLE, WHICH ONE WOULD IT BE?
EASY!
WELL, CAROLINE, IT WOULDN'T BE JUST ONE. I'D BE A WHOLE GROUP OF ELEMENTS...
THE "METALS"!!
DOOM METAL!
STONER METAL!
HEAVY METAL!
TRASH METAL!
DEATH METAL!!
AND SOMETIMES EVEN PROG METAL.
SLUDGE METAL!

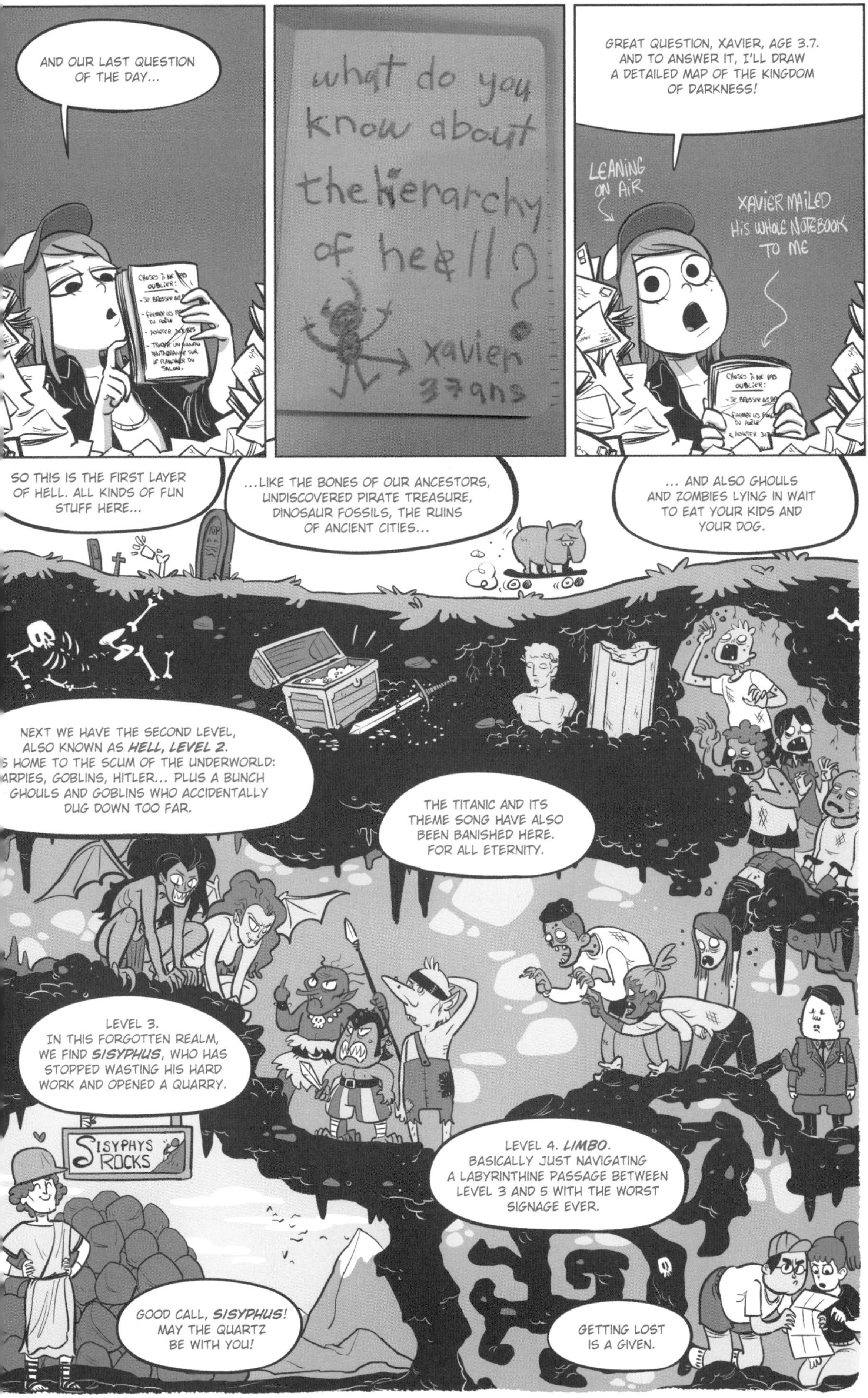
AND OUR LAST QUESTION OF THE DAY...
what do you know about the hierarchy of hell?
xavier 37ans
GREAT QUESTION, XAVIER, AGE 3.7. AND TO ANSWER IT, I'LL DRAW A DETAILED MAP OF THE KINGDOM OF DARKNESS!
LEANING ON AIR
XAVIER MAILED HIS WHOLE NOTEBOOK TO ME
SO THIS IS THE FIRST LAYER OF HELL. ALL KINDS OF FUN STUFF HERE...
...LIKE THE BONES OF OUR ANCESTORS, UNDISCOVERED PIRATE TREASURE, DINOSAUR FOSSILS, THE RUINS OF ANCIENT CITIES...
... AND ALSO GHOULS AND ZOMBIES LYING IN WAIT TO EAT YOUR KIDS AND YOUR DOG.
RIP
NEXT WE HAVE THE SECOND LEVEL, ALSO KNOWN AS *HELL, LEVEL 2.* S HOME TO THE SCUM OF THE UNDERWORLD: ARPIES, GOBLINS, HITLER... PLUS A BUNCH GHOULS AND GOBLINS WHO ACCIDENTALLY DUG DOWN TOO FAR.
THE TITANIC AND ITS THEME SONG HAVE ALSO BEEN BANISHED HERE. FOR ALL ETERNITY.
LEVEL 3. IN THIS FORGOTTEN REALM, WE FIND *SISYPHUS*, WHO HAS STOPPED WASTING HIS HARD WORK AND OPENED A QUARRY.
SISYPHYS ROCKS
LEVEL 4. *LIMBO*. BASICALLY JUST NAVIGATING A LABYRINTHINE PASSAGE BETWEEN LEVEL 3 AND 5 WITH THE WORST SIGNAGE EVER.
GOOD CALL, *SISYPHUS*! MAY THE QUARTZ BE WITH YOU!
GETTING LOST IS A GIVEN.

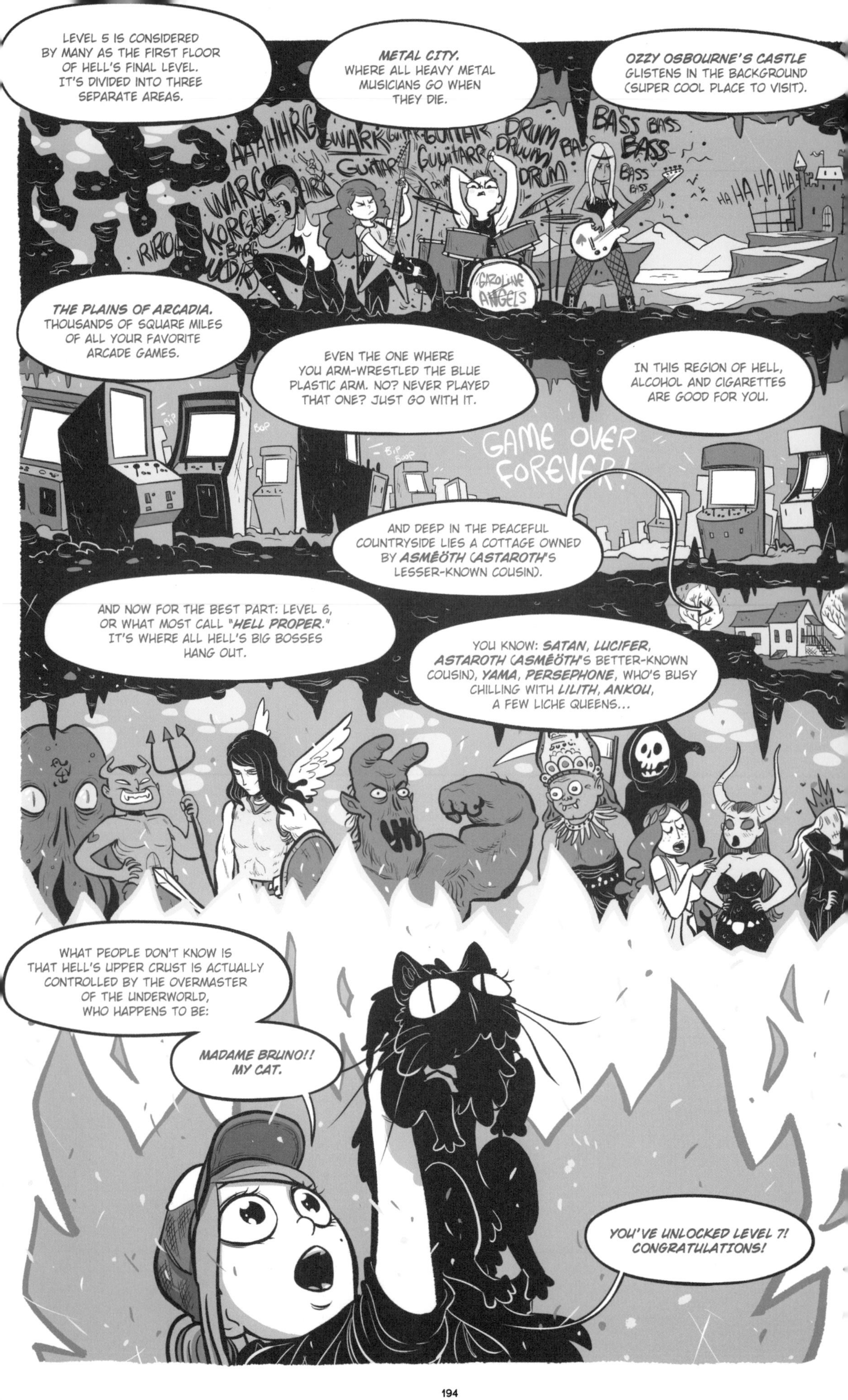
LEVEL 5 IS CONSIDERED BY MANY AS THE FIRST FLOOR OF HELL'S FINAL LEVEL. IT'S DIVIDED INTO THREE SEPARATE AREAS.
METAL CITY. WHERE ALL HEAVY METAL MUSICIANS GO WHEN THEY DIE.
OZZY OSBOURNE'S CASTLE GLISTENS IN THE BACKGROUND (SUPER COOL PLACE TO VISIT).
AAAHHRG
WARG
KORGH
GUITAR
GUIIITARR
DRUM
DRUUM
DRUM
BASS BASS
BASS
BASS
HA HA HA HA
CAROLINE ANGELS
THE PLAINS OF ARCADIA. THOUSANDS OF SQUARE MILES OF ALL YOUR FAVORITE ARCADE GAMES.
EVEN THE ONE WHERE YOU ARM-WRESTLED THE BLUE PLASTIC ARM. NO? NEVER PLAYED THAT ONE? JUST GO WITH IT.
IN THIS REGION OF HELL, ALCOHOL AND CIGARETTES ARE GOOD FOR YOU.
GAME OVER FOREVER!
AND DEEP IN THE PEACEFUL COUNTRYSIDE LIES A COTTAGE OWNED BY ASMÊÖTH (ASTAROTH'S LESSER-KNOWN COUSIN).
AND NOW FOR THE BEST PART: LEVEL 6, OR WHAT MOST CALL "HELL PROPER." IT'S WHERE ALL HELL'S BIG BOSSES HANG OUT.
YOU KNOW: SATAN, LUCIFER, ASTAROTH (ASMÊÖTH'S BETTER-KNOWN COUSIN), YAMA, PERSEPHONE, WHO'S BUSY CHILLING WITH LILITH, ANKOU, A FEW LICHE QUEENS...
WHAT PEOPLE DON'T KNOW IS THAT HELL'S UPPER CRUST IS ACTUALLY CONTROLLED BY THE OVERMASTER OF THE UNDERWORLD, WHO HAPPENS TO BE:
MADAME BRUNO!! MY CAT.
YOU'VE UNLOCKED LEVEL 7! CONGRATULATIONS!

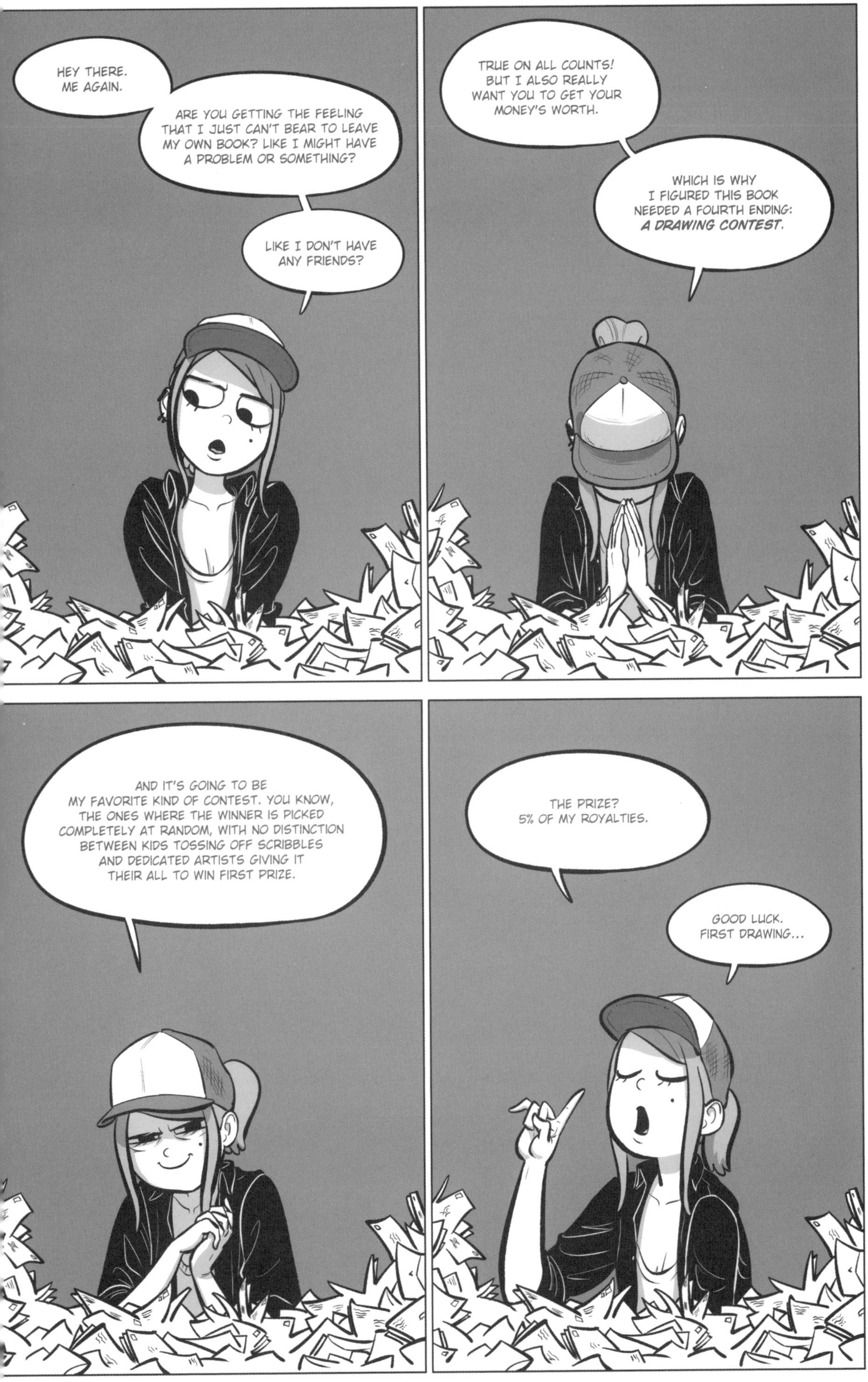

HEY THERE. ME AGAIN.
ARE YOU GETTING THE FEELING THAT I JUST CAN'T BEAR TO LEAVE MY OWN BOOK? LIKE I MIGHT HAVE A PROBLEM OR SOMETHING?
LIKE I DON'T HAVE ANY FRIENDS?
TRUE ON ALL COUNTS! BUT I ALSO REALLY WANT YOU TO GET YOUR MONEY'S WORTH.
WHICH IS WHY I FIGURED THIS BOOK NEEDED A FOURTH ENDING: ***A DRAWING CONTEST***.
AND IT'S GOING TO BE MY FAVORITE KIND OF CONTEST. YOU KNOW, THE ONES WHERE THE WINNER IS PICKED COMPLETELY AT RANDOM, WITH NO DISTINCTION BETWEEN KIDS TOSSING OFF SCRIBBLES AND DEDICATED ARTISTS GIVING IT THEIR ALL TO WIN FIRST PRIZE.
THE PRIZE? 5% OF MY ROYALTIES.
GOOD LUCK. FIRST DRAWING...

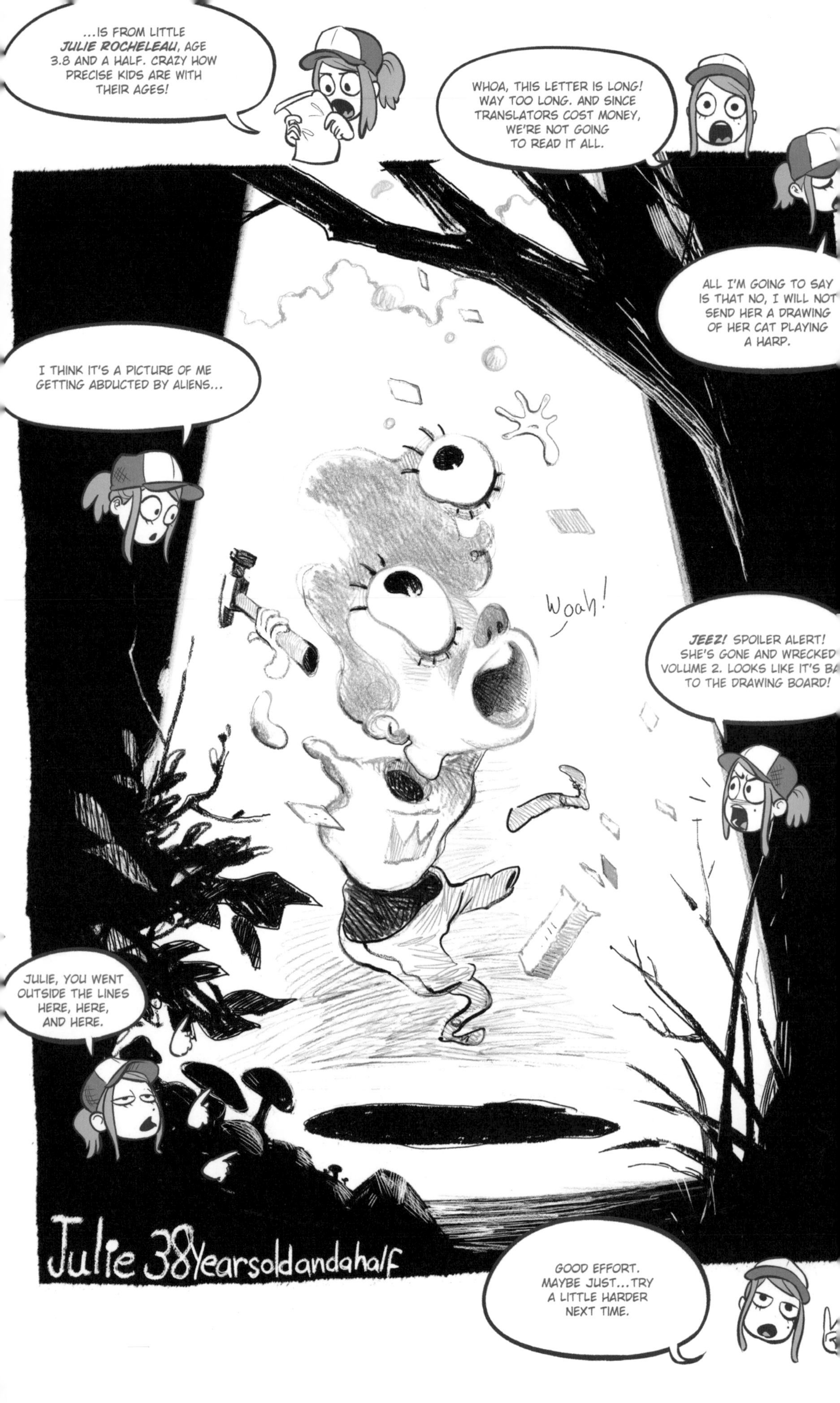

...IS FROM LITTLE *JULIE ROCHELEAU*, AGE 3.8 AND A HALF. CRAZY HOW PRECISE KIDS ARE WITH THEIR AGES!
WHOA, THIS LETTER IS LONG! WAY TOO LONG. AND SINCE TRANSLATORS COST MONEY, WE'RE NOT GOING TO READ IT ALL.
ALL I'M GOING TO SAY IS THAT NO, I WILL NOT SEND HER A DRAWING OF HER CAT PLAYING A HARP.
I THINK IT'S A PICTURE OF ME GETTING ABDUCTED BY ALIENS...
Woah!
JEEZ! SPOILER ALERT! SHE'S GONE AND WRECKED VOLUME 2. LOOKS LIKE IT'S BA TO THE DRAWING BOARD!
JULIE, YOU WENT OUTSIDE THE LINES HERE, HERE, AND HERE.
Julie 38Yearsoldandahalf
GOOD EFFORT. MAYBE JUST...TRY A LITTLE HARDER NEXT TIME.

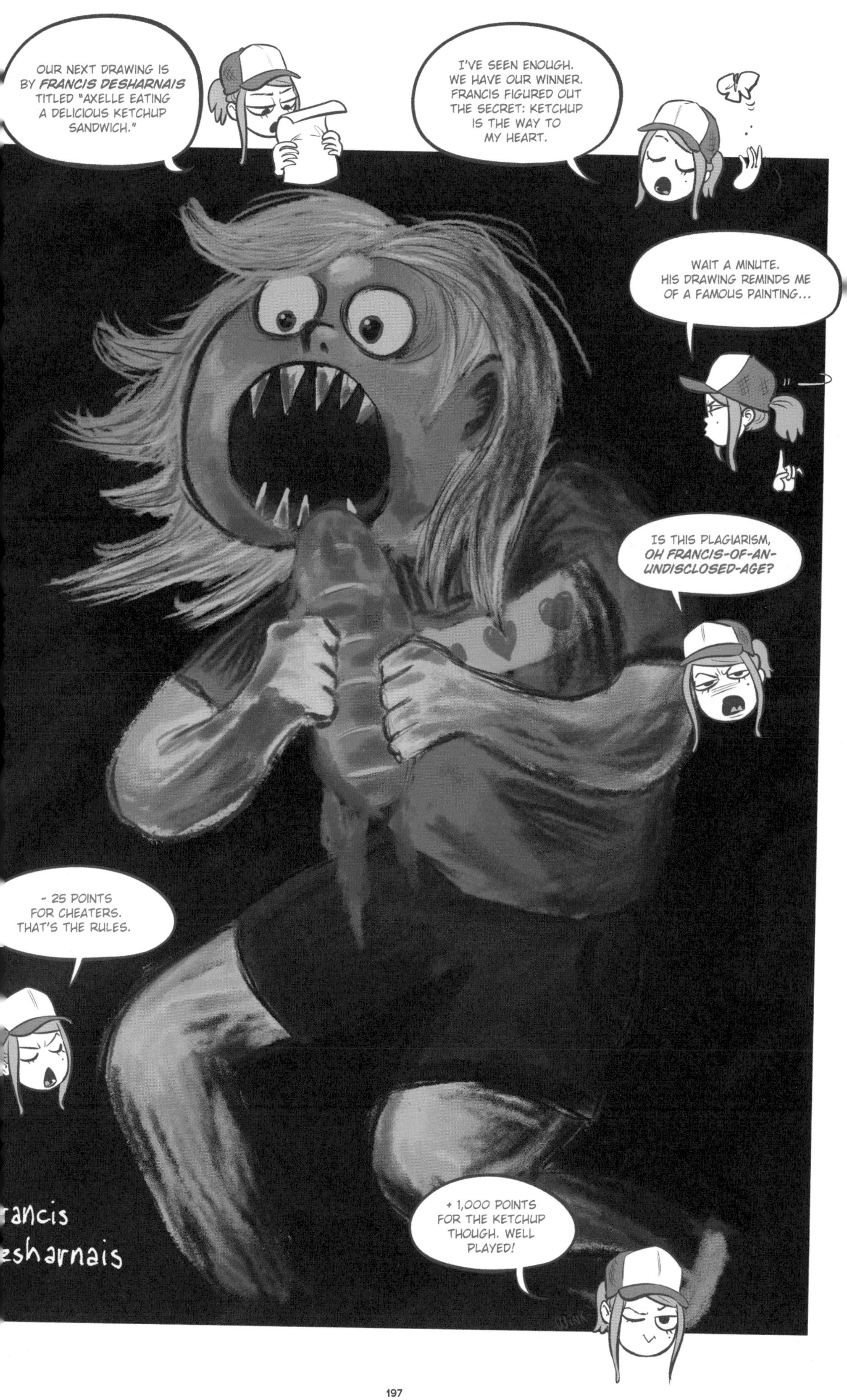

OUR NEXT DRAWING IS BY ***FRANCIS DESHARNAIS*** TITLED "AXELLE EATING A DELICIOUS KETCHUP SANDWICH."
I'VE SEEN ENOUGH. WE HAVE OUR WINNER. FRANCIS FIGURED OUT THE SECRET: KETCHUP IS THE WAY TO MY HEART.
WAIT A MINUTE. HIS DRAWING REMINDS ME OF A FAMOUS PAINTING...
IS THIS PLAGIARISM, ***OH FRANCIS-OF-AN-UNDISCLOSED-AGE?***
- 25 POINTS FOR CHEATERS. THAT'S THE RULES.
rancis
esharnais
+ 1,000 POINTS FOR THE KETCHUP THOUGH. WELL PLAYED!

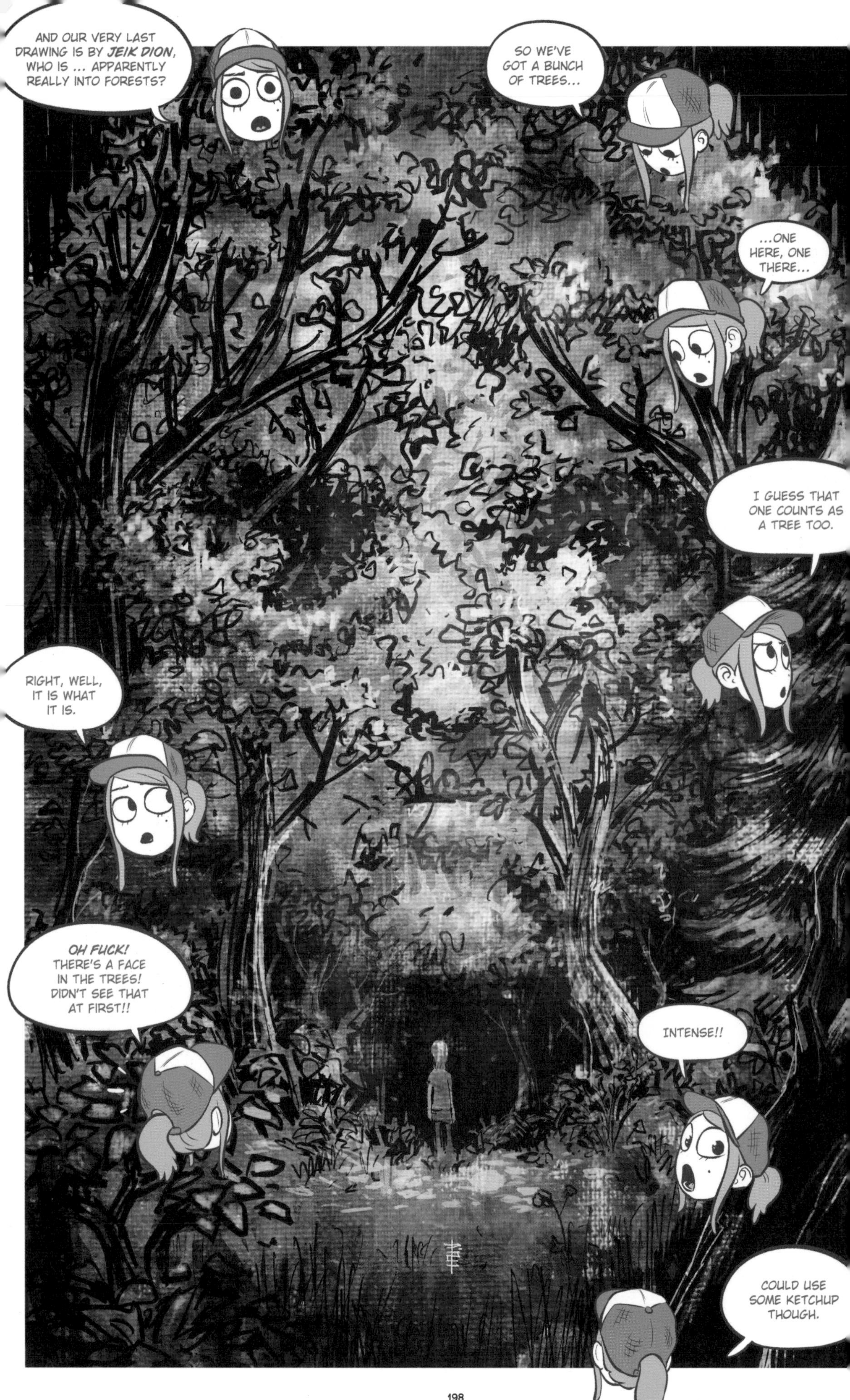
AND OUR VERY LAST DRAWING IS BY JEIK DION, WHO IS ... APPARENTLY REALLY INTO FORESTS?
SO WE'VE GOT A BUNCH OF TREES...
...ONE HERE, ONE THERE...
I GUESS THAT ONE COUNTS AS A TREE TOO.
RIGHT, WELL, IT IS WHAT IT IS.
OH FUCK! THERE'S A FACE IN THE TREES! DIDN'T SEE THAT AT FIRST!!
INTENSE!!
COULD USE SOME KETCHUP THOUGH.

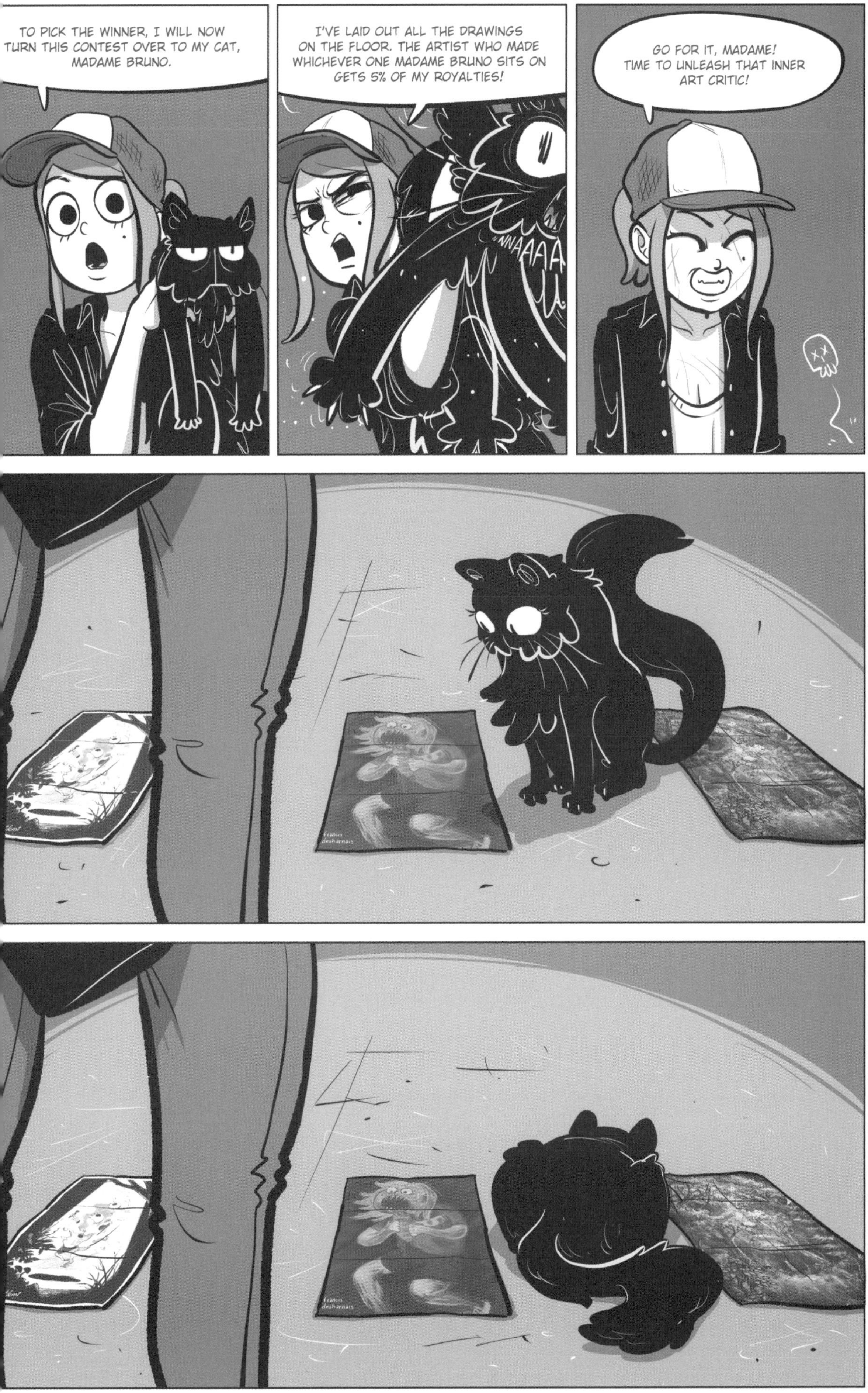
TO PICK THE WINNER, I WILL NOW TURN THIS CONTEST OVER TO MY CAT, MADAME BRUNO.
I'VE LAID OUT ALL THE DRAWINGS ON THE FLOOR. THE ARTIST WHO MADE WHICHEVER ONE MADAME BRUNO SITS ON GETS 5% OF MY ROYALTIES!
GO FOR IT, MADAME! TIME TO UNLEASH THAT INNER ART CRITIC!

Thanks to everyone who supported this project through Patreon:

Ju Marquette, Doan Trang Phan, Frank Hardcore, Stéfanie Tremblay, Xavier Cadieux, Noctis, David Price, Emilie Young-Vigneault, Jean-Dominic Leduc, Francis Gingras, François Vigneault, Bibbler, Étienne Cormier, Seiy, Olivier Gauthier, Joe Rivard, Pete Bonaro, Julie Rocheleau, Maude Laplante-Dubé, Jr Gauthier, Gilbert Falardeau, Octobre, Alexandre Bonneau, Marie-Josée Ouellet, Ph, Alexia Proulx, Mathieu Langlois, Annie Laflèche, Alice Bélanger, marc ou olivier, Isabelle Tremblay, David BRAMI, Satoji, Camille Proulx, François Lehoux, Christian, Murielle, L-A, Francis Desharnais, Jean-Michel Berthiaume, Gautier Langevin, Boum, Mélanie La Roche, Jeik Dion, Stéphanie L Charette, Cab, Pauline T., Jade Bérubé, Simon Chénier, Jessica Tourigny, Geneviève Boucher, Chase, Pen Write, Frank Boulay, Catherine Michaud, Patricia Favreau.

YOU'RE THE COOLEST!
HEE HEE!

Special thanks to Olivia Beauchamp, Cab, and Xavier Cadieux for participating in the Q&A. You sure made me laugh!

Thanks to Julie Rocheleau, Francis Desharnais and Jeik Dion for taking part in the drawing contest. It's an honor to have you in my book. See more great work at:

Julie Rocheleau: www.rocheleau.format.com
Francis Desharnais: www.instagram.com/fdesharnais
Jeik Dion: www.jeikdion.com

SUCH PRETTY DRAWINGS!... WAAAH!!

Thanks to Maude Laplante-Dubé, reviser extraordinaire, professional cousin!

Thanks to Aleshia Jensen and Pablo Strauss, for your patience and ability to make me laugh at my own jokes once they're translated into English.

Thanks to my family, for all the stellar material! xxx

LOUISE
DAD
DAVID
BING
BANG
TONIO...
MADAME

Think you recognized yourself in one of the characters in this story?
Well, you're wrong!
Still convinced?
Take a deep breath, it'll pass.
Bye!